Daniel Molkentin

The Book of Qt 4

The Art of Building Qt Applications

open
source
PRESS

Munich

NO STARCH
PRESS

San Francisco

Printed on recycled paper in the United States of America.

1 2 3 4 5 6 7 8 9 10 – 10 09 08 07

Publisher: William Pollock
Cover Design: Octopod Studios
U.S. edition published by No Starch Press, Inc.
555 De Haro Street, Suite 250, San Francisco, CA 94107
phone: 415.863.9900; fax: 415.863.9950; info@nostarch.com; http://www.nostarch.com

Original edition © 2006 Open Source Press GmbH
Published by Open Source Press GmbH, Munich, Germany
Publisher: Dr. Markus Wirtz
Original ISBN 978-3-937514-12-3
For information on translations, please contact
Open Source Press GmbH, Amalienstr. 45 Rg, 80799 München, Germany
phone +49.89.28755562; fax +49.89.28755563; info@opensourcepress.de; http://www.opensourcepress.de

Library of Congress Cataloging-in-Publication Data

```
Molkentin, Daniel
[Qt 4, Einführung in die Applikationsentwicklung.  English]
  The book of Qt 4:  the art of building Qt applications / by Daniel Molkentin.--
1st ed.
       p. cm.
  Includes index.
  ISBN-13 978-1-59327-147-3
  ISBN-10 1-59327-147-6
1. Qt (Electronic resource) 2. Graphical user interfaces (Computer systems) 3.
Application software--Development.  I. Title.  QA76.9.U83M6213 2007
  005.4'37--dc22
                              2007013181
```

Contents

Introduction   19

Preparations   23

1 Basics, Tools, and First Code   25

   1.1 Our First Qt Program 25

        1.1.1 Compiling a Qt Program   27

   1.2 Layouts, Object Hierarchy, and Memory Management   29

        1.2.1 How to Arrange Widgets Automatically   29

        1.2.2 Memory Management in Object Hierarchies   31

        1.2.3 Other Layout Types   33

   1.3 Signals and Slots   35

        1.3.1 The Simplest Case: A Slot Responds to a Signal   35

        1.3.2 Signals Carrying Additional Information and How They
               Are Processed   36

   1.4 Base Classes in Qt   39

        1.4.1 Classes Derived from QObject   39

        1.4.2 QString and Other Classes not Derived from QObject . . .   40

        1.4.3 The Qt Inheritance Hierarchy   41

   1.5 Qt at a Glance   42

        1.5.1 The Qt Libraries   42

        1.5.2 Tools and Utilities   47

        1.5.3 Examples and Demos   58

   1.6 How to Use the Documentation   59

2   The Tools Needed to Create Dialogs   **61**

2.1   What's the Difference Between Dialogs and Widgets? 62

2.1.1   Inheriting from QObject 64

2.1.2   More Complex Layouts 65

2.1.3   Increasing Usability   68

2.1.4   Implementing Slots   70

2.2   Separation of GUI and Processing Logic 74

2.2.1   Alternative Design   74

2.2.2   Declaring and Sending Out Signals 76

2.2.3   Using Your Own Signals 79

3   GUI Design Using the Qt Designer   **81**

3.1   Dialogs "By Mouse Click" 81

3.1.1   Making Layouts With the Designer 84

3.1.2   The Property Editor 85

3.1.3   The Preview 88

3.1.4   Signal/Slot Connections 88

3.1.5   The Tab Sequence   89

3.1.6   Shortcuts and Buddies 90

3.2   Integrating Designer-generated Files into Your Qt Project 91

3.2.1   Using Designer-generated Classes as Helper Classes 92

3.2.2   Always Having Designer-generated Widgets Available . . . 94

3.2.3   Multiple Inheritance 95

3.3   Automatic Signal/Slot Connections 97

3.4   Including Derived Classes in the Designer 99

3.5   The Resource Editor 99

4   Developing a GUI Application Based on a Main Window   **101**

4.1   The Anatomy of the Main Window 101

4.2   Deriving from QMainWindow 103

4.3   Creating a Main Window with the Qt Designer 106

4.3.1   Adding Menu Bars 107

4.3.2   Recycling Actions in the Toolbar   108

4.3.3   Integrating the Main Window with Your Source Code . . .   110

4.4   Making the Most of the Status Bar   118

4.4.1   Temporary Messages   120

4.4.2   Normal Messages   120

4.4.3   Permanent Messages   121

4.5   Toolbars   125

4.6   How Do Actions Work?   126

4.6.1   How to Instantiate QAction Manually   127

4.6.2   Selectable Actions   128

4.6.3   Grouped Actions   128

4.7   Dock Windows   130

4.7.1   Positioning Dock Windows   131

4.7.2   A Dock Window for Our Editor   133

4.8   Saving Preferences   136

4.8.1   Extending CuteEdit   139

5   Laying Out Widgets   141

5.1   Manual Layout   141

5.2   Automatic Layout   143

5.2.1   Horizontal and Vertical Layout   144

5.2.2   Grid Layout   148

5.2.3   Nested Layouts   149

5.3   Splitter   150

5.3.1   Behavior During Size Changes   150

5.3.2   Saving Splitter Positions and Determining the Widget Size   151

5.3.3   Defining Relative Sizes   152

5.3.4   Customizing Handles   153

5.3.5   Layout for Languages Written from Right to Left   156

5.4   Stacked Layouts   157

5.4.1   The Alternative: Stacked Widgets   157

5.4.2   When to Use Stacked Layouts and Widgets   157

6 Dialogs   **161**

6.1   Modal Dialogs 161

6.2   Non-modal Dialogs 163

     6.2.1   Usability Problems 163

6.3   Semi-modal Dialogs 164

6.4   Avoiding Bloated Dialogs 164

6.5   Ready-made Dialogs in Qt 166

     6.5.1   Message Dialogs 166

     6.5.2   Error Messages That Are Only Visible Once 174

     6.5.3   File Selection Dialogs 175

     6.5.4   Input Dialogs 179

     6.5.5   Font Selection Dialog 182

     6.5.6   Color Selection and Printing Dialog 183

7 Events, Drag and Drop, and the Clipboard   **185**

7.1   Event Loop and Event Handler 185

7.2   Handling Events 186

     7.2.1   Using Specialized Event Handlers 186

     7.2.2   Using the General Event Handler 189

7.3   Using Event Filters 190

7.4   Drag and Drop 194

     7.4.1   MIME Types 194

     7.4.2   The Drag Side 196

     7.4.3   The Drop Side 198

7.5   The Clipboard 201

8 Displaying Data Using "Interview"   **207**

8.1   Underlying Concepts 208

     8.1.1   The View Classes 210

     8.1.2   The Model Classes 211

8.2   Displaying Directory Hierarchies 212

     8.2.1   Using View Classes in the Designer 214

     8.2.2   Implementing the Functionality of the File Selection Dialog 216

8.3   The String Lists Model 221

8.4   Implementing Your Own Models 222

    8.4.1   An Address Book Model 222

    8.4.2   Making Your Own Models Writable 227

8.5   Sorting and Filtering Data with Proxy Models 231

    8.5.1   Adjustments to the User Interface 232

8.6   Making Entries Selectable with Checkboxes 234

8.7   Designing Your Own Proxy Models 237

8.8   Implementing Drag and Drop in Models 241

8.9   Your Own Delegates 245

8.10   Without Your Own Data Source: The Standard Model 249

8.11   Element-based Views Without Model Access 251

    8.11.1   Items 251

    8.11.2   The List View 251

    8.11.3   The Tree View 252

    8.11.4   The Table View 253

    8.11.5   Cloning Items 254

9   The QtSql Module   257

9.1   Structure of the QtSql Module 257

9.2   Selecting the Appropriate Driver 258

9.3   Making a Connection 260

9.4   Making Queries 261

9.5   Transactions 264

9.6   Embedded Databases 264

9.7   Using SQL Model Classes with Interview 265

    9.7.1   Displaying SQL Tables Without Foreign Keys in Table and
                Tree Views 265

    9.7.2   Resolving Foreign Key Relations 266

    9.7.3   Displaying Query Results 267

    9.7.4   Editing Strategies 268

    9.7.5   Errors in the Table Model 270

10 The Graphics Library "Arthur" **271**

10.1 Colors 271

    10.1.1 The RGB Color Space 272

    10.1.2 Other Color Spaces 273

    10.1.3 Color Selection Dialog 275

10.2 Painting with Qt 276

10.3 Geometrical Helper Classes 278

10.4 How to Paint on Widgets 280

    10.4.1 How to Prevent Monitor Flicker 282

10.5 Using QPainter in Practice 283

    10.5.1 Drawing a Pie Chart 284

    10.5.2 Defining the Widget Size 289

    10.5.3 The Diagram Application 290

10.6 Transformations of the Coordinate System 290

    10.6.1 Transformations in Practice 293

10.7 QImage 297

    10.7.1 Storage Formats, Transparency, and Color Palettes 297

    10.7.2 Reading out Pixels Line by Line 298

10.8 SVG Support 300

10.9 Printing with QPrinter 302

    10.9.1 Digression: Making Screenshots 304

    10.9.2 Printing an Image File 305

    10.9.3 Generating PDFs 306

    10.9.4 The Test Application 306

10.10 Complex Graphics 307

    10.10.1 Clipping 307

    10.10.2 Painter Paths 309

    10.10.3 Composition Modes 310

11 Input/Output Interfaces **317**

11.1 The QIODevice Class Hierarchy 317

    11.1.1 Derived Classes 318

    11.1.2 Opening I/O Devices 319

11.2 Access to Local Files 320

11.3 Serializing Objects 322

    11.3.1 Defining Serialization Operators 325

    11.3.2 Saving Serialized Data to a File and Reading from It 326

11.4 Starting and Controlling Processes 328

    11.4.1 Synchronous Use of QProcess 328

    11.4.2 Asynchronous Use of QProcess 330

11.5 Communication in the Network 332

    11.5.1 Name Resolution with QHostInfo 333

    11.5.2 Using QTcpServer and QTcpSocket 333

12 Threading with QThread   **337**

12.1 Using Threads 338

12.2 Synchronizing Threads 341

    12.2.1 The Consumer/Producer Pattern 342

12.3 Thread-dependent Data Structures 345

12.4 Using Signals and Slots Between Threads 347

12.5 Your Own Event Loops for Threads 350

    12.5.1 Communication via Events Without a Thread-based Event
    Loop 352

13 Handling XML with QtXml   **353**

13.1 The SAX2 API 354

    13.1.1 How It Works 354

    13.1.2 Reimplementing a Default Handler to Read RSS Feeds . . 355

    13.1.3 Digression: Equipping the RSS Reader with a GUI and
    Network Capability 361

13.2 The DOM API 366

    13.2.1 Reading in and Processing XML Files 367

    13.2.2 Searching for Specific Elements 370

    13.2.3 Manipulating the DOM Tree 371

    13.2.4 The DOM Tree as XML Output 372

14 Internationalization   **375**

14.1   Translating Applications into Other Languages 375

     14.1.1   Preparing the Application 376

     14.1.2   Processing Translation Sources with Linguist 377

     14.1.3   Using Translations in the Program 378

     14.1.4   Adding Notes for the Translation 380

     14.1.5   Specifying the Translation Context 380

     14.1.6   Internationalizing Strings Outside Qt Classes 381

Appendixes   **383**

A   Debugging Help   **385**

A.1   Debugging Functions 385

     A.1.1   Simple Debug Output 386

     A.1.2   Errors and Warnings 387

     A.1.3   Customizing the Output of Debugging Functions 388

A.2   Ways to Eliminate Errors 390

     A.2.1   Checking Assertions 390

     A.2.2   Checking Pointers 391

     A.2.3   Common Linker Errors 392

B   Tulip: Containers and Algorithms   **393**

B.1   Iterators 394

     B.1.1   STL-Style Iterators 395

     B.1.2   Java-Style Iterators 396

B.2   Lists 398

     B.2.1   Simple List (QList) 400

     B.2.2   Linked List (QLinkedList) 401

     B.2.3   Vectors (QVector) 401

B.3   Stacks and Queues 403

     B.3.1   Stacks (QStack) 403

     B.3.2   Queues (QQueue) 404

B.4   Associative Arrays 404

     B.4.1   Dictionaries (QMap) 404

B.4.2   Allowing Several Identical Keys (QMultiMap) 407

B.4.3   Hash Tables with QHash 409

B.4.4   Hash-based Amounts with QSet 411

B.5   Algorithms 412

B.5.1   The foreach Keyword 412

B.5.2   Sorting 413

B.5.3   Sorting in Unsorted Containers 414

B.5.4   Copying Container Areas 415

B.5.5   Binary Search in Sorted Containers 416

B.5.6   Counting the Number of Occurences of Equal Elements . . 418

B.5.7   Deleting Pointers in Lists 418

B.5.8   Checking that Data Structures Have Identical Elements . . 419

B.5.9   Filling Data Structures 420

B.5.10   Swapping Values 420

B.5.11   Minimum, Maximum, and Threshold Values 421

B.5.12   Determining Absolute Value 422

B.6   Qt-specific Type Definitions 422

B.6.1   Integer types 422

B.6.2   Floating-point Values 423

B.6.3   Shortcuts for Common Types 423

Index   425

Foreword to the English Edition

"We need an object-oriented display system," Haavard Nord said, as the two of us sat on a park bench in the summer sun outside the regional hospital in Trondheim, Norway, in the summer of 1991.

"Huh, what's that?" was my response.

Haavard went on to sketch what seemed like an obvious idea at the time. A C++ library of user interface components, or widgets, that would have the same API on all platforms.

We had both just gone through the transition from procedural programming to event-driven programming and were appalled at the tools available to do the job.

Almost three years, a couple of design iterations, and some serious hacking later, we incorporated what was to become Trolltech. At last we could work full time on our great passion: to make the lives of programmers more pleasant. We were sick and tired of using tools that detracted from the joy of creating software. We wanted to create tools that made you think, "Of course, this is the way it was always meant to be."

And we refused to compromise. We designed, redesigned, and threw away lots of code until we felt we got it just right. If a use case could be solved by one line less of code and still be easy to read a year after you had written the code (both are important), then we would ditch the current design and redo what had to be redone.

Today Trolltech has almost 250 employees and is a public company listed on the Oslo stock exchange. But still, that passion for making the best possible developer tools are evident in the hallways of our offices.

Haavard and I have left the control of Qt's destiny to much more capable programmers than ourselves. And I have to say they are doing an extraordinary job at it. Qt has developed into an exceptionally beautiful piece of software.

Today Matthias Ettrich (KDE founder) and Lars Knoll (of KHTML fame) lead the team of developers responsible for keeping Qt the kick-ass product you expect from Trolltech.

Qt 4 is more or less a total rewrite of Qt. And I know one of the parts the Trolltech developers are especially proud of is the new painting engine in Qt 4. It is called Arthur the paint engine, after "Thomas the Tank Engine,"[1] and it really is "the paint engine that could!" Arthur has developed into a state-of-the-art painting engine that makes it possible to easily create all those eye-catching visual effects end users have come to expect. And once you have created your breathtaking stuff, recompiling will make it run on all platforms supported by Qt.

From the very first version of Qt released back in May 1995, Trolltech has been using a dual-licensing business model with a free version of Qt available for developers of free and open source software. The first toe in the water back then was a binary-only version for development of free software under Linux only. This was quickly followed by a free version containing the complete source code. Today, Qt is available both under a standard commercial license and under the GPL (General Public License) on all platforms.

What this means in practice is that if you want to donate your work based on Qt to the community at large by licensing your work under the GPL, then go ahead and use our product for free. You can even modify and redistribute Qt under the terms of the GPL, no strings attached. If, on the other hand, you want to keep your software based on Qt proprietary and do not want to license your code under the GPL, then you also have an option. You can purchase Qt under a standard commercial license from Trolltech and you can license your code any way you want, no strings attached.

Qt is an open source product with a thriving community and at the same time a commercial product with the backing of a public company with a strong developer, support, and documentation muscle. It really is the best of both worlds.

And it is because of the feedback from the thousands of users out there, both commercial and open source developers, that Qt is such a high-quality toolkit. We still rely on and listen closely to all the feedback we receive on Qt. So, if you do find something you think can be improved in Qt or simply have a bug to report, do not hesitate to let us know, e.g., by sending an email to qt-bugs@trolltech.com. We have a team of eager engineers wanting to hear from you.

Well, I guess I have bragged enough about Qt now. The proof really is in the pudding. The only way to truly appreciate Qt is to start using it. So, start diving into this excellent coverage of Qt by Daniel Molkentin, and as you go along, play around with Qt as much as you can. I do hope and believe that you will be surprised and pleased by the programming universe of Qt.

Enjoy!

Eirik Chambe-Eng,
co-CEO and founder, Trolltech ASA

---

[1] See http://www.thomasandfriends.com/.

Foreword to the German Edition

Traditionally, getting applications to look "just right" on different operating systems and platforms has been the stuff of nightmares for programmers. Applications on Microsoft Windows look and feel different to those on Mac OS X, which in turn are different for those using Linux platforms. Applications written for Linux even behave differently on the various free desktop environments available, and much the same can be said of the various flavors of Windows.

While it is relatively easy to write code that works on all of these platforms, such code is either likely to feel alien on all but the one platform it was originally designed for, or it doesn't provide features that users expect to find in modern applications.

With Qt, our aims are much higher than this. We want applications written with Qt to be written in a platform-independent way, yet work as well as any other application on Microsoft Windows, Mac OS X, and Linux desktops—even on mobile devices. Writing code to make this possible is no easy task; it is one that provides a new—and welcome—challenge for the Trolltech team of developers each day.

The most difficult part of Qt to get right, and also the most visible, is the graphical user interface (GUI). The foundation for any GUI is the technology used to render the interface, and Qt contains its own technology for this purpose—namely "Arthur the Paint Engine." Partly inspired by "Thomas the Tank Engine," Arthur has come a long way in recent years. Its story is a good example of how Qt has continued to develop as users provide feedback and suggest solutions to problems they encounter.

Arthur began with just such a simple problem: Many Qt users make use of OpenGL in their software, and they increasingly wanted to be able to choose between drawing with OpenGL and drawing on conventional widgets, but use the same application programming interface (API) for both. We wanted to provide this ability with Qt 4. Easier said than done! The old paint device architecture, nearly 10 years old when we started, could not cope with this change, and so a little refactoring was necessary before Arthur could see the light of day. In the first Technology Preview of Qt 4, we were able to draw graphics not only with OpenGL, but also on the relatively new GDI+ on Windows, with both anti-aliasing and linear gradients.

Very nice, we thought, and far better than Qt 3, but we had failed to reckon with the high expectations of our users. Many changes had been taking place in the world of computer graphics. The XRender extension to X11 was becoming ever more powerful, the Cairo project was getting ready to close the gap with other systems once and for all, the Macintosh had CoreGraphics, and a new Scalable Vector Graphics (SVG) format had begun to indicate where modern toolkits were going at the beginning of the 21st century.

Arthur was on the right path, but we still had an enormous amount of ground to make up. Things that worked fast on the Mac were slow with GDI+ on Windows or with X11, and vice versa. And under X11—our core platform for the open source version—we were a long way behind, even when using extensions like XRender.

Team Arthur, headed by Gunnar Sletta, therefore set itself a new goal: to match the feature set offered by SVG. The team was determined not to rest until high-quality vector graphics could be displayed equally well on all platforms, and at high speed, too. All this happened, mind you, *after* the release of the first Qt 4 Technology Preview.

How would you have reacted as the project manager? We knew that our solution was not good enough, but we were already behind schedule. And how can you put your faith in two developers alone being able to write a new renderer that will compete with the giants of operating system vendors? Not only this, we also wanted it to be even better than GDI+, and platform independent as well. Team Arthur was given three weeks to build a prototype to show what it could achieve.

The two of them came up with the goods! The breakthrough success was due to the fantastic scan-line converter from the FreeType project, a piece of open source software that is generally used to display text. It took just three more days to display complex SVGs with floating-point precision, anti-aliasing, and powerful gradients.

What can we learn from this? Qt is continually being developed by highly motivated (and sometimes quite crazy) programmers who call themselves Trolls, who are spurred on to provide the best product for our users. It is also developed by dedicated people like Daniel and Patricia, to whom our thanks go for producing this wonderful book you are holding in your hands, and by many other contributors and users around the world.

Without this priceless community, Qt would not be where it is today, and the development team is gratefully aware of this. This is precisely the reason we will continue to strive for more and better. For you, our users—and because we enjoy it a little bit, of course. Welcome to Qt!

Matthias Ettrich,
Head of Development, Trolltech

Introduction

A number of years ago, I happened to come across an article on GUI programming with C++. I had just started learning C++ and was amazed at how little code the author[2] needed to produce a complete game, including the menus. Of course, there were a number of constructs that needed explanation, but after a short time I was hooked: The Qt library that he used turned out not only to have a very extensive collection of all kinds of useful *widgets* (also known to Windows programmers as *control elements*), but in addition had standard algorithms, data structures, and other nongraphic classes that made programming with C++ so intuitive, in a way that I had never seen before in any other toolkit.

The software company, Trolltech, was also promoting its own platform-independent API. This toolkit, which could produce programs for both Windows and Linux, simply by recompiling the code, attracted my attention. Shortly after this, nearly six years ago to the day, I joined the KDE project, which was developing an entire desktop based on Qt. Today, together with GNOME, KDE is one of the most important desktops under Linux. But Qt is also used by a substantial number of companies: Google Earth is based on Qt, as is the telephony software Skype and the video editing program MainActor.

When Trolltech published a pre-version of Qt 4 in 2005, I started trying out several of the new functionalities and was very impressed. For the first time there was a uniform licensing scheme for variations of Qt, which until then were different for Linux and Mac OS X: Quid pro quo—those companies that publish a program under an open source license may use the open source version of the library. But if the company is developing proprietary programs, then it pays for Qt license fees, thus supporting the development of the toolkit, and receives support from the manufacturer.

This structural level is of relevance as far as the licensing of the commercial Qt version. Trolltech has three editions of Qt 4 available: *Qt Console* for nongraphic development, and *Qt Desktop Light* and *Qt Desktop* as versions containing all features. The open source version in each case corresponds to the desktop edition, so it is not restricted in any way in terms of size.

---

[2] The article was written by Matthias Ettrich, the founder of the KDE project.

This book is based on the open source edition of Qt, but it can also be used without problem by those who have purchased the commercial version. The embedded version of Qt (*Qtopia Core*) is not covered in the book, because although the API is identical, apart from a few extra classes, there are so many items to be noted in embedded development that a separate book would be needed to describe them all.

Target Audience and Prerequisites

It is difficult to define a target audience for Qt programming because the areas of application for Qt are almost limitless. In general, however, it is aimed at all those who wish to have platform-independent results in a machine-oriented high-level language such as C++, results that can be compiled into native code, not least for reasons of performance.

The book assumes that you have a fundamental knowledge of C++. An interested reader should be familiar with the concepts of pointers and templates. The book also assumes that you know about things such as the overloading of operators.

Knowledge of the Standard Template Library (STL) in particular is not expected. Qt provides its own classes for the most common algorithms and containers, which are explained in Appendix B.

Structure of the Book

The book first explains the basic structure of the Qt toolkit, together with its most important specific properties. The subsequent chapters concentrate on writing your own small applications. All other technologies, presented in the final chapters, are demonstrated as short, independent examples for the sake of clarity. But they are arranged in such a way that it should be no problem to use them in a real program at the correct position.

Nearly all of the examples printed in this book are based on a complete and compilable test program. These examples begin with the name of the quoted source text file in C++ comments, such as

```
// program_name/file_name.cpp
```

For a better understanding, explanations are often added between code segments, so that the code is interrupted. When the code continues in such cases, it is also marked as a comment:

```
// program_name/file_name.cpp (continued)
```

If you prefer to read the examples in context, or want to try them out yourself, you can download a complete archive with all the examples described in the book. This file, as well as other hints and link recommendations, is available at the website for the book:

```
http://www.qt4-book.com/
```

This book is aimed at beginners and is not intended to be a reference. The excellent online documentation—which can be called via the Qt Assistant incorporated in the distribution or online at http://doc.trolltech.com/—provides a detailed API documentation on all the classes introduced here, and would be hard to beat.

Instead, the book aims to explain contexts and basic techniques by the use of examples, and to simplify getting started with programming, just as that magazine article back then helped me when I was starting to get to grips with Qt.

Note of Thanks

It would have been impossible to read this book without a number of people giving me support with their advice. In particular, Patricia Jung and her colleagues from Open Source Press made a significant contribution as far as the form and contents of the book were concerned. Further thanks go to Rainer M. Schmid, who also helped in getting the project off the ground, and Steve Tomlin, who did a fantastic job in translating this book.

I would also like to thank the people who proofread the book, providing me with valuable feedback. Thorsten Stärk and Stephan Zeissler deserve special mention here, as well as Axel Jäger, with whom I had many valuable discussions.

I would never have written this book, of course, if I had not bumped into the KDE project and met Harri Porten, a patient maintainer who looked after my first patches and commented on them with great patience.

As the book was being written, I also found support from the extremely helpful members of the #kde4-devel channel at irc.freenode.net who provided important tips and advice. The mailinglist archive of Trolltech and the community forum http://www.qtcentre.org/ also provided valuable tips, clarifying some tricky questions.

Trolltech itself deserves special thanks, because due to the dual licensing, the company supports the ideals of free software. In some cases the source text was the last possibility of confirming certain technical issues, where gaps were to be even in the excellent API documentation.

The Linux/Unix Usergroup Sankt Augustin and the Bonner Netzladen also deserve a special mention. Their excellent provision of Club-Mate iced tea always kept me wide awake during my work.

Many of my friends have given me encouragement and motivation on this project, and many thanks should also go to my family. They provided support, particularly in the critical phases, which was a great help in my work. This book is therefore dedicated to the best family I could ask for.

Daniel Molkentin

Preparations

You should always use the most recent Qt version from Trolltech[3] to ensure having as many bugfixes covered as possible. Linux users may also use the precompiled packages from their Linux distribution, but they should be prepared to meet some—often subtle—problems with older distributions like Ubuntu Dapper Drake, where problems with the debug libraries have been reported. In these cases, it is safer to obtain the source texts from Trolltech, and compile the sources yourself as described below.

On OS X, you can choose between compiling Qt yourself or using a diskimage (.dmg) archive, which installs precompiled libraries to /opt/qt4. The latter will install only the static libraries, which are easily identified via their extension (.a). At link time, these libraries become part of the binary. A second .dmg archive contains the debug version of all Qt libraries, which should be installed on development systems, too.

Although Qt can be configured to build static libraries on all platforms, this is mostly used on Mac OS X, where static linking is the preferred way to avoid library problems, at the expense of disk space.

If you choose to build the sources on Linux or Mac OS X, it is sufficient to unpack the archive, and—provided you have a compiler installed—run the command

```
./configure -qt-gif -debug
make
```

from within the package directory. Beforehand you should check, using ./configure -help, whether the system takes account of specific modules during compilation, such as particular database drivers, which you may require for your work. More detailed notes, especially on the SQL modules, are available in the corresponding chapters of this book.

The parameters specified here for configure have turned out to be the smallest common denominator for many application cases: -qt-gif adds support for the GIF file format, disabled by default for reasons of licensing, to be included in the library. -debug ensures that a version with debugging icons is built, apart from the normal

---

[3] See ftp://ftp.trolltech.com/Qt/qt/source.

libraries. For developing, you should always use the debug version of the libraries. If you don't do this, several of the examples in this book will provide no output, since they use debugging functionality for this purpose.

A make install installs Qt under Unix to the directory /usr/local/Trolltech/Qt-*version*. If you would prefer a different directory, you pass the desired installation path to configure, using the -prefix option. Qt can be used straight out of the directory in which it was built, however. To do this you just have to include the bin directory in the path and the lib directory under Unix in the environment variable LD_LIBRARY_PATH.

Users of the Windows open source edition can download a precompiled archive as an executable file. It will run an installer that does not only install Qt, but also offers to download MinGW.[4] MinGW (*Minimalist GNU for Windows*) is a port of the GNU Compiler Collection (GCC) to Windows, which produces native Windows executables without the need for a Unix compatibility library, as is the case with Cygwin.

After a successful installation, Qt is available from C:\Qt*version*. On Windows, Trolltech provides both static and dynamic versions of Qt: The static libraries can be found in lib, while the dynamically linked ones "live" in bin along with the helper tools. The reason for this hodgepodge is that Windows looks for libraries only in special places (like in the system32 directory) and in the path where the binary resides.

If you prefer to build Qt from scratch, you will need to download and install MingGW yourself. After having done this successfully, you install Qt as described above, except that the configure command in this case is an .exe file, so that the configuration command must be written as

```
configure.exe -qt-gif -debug
```

Corresponding graphic development environments are presented in the first chapter.

---

[4] See http://www.mingw.org/.

Basics, Tools, and First Code

1.1 Our First Qt Program

Following in the tradition of many programming books and tutorials, this book will start with the obligatory "Hello, world!" program. This minimal Qt application, which we will save in a file called main.cpp, simply opens a window displaying the text Hello, world! when it is run:

```
// helloWorld/main.cpp

#include <QApplication>
#include <QLabel>

int main(int argc, char *argv[])
{
    QApplication a(argc, argv);
```

```
QLabel label("Hello World");
label.show();

return a.exec();
}
```

For this purpose, the first two lines of code include the header files for the Qt classes that we want to use in the following code. In our case these header files contain the interface descriptions for the classes QApplication and QLabel.

In Qt 4 there is precisely one header file for each Qt class, which is named *without* the otherwise standard filename extension .h: Its name corresponds exactly to the class name.[1] When you give the #include directive, make sure that you capitalize the header filename correctly.

The fourth line of the listing onward shows what a typical main() function of a Qt program looks like. First you create a QApplication object and pass to its constructor the command-line arguments that the user supplied when invoking the finished program. No GUI program can manage without a QApplication object, because, among other things, QApplication makes available an *event loop*. This loop ensures that the application continues running until its window is closed.

Next we create a QLabel object that displays the text "Hello, world!". Initially, this object is invisible. We must call its show() function in order to make it appear—as shown in Figure 1.1—in a window.

Figure 1.1:
The first Qt program

Finally the call to exec() starts the event loop which is in charge of forwarding application events to the appropriate objects. Such events are caused by user actions, such as clicking a button. In our first example we will leave event handling entirely to Qt itself. Section 1.3 (page 35) shows how additional user interaction can be implemented.

The event loop is terminated when the quit() function of the QApplication object is called. In our example, this happens indirectly when the last main window of the application (which in this case is label) closes and is deleted from memory.

---

[1] In reality, these files themselves just contain a directive that loads the corresponding .h file. These are not documented, however, so that you can never be quite sure whether Trolltech might have made unannounced changes.

1.1.1 Compiling a Qt Program

When compiling this program, you are faced with a problem: Qt is supported on various platforms, and the details of the compilation process differ for each type of system. The Qt vendor Trolltech solves this problem with a simple program that is used to create projects on a cross-platform basis: qmake.

qmake generates a Makefile from a project file that describes the application in a form that is independent of the operating system on which the application is actually compiled. The generated Makefile contains all the information required to compile the C++ application code on a specific platform. (In Windows it is also possible to generate Visual Studio projects from qmake project files.)

Generating Project Files and Makefiles with qmake

To generate a project file for the "Hello, world!" program, it is sufficient to call qmake with the -project option.[2] To do this, open a shell and change the current directory to the directory containing the source file. If the source text is located in the directory helloWorld and has the name, as in our case, main.cpp,[3] then the command

```
user@linux:helloWorld$ qmake -project
```

will generate a file called helloWorld.pro with the following contents:

```
#helloWorld/helloWorld.pro

#####################################
# Automatically generated by qmake
#####################################

TEMPLATE = app
CONFIG -= moc
DEPENDPATH += .
INCLUDEPATH += .

# Input
SOURCES += main.cpp
```

[2] Please make sure that you really do use the Qt 4 qmake, which differs significantly from the Qt 3 version. Use of the latter on Qt 4 projects causes errors. Many Linux distributions contain both Qt 3 and Qt 4; in Ubuntu Breezy Badger and Dapper Drake, for example, qmake is linked by default to qmake-qt3. The Qt 4 version of the tool can be run with qmake-qt4; if you seldom need the third edition, change the corresponding link to /etc/alternatives.

[3] Although qmake does not require main.cpp to contain the main() function, this convention has become established.

The interesting entries here are the ones for TEMPLATE and SOURCES.[4] The value of TEMPLATE specifies whether we want to create an application (app) or a library (lib); that of SOURCES specifies the source text files of which the project consists.

Simply running qmake is then sufficient to generate the Makefile from the project file:

```
user@linux:helloWorld$ qmake
```

In Windows this command generates three files: Makefile, Makefile.Debug, and Makefile.Release. Makefile here is a metafile that refers to the two other files. Makefile.Debug and Makefile.Release describe how the make program should put the project together.

On Unix platforms (including Linux and Mac OS X projects built with qmake -spec mac-g++, as described below), qmake generates only the Makefile file, which creates an executable of the program that includes debug output after make is run, unless the debug variants of the Qt libraries used by the program are missing.[5] To ensure that these are installed, on Unix systems you should search for the library files with _debug.so in the name, for example, libQtCore_debug.so.4 for the debug version of the QtCore library. In Windows you should look for the corresponding DLL files with names ending in d before the version number, for example, qtcored4.dll for the debug version of QtCore. Clicking the entry Build debug libraries in the start menu folder Program ensures that Qt builds its debug libraries.

Furthermore, in order to achieve the same results with qmake in Unix as in Windows, not only must the debug libraries be available, but the following line must also be included in helloWorld.pro:

```
CONFIG += debug_and_release
```

The operator += here has the same function as in C++: It adds a further option to the variable, without overwriting the ones already set. The -= operator is used similarly to remove individual options.

Alternatively you can set the environment variable QMAKEFLAGS to the value 'CONFIG+=debug_and_release' (don't forget the apostrophes!) before running qmake. But the entry in the .pro file simplifies development if several programmers are all working on the code (or working with one program on several computers) using a version control system such as CVS, Subversion, or Visual Source Safe.

---

[4] The other entries are not required; qmake can be too cautious when automatically generating a project. CONFIG = -moc specifies that we do not need the meta-object compiler for this project, and in the entries for INCLUDEPATH and DEPENDPATH we can specify directories in which the compiler should search for include files.

[5] The debug libraries may need to be installed separately in, for example, Kubuntu (libqt4-debug, libqt4-debug-dev) and SUSE (qt-debug, qt-devel).

If you just want the debug-enabled variation of the executable application, the CONFIG variable should include the value debug. Likewise, you can include release if you just want to generate executable files without extra debugging support, suitable for release to the end user.

Compiling the Project

The make command issued without any target or with the release target, for example,

```
user@linux:helloWorld$ make release
```

creates a release version of the project, whereas

```
user@linux:helloWorld$ make debug
```

accordingly creates a debug version. If you use Microsoft Visual Studio, change the command make to nmake. In either case, the executable file is stored in the release or debug subdirectory, as appropriate.

Once the application is compiled in this way and executed on Unix systems with either ./release/helloWorld or ./debug/helloWorld, the window opens as shown in Figure 1.1 on page 26.

1.2 Layouts, Object Hierarchy, and Memory Management

1.2.1 How to Arrange Widgets Automatically

In order to extend the "Hello, world!" program so that it doesn't just show text in a single QLabel object, but arranges two QLabels one under the other, as shown in Figure 1.2, we use the layout system included in Qt. This automatically arranges the GUI elements, referred to in Qt as *widgets* or *controls*. In language similar to that used in the field of printing, we talk here of *layouting*.

Figure 1.2:
A widget with vertical layout

Figure 1.2 is created with the following source code:

```cpp
// layout/main.cpp

#include <QApplication>
#include <QVBoxLayout>
#include <QLabel>

int main(int argc, char *argv[])
{
    QApplication a(argc, argv);

    QWidget window;

    QVBoxLayout* mainLayout = new QVBoxLayout(&window);
    QLabel* label1 = new QLabel("One");
    QLabel* label2 = new QLabel("Two");

    mainLayout->addWidget(label1);
    mainLayout->addWidget(label2);

    window.show();

    return a.exec();
}
```

In addition to the QApplication and QLabel classes already used in Section 1.1, we now include a class, QVBoxLayout, that is used to arrange widgets vertically—the "V" in the name stands for *vertical*. This time, instead of the QLabel object, there is a simple QWidget object for the main window of the application, which we call window. Use of this variable name is just a convention. The object only becomes a separate window after two steps. First, the QWidget constructor is called. If no arguments are supplied, as in this case, the new object has no parent widget and thus itself forms the root of an object hierarchy. Second, a widget becomes a window only when it is displayed using its show() method.

After creating the QWidget, we create a QVBoxLayout object. The reason why the new operator is used here instead of

```cpp
QVBoxLayout mainLayout(&window);
```

is explained in the following Section 1.2.2. So that the new QVBoxLayout will know that it is responsible for the layout of window, its constructor is given a pointer to this QWidget object as an argument.

Similarly, the two QLabel objects with the texts One and Two are created. In order for these to be managed by the layout object, we add them to the QVBoxLayout object with the QVBoxLayout function addWidget().

Otherwise the rest of the program hardly differs from the first example. Observe that we only have to make the QWidget object visible by calling its show() method. This causes all widgets that the QWidget contains to be displayed on the screen as well, which in our case is both QLabels.

Finally we start the event loop as before and pass the return code from the event loop back as the application's return value. A simple return 0; would terminate the application immediately without even displaying the window.

This application demonstrates the main advantage of layouts: You don't need to worry about the exact positioning of the widgets. In addition, the user can enlarge or scale down layout windows, and the layout automatically ensures that the components of the window will adjust to sensibly fill the space available, without the need for the programmer to write explicit code to implement this behavior.

The programmer may also define what behavior is allowed for individual widgets in a layout: for example, whether a control element (such as a widget to display multiple line texts) should occupy as much space as possible or be constrained in size; or how to handle widgets which don't need more vertical space, such as checkboxes. Chapter 5 (page 141) describes the possibilities here in more detail.

1.2.2 Memory Management in Object Hierarchies

The application shown in Figure 1.2 and described in the previous section not only introduces automatic layouts, but also differs from "Hello, world!" from Section 1.1 in another respect: Although the variable declaration QWidget window; is used to allocate the QWidget object, the new operator is used to allocate the QVBoxLayout and the QLabel objects. We used

```
QVBoxLayout* mainLayout = new QVBoxLayout(&window);
```

rather than

```
QVBoxLayout mainLayout(&window);
```

to create the layout.

We've taken this approach because C++ does not provide automatic memory management. In general, the application programmer must take care of this himself. However, Qt can take over some of the work of memory management, as follows. Objects of classes that are derived from the QObject class can be arranged to form a tree structure: Objects may possess "child" objects. If such an object is deleted, then Qt automatically deletes all of the child objects, and these "children" in turn delete their own "offspring," and so on.

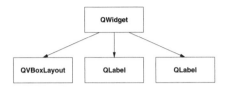

Put another way, if the root of an object tree disappears, Qt automatically deletes the entire tree. This relieves the programmer from having to track down the descendants of the object and release the memory that they occupy. However, in order for this automatic memory management to function, all children (and the children's children, and ...) must lie on the *heap*, which is brought about by creating them using new. Objects that are created using new are then referenced with a pointer into the heap. This is why mainLayout was declared as a pointer to a QVBoxLayout, rather than as a QVBoxLayout.

Not placing objects on the heap (that is, *not* allocating them with new) is a common beginner's mistake: Widgets that are created only on the stack, for example, in a class constructor, are deleted by the compiler after processing is finished. Although the application does generate the widget briefly, it is never visible to the eye.[6]

Also, this declaration not only creates the QVBoxLayout object but also makes it a child of the QWidget object window, by means of the constructor provided by the QVBoxLayout class. In contrast, when they are created, the two labels initially have no parent object; the QLabel constructor initializes only the label's text:

```
QLabel* label1 = new QLabel("One");
```

We use the subsequent QVBoxLayout::addWidget() calls to ensure that the QWidget object assumes parentage of each of the new labels. (In fact, the GUI elements contained in a widget must be the children of the overlying widget. For this reason, the QWidget object becomes the parent of the QLabel object, and not the

---

[6] Of course, all allocated objects will go out of scope after exec() returns. However, the problem here is that we *implicitly* create an object hierarchy via the layouts for the first time ((foo->addWidget(bar) automatically assigns the widget that layout foo manages to be the parent of bar). When the parent widget goes out of scope, it will try to delete its children, which may already have gone out of scope, depending on the order that the compiler chooses to place the objects on the stack (this should be deterministic in order of creations but has allegedly been nondeterministic in special situations with some compilers). And even if you do it correctly, there is still a lot of stuff to get wrong. Now if you just create all QObject derivatives (and thus QWidget derivatives) on the heap, you don't have to deal with those issues and, as a benefit, the code is a lot easier to refactor later on. This is why it really is advisable to create all objects on the heap rather than on the stack, with the exception of the parent widget.

QVBoxLayout object, as might be assumed.) A tree structure as shown in Figure 1.3 is thereby created.

Both the layout object and the two labels, which are subobjects of the window object, must be generated on the heap using new. On the other hand, we generate the window on the stack using QWidget window;, so that we don't have to delete it by hand when the application is terminated. (You can do this only with objects that have no parent object.) Therefore, in most cases you should create objects of classes derived from QObject on the heap using new.

1.2.3   Other Layout Types

The class QHBoxLayout is used to arrange elements horizontally, in the same way that the QVBoxLayout class is used for vertical layouts. Its interface is just like that of the QVBoxLayout. If you replace QVBoxLayout with QHBoxLayout in the example from Figure 1.2, the result will appear as shown in Figure 1.4.

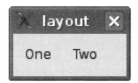

Figure 1.4:
The two labels
arranged horizontally
instead of vertically

There is also a class that arranges widgets in a grid, QGridLayout:

```
// gridLayout/main.cpp

#include <QApplication>
#include <QGridLayout>
#include <QLabel>

int main(int argc, char *argv[])
{
    QApplication a(argc, argv);

    QWidget window;

    QGridLayout* mainLayout = new QGridLayout(&window);
    QLabel* label1 = new QLabel("One");
    QLabel* label2 = new QLabel("Two");
    QLabel* label3 = new QLabel("Three");
    QLabel* label4 = new QLabel("Four");
    QLabel* label5 = new QLabel("Five");
    QLabel* label6 = new QLabel("Six");

    mainLayout->addWidget(label1, 0, 0);
    mainLayout->addWidget(label2, 0, 1);
```

```
mainLayout->addWidget(label3, 1, 0);
mainLayout->addWidget(label4, 1, 1);
mainLayout->addWidget(label5, 2, 0);
mainLayout->addWidget(label6, 2, 1);

window.show();

return a.exec();
}
```

This program is like the previous example: Instead of the QVBoxLayout, now a QGridLayout is used as a "container," this time for six QLabel objects. Unlike the addWidget() function of the horizontal or vertical layout class, QGridLayout::add-Widget() requires three arguments: the widget to be allocated, as well as the line and column number of the grid cell in which it should take its place. The first cell of the grid has the coordinates (0,0) and is located at the top left corner. The result can be seen in Figure 1.5.

If the text Five is not displayed correctly, the typical reason is that the editor used has saved the source file in UTF-8 encoded form. In this case it needs to be converted to the ISO-8859-1 or ISO-8859-15 format. In the KDE editor Kate, this option can be found in the Save as... dialog.

Figure 1.5:
A program that uses
QGridLayout

You will find further details on the subject of layout in Chapter 5 which explains how you can design complicated layouts, for example, through nesting, and also looks at manual layout, *splitters*, and the QStackedLayout class.

Splitters behave like vertical or horizontal layouts, but display so-called *handles* in an otherwise empty space. The user can pull these handles in either direction to make more space for the widget lying next to it on the side opposite the motion. When a handle is pulled, the widgets shrink on the side toward which the handle is pulled.

The QStackedLayout class, on the other hand, manages layouts with several "panels" that can each contain various groups of widgets, of which only one is ever visible. Configuration dialogs can be created using this class. When, for example, the user selects a category on a left-hand panel of such a configuration dialog, this causes the right-hand panel to show the widgets that can be used to change the configuration of the chosen category. When the user changes the category on the left side, the QStackedLayout object knows that it should display a different "page" on the right side.

1.3 Signals and Slots

The programs discussed until now generate output only. But if we need to handle user input, we cannot manage without communication between objects.

Many GUI toolkits use *callback functions* or *event listeners* to manage communication between objects, but Qt uses the *signal/slot concept.*[7] Compared with callback functions, this mechanism has the advantage that Qt automatically dismantles a connection if either of the two communicating objects is deleted. This avoids crashes, and makes programming simpler.

1.3.1 The Simplest Case: A Slot Responds to a Signal

The easiest way to explain how signals and slots allow objects to communicate is with a simple example. Consider the following program, which displays a simple button with the text Quit. If the user clicks this button, the application ends.

```
// signalSlot/main.cpp

#include <QApplication>
#include <QPushButton>

int main(int argc, char *argv[])
{
    QApplication a(argc, argv);

    QPushButton button("Quit");
    button.show();

    QObject::connect(&button, SIGNAL(clicked()),
                     &a, SLOT(quit()));

    return a.exec();
}
```

Compared with the "Hello, world!" program from Section 1.1 on page 25, only two things have changed. First, the QLabel object used there has been replaced by a

---

[7] There are also events and event handler functions in Qt. The difference between signals and events is that a signal may be connected to as many slots as desired, including slots from different objects. In contrast, an event handler handles events determined for other objects. It's a kind of event interceptor. Chapter 7 provides more details of events.

QPushButton. This class is used to display a button and process mouse clicks on this button.

The second difference consists of the call to QObject::connect(). connect() is a static function of the QObject class that creates a connection between a signal originating from one object and a slot in a destination object. The first two arguments specify the object sending the signal and the signal that we want to bind to the receiving slot. The last two arguments specify the object that is the recipient of the signal, and the receiving slot. The & characters are necessary because the function expects the addresses of the sending and receiving objects as arguments. Here this function is used to determine the action that is executed by the application when the user presses the button: The application terminates.

Slots are normal functions of a class that are specially marked so that they can react to signals. Signals on the other hand are "sent" by objects. A signal from an object can be connected to one or several slots of a single receiving object or of several different receiving objects. If an object sends out a signal, then all the slots are called that are connected to the signal. If there is no matching link, nothing happens.

The call to the QObject::connect() function in the example connects the clicked() signal of the QPushButton object with the quit() slot of the QApplication object. The button sends out the clicked() signal whenever the user presses the button, thus causing the button's clicked() function to be called. In response to this signal, the quit() function of the application is called. Calling this slot ends the event loop, and thus the entire application.

When linking signals and slots with the QObject::connect() function, you must use the macros SIGNAL() and SLOT(), as shown. For its second (signal) and fourth (slot) arguments, the connect() function expects to be passed string values that contain a prefix describing the type (signal or slot) and otherwise comply with an internal Qt convention, about which we need not be concerned. Using the two macros will ensure that the expected strings are generated correctly.

1.3.2 Signals Carrying Additional Information and How They Are Processed

The link between a signal and a slot can also be used to transmit additional information that controls the precise reaction of the slot. For example, see the application shown in Figure 1.6. This program consists of three control elements: a label, which displays a numeric value; a spin box, which can be used to change the value via the keyboard or mouse (and which also displays the value); and a slider, which shows the current value graphically and can be manipulated to change the value.

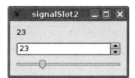

Figure 1.6:
All three elements should display the same changeable value.

The aim is for all three widgets to always display the same value. If the user changes the value via the slider, the value must also be adjusted in the spin box and in the label. The same applies to the slider and label if the user adjusts the value in the spin box. This is accomplished with the following code:

```cpp
// signalSlot2/main.cpp

#include <QApplication>
#include <QVBoxLayout>
#include <QLabel>
#include <QSpinBox>
#include <QSlider>

int main(int argc, char *argv[])
{
    QApplication a(argc, argv);

    QWidget window;

    QVBoxLayout* mainLayout = new QVBoxLayout(&window);
    QLabel* label = new QLabel("0");
    QSpinBox* spinBox = new QSpinBox;
    QSlider* slider = new QSlider(Qt::Horizontal);

    mainLayout->addWidget(label);
    mainLayout->addWidget(spinBox);
    mainLayout->addWidget(slider);

    QObject::connect(spinBox, SIGNAL(valueChanged(int)),
                     label, SLOT(setNum(int)));
    QObject::connect(spinBox, SIGNAL(valueChanged(int)),
                     slider, SLOT(setValue(int)));
    QObject::connect(slider, SIGNAL(valueChanged(int)),
                     label, SLOT(setNum(int)));
    QObject::connect(slider, SIGNAL(valueChanged(int)),
                     spinBox, SLOT(setValue(int)));

    window.show();

    return a.exec();
}
```

We will place the three widgets in turn (that is, from top to bottom) into a vertical layout. To do this the QSpinBox class contributes the spin box element, and the QSlider is correspondingly responsible for the slider.

To ensure synchronization of the widgets, we use four connect() calls (Figure 1.7): if the value of the spin box changes, then the label and the slider must be updated; if the status of the slider varies, the label and the spin box need to be brought up-to-date. (Note that because the spinBox, label, and slider variables are already pointer variables that reference the widgets, we don't have to take their addresses using the & operator, as we did in the previous example.)

Figure 1.7:
The example program shows that a signal can be connected to several slots.

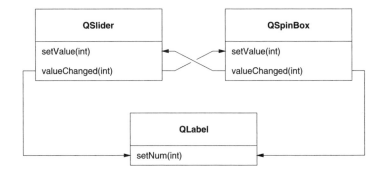

A change made to the value by the user is reported by the QSpinBox and QSlider classes via the signal QSpinBox::valueChanged(int) or QSlider::valueChanged(int). In each case, the integer argument indicated by the int keyword, which the signal transmits to the slot, specifies the new value of the spin box or the slider.

A new value for the label is set using the QLabel::setNum(int) slot, a function that is called with an integer value as an argument. The spin box and the slider are handled similarly using the slots QSpinBox::setValue(int) and QSlider::setValue(int).

The arrows in Figure 1.7 show that a signal can be connected to several slots and that a slot can react to several signals. For example, if the QSpinBox object sends out the signal valueChanged(int) with the value 5, both the setNum(int) slot of the QLabel object and the setValue(int) function of the QSlider object are called with the value 5.

Qt does not specify the order in which this happens. Either the label or the slider can be updated first, and the exact behavior may be unpredictable. Still, all three widgets will eventually display the value 5.

In this example the signals and slots use the same argument list because no type conversion takes place in signal/slot connections. Thus the setText() slot of the QLabel object, which takes a string as an argument and displays it, cannot be connected to the valueChanged(int) signal, since the int argument will not be converted to a string.

If a type conversion cannot be avoided, then you must make a derived class and implement a corresponding slot. This new slot performs the type conversion on the value sent by the signal and then calls the actual, desired slot. This is possible since slots are normal functions of a class. However, the reverse is not true: You cannot use any function you like as a slot, since slots must specifically marked so that they are detected as such by Qt. Chapter 2 explains in detail how to inherit from QObject and define your own signals and slots.

Even though signal/slot connections do not automatically adjust argument types, you may connect a signal to a slot that accepts fewer arguments than those sent by the signal; the slot simply ignores the extra arguments. In this way the valueChanged(int) signal of the QSlider could be connected, say, to the quit() slot of the QApplication object. While this would terminate the application as soon as the value of the slider is changed (admittedly not an especially useful behavior), it does show that quit() ignores the int sent by the signal. The types of the arguments used by the slot must match those of the signal arguments. For example, you can connect the signal signalFoo(int, double) to the slots slotFoo(), slotFoo(int), and slotFoo(int, double). However, you cannot link the signalFoo(int, double) signal with the slotFoo(double) slot using connect().

If you try to create an invalid signal/slot connection, neither the compiler nor the linker will complain. Only when the application is run will you see a warning that the signal and slot were not connected properly. For example, if the erroneous connect() call described in our previous paragraph is executed, the terminal window from which the program was called displays the following warning:

```
Object::connect: Incompatible sender/receiver arguments
        SomeClass::signalFoo(int,double) --> SomeClass::slotFoo(double)
```

A slot that expects more arguments than the signal contains cannot process the signal. Thus we can't connect the signalFoo(int, double) signal to the slotFoo(int, double, double) slot.

1.4 Base Classes in Qt

1.4.1 Classes Derived from QObject

Both the automatic memory management mechanism (see Chapter 1.2.2, page 31) and the signal/slot mechanism require the classes involved to be derived from the QObject class.[8]

---

[8] In addition to support for these mechanisms, there are further requirements demanded of classes having QObject as a base class: the treatment of events and the translation of strings from one language to another. These are explained in detail in Chapters 7 and 14.

Several Qt classes have QObject as a base class. Thus all widgets (that is, all elements that display something on the screen) are derived from the QWidget class, which, in turn, is derived from QObject. The layout classes are also inherited from QObject, so that their objects can also be formed into hierarchies which derive benefits from the automatic memory management. As nonvisual objects, however, they are not derived from QWidget.

Other nongraphical classes also originate from QObject, such as QThread for lightweight processes (see Chapter 12) or QTcpSocket, a class that provides objects for network communication via sockets. These classes have QObject as the base class so that they can communicate through signals and slots.

1.4.2   QString and Other Classes not Derived from QObject

However, Qt also contains many classes that do not inherit from QObject, since they require neither signals and slots, nor automatic memory management. These classes include, for example, one of the most important classes, QString, which is responsible for strings. The strings in QString are stored and processed by Qt in Unicode format, enabling text in almost all notation systems in the world to be used; that is, not only West European characters, but also Cyrillic, Arabic, Hebrew, Chinese, and many more. For this reason, Qt can be used very efficiently for programs that must deal with different languages—provided that you use QString for manipulating text that the user may see. The classes QImage (used for loading and saving images), QColor (which saves a color), and many others are also not inherited from QObject; they all work in a value-based manner.

Figure 1.8:
Implicit sharing using
two QString *instances*

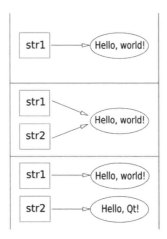

Qt ensures that when these classes are used, two instances never have the same contents. For example, it would be wasteful to have distinct copies of the string "value" "Hello, world!", instead of one copy that is shared among all of that object's clients. However, it takes special management to avoid unnecessary duplication. Figure 1.8 displays the value-based object management procedure at work on the string "Hello, world!" using the following code example:

```
QString str1 = "Hello, world!";
QString str2 = str1;
str2.replace("world", "Qt");
```

As you can see, we first set up the QString instance str1. This automatically stores the string's text, "Hello, world!", in an underlying object, to which str1 is a reference. In the second line the instance str2 is is "assigned" the "value" of str1, but what actually happens, because strings are value-based objects, is that str2 gets a reference to the common underlying object. In the third step we change str2, but before the str2 object implements the change, Qt creates a new underlying data object and sets str2 to now refer to it, so that str1 remains the same afterward, which is the "value-oriented" behavior one expects from string objects. This all happens without the intervention of the programmer.

Qt's use of this copy-when-needed memory management procedure allows data of this kind, for example, strings or QImage objects, to be passed around and shared without using up much memory.

1.4.3 The Qt Inheritance Hierarchy

Figure 1.9 shows a small excerpt from the inheritance hierarchy of Qt. Notice that QLabel inherits not only all the properties of a QObject and a QWidget, but also those of QFrame. This is a base class for all widgets that can have a visual frame surrounding them.

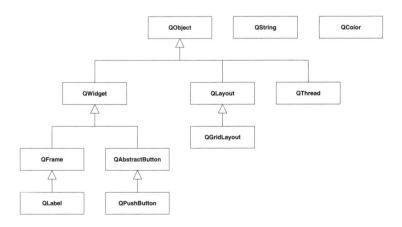

Figure 1.9:
Not all Qt classes are inherited from QObject.

The base class QAbstractButton is also inherited from QWidget. It serves as a base class for all classes that display a button (that is, an element that the user can operate via mouse click). Apart from the QPushButton class that we have seen, this also includes QCheckBox and QRadioButton.

The layout classes are located in a separate branch, which does not lead back to QWidget and for which QLayout is the base class. QGridLayout inherits directly from this,[9] whereas QVBoxLayout and QHBoxLayout are derived from the QBoxLayout class.

The classes QFrame, QAbstractButton, QLayout, and QBoxLayout are used directly only in very few cases. They merely summarize common properties and functions of their "children" in a base class. The classes QString and QColor, on the other hand, have no base class (except themselves).

If you want to implement your own widget, you will usually do so with a class derived from QWidget.

1.5   Qt at a Glance

In reality, Qt 4 is not just *one* monolithic programming library, but rather seven libraries, supplemented by several utility programs. qmake is one of these utilities.

1.5.1   The Qt Libraries

Today, the common usage of the term *GUI toolkit* conveys just a small part of what such a system offers. Qt in particular includes relatively extensive classes for various aspects of application development. Many of these relate to the programming of graphical interfaces, but there are also classes for network programming, OpenGL support, database and XML development, and many more. The focus throughout lies on the platform independence of the classes: With very few exceptions, the same classes are available on all supported operating systems, with the same functions and the same behavior.

Qt 4.0 consists of the following program libraries:

- QtCore contains base classes that do not generate any GUI output.

- QtGui contains the base GUI classes.

- QtNetwork contains the network classes.

- QtOpenGL contains the OpenGL support.

[9] See http://doc.trolltech.com/4.2/hierarchy.html.

- QtSql contains the SQL database classes.

- QtXml contains the XML and DOM classes (see page 45).

- QtAssistantClient allows you to use Qt assistant as a documentation browser in your application.

- Qt3Support includes classes that ensure compatibility with Qt 3.

Qt 4.1 added the QtSvg library, which provides support for the SVG vector graphics format, as well as the QtTest library, also called QTestLib, which contains a framework for writing unit tests.

Finally in Qt 4.2, Trolltech added the QtDBus module, which provides the Qt bindings for the message bus system from Freedesktop.org.[10]

You may need to link an application's code to several libraries, often including QtCore and QtGui. For this reason, qmake uses both libraries by default.

The libraries to be linked are specified by the qmake variable QT. By default it contains the values core and gui. For example, to write a GUI program with network support, you would add the value network to this variable. This is brought about in the .pro file with the line

```
QT += network
```

To write a command-line program with XML support that merely links with QtCore and QtXml, and not with QtGui, you must add xml and remove the value gui. This is done with the following lines:

```
QT -= gui
QT += xml
```

To use all of the libraries in Qt 4.0, write:

```
QT += network opengl sql xml support
```

In addition to specifying project files, there is another topic for which knowledge of the contents of the Qt libraries is of particular interest. Besides the header files for individual class definitions, whose filenames match the names of the classes they describe, Qt also provides header files for its libraries. Each of these files contains the interface descriptions of all of the classes of a library; the name of the header file matches the name of the library. Thus, in the examples so far, which have only used classes from QtGui, instead of the many separate #include statements, we could simply have written

---

[10] See http://www.freedesktop.org/wiki/Software/dbus.

```
#include <QtGui>
```

However, these library header files are very long, which considerably increases the length of the compiling process. This won't be a problem if the compiler supports precompiled header files, but only the more recent compilers do (such as with GCC from version 3.4 on).

The Base Library QtCore

QtCore is a partial library required by every Qt program. Among other things, it makes available the following:

- Basic data types, such as QString and QByteArray

- Basic data structures, such as QList, QVector, and QHash

- Input/output classes such as QIODevice, QTextStream, and QFile

- Classes with which multiple threads can be programmed (including QWaitCondition and QThread)

- The classes QObject and QCoreApplication (the base class for QApplication)

None of these classes depends on GUI components. This separation from the GUI allows Qt applications (such as command-line programs) to be written that do not implement a GUI

In nongraphical programs the QCoreApplication class takes on the role of the QApplication class in GUI applications: It makes an event loop available. This is useful if you require asynchronous communication, whether between different threads or via network sockets.[11]

The GUI Library QtGui

The QtGui library contains all classes that are necessary for programming graphical user interfaces, including the following:

- The QWidget class and classes derived from it, such as QLabel and QPushButton

- The layout classes (including QVBoxLayout, QHBoxLayout, and QGridLayout)

- Classes such as QMainWindow and QMenu, which are needed if you want to add menus to an application

[11] QtCore does not contain any network classes, but the QtNetwork library can be used with QtCore if networking is required.

- Classes for drawing, such as QPainter, QPen, and QBrush

- Classes providing ready-to-use dialogs (including QFileDialog and QPrintDialog)

- The QApplication class

QtGui requires the QtCore library.

The Network Library QtNetwork

The partial library QtNetwork provides classes for writing network applications. In addition to supporting simple socket communication via the QTcpSocket and QUdpSocket classes, this library also enables client-side HTTP and FTP with QHttp and QFtp.

Unlike QtGui, QtNetwork requires the QtCore library, but it can, of course, be used together with QtGui and the other libraries.

The OpenGL Library QtOpenGL

The QtOpenGL library enables OpenGL to be used in a Qt program. It provides the QGLWidget class—a Qt widget in which you can draw using OpenGL commands.

QtOpenGL uses the QtCore and QtGui libraries.

The Database Library QtSql

The QtSql library classes provide access to SQL databases in Qt programs. This library includes classes that are used to establish a connection with an SQL database and to query and modify data. Qt supports a range of SQL databases, including the open source databases PostgreSQL, MySQL, and SQLite.

QtSql requires the QtCore library, and it is discussed at length in Chapter 9 (page 257).

The XML Library QtXml

A simple, nonvalidating XML parser is provided by the partial library QtXML. It can be addressed directly through a SAX2 interface (*Simple API for XML*).

QtXml also contains an implementation of the DOM standard (*Document Object Model*). The corresponding classes allow you to parse an XML document, manipulate its tree structure, publish the modified document again as an XML document, or to create a new XML document with DOM.

This library requires only the QtCore library, and it is discussed in more depth in Chapter 13 (page 353).

The Compatibility Library Qt3Support

Compared with its predecessor, Qt 3, Qt 4 has undergone considerable development: Some classes contain changes that are incompatible with the Qt 3 versions, and others have been replaced in Qt 4 with completely new classes with different names. In order to simplify the porting of Qt 3 programs to Qt 4, Trolltech includes the corresponding Qt 3 classes in the Qt3Support library. However, you should not use this library for new programs, since development of their classes has stopped. Since this book explains programming with Qt 4, we will not use these classes and will not discuss them further.

The Vector Graphics Library QtSvg

The SVG vector graphics format, published by the W3 consortium and based on XML, has great potential. From Qt 4.1 onward the QtSvg library supports the SVG profiles *SVG Basic* and *SVG Tiny*,[12] which can be used to display SVG files and animations, although it cannot as yet create them or, as in XML, manipulate them through a DOM tree.

The QtAssistantClient Library

The assistant client library allows you to remotely control the Qt assistant application. This allows you to use the assistant as a platform-independent help browser for your application. The heart of the module is the QAssistantClient class.

Customized help pages for use with Qt assistant are provided in basic HTML markup, along with an XML file that describes the structure of the documentation.

The Test Case Library QTestLib

Originally released outside the Qt core distribution for paying customers, QTestLib entered the regular Qt distribution starting with the Qt 4.1.0 release. The library contains facilities to write proper unit tests for newly written classes, and covers a scope similar to JUnit in Java.

---

[12] See http://www.w3.org/TR/SVGMobile/.

The QtDBus Library

DBus is a messaging protocol that has emerged as a de facto standard on Linux and other Unix derivates. For instance, the Linux Hardware Abstraction Layer (HAL) and the upcoming KDE 4 are using DBus for interprocess communication. Even though ports for Windows and Mac OS X exist, Qt 4.2 will offer to build this library only on Unix. This may, however, change in future versions.

ActiveQt and Migration Classes

The platform-specific extension ActiveQt for Windows makes it possible to implement Active X components with Qt and to use them in Qt programs. It is available only in the commercial Qt desktop edition, however.

Trolltech also provides migration solutions for MFC-, Motif-, and Xt-based applications. Like ActiveQt, however, they are available only as separate commercial add-ons for Qt 4, the *Qt Solutions*,[13] and will not be discussed in this book.

1.5.2 Tools and Utilities

In addition to all this, Qt includes three GUI programs that can be used to display Qt documentation, create dialogs according to the WYSIWYG principle (*What You See Is What You Get*), or translate programs into other languages. The toolkit also provides a series of command-line programs for performing various tasks.

The Documentation Browser "Qt Assistant"

The Qt documentation consists of simple HTML files that can be viewed with any web browser or with the Qt Assistant. Unlike a web browser, the Assistant displays an index of the entire Qt documentation and allows for a full-text search of that documentation (Figure 1.10).

The Assistant's keyword directory is particularly useful when working with Qt daily. For example, if you require documentation on a class, on QLabel, simply enter qlabel in the index input box. With (Enter) you are taken immediately to the excellent class documentation.

---

[13] See http://www.trolltech.com/products/solutions/.

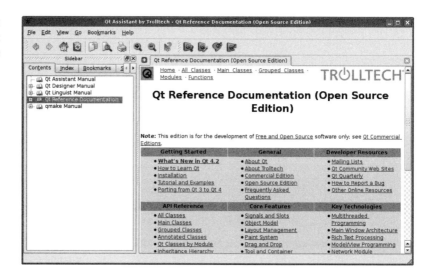

Figure 1.10:
The Qt Assistant
displays the Qt
documentation.

The Assistant is an important complement to this book because it not only documents newly added API calls (or ones not discussed in this book due to lack of space), but also provides additional usage examples.[14]

The GUI Editor "Qt Designer"

The Qt Designer allows you to create application dialogs and the main application window in a WYSIWYG fashion (Figure 1.11), which is particularly useful when creating complex dialogs and layouts. You can add widgets in the Designer via drag and drop and set their properties. For example, you can change the text of a QLabel or its color and typeface.

You can use the Designer to combine several widgets in a layout, and immediately see the effect that the layout has on the window. You can even set up signal/slot connections between the widgets and the Designer, if necessary.

The Designer's preview mode allows you to check the GUIs you've created: You can see how the layouts react to changes in size, test the widgets, and see whether the signal/slot connections have the desired effects.

The Designer also has a mode that specifies the *tab sequence* of the widgets; that is, the order in which the user accesses the individual widgets when pressing (tab) repeatedly. This is an important aspect of a user interface, and one that you should always check. A program can only be operated intuitively from the keyboard if the

---

[14] For those who prefer to read it in the web browser, the Qt class documentation can be found on the Trolltech website at http://doc.trolltech.com/.

tab sequence makes sense. Note that if you do not set the sequence yourself, Qt sets it automatically, which may not always lead to desirable results.

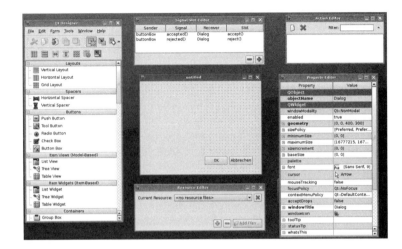

Figure 1.11:
The tools of the
Designer as multiple
top-level windows

In order to use dialogs created with Designer in an application program, you will need a separate conversion program. The Qt Designer saves the description of the draft versions of an interface in a separate XML-formatted file with the filename extension .ui. To use this interface in a program, C++ code must be created from the XML description with the command-line tool uic (*User Interface Compiler*).

If you use qmake to create a project, uic can be used to integrate a Designer-created interface very easily: Each .ui file to be used is added to the FORMS variable by a line in the .pro file. For example, the following line in the .pro file adds the description of the dialog from mydialog.ui to the project:

```
FORMS += mydialog.ui
```

qmake then creates a corresponding rule that generates the C++ file ui_mydialog.h from mydialog.ui, using uic. The latter contains the interface description of the code that implements the dialog. (We explain this file and its use in the rest of the code for the application program in more detail in Chapter 3 on page 91.)

The Translation Tool "Qt Linguist"

Qt Linguist is used to translate application programs from one language to another. As a separate GUI tool it allows you to integrate language translators in the work process of a software project more easily. Like Qt Designer, Qt Linguist is used in conjunction with external command-line programs, namely lupdate and lrelease, to update the binaries of a software project and replace the words and phrases that are displayed to the user with their equivalents in a different language. lupdate extracts the texts to be localized from the source code of the program and generates translation files according to a definition given in the project file:

```
TRANSLATIONS = application_fr.ts \
               application_nl.ts
```

The GUI application Linguist serves as a graphical utility when translating (i.e., editing) the translation files generated in this way (Figure 1.12). Finally, lrelease creates additional binary files containing the translations that the application, on request, will load at startup, and hence appear translated. By using lupdate, Linguist, and lrelease together in this way, the application code does not have to be rewritten and recompiled in order to produce a release that supports another language.

In order for all this to work, the source code of the application must follow certain conventions. Specifically, strings representing text that is to be translated must be passed on to the functions QObject::tr() or QApplication::translate(). This accomplishes two things.

- It allows Qt to change strings dynamically. If you specify only the string "Hello, world!" in the source code, then only this will be used when the application runs. But if you send the string first through the QObject function tr() or to the translate() function of the QApplication class, then this function will look up the translation and return a string containing it, which will be used instead of the original "Hello, world!".

- It allows the lupdate utility to look for such function calls and thus identify passages in the source code that are to be translated.

Figure 1.12:
The Qt Linguist
enables applications
to be translated into
other languages.

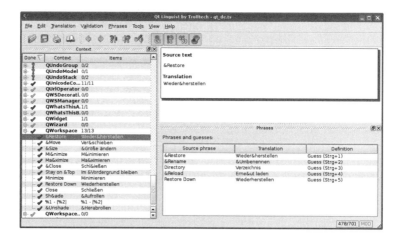

Unfortunately, the simple "Hello, world!" program from Section 1.1 cannot be translated into other languages, since we used neither tr() nor translate() for the string "Hello, world!". To rectify this shortcoming we replace the line

```
QLabel label("Hello, world!");
```

with

```
QLabel label(QApplication::translate("MyLabel", "Hello, world!"));
```

The function QApplication::translate() takes as the first argument a context label for the text, whereas the QObject::tr() function the class name of the widget in question is automatically used as the context label.[15] If, for example, you call up tr() for a QLabel object, Qt automatically uses the context name QLabel. This is possible because QLabel is derived from QObject as the base class and therefore inherits the tr() function.

The context label is important because the same text may appear in several places, with different meanings. If the target language uses distinct terms for these varia-tions, the appropriate translations for the instances of original text will depend on the context. For example, the English text Open may occur in one dialog with the meaning *open file*, but in another dialog with the meaning *open Internet connec-tion*; the German version of the program should render the first instance as Öffnen and the second as Aufbauen. When the two instances are given different context labels, Qt Linguist can distinguish them.

You should send all text in your program through the tr() or translate() function. You will find that the program can generally be translated without great difficulty when it is done during code development, and that it is very tedious to go through the entire source text of a large program by hand and add tr() or translate() calls once the coding is finished. The example programs in the remainder of this book therefore will use tr() right from the beginning.

(You'll find details on internationalization and localization in Chapter 14.)

Creating the Project

As demonstrated in Section 1.1.1, qmake creates platform-specific Makefiles from system-independent project files. The rules stored in the Makefile, make, or nmake are then used to compile and link the application. nmake, however, only works with the commercial Qt version, not with the open source edition.[16] The GPL variant of

---

[15] See also page 380.
[16] The EULA of Visual Studio is incompatible with the GPL anyway once the libraries from Visual Studio are included.

Qt 4 for Windows uses the GCC port MinGW, which instead of nmake provides the GNU make known from Linux.

qmake project files don't require us to worry about either the compiler or linker options. For this reason we will use qmake for all the examples in this book.

In Windows you can also create project files for Microsoft Visual Studio with qmake, if you own a commercial Qt license. (The Qt integration does not function in the free variant of Visual Studio Express; these users are also dependent on the command-line–based version, qmake.)

Figure 1.13:
Code::Blocks builds
our "Hello, world!"
program.

For open source developers in Windows, the development environment Code::Blocks[17] provides a useful alternative. It works together with the MinGW included in Qt, and even has a template for Qt 4 projects. In order for it to work together with qmake, however, you first have to stop it from generating the Makefile itself. To do this, select Project→Properties and mark the option This is a custom Makefile. Then look for the dialog under Project→Build options and activate the Commands tab. Then, in the Pre-build steps field, enter the following commands:

```
qmake -project
qmake
make.bat
```

[17] See http://www.codeblocks.org/.

To ensure that qmake is called even when other programs (such as the Qt Designer) add new files, select the option Always execute, even if target is up-to-date. Figure 1.13 shows Code::Blocks after the "Hello, world!" program has been compiled.

It is useful to store the menu items for starting the Designer, the Assistant, or make in the Tools menu. You can also use this, to a certain extent, to quickly start your own programs, which you can specify in the subitem Configure tools....

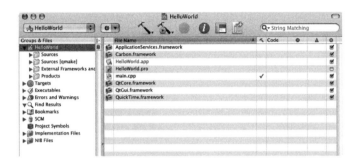

Figure 1.14:
Apple's Xcode IDE enables efficient project management, for which qmake generates the necessary files.

On Mac OS X, the preferred development environment is the Xcode IDE. Apple provides this software free of charge since OS X version 10.3 (Panther), but it needs to be installed separately. qmake on the Mac conveniently creates project files for Xcode instead of Makefiles. However, if you prefer to avoid Xcode and rely on command line tools only, simply append -spec macx-g++ to generate a Makefile:

```
qmake -spec macx-g++
```

In contrast,

```
qmake -spec macx-xcode
```

will cause qmake to generate Mac OS X project files for Xcode in all Qt editions. qmake generates an Xcode project from a .pro file, which then turns up in the project management tool of Xcode.

```
qmake -spec macx-g++
```

creates a Makefile for direct use with GCC.

When creating your application under Linux, the development environment KDevelop[18] is probably the best choice. Version 3.4 provides support for Qt 4 projects. KDevelop includes both, a project template and a graphical management utility for qmake project files, which can be integrated seamlessly into the IDE.

[18] See http://www.kdevelop.org/.

Upon first startup, KDevelop will present an almost blank main window. Choosing Project→New Project will start the project wizard which guides through the initial steps of creating a KDevelop-based project. To create a Qt 4 project that uses qmake, select C++→QMake project→Basic Qt4 application from the treeview as shown in Figure 1.15. For the first step to complete, the wizard also needs a name for the application, as well as a directory location to store all files in.

Figure 1.15: KDevelop provides a qmake-based project support.

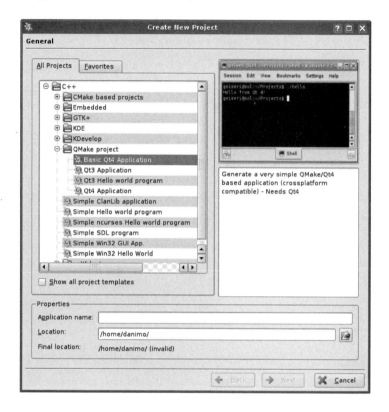

In the next step, KDevelop asks for the name of the default author, an initial version number, and the license for the project. Also it is important that you specify the full path to the Qt 4 versions of qmake and designer in this step. This ensures that KDevelop will not pick the Qt 3 version by accident if both are installed in parallel.

The next step allows you to pick a source code control. If you are not using source code management system, just keep the None default. The remaining steps allow for customizing the templates that are inserted into all header and implementation files. These usually contain the license as well as the author's name. Figure 1.16 shows a mainwindow with the example main.cpp file after the wizard has completed.

Pressing (Shift+F9) will build and execute a given project; the textual output is visible in the Messages and Application tab on the bottom, which will automatically open during build and execution phases, respectively.

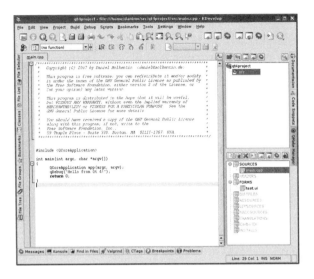

Figure 1.16:
The KDevelop main window after the setup

The qmake-project manager (**QMake Manager**) is hidden behind a tab on the right bearing the Qt symbol. Upon expansion, you can use it to graphically add, remove, or open files. The project manager view separates between different types of sources: KDevelop opens a new tab for common source files, while ui files are automatically launched with the Qt Designer.

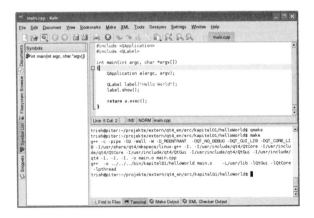

Figure 1.17:
The KDE editor Kate can quickly be converted to a powerful source code editor.

A good alternative for those who dislike a fullblown IDE is the Kate editor (*KDE Advanced Text Editor*), which includes a pull-down menu from which you can run the compiler directly, as shown in Figure 1.17. Depending on your distribution, you may want to install the kate-plugins package first which—among others—provides a plugin for code completion. Equipped this way, Kate gives an overview of methods and member variables in C and C++ files, and even allows for code snippet administration under Settings→Configure Kate→Application→Plugins.

Kate's setup dialog provides a subitem, External Tools, in which you can store your own commands, as with Code::Blocks, which then appear under Tools→External Tools. Settings→Configure Shortcuts lists keyboard shortcuts.

The Meta-object Compiler moc

The signal/slot concept in Qt is not pure C++, but rather an extension of the C++ standard. For this reason the command-line program moc (*meta object compiler*) is used to convert the signal and slot constructs into standard C++. moc generates additional C++ code for each class derived from QObject. This ensures that signal/slot connections can be dynamically generated at runtime. It also allows the names of classes that have QObject as a base class to be dynamically determined at runtime, and even to determine whether a class is a base class for another class.[19]

Qt also includes a *property system*, for which moc generates the necessary code. Properties are special characteristics of a class that can be queried and set. For example, the QLabel class has a text property, whose value is a string containing the text that the label displays. For each property there are two functions: one that reveals its current value, also called the *get method*, and one that changes it, also known as the *set method*. In the case of QLabel, text() is the get method returning the label's text, and setText() is the set method providing the label with a new text.

These two functions, marked in the class definition as properties, allow the text to be queried via QObject::property() and be set with QObject::setProperty(). Both require a string, namely, the name of the property, as an argument. The *Property Editor* of the Designer determines the value of properties at runtime and allows these properties to be changed. If you require properties in a separate class, these must be derived from QObject.

In short, moc is needed whenever a class uses QObject as a base class. The meta-object compiler must preprocess every file that implements the definition of such a class before the C++ compiler is run. In each case this creates a file beginning with the prefix moc_.

For example, if you write your own dialog class MyDialog with QObject as a base class, with the class definition in the file MyDialog.h and the actual implementation

---

[19] By *base class* we mean not just the class from which a class is directly derived, but *all* classes in the inheritance sequence beginning from a root of the class hierarchy. Thus QVBoxLayout has three base classes (QBoxLayout, QLayout, and QObject), because QLayout inherits from QObject, QBoxLayout from QLayout, and QVBoxLayout from QBoxLayout.

in MyDialog.cpp, the meta-object compiler has to process MyDialog.h, then generate the file moc_MyDialog.cpp, and integrate the generated file into the complete project. qmake does all of this automatically.

The Qt Resources Compiler rcc

Almost every program uses external resources such as images or graphics. These resources can either lie in separate files or be embedded directly in the executable files to be generated. Qt 4 uses the resources compiler *rcc* for generated files. The resource compiler obtains its information from resource description files, the names of which end in the extension .qrc. A .qrc file specifies filesystem paths to resources used by the program, beginning from the directory in which the .qrc file resides.

If you include the resource file in the qmake project, Qt automatically generates arrays encoded in hexadecimal form, in which it stores the contents of the resource files. The *Qt resource system* ensures that the application program can access the resources encoded in this way using the old directory and file names. A .qrc file describes (using XML) which files are needed by the finished program. It looks something like this:

```
<RCC>
    <qresource>
        <file>pics/symbols/stop.png</file>
        <file>pics/symbols/start.png</file>
        <file>pics/symbols/pause.png</file>
    </qresource>
</RCC>
```

The path details are always understood as relative to the directory in which the resource file is located. For this example we assume that the above resource file is called symbols.qrc and that the directory pics/symbols, which contains the required images, is beneath the directory with the source code (including the resource file).

In order for qmake to be able to take the information from the resource file into account, a corresponding RESOURCES directive must be added to the project file:

```
RESOURCES    = symbols.qrc
```

The image file stop.png under pics/symbols can now be referenced in the application code as follows:

```
myLabel->setPixmap(QPixmap(":/pics/symbols/stop.png"));
```

That is, in order to refer to a resource, you need only place a colon in front of the path details specified in the .qrc file. (The leading slash is not a typo; relative paths in the file system are specified in the logical path notation as absolute paths, with the code directory as the root.) If the resource description file is properly integrated into the project, a call to QPixmap() can correctly resolve the path, and the label will display a stop icon.

A file in a resource can also be addressed with a logical path completely different from its actual file system path, as shown here:

```
<RCC>
  <qresource prefix="/player">
    <file alias="stop.png">pics/symbols/stop.png</file>
    ...
  </qresource>
</RCC>
```

The prefix attribute for the qresource tag specifies a prefix to be used before the path details, whereas the alias attribute specifies an alternative name or path that can be used instead of the actual path details. With the combination shown above, the stop icon can now also be addressed in the application code as follows:

```
myLabel->setPixmap(QPixmap(":/player/stop.png"));
```

With the help of the lang attribute and alternative qresource entries, the system can load other graphics depending on the current language setting:

```
<RCC>
  <qresource>
    <file>pics/symbols/stop.png</file>
    ...
  </qresource>
  <qresource lang="de">
    <file>pics/symbols/de/stop.png</file>
    ...
  </qresource>
</RCC>
```

Beginning with version 4.1, Qt Designer includes a Resource Editor (see page 99). Unfortunately, in Qt 4.1.0 this does not display the relative paths to the individual resources, nor will it handle the alias attribute. Therefore, you should always check the resource description file that is generated.

1.5.3 Examples and Demos

A complete Qt installation contains a series of example programs in the examples directory and several demo programs in the demo folder.

The example programs are of particular help if you have problems using specific Qt classes, whereas the demo programs mainly demonstrate all the things that Qt can do and are not appropriate as a reference for how to use the class libraries.

1.6   How to Use the Documentation

The HTML documentation included by Trolltech is recommended as a constant companion in Qt programming, especially because it describes all Qt classes in detail. Also, you may find it useful when reading this book to look up the documentation for the classes used in the various examples.

When Qt Assistant starts, the program automatically loads the start page doc/html/index.html (Figure 1.10 on page 48); it can also be viewed in any web browser, and is available online.[20] In addition to the precise documentation of the Qt classes already mentioned, the documentation includes introductory texts; overviews of the signal/slot concept, layouts, and the SQL, network, XML, and OpenGL modules; and detailed descriptions of the tools and utilities.

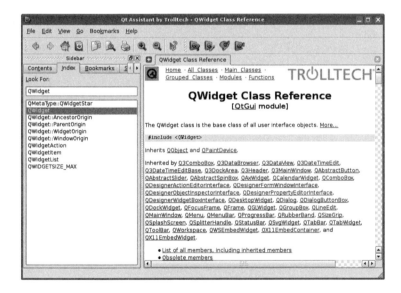

Figure 1.18:
The class
documentation of the
QWidget class

The class documentation is what is most frequently used in day-to-day work with Qt. If you know the class names, you can enter them in the Index tab of the Assistant. From the start page you can also access a list of all classes and a list grouped according to topics.

---

[20]   For Qt 4.1, see http://doc.trolltech.com/4.1/.

The documentation of each class begins with a short description of what the class does, followed by the name of the header file that needs to be integrated in order to use it. The keyword Inherits reveals from which direct base classes the class is derived, Inherited by lists the classes that inherit from this one (Figure 1.18).

This information is followed by a list of the functions of the class which is divided into several categories. These categories include the get and set methods for properties of the class, public and protected functions, signals, and slots.

Only the functions that are defined in the class itself appear in this list; the documentation does not discuss methods that the class obtains through inheritance from base classes. Remember that if you are looking for a specific function and do not find it in the list—it may be documented in a base class. Alternatively, the link List of all members, including inherited members at the beginning of the class documentation, leads to a list of all functions of the class, including inherited functions.

The function list is followed by a detailed description of the class. In addition to a description of the tasks that the class carries out, it also explains some typical ways in which the class is used.

2

The Tools Needed to Create Dialogs

Now that you have an overview of Qt, we will turn to a more practical example to see how the classes work together. Our first extensive program will convert numbers between decimal, hexadecimal, and binary notation; it's shown in Figure 2.1.

Figure 2.1:
Our example program converts numbers between decimal, hexadecimal, and binary notation.

The user of this program can enter any one-byte number (from 0 to 255) in any of the three input fields. The program updates the other two *Line-Edits* input fields with the converted value.

2.1   What's the Difference Between Dialogs and Widgets?

The program's main() function is almost identical to the main() function of the "Hello, world!" program discussed in Section 1.1:

```
// byteConverter/main.cpp

#include <QApplication>
#include "ByteConverterDialog.h"

int main(int argc, char *argv[])
{
    QApplication a(argc, argv);

    ByteConverterDialog bc;
    bc.setAttribute(Qt::WA_QuitOnClose);
    bc.show();

    return a.exec();
}
```

There is just one exception: The class QLabel has been replaced by ByteConverterDialog. This class inherits from QDialog, and its class definition is placed in the header file ByteConverterDialog.h.[1] The #include directive that integrates this header file into the application code uses quotation marks (") instead of angle brackets (<>), since the file is in the same directory as main.cpp.

We've also added the WA_QuitOnClose attribute to the dialog to ensure that the program ends when the dialog is closed. This was not necessary in the previous examples, because we did not use any classes inherited from QDialog as the main window. Since dialogs usually only provide in-between information, the attribute is not active by default for QDialog. After all, closing a dialog shouldn't terminate the application unless there's a serious bug.

We surround the contents of the file ByteConverterDialog.h with *include guards*, consisting of the three preprocessor instructions #ifndef *label*, #define *label* and #endif:

---

[1] For header files that we create ourselves, we use the C/C++ standard file extension .h, to make the file type clear.

```
// byteConverter/ByteConverterDialog.h

#ifndef BYTECONVERTERDIALOG_H
#define BYTECONVERTERDIALOG_H

#include <QDialog>
class QLineEdit;

class ByteConverterDialog : public QDialog
{
    Q_OBJECT

public:
    ByteConverterDialog();

private:
    QLineEdit* decEdit;
    QLineEdit* hexEdit;
    QLineEdit* binEdit;
};

#endif
```

Using include guards is a standard technique in C/C++ programming to avoid problems that occur if more than one source file tries to #include a header file, which can happen in large programs with many independently developed modules. Here, the first time ByteConverterDialog.h is processed, the keyword BYTECONVERTER-DIALOG_H is defined. If a later source file attempts to #include ByteConverterDialog.h again, the #ifndef...endif ("if not defined") directive causes the preprocessor to skip the header file's contents. Without the include guards, the compiler would notice that the keywords and classes are being multiply defined and signal an error.

We include the header file QDialog, since the ByteConverterDialog class inherits from QDialog. In order for the functions of QDialog to be available outside the ByteConverterDialog class we use the access control public.

The class declaration class QLineEdit; is a *forward declaration*. Objects of the ByteConverterDialog class contain three private variables that point to QLineEdit objects, and so the C++ compiler needs to know that QLineEdit is a class in order to process the ByteConverterDialog declaration, but it does not need to know the exact class definition at that point.[2]

The Q_OBJECT macro must be used in all derivations from the QObject base class, including indirect ones, because it defines functions without which the signal/slot concept cannot work. (More on this in Section 2.1.1.)

---

[2] Alternatively, you could include the QLineEdit header file before the declaration of ByteConverterDialog, but then the parser would need to read this, which would slow down compiling considerably, especially on slower machines. For this reason, we try, in this book, to optimize the header files so that only the necessary ones are included.

The constructor is the only public function of the class. We will store pointers to the QLineEdit objects displayed by the byte converter widget in the three member variables (decEdit, hexEdit, and binEdit) because we wish to update the input fields in which the user does not enter data immediately to ensure that all three line edits display the same text. Because this is an implementation detail of our ByteConverterDialog class, we declare them as private variables.

2.1.1 Inheriting from QObject

As mentioned previously, you must always use the Q_OBJECT macro when a class inherits, directly or indirectly, from QObject.[3] This macro defines several functions that implement the signal/slot concept. Unfortunately, if the macro is missing in the definition of a class that inherits from QObject, neither the compiler nor the linker will report an error. Instead, the signals and slots of the class will remain unknown to Qt, and at runtime the corresponding connections will not work.

Applications compiled with debugging information will warn at runtime (in a terminal window) that a signal or slot does not exist whenever code is executed that tries to access an unknown signal or slot. The error message is:

```
Object::connect: No such slot QObject::decChanged(QString)
```

However, this error message is a bit non-specific. You will also see it if you have written the name of the signal or slot incorrectly or if the argument list is incorrect.

Every file that uses the Q_OBJECT macro must be submitted to the command-line program moc (see page 56). This tool automatically generates the code converted into pure C++ code by the signal/slot concept.[4]

If you use qmake to create your project, the qmake tool searches all header and source text files named in the .pro file for the Q_OBJECT macro. When it finds one, qmake automatically generates the necessary build instructions for moc based on the contents of those files.[5]

For this to work you must, of course, specify the project's header files in the .pro file. To do so, use the qmake variable HEADERS, as you would the SOURCES variable for source text files:

---

[3] Some compilers issue errors if the Q_OBJECT macro is terminated with a semicolon, which is why, for reasons of portability, we recommend that you always omit it.

[4] moc does not modify your files; it provides the new code in separate files which you have to take care of when writing your Makefiles by hand. If you use qmake as we recommend, you don't have to care.

[5] qmake will not automatically notice if the Q_OBJECT macro is inserted into a file later on.

```
#byteConverter/byteConverter.pro

TEMPLATE = app

SOURCES  = main.cpp \
           ByteConverterDialog.cpp
HEADERS  = ByteConverterDialog.h
```

If moc is not invoked for files containing the Q_OBJECT macros, the linker complains of undefined symbols, and GCC issues this error message:

```
ld: Undefined symbols:
vtable for ByteConverterDialog
ByteConverterDialog::staticMetaObject
```

If you see this error message, check the following:

- Have the qmake variable HEADERS been properly defined?

- Is the problem resolved if the Makefiles are regenerated with qmake?

2.1.2   More Complex Layouts

We now turn to the implementation of the ByteConverterDialog class. When creating instances of this class, the constructor function generates all the QLineEdit widgets displayed by the new ByteConverterDialog object and inserts them into a layout. However, this is no longer as simple as before: In order for the application to behave in an intuitive manner when the user changes the size of the dialog, we need to use nested layouts. Figure 2.2 shows how Qt ensures that the input fields always appear at the top of the window and that the Quit button always appears at the lower right corner of the window.

Figure 2.2:
How Qt layouts react
to a size change in
the dialog

But don't panic: Even though the source code for the constructor becomes quite long, it uses only simple functions:

```cpp
// byteConverter/ByteConverterDialog.cpp

#include "ByteConverterDialog.h"
#include <QLabel>
#include <QLineEdit>
#include <QPushButton>
#include <QVBoxLayout>
#include <QHBoxLayout>
#include <QGridLayout>

ByteConverterDialog::ByteConverterDialog()
{
    // Generate the necessary layouts
    QVBoxLayout* mainLayout = new QVBoxLayout(this);
    QGridLayout* editLayout = new QGridLayout;
    QHBoxLayout* buttonLayout = new QHBoxLayout;

    mainLayout->addLayout(editLayout);
    mainLayout->addStretch();
    mainLayout->addLayout(buttonLayout);

    // Generate the labels and line-edits and add them
    // to the object pointed at by editLayout
    QLabel* decLabel = new QLabel(tr("Decimal"));
    QLabel* hexLabel = new QLabel(tr("Hex"));
    QLabel* binLabel = new QLabel(tr("Binary"));
    decEdit = new QLineEdit;
    hexEdit = new QLineEdit;
    binEdit = new QLineEdit;

    editLayout->addWidget(decLabel, 0, 0);
    editLayout->addWidget(decEdit, 0, 1);
    editLayout->addWidget(hexLabel, 1, 0);
    editLayout->addWidget(hexEdit, 1, 1);
    editLayout->addWidget(binLabel, 2, 0);
    editLayout->addWidget(binEdit, 2, 1);

    // Create the Quit button and add it to the object pointed
    // at by buttonLayout
    QPushButton* exitButton = new QPushButton(tr("Quit"));

    buttonLayout->addStretch();
    buttonLayout->addWidget(exitButton);
    ...
```

Figure 2.3 shows which layouts are involved with which widgets. Keep an eye on it when we now walk through the code above.

The mainLayout object, a vertical box layout, is responsible for the layout of the entire dialog. Therefore, we pass a pointer to the ByteConverterDialog object when we call its constructor. To do this we use the this pointer, since we are in a function of the ByteConverterDialog class itself.

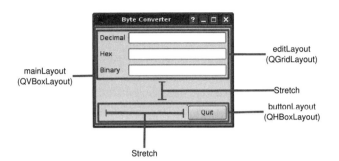

Figure 2.3:
The layouts as used
by
ByteConverterDialog

The editLayout object is responsible for the layout of the labels and line-edit widgets. In order to be able to stack these elements neatly, and to organize the widgets in a single column, we use a grid layout.

The buttonLayout, which we create with the third new call, will be responsible for managing the Quit button. However, before we can generate widgets like this button and add them to editLayout and buttonLayout, we must add those two layouts to the mainLayout using addLayout(), which is the layout equivalent of addWidget(). If you add widgets to a layout not yet associated with a widget, you will receive this runtime error in a terminal window:

```
QLayout::addChildWidget: add layout to parent before adding children to
layout.
```

and the widgets will remain invisible. Therefore, you should always generate the basic layout for your class first, then continue with the next layout "layer," and so on.

To ensure that input fields are always placed at the top of the ByteConverterDialog and that the Quit button is always positioned at its lower right, we use *stretches*.

Figure 2.4:
The dialog after a
change in size when
stretches are not used

Stretches occupy the space not required by the widgets and thus create empty spaces in your dialog. If you were to omit stretches in our example, the widgets would occupy the entire space. Were the user to enlarge such a dialog, without stretch, he would see something like Figure 2.4.

To avoid this behavior, we add a stretch between the editLayout and the button-Layout with the addStretch() function.

Now we can generate the labels and line edits and entrust them to the editLayout. We save the line edit objects in the private class variables decEdit, hexEdit, and binEdit, because we want to change their contents through code stored in other functions. For all other objects, we can manage without corresponding pointers because we do not need to access them outside the constructor.

To ensure that the Quit button is always displayed at the far bottom right of the dialog, we first fill the horizontal layout buttonLayout with a stretch before we adjust the button itself.

By adding all the widgets and sublayouts to the mainLayout object or its children using QObject::addWidget() and QObject::addLayout(), we ensure that all objects generated by the constructor with new are inherited from the ByteConverterDialog object. Since they now form a heap-allocated object hierarchy that Qt's memory management will handle for us, we do not need to delete any of them manually. When the ByteConverterDialog object is deleted, all its children disappear automatically.

Are you becoming slightly disillusioned because of the not insignificant amount of code that we had to write just to create a really simple dialog? Help is on the way in Chapter 3, which explains how a dialog can be created using the Qt designer, and code automatically generated. More details and background information on layouts is provided in Chapter 5.

2.1.3   Increasing Usability

Despite the improved layout, the dialog does not yet behave ideally in certain respects:

- The window title at the moment shows the program name byteConverter. Something more descriptive might be better.

- The Quit button should become the *default button* of the dialog. The default button is activated by (Enter) even if it currently does not have keyboard focus. Most widget styles highlight the default button in a particular way.

- Currently you can enter any numbers in the line-edit widgets. We should restrict this to valid values, that is, only whole decimal numbers between 0 and 255, hexadecimal numbers with a maximum of two digits, and binary numbers with a maximum of eight bits.

We can solve these three problems by adding the following lines to the constructor:[6]

```
// byteConverter/ByteConverterDialog.cpp (continued)

    ...
    exitButton->setDefault(true);

    // Limit input to valid values
    QIntValidator* decValidator =
        new QIntValidator(0, 255, decEdit);
    decEdit->setValidator(decValidator);

    QRegExpValidator* hexValidator =
        new QRegExpValidator(QRegExp("[0-9A-Fa-f]{1,2}"), hexEdit);
    hexEdit->setValidator(hexValidator);

    QRegExpValidator* binValidator =
        new QRegExpValidator(QRegExp("[01]{1,8}"), binEdit);
    binEdit->setValidator(binValidator);

    setWindowTitle(tr("Byte Converter"));

    ...
```

Setting the Window Title

The first two problems are each solved with a single line of additional code. To solve the first problem, we use the function setWindowTitle(), which sets the window title of a widget if the widget occupies a top-level window. This function is a method of the QWidget class. Since ByteConverterDialog has QWidget as its base class, it inherits this function, and we can simply call it up.

Specifying the Default Button

The default button for a dialog is specified by informing the button (rather than the dialog, as you might expect) that it is indeed the default button. (Note, however, that calling setDefault(true) on a QPushButton object only has an effect if the button is used in a dialog—in a main window there are no default buttons. If you try to define a default button for a main window, Qt will make it look like one, but it doesn't activate it when the user presses the (Enter) key.)

---

[6] To compile the resulting code, please also add the missing #include lines (omitted above for the sake of clarity) for the classes used for the first time here, QIntValidator and QRegExpValidator!

Checking User Input

The third problem, restricting the input in the line-edit widgets to valid values, requires somewhat more work, but can be resolved through *validators*. These inherit from QValidator as the base class. A validator is associated to a parent object that receives input and informs that object whether or not it should accept the current input value.

To check the validity of the decimal number, we use a QIntValidator object. It is created by invoking the constructor and passing to it, as the first and second arguments, the minimum and maximum input values allowed. The third argument, here decEdit, is a pointer to the line-edit object that we want to make the parent object of the validator. This invocation, besides binding the validator to the input widget, also makes it subject to automatic memory management, so that the validator will be deallocated when the widget is. The setValidator() call then causes the validator to keep an eye on the input given to the object pointed to by decEdit. Now the user can type only whole numbers between 0 and 255 in the input field.

To check the validity of hexadecimal numbers, we must make use of another type of validator: QRegExpValidator. This compares the input, viewed as a string, against a regular expression. In our case, the regular expression is [0-9A-Fa-f]{1,2}. The first subexpression in square brackets specifies the characters permitted in the input string: the digits 0 to 9 and the letters A to F (written either in upper or lower case). The following subexpression, {1,2}, restricts the length of the input string to at least one, and at most two, characters.

Regular expressions in Qt are related to those from Perl, but there are some significant differences. For example, it is necessary to escape a *backslash* (\) in a Perl-style regular expression with another backslash to get the corresponding Qt-style expression, because a single backslash already acts as an escape character in C/C++. QRegExp then recognizes the double backslash as a simple backslash. It follows from this that we need to type in four backslashes if we want to specify a literal backslash within a Qt-style regular expression.

We also use a QRegExpValidator with the regular expression [01]{1,8} as a validator for the input field for binary numbers. This expression allows only the characters 0 and 1 in the input string, but the string can be anywhere from one to eight characters in length.

2.1.4   Implementing Slots

Finally, we need to implement the functional connections that make the Quit button work as expected and synchronize the three input fields with one another.

To ensure that clicking the Quit button will close the byte-converter dialog, we extend the ByteConverterDialog constructor to associate the clicked() signal of the button with the accept() slot of the dialog. The slot is provided by QDialog, which the ByteConverterDialog class inherits from:

```
// byteConverter/ByteConverterDialog.cpp (continued)

    ...
    connect(exitButton, SIGNAL(clicked()),
            this, SLOT(accept()));
    ...
```

The accept() method, when invoked, simply closes the dialog. Our use of *accept()* here follows a general convention: A large number of dialogs have an Ok and a Cancel button at the bottom; Ok corresponds to the accept() slot, Cancel to the reject() slot. Both slots close the dialog, the first exiting with a positive return value, the second with a negative one (see Chapter 6, page 161). In this example we only have one button and therefore are not interested in the return value, just the action.

However, the real event-processing logic of our byte converter application consists of augmenting the customary signals and slots with several custom-built connections, specific to the functionality of our ByteConverterDialog class. These signal/slot connections should come into action when any one of the QLineEdit objects sends out the signal textChanged(), indicating that the text in that object's input field has changed. For this purpose, we expand our class definition as follows:

```
// byteConverter/ByteConverterDialog.h (continued)

class ByteConverterDialog : public QDialog
{
    ...

private slots:
    void decChanged(const QString&);
    void hexChanged(const QString&);
    void binChanged(const QString&);
};
```

Slots are declared in the same way as normal functions, except that for access control we use the designators public slots:, protected slots:, and private slots:, instead of the usual public:, protected:, and private: protection modes.

Each of our three slots accepts an argument of the type const QString&. In this way the textChanged() signal of the function can pass the new text of the line edit.

As the argument type for the signals/slots to be, we do not choose simply QString, but a reference to a const QString. There are two reasons for this. First, by using call-by-reference rather than call-by-value, the QString object containing the updated input to be passed to the signals/slots will not be copied when the signals and slots are invoked, and the code becomes more efficient. However, use of call-by-reference allows the function to modify the actual parameter, which the signals and slots should not do, so the parameter is also declared to be a reference to const data. This second step is a recommended "defensive programming" practice whenever a function should not change an actual parameter that is passed by reference.

Even though the declaration of a slot differs slightly from that of other functions, it is still an ordinary function, which is implemented and can be called in the usual way. Here is the definition of the decChanged() slot in the file ByteConverterDialog.cpp:

```
// byteConverter/ByteConverterDialog.cpp (continued)

void ByteConverterDialog::decChanged(const QString& newValue)
{
    bool ok;
    int num = newValue.toInt(&ok);
    if (ok) {
        hexEdit->setText(QString::number(num, 16));
        binEdit->setText(QString::number(num, 2));
    } else {
        hexEdit->setText("");
        binEdit->setText("");
    }
}
```

The function receives the new string displayed by the decimal line-edit widget as the actual value for its newValue parameter, and it updates the strings displayed by the hexadecimal and binary line-edit widgets. First, we need to determine the numeric value that corresponds to the input string. As an object of the QString class, newValue knows several functions that convert strings to numbers. We will use the toInt() function, as the input is a string representing an integer value.

toInt() accepts a bool pointer as an optional argument: If this argument is specified, the function sets the variable to which it points to true if the string is successfully converted to a numeric value, and to false if the conversion fails, that is, if the string does not represent an integer value.

If the conversion is successful, we set the texts displayed by the two other line edits (hexEdit and binEdit) to the hexadecimal and binary equivalents of the new value. To do this, we convert the number to a string that represents the new value in hexadecimal form and to a string that represents the new value in binary form. For this purpose the QString class has the static function number(), which returns the representation of a number as a string. The number itself is its first argument. As a second argument, number() expects the base for the number system used, in our case 16 for hexadecimal and 2 for binary. The second argument is optional, and if it is not specified, number() assumes base 10 (the decimal system), which is the most common case.

If the toInt() function could not convert the string that was entered in the decimal line-edit widget into a number, we write an empty text to the other two line-edit widgets, with setText(). Thanks to the validator we used for the decEdit object, which ensures that only numbers in the range 0 to 255 can be entered, the conversion will only fail in one single case: if the user deletes the input completely.

We implement the two remaining slots in the same way:

```
// byteConverter/ByteConverterDialog.cpp (continued)

void ByteConverterDialog::hexChanged(const QString& newValue)
{
...
    if (ok) {
        decEdit->setText(QString::number(num));
        binEdit->setText(QString::number(num, 2));
    } else {
...
    }
}

void ByteConverterDialog::binChanged(const QString& newValue)
{
...
    if (ok) {
        decEdit->setText(QString::number(num));
        hexEdit->setText(QString::number(num, 16));
    } else {
...
    }
}
```

In these functions, when transforming the string to an integer value, we specify the base in an optional second argument to toInt(); like QString::number(), toInt() uses base 10 by default if this argument is omitted.

In order for these parts of our application to work together according to our design, we must connect the textChanged() signals of each of our QLineEdit objects with the corresponding slots. To do this, we extend the constructor for the last time:

```
// byteConverter/ByteConverterDialog.cpp (continued)

    ...
    connect(decEdit, SIGNAL(textChanged(const QString&)),
            this, SLOT(decChanged(const QString&)));
    connect(hexEdit, SIGNAL(textChanged(const QString&)),
            this, SLOT(hexChanged(const QString&)));
```

```
connect(binEdit, SIGNAL(textChanged(const QString&)),
        this, SLOT(binChanged(const QString&)));
}
```

The code for the constructor of our ByteConverterDialog class is now complete, and performs three different tasks:

- It generates all the widgets of a dialog, incorporates them into the appropriate layouts, and sets up the object hierarchy of the dialog.

- It restricts the user input to sensible values.

- It sets up all the necessary signal/slot connections.

The entire logic of the application is contained in the code for slots and in their connections to the corresponding signals.

2.2   Separation of GUI and Processing Logic

2.2.1   Alternative Design

In the previous example program, we defined a single ByteConverterDialog class that implements both the graphical interface and the processing logic for the application: If the user changes the value in one of the line-edit widgets, the ByteConverterDialog class calls the corresponding slot, which adjusts the value of the two other line edits. Figure 2.5 depicts this.

Such a dovetailing of the GUI and the application logic brings the risk of a program design that is confusing and difficult to maintain. If, for example, crucial application logic has been embedded in methods responsible for setting up layouts and widgets, and it's later decided to change the look and feel of the interface, then the code responsible for the functionality will have to be painstakingly factored out.

This problem cannot be completely avoided, but it can at least be minimized by separating user interface code and data processing code, as shown in Figure 2.6. The possibility of using signals and slots simplifies the abstraction here, because unnecessary dependencies of the dialog class on the processing class (and vice versa) can be avoided.

In this design, the ByteConverterDialog class is responsible only for the GUI; conversion of the numbers is taken over by an additional class, ByteConverter. This class has the slots setDec(), setHex() and setBin(). If you call the setDec() slot with a string, the class sends out the signals hexChanged() and binChanged() with the corresponding values in hexadecimal or binary form, and similarly for the other two slots.

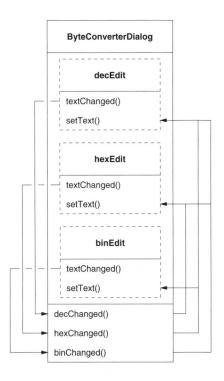

Figure 2.5:
GUI elements and
processing logic of
the
ByteConverterDialog
class until now

We can connect the signals and slots of the line-edit widgets from the ByteConverterDialog to the signals and slots of the ByteConverter class, for example, the hexChanged() signal of the decEdit object in a dialog to the setDec() slot of the associated ByteConverter. If the user enters a new decimal value, the line-edit widget sends out the textChanged() signal and setDec() is applied. This slot in turn sends out the signals hexChanged() and binChanged(). Since we have connected them to the setText() slot of the hexEdit or binEdit object, the program updates the hexadecimal and binary values in the graphical user interface.

The ByteConverter class "knows" nothing about the GUI components. It has a clearly defined interface and can still be used if the appearance of the application changes.

Separating data processing from the GUI in this way should always be considered if the processing logic can be separated naturally from the user interface. If, on the other hand, you only want to synchronize individual GUI elements with one another, you should decide against such a splitting-up: In this case you will not attain any independence, but only shift responsibility to a new class.

Our example program is a borderline case in this respect: Its data processing task consists of converting numbers from one base to another—a functionality not linked to a particular user interface. If you were to write a hex editor, on the other hand, whose outputs can be switched between decimal, hexadecimal, and binary notation, it would probably not be justifiable to separate the GUI from the calculation logic for the synchronization of the corresponding line edits.

Figure 2.6:
Separation of GUI
elements from the
processing logic

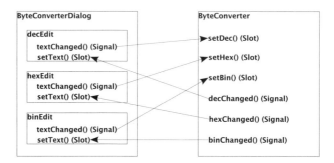

It can already be seen that there is no easy answer as to what you should separate and what you should leave together. To a certain extent the answer depends on the programming style and the project organization. Qt provides the necessary freedom for both methods.

2.2.2 Declaring and Sending Out Signals

The new ByteConverter class has signals and slots, and must therefore ultimately inherit from QObject. Since it displays nothing on the screen, is not a widget, and requires no other functionality that Qt makes available in other subclasses of QObject, it can inherit directly from QObject:

```
// byteConverter2/ByteConverter.h

#ifndef BYTECONVERTER_H
#define BYTECONVERTER_H

#include <QObject>

class ByteConverter : public QObject
{
    Q_OBJECT

public:
    ByteConverter(QObject* = 0);

public slots:
    void setDec(const QString&);
```

```
    void setHex(const QString&);
    void setBin(const QString&);

signals:
    void decChanged(const QString&);
    void hexChanged(const QString&);
    void binChanged(const QString&);
};

#endif
```

Again it is important here not to forget the Q_OBJECT macro, otherwise Qt will not know about the signals and slots declared.

The constructor accepts a pointer to a QObject object as an argument. This becomes the "father" of the new object in the object hierarchy. As the default value (exactly as in the signature of the QObject constructor) is 0, the zero pointer is used—a corresponding ByteConverter object therefore has no parent.

The class has three slots, setDec(), setHex(), and setBin(). This time we want to access them from outside the class, namely from the ByteConverterDialog class, and we allow this with the keyword public.

Signals are declared with the signals: designator. There is no access control mode specified—they are always public. Any private or protected signals would be invisible outside the class, and therefore would be useless for communicating between different classes. Within a single class (as in our previous implementation), straightforward function calls can be used. Apart from the signals: designator, signal declarations look just like function declarations.

In contrast to member functions and slots, however, the implementation of the class omits defining the signals, since all they do is call the slots to which they are connected.[7]

The ByteConverter constructor is quickly implemented:

```
// byteConverter2/ByteConverter.cpp

#include "ByteConverter.h"

ByteConverter::ByteConverter(QObject* parent) :
    QObject(parent)
{
}
```

We pass only the parent argument to the QObject constructor (that is, the constructor of the base class).

[7] Of course, signals *are* also implemented automatically by moc. The code generated for a signal calls the corresponding slots, but it is not possible to write a separate implementation for signals.

The implementation of the slots corresponds more or less to that from Section 2.1.4 on page 70:

```cpp
// byteConverter2/ByteConverter.cpp (continued)

void ByteConverter::setDec(const QString& newValue)
{
    bool ok;
    int num = newValue.toInt(&ok);
    if (ok) {
        emit hexChanged(QString::number(num, 16));
        emit binChanged(QString::number(num, 2));
    } else {
        emit hexChanged("");
        emit binChanged("");
    }
}

void ByteConverter::setHex(const QString& newValue)
{
    bool ok;
    int num = newValue.toInt(&ok, 16);
    if (ok) {
        emit decChanged(QString::number(num));
        emit binChanged(QString::number(num, 2));
    } else {
        emit decChanged("");
        emit binChanged("");
    }
}

void ByteConverter::setBin(const QString& newValue)
{
    bool ok;
    int num = newValue.toInt(&ok, 2);
    if (ok) {
        emit decChanged(QString::number(num));
        emit hexChanged(QString::number(num, 16));
    } else {
        emit decChanged("");
        emit hexChanged("");
    }
}
```

Again we convert a numerical value into each of the three number systems with the QString functions toInt() and number(). However, the slots do not change the value of the line-edit widgets themselves, but merely send the corresponding signals. To do this, we simply call the signal like a function.

To make it clear that this is not a normal function call, we prefix the call with the emit designator. This is not necessary, but merely intended as an aid for the programmer, who can immediately see from this that a signal is being sent. It is good programming practice to consistently mark signal emissions with emit.

Now we only need to enter the new header and source text files in the .pro file so that qmake can generate the necessary moc calls:

```
#byteConverter2/byteConverter2.pro

TEMPLATE = app

SOURCES  = main.cpp \
           ByteConverterDialog.cpp \
           ByteConverter.cpp
HEADERS  = ByteConverterDialog.h \
           ByteConverter.h
```

If you forget to process a file that declares a class with signals using moc, the linker will complain of undefined symbols; GCC issues the following error message, for example:

```
ld: Undefined symbols:
ByteConverter::binChanged(QString const&)
ByteConverter::decChanged(QString const&)
ByteConverter::hexChanged(QString const&)
```

If the class only declares slots, however, and you do not process it with moc, then you will unfortunately only receive an error message at runtime that the signal/slot connection could not be created, since the slot is not known.

2.2.3 Using Your Own Signals

With the ByteConverter class, the ByteConverterDialog class has been simplified— we require neither class variables nor slots; the constructor is sufficient:

```
// byteConverter2/ByteConverterDialog.h

#ifndef BYTECONVERTERDIALOG_H
#define BYTECONVERTERDIALOG_H

#include <QDialog>

class ByteConverterDialog : public QDialog
{
    Q_OBJECT

public:
    ByteConverterDialog();
```

```
};

#endif
```

We generate the widgets as in the previous example and pass them in the same way as before to the care of the layout, and there are also no differences in the adjustments, including the validators. We merely require different signal/slot connections:

```
// byteConverter2/ByteConverterDialog.cpp

ByteConverterDialog::ByteConverterDialog()
{
    ...
    // Signal/slot connections
    connect(exitButton, SIGNAL(clicked()),
            this, SLOT(accept()));

    ByteConverter* bc = new ByteConverter(this);

    connect(decEdit, SIGNAL(textChanged(const QString&)),
            bc, SLOT(setDec(const QString&)));
    connect(hexEdit, SIGNAL(textChanged(const QString&)),
            bc, SLOT(setHex(const QString&)));
    connect(binEdit, SIGNAL(textChanged(const QString&)),
            bc, SLOT(setBin(const QString&)));

    connect(bc, SIGNAL(decChanged(const QString&)),
            decEdit, SLOT(setText(const QString&)));
    connect(bc, SIGNAL(hexChanged(const QString&)),
            hexEdit, SLOT(setText(const QString&)));
    connect(bc, SIGNAL(binChanged(const QString&)),
            binEdit, SLOT(setText(const QString&)));
}
```

We connect the clicked() signal of the Quit button to the accept() slot of the dialog, which closes the dialog. The remaining signal/slot connections correspond to those shown in Figure 2.6 on page 76.

In the ByteConverter constructor we enter the this pointer as an argument so that the new object will become a child of ByteConverterDialog. This causes the automatic memory management to delete the ByteConverter object as soon as the GUI is deleted. In addition, this parent/child relationship ensures that the ByteConverter object is available for the entire lifetime of the ByteConverterDialog object.

The example demonstrates that whether you connect slots with your own signals or with signals of the Qt classes, it makes no difference as far as the syntax is concerned.

GUI Design Using the Qt Designer

While simple graphical interfaces such as the one for the converter created in Chapter 2 can be programmed "manually" without too many problems, there is a need for a graphical interface design tool, especially when designing dialogs in which many GUI elements must be placed. Qt provides this very thing in the form of the *Qt Designer*.

3.1 Dialogs "By Mouse Click"

Below we will create the ByteConverter dialog from the previous chapter using this GUI tool.

The fact that many different windows open when the Designer starts is something to which some Windows users are unaccustomed. If you want to use the dock window mode instead, which is the default mode in Visual Studio, for example, you can switch this on under Edit→User Interface Mode→Docked Window.

One of the windows is the "New Form" dialog, which expects a template to be selected. Templates are generally available here for main windows, dialogs, and widgets. Qt 4 makes a distinction between dialogs that place the buttons for the user actions OK (confirm) and Cancel on the bottom edge and those that place them in the right corner. We select one of these as a template for the ByteConverter dialog; Figure 3.1 shows the Dialog with Buttons Bottom type.

Figure 3.1:
The dialog template
with standard
buttons arranged
below

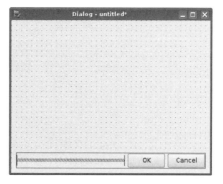

We no longer require the buttons specified. To delete them, we draw, using the left mouse button, a selection frame surrounding the buttons and the space marker (*spacer*). Pressing the (Del) key removes the widgets that are surplus to requirements in our case.

The next step is to add the input lines and labels to the dialog framework. These can be found in the Widget Box, which the program normally places on the left side of the screen. To create a new label, we look for the Display Widgets group (at the bottom of the box) and pull the Label entry onto the dialog via drag and drop.

Figure 3.2:
The dialog contains
the first widgets.

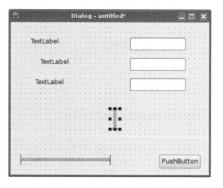

Now we add the line-edit widgets. As an input element, this user interface component belongs to the category of Input Widgets and is also moved into position via drag and drop. In addition to the three text labels and line edits, we need a button (Buttons→Push Button) and both a horizontal and vertical spacer. These placeholders in the Designer work like stretches; they adjust the distance between widgets when the window containing them is resized.

A GUI element that has been positioned can be repositioned by dragging it with the left mouse button. Figure 3.2 shows the form for the ByteConverter dialog after all required Widgets have been placed.

Users of Qt 4.2 and newer might not find the Designer template as described above, as Trolltech has slightly altered the default dialog template. The motivation was to overcome problems with regard to the button order on different platforms: The current style defines the order of the buttons. On Mac OS X and GNOME, the destructive action (e.g., Cancel) is located on the left side, while the constructive action (e.g., OK) is located on the right hand side. On Windows and KDE, the button order is the other way around.

Trolltech's solution was to introduce a new class called QButtonBox in Qt 4.2, which automatically provides what the user had to set up manually before: a set of default buttons and a spacer. By using QButtonBox, the application will automatically pick the right order for the style chosen. Figure 3.3 shows the default template in Cleanlooks (GNOME) and Plastique (KDE) style.

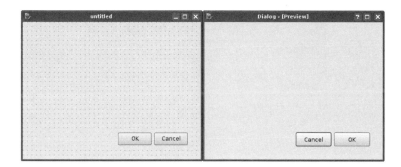

Figure 3.3:
QButtonBox *adapts the button order to the environment's style guide.*

If Qt Designer can make use of QButtonBox, the best solution is to neither remove it as advised for the buttons above nor add a new button. Instead, we modify the standardButtons property in the Designer's Property Editor in a way that it will only use the Close button. This is done by deselecting both active entries from the drop-down box of the standardButtons property and then selecting QDialogButtonBox::Close.

Users unfamiliar with property editors, e.g., from other graphical GUI builders, should first read section 5 to obtain a short introduction.

3.1.1   Making Layouts With the Designer

The widgets do not yet have a clean arrangement. To avoid having to explicitly position interface elements down to the last pixel, the Qt Designer provides some standard layouts. To group a number of widgets together, you can first highlight them by drawing a rectangle around them all with the left mouse button, and then choose the desired layout, either from the context menu which appears in the selection if you click the right mouse button, or from the toolbar. The latter is recommended specifically for Mac users with a one-button mouse.

In the case of the line edits and labels, a *grid layout* is the best choice; this is selected in the context menu through the item Lay out→Lay Out in a Grid. The layout is then outlined in red and the objects appear, grouped together, as they will be in the final application.

When applying a layout, the Designer tries to tolerate any pixel imprecisions that the developer may have caused in placing the widgets. If the selected layout does not arrange the widgets as you intended, or if there are the wrong number of elements for the layout, the arrangement can be canceled through the context menu entry Lay out→Break Layout.

If we chose not to use QButtonBox above, we choose a horizontal layout for the spacer and the buttons, as QButtonBox already includes a horizontal layout with a spacing (Lay out→Lay Out Horizontally).

Figure 3.4:
Layouts group
widgets together.

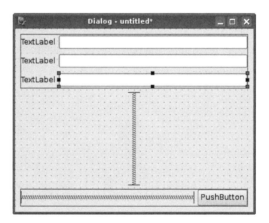

Finally, we bring together both layouts, along with the until now ungrouped vertical spacers, by selecting the context menu entry Lay out→ Lay Out Vertically into a single, vertical layout. This "global" layout does not need to be specifically selected: The Designer does not highlight it with a separate frame, and its context menu opens if you click an empty space in the dialog. It affects all the previously formed layouts and until now ungrouped elements (e.g., the vertical spacer).

The result, shown in Figure 3.4, is close to our desired GUI. The labels, however, are not yet correct. This can be changed via the context menu entry Change text... or via the *Property Editor* to the right of the screen. To better understand the latter, it is worth taking a look at the property concept of Qt.

3.1.2   The Property Editor

QObject-based classes have special *properties* that can be set with setProperty() and queried using property(). Examples of user interface information that can be represented by properties include size, labeling, formatting details, help texts, and many other things.

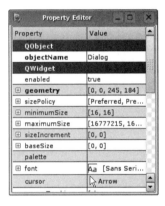

Figure 3.5:
The Property Editor
classifies each
property of a class
according to the class
in which it was first
defined (either the
class itself, or one of
its parents).

This is done in the *Property Editor* (Figure 3.5). It lists the changeable properties, arranged by the class in which each property was first implemented—either the class itself, or one of its parents. For example, a QLabel inherits from the QFrame class, which in turn is a descendant of QWidget; accordingly, one can get and set not only a label's QLabel-specific properties such as the labeling text (text property), but also its QFrame properties such as the frameShape[1] and its QWidget properties such as the size (geometry).

Since all widgets inherit from QObject, you can always get and set the QObject property objectName, which provides an internal description and should not be confused with a label to be displayed on the widget in the user interface—for example, the text on a label or button (which is specified with the text property). The name of the object variable and other things are derived from objectName.

Since we don't want to change the labels in the code we are going to write later, their variable names play no further role. That is why we continue using the object names generated by the Designer.

---

[1]   Labels are normally without frames, which is why frameShape is set to QFrame::None by default.

On the other hand, we need to manually access the line-edit widgets later on, which is why we give them the same names as the ones they had in Chapter 2 (that is, decEdit, hexEdit, and binEdit) using the Property Editor. This ensures that in the code that will be generated by the User Interface Compiler, the corresponding pointers also have the same names. How we can access the line-edit widgets created by the Designer is explained on page 92.

To change properties in the Designer, you highlight the relevant widget with a (left) mouse click. The contents of the Property Editor window are adjusted accordingly, and you can change the properties of the highlighted widget. The properties whose values are (already) different from the default are shown in bold type.

Changing Window Titles

To change the window title of the entire dialog, we click any point in the widget construction window not covered by child widgets or layouts, such as the area between the layout frame and the dialog margin. The Property Editor now displays the windowTitle property in the QWidget section. Clicking the corresponding line enables you to change the value of the property, for example, to turn the Dialog into a number converter.[2] The button with the small red arrow, next to the value of the property, allows the property to be reset to the default value.

Although every widget has the windowTitle property, it becomes visible only in the case of *top-level widgets*, that is, windows and dialogs.

Adjusting Lettering

Our dialog still does not display the correct text strings on its labels and buttons. In order to do this, the text property is required.

Figure 3.6:
The labels contain the
correct text.

---

[2] For new projects, the Designer only displays the changed window title after the user has saved the dialog. Before the dialog is saved for the first time, the title bar contains only the word *untitled*.

We set this property in the three QLabels, in turn, to decimal, hexadecimal, and binary. For the button, we set the property value (in the QAbstractButton section of the parent class) to Exit. Figure 3.6 shows the result.

Defining the Default Button

If you want, you can also switch on the default property for the QPushButton. If it is set to true, pressing the (Enter) key anywhere within the dialog activates the button. However, this hardly makes sense, because when the button is activated, the application carries out a destructive action (that is, it closes), which would probably irritate the user if he activated it by mistake.

Although the Designer allows the default property of several buttons in a widget to be set to true, only one of them can function as the default button. Qt treats the last button of the widget to have its default property set to true as the widget's actual default button.

If the widget involved is a dialog, Qt from version 4.1 onward also automatically enables the autoDefault property for all buttons arranged on it. This property comes into effect if the user "jumps" from one widget part to the next using the (Tab) key (see page 89): If he reaches a line edit when doing this, for example, pressing the (Enter) key activates the next button in the tab sequence, provided its autoDefault property has been set.

When using QButtonBox, the default property is automatically assigned to constructive button. Close, being a destructive action, cannot become the default button in this case.

Changing the Window Size

Only one detail now spoils the picture: The dialog as a whole is much too large. It is possible, of course, to click the plus sign in front of the geometry property and define the width and height precisely, down to the pixel.

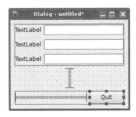

Figure 3.7:
Adjust Size *provides the dialog with the correct size.*

Alternatively, the dialog can be scaled down to the required size using the mouse. But as a rule it is simpler to select the Adjust Size function from the Form menu or from the toolbar (via the icon with the diagonal arrow on the far right), provided you activated the dialog yourself beforehand. This will now shrink the dialog to a suitable size calculated by the Designer (Figure 3.7).

3.1.3   The Preview

To check the result, you can use the preview function provided in the Form menu of the Designer. If you want, you can even view the dialog in other widgets' styles, via the Preview in submenu. Figure 3.8 shows the preview under Linux. Trolltech defines the *Plastique* style as the default, which is similar to the default style of KDE 3. Under Mac OS X, Qt uses the native Aqua style, using the drawing routine of Mac OS X. Likewise, the Windows XP style uses Windows APIs to draw the style. Therefore, the Aqua and XP styles are available only on those respective operating systems.

Figure 3.8:
A preview of the
finished widget

3.1.4   Signal/Slot Connections

Besides the interface design mode, the Designer also contains a view in which the signals of widgets in an existing design can be graphically linked to slots. Press the (F4) key or select the entry Edit Signals/Slots from the Edit menu to switch to this mode; you can leave this mode with Edit→Edit Widgets or the (F3) key.

Connecting signals and slots in the Designer is a two-step process. First, you pull a connection from the widget with the desired signal onto a widget with a corresponding slot. The backgrounds of the widget or dialog can themselves be drop targets here. Connections that land there are provided with a ground icon by the Designer; all other connections end with an arrow on the target widget (Figure 3.9 demonstrates both cases).

Figure 3.9:
Signal/slot
connections are
created in the
Designer via drag and
drop.

Step two consists of specifying the desired signal and slot pair for the two widgets. As soon as you release the mouse button over the target widget, the Designer opens a dialog, as shown in Figure 3.10: On the left it shows a menu of the most frequently used signals. If the signal you are looking for is not there, click the Show all signals and slots checkbox to display all possible signals of the source widget. The right selection box will show all the slots of the target widget matching the signal selected on the left. If you confirm the choice, the connection is established.

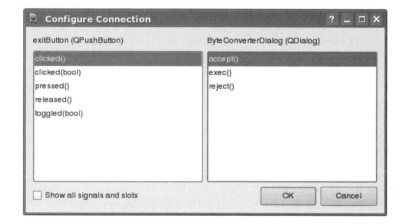

Figure 3.10:
Signals and slots of
two selected widgets
are connected by the
developer in this
dialog.

A click on the connecting line, followed by pressing the (Del) key, will remove the connection.

3.1.5   The Tab Sequence

The so-called *tab sequence* is important for keyboard users. This function allows the input focus to be shifted, via the (Tab) key, to the next widget that expects input. The Designer specifies the tab sequence so that initially the first widget in the dialog has the keyboard focus. The focus is moved to the next inserted GUI element when the (Tab) key is pressed. When designing a user interface, you should pay attention to the default tab sequence and modify it as necessary in order to make your application as user friendly as possible.

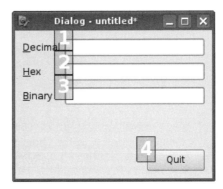

To do this, you switch to the *Tab Order mode*, via Edit→Edit Tab Order or the icon with the numbers 123 and an arrow in the toolbar. Now the Designer displays each widget's current position in the tab sequence in a blue box (Figure 3.11). A click on the corresponding box increases the rank in the sequence by one.

3.1.6   Shortcuts and Buddies

Those who prefer keyboard control will thank you if they can jump directly to as many commonly used widgets as possible. GUI elements that display a user-defined text, such as buttons, are assigned a key abbreviation by placing an *ampersand* (&) before the character that will serve as the keyboard shortcut. If the text itself contains a real ampersand, it is masked by duplicating it: &&.

If the user presses the combination of (Alt)+(character) from now on, the widget obtains the focus and is activated. In Figure 3.12 we use this technique with the Quit button.

QLabel objects form an exception, however. Since they usually occur in a layout for the purpose of describing an adjacent "partner" widget, they themselves do not accept a focus. However, the Buddy property of a label can be used to specify a keyboard shortcut to be associated with the partner widget, as though the descriptive text of the label were directly attached to the partner element itself.

In the Designer view mode Edit Buddies, you can now specify with which widget a label is a partner. To do this, click the future Buddy label, which will then light up in red. Holding down the mouse button, you now pull a connection over to the widget that in future should be associated to the label.

Figure 3.12:
Labels are friends to
other widgets: The
Buddy allocations can
be found in the Buddy
mode of the Qt
Designer.

In the example from Figure 3.12, the respective line edit now has the focus if the user presses the letters underlined in the label inscription while holding down the (Alt) key.

Alternatively, while in the normal design mode, you can set the name of the desired Buddy widget in the Property Editor, using the Buddy property.[3] Using this approach, we would set the value of the Buddy property of the QLabel object that displays the Decimal text in our byte converter dialog so that it matches the value of the objectName property of the corresponding line-edit object, namely, the string decEdit.

To undo the relationship, all you need to do is click the connection line in the Buddy mode and press the (Del) key.

3.2 Integrating Designer-generated Files into Your Qt Project

When saving with the menu item File→Save Form or Save Form As..., the Designer generates a .ui file from the information it has for each widget in the form.[4] This .ui file is specified in the qmake project file, as shown in the following line:

```
FORMS = byteconverterdialog.ui
```

In our case, qmake takes into account the user interface file byteconverterdialog.ui; several files can be specified, separated by a space, or other lines can be added according to the pattern FORMS +=*file.ui*.

---

[3] Although this property has been there since Qt 3.*x*, the Designer for Qt 4.0 does not display it. Only in version 4.1 does it appear again.

[4] Using the third menu item, Save Form As Template..., you can save your form as a template, which then appears in the selection dialog for new *Forms*.

When building the project, make then relies on the *user interface compiler* uic to convert Designer-generated .ui files into C/C++ header files.[5] There is a fixed naming convention in this step: for example, if the class represented by the .ui file generated by the Designer is called ByteConverterDialog (the value of the object-Name property can be examined to determine the class name), then the resulting header file is given the name ui_byteconverterdialog.h by uic.

It is important here that at least one other file in the project includes this generated header file. You must add the appropriate #include statements *before* qmake is run. Otherwise, make won't call uic with the relevant interface description file as an argument on its next run.

Notice that the generated header file contains only a help class with two methods: setupUi(), which generates the GUI, and retranslateUi(), which can be called if the program is to allow the user to change the language while it is running.

Both methods expect (as an argument) a pointer to the widget to which the GUI object described in the Designer is to be bound. Even if you have already chosen a template in the Designer, you can freely choose at this point the widget class for which the interface is intended. The MainWindow template is the only one that must be used together with a QMainWindow.[6]

The class generated by the uic is now available as Ui::ByteConverterDialog or Ui_ByteConverterDialog, in general as Ui::*classname* or Ui_*class name*, whereby the class name corresponds to the objectName attribute of the form created in the Designer.

There are now three ways of using and functionally developing the widget created. Which of these is best to use depends on the particular context.

3.2.1 Using Designer-generated Classes as Helper Classes

If you only want to display a Designer-created user interface once, without touching the corresponding object again after it is initialized, it is appropriate to directly instantiate the generated class and bind the instance to a previously created widget with setupUi(). This method fixes the GUI elements described in the .ui file on to the widget and anchors them—provided this was specified in the Designer—with layouts.

We shall demonstrate this technique using our Designer-generated ByteConverter-Dialog:

---

[5] Note for Qt 3 users: uic no longer generates a complete QObject-based class in Qt 4, but merely a framework which can be applied to the widget of the matching type.

[6] The widget created in the Designer is used in this case as the central widget for the QMainWindow instance, and it is positioned with setCentralWidget(), instead of with the help of a layout, as normal. In addition, the Designer menu bars and toolbars are treated separately from Qt 4.1, a functionality that is equally available only for QMainWindow instances.

```
// simple/main.cpp

#include <QtGui>

#include "ui_byteconverterdialog.h"

int main(int argc, char*argv[])
{
  QApplication app(argc, argv);
  QDialog dlg;
  Ui::ByteConverterDialog ui;
  ui.setupUi(&dlg);
  dlg.setAttribute(Qt::WA_QuitOnClose);
  dlg.show();
  return app.exec();
}
```

Since the widgets of the Designer-generated dialog are available as publicly accessible members of the UI class, they can be fine-tuned in the code later on by calling the methods of the respective widgets. Their signals and slots can participate in signal/slot connections. Whether the class Ui::ByteConverterDialog is now instantiated in the main() function or in the constructor of a class inheriting from QDialog makes no difference.

In our example, however, the approach shown in the listing above causes problems: We could connect the Quit button's clicked signal to the accept() slot of the dialog, and we would then be able to connect the slots binChanged(), hexChanged(), and binChanged() to the textChanged() signals of the respective QTextEdit widgets. But then we would not be able to access the pointer to any uic-generated widget in the slot itself.

For this reason, the use of directly calling setupUi() is very limited: If we do so, we shall restrict ourselves to applying instances of the class generated by uic to instances of a standard class like QWidget or QDialog. However, in some situations this procedure could be completely sufficient, for example, in simple modal input dialogs which are called with exec(). The exec call starts a separate event loop and returns only if accept(), reject(), or another method closes the dialog. Since the dialog object does not cease to exist when the dialog has been closed, the subsequent code can fetch the values of the widgets placed inside the dialog by setupUi() without any danger, so that you can get by without the QDialog subclass in those cases.

It is important that you always call the setupUi() method of an instance of a Designer-generated class first, before trying to access member variables of the interface object (in the current example, those of ui). Otherwise, the program will mess around with uninitialized pointers and crash.

An argument for not instanciating Designer-generated classes directly results from the fact that public-member varibles are accessible from the outside, causing a violation of secrecy, one of the most important principles of object-oriented pro-gramming. Secrecy enforces abstraction by only granting the class members access to their own methods.

The internal details of the class are thus "cut off" from the other classes, and you can change the internal design of the class without having to adjust the rest of the program that uses this class. As long as you use only the UI class as a short-term setup class, the infringement of the encapsulation principle is not really of any consequence.

3.2.2   Always Having Designer-generated Widgets Available

In order to deal with the shortcoming just demonstrated, it is a good idea to include the class generated by uic as a member variable. To do this, we first inherit from the desired class, which in our case is QDialog.

The main() function matches the one from Chapter 2, since ByteConverterDialog from its point of view is again a "black box."

The crucial difference is in the declaration of the class. We declare the class gen-erated by uic as a private member of a QDialog subclass. This allows for abitrary access to the widgets within the Designer-generated class via this newly created ui member variable of the ByteConverterDialog class inherited from QWidget:

```
// member/byteconverterdialog.h

...
#include <QDialog>
#include "ui_byteconverterdialog.h"

class QLineEdit;

class ByteConverterDialog : public QDialog
{
    ...
private:
    Ui::ByteConverterDialog ui;
};
```

The constructor and all slots now access the generated class via the ui member variable:

```
// member/byteconverterdialog.cpp

...
ByteConverterDialog::ByteConverterDialog(QWidget *parent)
  : QDialog(parent)
```

```
{
  ui.setupUi(this);

  connect(ui.decEdit, SIGNAL(textChanged(const QString&)),
          this, SLOT(decChanged(const QString&)));
  connect(ui.hexEdit, SIGNAL(textChanged(const QString&)),
          this, SLOT(hexChanged(const QString&)));
  connect(ui.binEdit, SIGNAL(textChanged(const QString&)),
          this, SLOT(binChanged(const QString&)));

}

void ByteConverterDialog::decChanged(const QString& newValue)
{
    bool ok;
    int num = newValue.toInt(&ok);
    if (ok) {
        ui.hexEdit->setText(QString::number(num, 16));
        ui.binEdit->setText(QString::number(num, 2));
    } else {
        ui.hexEdit->setText("");
        ui.binEdit->setText("");
    }
}
...
```

The overlying principle also applies here: It is essential that setupUi() is called first before we can use the UI class in any way at all. The disadvantage of this method is its indirectness, via the member variable. But the advantage of this approach is that it defuses the encapsulation problem, limiting the problem to scope of the dialog class. Any since access from outside of the dialog is not possible under any circumstances. A further bonus: It is clear from the code which widgets were generated in the Designer. In addition, this approach is particularly suited for widgets in libraries that have to remain binary-compatible, because only the pointer to the instance of the generated class changes the binary layout in the compiler output.[7]

3.2.3 Multiple Inheritance

As the ideal solution, Trolltech recommends multiple inheritance. But like the previous solution, this works only if you plan your own subclass.

In this method, the new widget inherits not only from QWidget, but also from the UI class generated by uic. A particular highlight is the use of the private keyword in the inheritance instruction. This ensures that all methods from the UI class

---

[7] More details of binary compatibility in C++ have been compiled by the KDE project at http://developer.kde.org/documentation/other/binarycompatibility.html.

are given the status of private class variables in the new class, although they are actually publicly accessible in the former class itself:

```
// inherit/byteconverterdialog.h

...
class ByteConverterDialog : public QDialog,
                             private Ui::ByteConverterDialog
...
```

This method thus solves several problems at one stroke: We can use the widget pointers generated by uic as standard member variables, without going the long way round, via a help object, and they remain private, so that encapsulation to the outside is maintained.

For our example, this means that the constructor changes as follows:

```
// inherit/byteconverterdialog.cpp

...
ByteConverterDialog::ByteConverterDialog(QWidget *parent)
 : QDialog(parent)
{
  setupUi(this);

  connect(decEdit, SIGNAL(textChanged(const QString&)),
          this, SLOT(decChanged(const QString&)));
  connect(hexEdit, SIGNAL(textChanged(const QString&)),
          this, SLOT(hexChanged(const QString&)));
  connect(binEdit, SIGNAL(textChanged(const QString&)),
          this, SLOT(binChanged(const QString&)));

}

void ByteConverterDialog::decChanged(const QString& newValue)
{
    bool ok;
    int num = newValue.toInt(&ok);
    if (ok) {
        hexEdit->setText(QString::number(num, 16));
        binEdit->setText(QString::number(num, 2));
    } else {
        hexEdit->setText("");
        binEdit->setText("");
    }
}

...
```

As before, we only need to call the setupUi() method in first position, and as the argument we again use a pointer to the widget that is our current class scope.

Caution: In this approach the inheritance sequence is important. First the class must inherit from QDialog, and then from the Designer class. If this is not the case, the compiler will throw an error that is difficult to understand, and which quickly brings the programmer to despair:

```
moc_byteconverterdialog.cpp:43: error: 'staticMetaObject' is not a
    member of type 'Ui::ByteConverterDialog'
moc_byteconverterdialog.cpp: In member function 'virtual void*
    ByteConverterDialog::qt_metacast(const char*)':
moc_byteconverterdialog.cpp:60: error: 'class Ui::ByteConverterDialog'
    has no member named 'qt_metacast'
moc_byteconverterdialog.cpp: In member function 'virtual int
    ByteConverterDialog::qt_metacall(QMetaObject::Call, int, void**)':
moc_byteconverterdialog.cpp:66: error: 'class Ui::ByteConverterDialog'
    has no member named 'qt_metacall'
make: *** [moc_byteconverterdialog.o] Error 1
```

The reason is the behavior of the meta-object compiler, which checks only in the first parent class of the inheritance list whether this inherits from QObject or not. This also means that it is generally not possible to inherit from several classes that all have QObject as a base class.

3.3 Automatic Signal/Slot Connections

Developers versed in Visual Basic or Delphi who start on Qt/C++ development find the signal/slot concept unusual, and they miss the event handler. Qt 4 allows them to stick to the semantics they are used to, permitting slot declarations of the form

```
void  on_objectname_signalname();
```

that are converted into connect() instructions that uic saves in setupUi(). Incidentally, this naming convention increases the readability of the source text.

The whole point of this functionality is the static QMetaObject::connectSlotsBy Name() method: It expects a pointer to a QObject and searches through it for slots with matching names. Then QMetaObject::connectSlotsByName() connects the found slots with the appropriate signal. To do this it uses information from the meta-object generated by the meta-object compiler, moc. This meta-object adds the capability known in C++ as *introspection* (also known in Java as *reflection*) to all classes inheriting from QObject. At runtime the class therefore "knows" its methods, signals, and slots. connectSlotsByName() recursively looks at the slot names of the object behind the pointers and all its children, connecting the respective signals to them.

Trolltech recommends the semantics shown above only with the Designer-generated classes, since in this case the object name and the name of the uic-generated pointer to the widget match, and because the setupUi() method subsequently calls connectSlotsByName(). But for those who find this consistent naming pattern irresistible, all the relevant objects must be assigned a name via setObjectName(), must be called in the constructor or from outside QMetaObject::connectSlotsByName(), and must pass a pointer to the current class (this) to this call.

Because the shown semantics are very prone to errors,[8] you should use automatic connection only with Designer-generated widgets with multiple inheritance.

We will modify our examples from above so that the slot names follow the conventions for automatic connection. At the same time the connect() calls in the constructor cease to apply, so that only the setupUi() instruction is left:

```
// autoconnect/byteconverterdialog.h

...
private slots:
    void on_decEdit_textChanged(const QString&);
    void on_hexEdit_textChanged(const QString&);
    void on_binEdit_textChanged(const QString&);
...


// autoconnect/byteconverterdialog.cpp

...

ByteConverterDialog::ByteConverterDialog(QWidget *parent)
 : QDialog(parent)
{
  setupUi(this);
}

void ByteConverterDialog::on_decEdit_textChanged(const QString& newValue)
{
    bool ok;
    int num = newValue.toInt(&ok);
    if (ok) {
        hexEdit->setText(QString::number(num, 16));
        binEdit->setText(QString::number(num, 2));
    } else {
        hexEdit->setText("");
        binEdit->setText("");
    }
}

...
```

---

[8] Remember that only the object name is relevant and that in this procedure, Qt cannot issue warnings about connections that fail at runtime.

3.4 Including Derived Classes in the Designer

It is sometimes necessary to make minor modifications to a Qt standard widget. In such cases you can no longer use the Designer without registering the new widget there as a so-called *custom widget*, which involves a fair amount of work.[9]

To still be able to use such a widget in the Designer, you select its Qt base widget in the Designer and click it with the right mouse button after it has been adjusted. From the context menu, you now select the entry Promote to Custom Widget. In the dialog that appears (see Figure 3.13), you specify the name of the new class and that of its header file. Although the Designer continues to show the original Qt widget, the finished program uses the modified widget; so in the implementation you obtain a pointer to an object of the type of the inherited widget.

Figure 3.13:
Using inherited
classes in the
Designer is very
simple, thanks to
widget promotion. It
is often all you need.

To undo such a promotion, the entry Demote to *base class* can be found at the same position in the context menu.

For more complex modifications, such as fundamental changes to the layout behavior or adding properties, this procedure is not suitable, however, since the Designer does not take them into account.

3.5 The Resource Editor

From Qt 4.1 on, the Designer supports the setting up and administration of the resources already discussed on page 57. The editor integrated in this (Figure 3.14) can be called from the entry Tools → Resource Editor, in case it is not already visible. Navigating in it takes some getting used to, however. The drop-down box next to the New and Open entries shows a list of already opened resource files. It does not include a save action, as this is performed implicitly by the editor.

---

[9] Notes on this are provided in the online documentation for Qt.

Figure 3.14:
The resources
example from page
57 in the Resource
Editor of the Designer

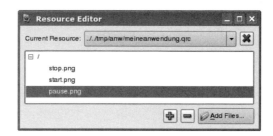

In addition, the list of resources displayed in the Designer is independent of those in the .pro file. This is why it is important to ensure that all the resources really are entered there under the keyname RESOURCES. By subsequently running qmake, the resources become a part of the project.

To assign an image from a resource to a QLabel in the Designer, for example, you first search in the Property Editor for the pixmap property and click there on the folder icon. In the following dialog you reach the Resource Editor by selecting Specify a resource, where you can choose one of the images. To display the desired graphics in the current widget size, the scaledContents property in the Property Editor must be set to true; otherwise it will remain in the original size of the image.

4

Developing a GUI Application Based on a Main Window

In the following section we will develop an application step by step, one which displays all the typical features of a genuine graphical application and which also performs a useful task: a small text editor called *CuteEdit*.

We design its *main window* using the Designer, which allows the basic graphical framework of most applications to be put together "by mouse click" in Qt versions 4.1 and later. The basis of this is the QMainWindow Qt class.

4.1   The Anatomy of the Main Window

The QMainWindow class forms the basis of an application window: Menu bar, status bar, toolbars, and dock windows can be brought into this main window. Figure 4.1 shows the individual components. The *central widget* provides the workspace for the user.

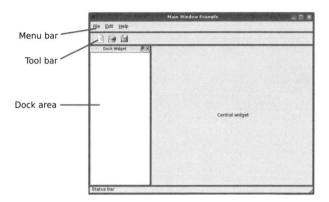

Figure 4.1:
Anatomy of a main
window

A bare main window, as shown in Figure 4.2, initially consists only of the central widget and frame, plus a title bar.[1]

In order to conjure this minimal arrangement onto the screen, nothing more than a simple program that instantiates a QMainWindow object and sets a label announcing it as the central widget is required. So that the lettering is displayed with centered alignment by the label, we use the <center> tag: QLabel interprets certain HTML tags as markup, rather than as text:

```
// mainwindow/main.cpp

#include <QApplication>
#include <QMainWindow>
#include <QLabel>

int main(int argc, char *argv[])
{
    QApplication a(argc, argv);

    QMainWindow mainWindow;
    QLabel *label = new QLabel("<center>Central Widget</center>");
    mainWindow.setCentralWidget(label);
    mainWindow.show();

    return a.exec();
}
```

This example is therefore different from the one introduced in Chapter 1.1 (page 25), in particular because we display a label within a QMainWindow instance. The result is shown in Figure 4.2.

[1] Under X11, there are a few window managers that do not show any decoration around the window.

Since the label is no longer the top-level widget, it is vital that it is created on the heap, with new. Otherwise, the program may try to delete it twice after the main() function has ended: First the computer would remove the label from the stack, and only then remove the main window, which in turn would also like to delete the label, which it too has adopted as a child through setCentralWidget(). Under certain circumstances this can cause the program to crash after it has run normally.

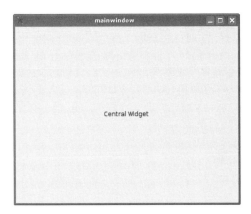

Figure 4.2:
Our MainWindow
example
program—without
menu bar, status bar,
toolbar, and dock
window

4.2 Deriving from QMainWindow

More serious applications usually inherit from QMainWindow, adding features that provide more control. In contrast to the above example, we shall derive a separate class called MainWindow from QMainWindow, on the basis of which we shall construct CuteEdit. At the same time we will get to know other essential widgets, such as QTextEdit, a flexible editor widget.

```cpp
// cuteedit1/main.cpp

#include <QApplication>
#include "mainwindow.h"

int main(int argc, char *argv[])
{
    QApplication a(argc, argv);

    MainWindow mainWindow;
    mainWindow.show();

    return a.exec();
}
```

The main() function is almost identical to the one from our "Hello, world!" program from Section 1.1. Instead of the QMainWindow class from the mainwindow example on page 102, we now use our own MainWindow class, derived from QMainWindow. The corresponding class definition can be found in the header file mainwindow.h.[2] The #include directive which incorporates the contents of this header file uses quotation marks instead of angle brackets, since the file is not a standard header file.

We again surround the file contents of mainwindow.h with an #ifdef construction providing the *include guards* to avoid compilation errors if this header file is included by more than one source file.[3] MAINWINDOW_H will be defined when the header file is processed for the first time, and the preprocessor ignores the entire file contents for all subsequent inclusion attempts:

```
// cuteedit1/mainwindow.h

#ifndef MAINWINDOW_H
#define MAINWINDOW_H

#include <QMainWindow>

class MainWindow : public QMainWindow
{
    Q_OBJECT

public:
    MainWindow();
};

#endif // MAINWINDOW_H
```

Since the MainWindow class is derived from QMainWindow, we first issue a directive to include the header file for the QMainWindow class. To ensure that the QMainWindow methods remain accessible even outside the MainWindow class, we grant the derivation public access.

Because our new class also inherits from QObject as a base class, we must not forget the Q_OBJECT macro. Otherwise the linker will complain of undefined symbols, which, in the case of self-defined signals, results in an error message. In the case of a Tool class, which defines a signal called switchTool(Tool*), this will appear as follows:

```
tool.o: In function 'Tool::activateTool(bool)':
tool.cpp:(.text+0x5f): undefined reference to 'Tool::switchTool(Tool*)'
collect2: ld returned status 1
```

---

[2] For header files that we create ourselves, we use the filename extension common in C/C++, .h, to make clear the file type. We do not use uppercase in any filenames.

[3] See page 62.

In the MainWindow class itself, we only have to define the constructor. For this reason, the source text file mainwindow.cpp is also rather short:

```
// cuteedit1/mainwindow.cpp

#include "mainwindow.h"
#include <QLabel>

MainWindow::MainWindow()
{
    setWindowTitle(tr("CuteEdit"));
    resize(600, 400);

    QLabel* label = new QLabel(tr("Central Widget"));
    setCentralWidget(label);
    label->setAlignment(Qt::AlignCenter);
}
```

In the constructor we the first call the QWidget function setWindowTitle(). Since the MainWindow class is derived from QWidget as the base class, it inherits this function, and we can use it to set the text displayed by the title bar of the window. If you leave this step out, Qt uses the program name as the title text.

We set the text for the title bar via the tr() method, which inherits MainWindow inherits from QObject. If the user wants, this will translate the text to another language at runtime; if not, it returns the string unchanged.[4]

The resize() function that MainWindow also inherits from QWidget specifies the size of the window. The two arguments determine the width and height of the window in pixels. If the size is not set explicitly, Qt will determine it automatically, based on the content to be displayed. But in our case this would be too small, since we will soon fill the window with more content.

In order to display something in the main window, we create a QLabel object with the central widget text and make it the focal point of the application with the set-CentralWidget() function, which MainWindow inherits from QMainWindow. With this call the MainWindow object adopts the new QLabel. Accordingly we must allocate it on the heap with new, from which it will ultimately be deleted by the memory management provided by Qt for instances of QObject.

The setCentralWidget() call packs the QLabel object into a layout so that it fills the entire space in the window. By default the QLabel class arranges text centered vertically, and horizontally aligned at the left margin. To center text in both directions, we change the alignment with setAlignment(). This function takes as an argument values from the enumeration type (enum) alignment, which is defined in the Qt *namespace*[5]—hence the value AlignCenter is prefixed with Qt::.

---

[4] See also page 49 and Chapter 14 from page 375 for a detailed discussion.
[5] Qt uses the namespace Qt for a large number of enumeration types, in order to avoid conflicts when the same symbolic names are used in several contexts.

So that qmake can unite the existing files into a project, we use the following .pro file:

```
#cuteedit1/cuteedit1.pro

TEMPLATE = app
SOURCES  = main.cpp mainwindow.cpp
HEADERS  = mainwindow.h
FORMS    = mainwindow.ui
```

Apart from the already known variables TEMPLATE and SOURCES, which we use to specify that we are compiling an application and to specify the source text files, the HEADERS variable is also used. This specifies the header files to be used in the project: qmake searches through those header files for the Q_OBJECT macro and creates appropriate rules for the moc calls.

4.3   Creating a Main Window with the Qt Designer

Ever since Qt 4.1, the Qt Designer has enabled the user to design main windows as well as dialogs. When used for this purpose, all the descriptions from Chapter 3 apply. In particular, just as explained there, the user interface compiler uic creates a class from the .ui file generated by the Designer; the setupUi() method then "decorates" a main window to a certain extent.

After the Designer has started, we select the Main Window item from the template menu. When designing our editor window, we borrow ideas from the designs of other editors. The central widget will be a widget that enables text to be displayed and edited. Qt provides a class called QTextEdit for this purpose.

Accordingly we pull an empty text edit element from the input widget category to the middle of our new main window, and then click the gridded window background.

We now select a layout strategy, either from the Context menu or from the Form menu. It is completely irrelevant which one we choose. The 9-pixel-wide *margin* that is created, which makes available the necessary space in dialog widgets, is out of place in the main window, however. To remove it, we select the centralwidget entry in the object inspector window and enter a margin value of 0 to its layout.

For the text editor itself it is recommended that the font type be changed to a monospaced font, using the Property Editor. To do this we open the font entry in the Property Editor and select the Courier font type, for example. In addition we set the lineWrapMode mode to NoWrap, since line wraps are seldom wanted in editors. If you do want them, an action is feasible that would switch on the lineWrapMode property.

In addition we equip the editor with a menu bar from which the program functions can be controlled. To guarantee rapid access to the most important functions, such as loading and saving, we also insert a toolbar beneath this containing an icon for each of these commonly invoked actions. A status bar provides space for display of permanent and/or contextual information, such as the current position of the cursor or the purpose of the current menu entry.

4.3.1   Adding Menu Bars

First we will look at the menu bar. We provide it with the standard entries that we are accustomed to from standard applications: the File menu, which takes care of the file to be edited, the Edit menu, which controls manipulation of the text, and a Help menu.

To do this, we select the Type here entry in the already existing menu bar and create the three entries. When doing this we should remember to place an ampersand (&) before each entry, so that the (Alt) key will call up the respective menu in combination with a (F), (E), or (H) key.

The & instructs the menu to define a window-wide shortcut (called *accelerator*), which, in combination with the (Alt) key, jumps to the corresponding menu item. It is appropriate to take the first letter of a menu entry, but the same letter may not be used twice, so you may need to use another letter for the shortcut when two menu entries begin with the same letter. The letter in the entry chosen as the shortcut character should be as intuitive as possible.

Figure 4.3:
Now our editor has
an input window and
a menu bar.

Accelerators like this allow experienced users to operate the application with the keyboard, which can often be much quicker than using the mouse and can improve the user friendliness of the software. They should therefore be provided as a matter of course in the design of user interfaces. With the accelerators in place, the design view of the editor should correspond to that shown in Figure 4.3.

To define the subitems of an individual menu entry, we select the entry in the menu bar. A drop-down menu then appears and, for each desired subitem, we select Type here... and enter its name.

Let's start in the File menu, to which we will assign the subentries New, Open..., Save, Save as ..., and Quit. We recommend that you add a separator before the Quit entry, so that this special action has visual distance from the other entries.

There is a reason behind the fact that only some entries end with dots (...)—these denote entries that require further user interaction through a dialog.

In the same way we equip the Edit menu with the entries Undo, Repeat, and after a separator, Cut, Copy, and Paste. The Help menu gets by with the Info... item, the implementation of which we will deal with on page 117.

4.3.2   Recycling Actions in the Toolbar

If you want to make the most important entries in the menu bar easily accessible for mouse users, this raises the following question: Is it possible to recycle the entries from the menu entries? Luckily the answer is yes, since Qt encapsulates menu and toolbar entries in so-called *actions*, for which the QAction class is responsible.

When we created the entries in the menus of the menu bar, the Designer created a separate action for each entry, which we will now reuse. An overview of all existing actions is provided by the *Action Editor*. If it is not already displayed as shown in Figure 4.4, you can make it visible with Actions→Action Editor.

*Figure 4.4:
The* Action Editor *lists all available actions that can be adjusted in the Property Editor like widgets.*

At the moment, no icons are assigned to the actions listed in it, in which case the full text is displayed instead of an icon, taking up significantly more space. Icons can also be of great help here because the human brain can rerecognize them more easily, since it can apply a simple pattern matching instead of having to parse a textual description.

In general there are two ways of rectifying the lack of icons. First we select the appropriate action in the Action Editor. Its properties now appear in the Property Editor. We are interested in the Icon property, and we select the Open icon in the value column. The dialog now allows us to choose whether we want to search for an icon from a resource (see page 99) or use an image file directly from the filesystem.

For our example, we copy the items from the Crystal Icons series as used by KDE 3 and combine them into a resource, using the Resource Editor in the Designer. For each action we can now select a matching icon. We save the resource file in the same directory as the .ui file.

Figure 4.5:
The toolbar provides
quick access to
important actions.

To add a new toolbar, we move the mouse cursor to the status bar at the bottom of the window and select Add Tool Bar from the context menu. We now drag the actions New, Open, and Save from the Action Editor into the bar that now appears.

Cut, copy, and paste are also frequently used actions in editors. If you want to include them in the same toolbar, as is the case in Figure 4.5, you should separate them from the other entries in the File menu with a separator (right mouse button →Insert Separator).

Actions have other properties that the Property Editor allows to be set. These include the application-wide shortcut (the so-called *shortcut*). In contrast to accelerators, shortcuts are activated with the (Ctrl) key. The user can often get to the action he wants more quickly with shortcuts than with accelerators.

This becomes clear in the example of the Open file action: (Ctrl)+(O) is quicker to type than (Alt)+(F), followed by (Alt)+(O). For the sake of clarity, you should not use an excess of shortcuts, but experienced users highly value shortcuts for frequently used operations. The Qt documentation provides an overview of the standard shortcuts for programs in English.[6]

It is interesting that the entry for a shortcut in the Designer is a string. There is no syntax check when this is done, so you should always check the entries yourself. The format is Ctrl+*key*.

The reason Qt interprets shortcuts as strings is due to internationalization: The code generated by the Designer and the user interface compiler passes the string to the localization routine tr(), so that the shortcut can be customized. This is a useful feature, since abbreviations that no one can remember (ones held over from an implementation in another language, for example) are just not used, whereas many users will remember them if the abbreviations are mnemonics for the action to be triggered.

Another feature of the QAction class is the tooltip. Tooltips, which the application displays to the user as a "pale yellow note" if the mouse cursor is held over a menu or toolbar entry, are set in the code using setToolTip().

The text set via the statusText property shows up in the status bar (if the current window has one) as the mouse hovers over the respection action. Finally the what-sThis property allows longer help texts on individual widget parts to be displayed.

4.3.3   Integrating the Main Window with Your Source Code

It is now time to turn the GUI generated in this way into a program. We can save ourselves a bit of work doing this and use the file main.cpp from the example on page 103:

```
// cuteedit2/main.cpp

#include <QApplication>
#include "mainwindow.h"

int main(int argc, char *argv[])
{
    QApplication a(argc, argv);

    MainWindow mainWindow;
    mainWindow.show();

    return a.exec();
}
```

[6] See http://doc.trolltech.com/4.1/accelerators.html.

In the implementation, we now make a multiple derivation from both the QMain-Window class and from the helper class Ui::MainWindow class generated from the uic; the latter is a private derivation so that—as already described in Chapter 3—the objects generated in the Designer are made available as member variables for the new MainWindow class with the correct visibility:

```
// cuteedit2/mainwindow.h

#ifndef MAINWINDOW_H
#define MAINWINDOW_H

#include <QMainWindow>
#include "ui_mainwindow.h"


class MainWindow : public QMainWindow,
                   private Ui::MainWindow
{
  Q_OBJECT
  public:
    MainWindow(QWidget *parent = 0);
    ~MainWindow();

  protected:
    void setupActions();
  ...
```

Before discussing the rest of the declaration on page 112, we will first turn to the implementation of the constructor. It is important that we correctly initialize the parent class. C++ does guarantee the automatic initialization of QMainWindow, so the chain of inheritance has not been interrupted. The parent object is no longer passed on when this is done, however, which can lead to memory leaks and problems when using layouts. Details are explained in Section 1.2.2 on page 31.

The first thing the constructor itself contains is the setupUi() call, which guarantees the initialization of all member variables from Ui::MainWindow:

```
#include <QtGui>
#include "mainwindow.h"

MainWindow::MainWindow(QWidget *parent)
 : QMainWindow(parent)
{
  setupUi(this);
  setupActions();
}
```

Linking Actions to Functionality

The next step is to link a number of actions manually to slots and provide them with functionality. To achieve better clarity, we will move this task to a separate method called setupActions().

Here we will breathe a bit of life into the actions through a signal/slot connection. If the user sets off an action, such as clicking the menu entry, this will send out the triggered(bool) signal. The parameter does not interest us, since it is only relevant for alternating ("toggled") or grouped actions. We must include it nevertheless so that connect() can find the signal:

```
// cuteedit2/mainwindow.cpp

void MainWindow::setupActions()
{
  connect(action_quit, SIGNAL(triggered(bool)),
          qApp, SLOT(quit()));
  connect(action_open, SIGNAL(triggered(bool)),
          this, SLOT(loadFile()));
  connect(action_save, SIGNAL(triggered(bool)),
          this, SLOT(saveFile()));
  connect(action_saveas, SIGNAL(triggered(bool)),
          this, SLOT(saveFileAs()));

  connect(textEdit, SIGNAL(copyAvailable(bool)),
          action_copy, SLOT(setEnabled(bool)));
  connect(textEdit, SIGNAL(undoAvailable(bool)),
          action_undo, SLOT(setEnabled(bool)));
  connect(textEdit, SIGNAL(redoAvailable(bool)),
          action_redo, SLOT(setEnabled(bool)));

  connect(action_copy, SIGNAL(triggered(bool)),
          this, SLOT(copy()));
  connect(action_undo, SIGNAL(triggered(bool)),
          this, SLOT(undo()));
  connect(action_redo, SIGNAL(triggered(bool)),
          this, SLOT(redo()));

  connect(action_about, SIGNAL(triggered(bool)),
          this, SLOT(about()));
}
```

We link the quit action with the quit() signal of the QApplication object, which is accessible from the entire application via the global pointer qApp. This causes the application to leave the event loop and terminate itself.

In order for other connections to work, we still need to declare a number of slots in mainwindow.h, the contents of which are discussed on the following pages. Since we only use them in the MainWindow class itself, we declare them as protected methods:

```
// cuteedit2/mainwindow.h (continued)

...
  protected:
    bool mayDiscardDocument();
    void saveFile(const QString&);
  protected slots:
    void newFile();
    void loadFile();
    void saveFile();
    void saveFileAs();
    void undo();
    void redo();
    void copy();
    void about();
  private:
    QString mFilePath;
};
#endif // MAINWINDOW_H
```

The variable mFilePath specifies the path to the current file. If the document has not been saved until now, this string is empty.

Since we do not need to destruct anything manually, the destructor remains empty. All Widget destruction is taken care of by the QObject hierarchy when the Main-Window instance is destructed at the end of main().

Opening Files

The first function that CuteEdit should master is the loading of a file, usually called a *document* in the terminology of text editors. To do this, we first require a file-name, for which we query the user via an object of the QFileDialog class.

It is normally completely sufficient to use the static methods of this class, which merely require a pointer to the parent widget, as well as an optional window title and a filter for various file types. We will use the getOpenFileName() static method, which returns precisely one filename as a QString. A more detailed description of various dialog types is provided in Chapter 6.

To open a file, Qt uses the QFile class, which allows platform-independent access to files. This is part of the Qt input/output concept that is explained in more detail in Chapter 11 and occurs in place of the FILE pointer familiar from C.

The open() method, similar to the C function fopen(), opens the file, in this case in read-only mode:

```
// cuteedit2/mainwindow.cpp (continued)

void MainWindow::loadFile()
{
```

```
QString filename = QFileDialog::getOpenFileName(this);
QFile file(filename);
if (file.open(QIODevice::ReadOnly|QIODevice::Text)) {
  textEdit->setPlainText(QString::fromUtf8(file.readAll()));
  mFilePath = filename;
  statusBar()->showMessage(tr("File successfully loaded."), 3000);
}
}
```

We use the QIODevice::Text flag so that the editor can cope with the differences between Unix and Windows with respect to text files. Unix uses just a line feed (\n) to separate lines, whereas Windows in addition requires the control character for a carriage return (\r\n). Qt classes are internally based on Unix conventions wherever possible, which is why QTextEdit only works with line feeds, and so we have QFile remove all the carriage returns when it opens a text file on Windows platforms by specifying QIODevice::Text.

Now the readAll() method reads the entire contents of the file into a QByteArray. We could import this directly into the textWidget, using setPlainText(), but we do not know the encoding format of the files. QByteArray contains the text in its 8-bit encoding, while QString uses 16-bit Unicode characters. In Windows, text files are normally saved in UTF-8 format. This mirrors the Unicode characters in 8-bits, and is compatible to ASCII encoding. In Linux, text files are available either as UTF-8 or in country-specific encoding, such as ISO Latin 1 (also known as ISO 8859-1).

For the sake of simplicity, CuteEdit assumes that files are always encoded in UTF-8 and therefore converts the text contents using QString::fromUtf8() into a QString.[7]

We will remember the filename for later operations, for example to save the file again when we need to.

To report the successful opening of the selected file, we use the status bar. Its showMessage() method in this example shows the message *File successfully loaded.* for three seconds, and then removes it.

Saving Files

Now we have to implement the CuteEdit function that makes the program usable in the first place, namely, the ability to save the current document:

```
// cuteedit2/mainwindow.cpp (continued)

void MainWindow::saveFile()
```

[7] In a real editor the program should first ask the user about the encoding of his file or—even better—find out the encoding method itself. Valuable work in implementation is provided by the QTextCodec class, which also provides a list of the available codecs, with the availableCodecs() static methods.

```
{
  if(mFilePath.isEmpty())
    saveFileAs();
  else
    saveFile(mFilePath);
}

void MainWindow::saveFile(const QString &name)
{
  QFilc file(name);
  if (file.open(QIODevice::WriteOnly|QIODevice::Text)) {
    file.write(textEdit->toPlainText().toUtf8());
    statusBar()->showMessage(tr("File saved successfully."), 3000);
  }
}


void MainWindow::saveFileAs()
{
  mFilePath = QFileDialog::getSaveFileName(this);
  if(mFilePath.isEmpty())
    return;
  saveFile(mFilePath);
}
```

If no file is currently opened and mFilePath is therefore empty, the saveFileAs()
method comes into play. It is also directly called from the menu item File→Save
as..., but serves the same purpose in both cases: to store the file under a name
specified by the user.

Internally saveFileAs() uses the overloaded method, not declared as a slot, save-
File(const QString &name), which takes on the actual work: To do this, it makes
use of the toPlainText() method of the QTextEdit instance, which returns a QString.
The resulting text is encoded by toUtf8() again as an 8-bit text. Before this, it
opens the file, as loadFile() did before, with the QIODevice::Text flag, in order to
guarantee the correct conversion in Windows. But this time we only open the
file for writing (QIODevice::WriteOnly). Afterward, this method also reports the
successful completion of the action via the status bar.

Even if he has already loaded a file, the user should be able to create another new
document. Since CuteEdit, for the sake of simplicity, can only manage one open
file at a time, we have a problem if the first document has been modified but not
yet saved.

Whether this is the case or not is known by the document object which is managed
by QTextEdit:

```
// cuteedit2/mainwindow.cpp (continued)

bool MainWindow::mayDiscardDocument()
```

```
{
  if (textEdit->document()->isModified()) {
    QString filename = mFilePath;
    if (filename.isEmpty()) filename = tr("Unnamed");
    if (QMessageBox::question(this, tr("Save Document?"),
      tr("You want to create a new document, but the "
         "changes in the current document '%1' have not "
         "been saved. How do you want to proceed?"),
         tr("Save Document"), tr("Discard Changes") ))
      saveFile();
    return true;
  }
  return false;
}

void MainWindow::newFile()
{
  if (!mayDiscardDocument()) return;
  textEdit->setPlainText("");
  mFilePath = "";
}
```

Before CuteEdit opens a new document in the newFile() slot, it should ask the user what he intends to do with these changes. Since this function can be used universally, we shall move it to the mayDiscardDocument() method, which returns a true value.

For the actual requests to the user, we use a QMessageBox. In a similar way as for QDialogBox, for this class we use mainly the static methods that are appropriate for most situations and only need to be provided with the corresponding arguments. Although a title and the message contents would be sufficient in this case, the example replaces the standard responses of Yes and No with more descriptive responses, for the sake of better usability.

Ideally, message boxes should clearly inform the user what action is to be carried out—unfortunately the number of applications with dialog box texts that lead to misunderstandings is very high. Since buttons specify responses directly, this reduces the probability that the user will select the wrong action.

If mayDiscardDocument() returns true, we delete the text of the current document and reset the file path so that other functions do not access the file just edited by mistake. An even more efficient method would be to set a new document through textEdit->setDocument(), but since all signal/slot connections to the document are lost, these would have to be recreated afterwards.

In addition the method here has the side-effect that the undo buffer remains. This could be an advantage for people who can click faster than they can read, but it could also involve possible data protection problems (such as if several users are using the same workplace).

The Undo/Redo Function

Programs that do not allow the user to undo actions can be frustrating. This applies particularly to text editors. Since QTextDocument already provides an *undo stack*, we can equip CuteEdit quickly and easily with an undo function:

```
// cuteedit2/mainwindow.cpp (continued)

void MainWindow::undo()
{
  textEdit->document()->undo();
}
```

The redo is to a certain extent the opposite operation to undo: It recreates a status that has been undone. This has also been implemented already, so that we just need to make it accessible as a slot.

```
// cuteedit2/mainwindow.cpp (continued)

void MainWindow::redo()
{
  textEdit->document()->redo();
}
```

The copy method, with which the user copies highlighted text to the temporary buffer, is also made available directly by QTextEdit, so we just need a wrapper method here:

```
// cuteedit2/mainwindow.cpp (continued)

void MainWindow::copy()
{
  textEdit->copy();
}
```

The undo(), redo(), and copy() slots therefore simply call the matching methods of the QTextEdit or QTextDocument classes. If the undo stack is empty, the first two actions in the menu and icon bars are grayed out, since we disable them in setupActions() through signals undoAvailable() and redoAvailable() of QTextEdit, if QTextEdit or QTextDocument consider them to be not applicable. We discussed setupActions() on page 112.

Information on the Program

Of course, the obligatory info box must not be missing in any program. QMessage-Box (see page 166) provides its own static method for this, called about(), which expects a heading and a short text:

```
// cuteedit2/mainwindow.cpp (continued)


void MainWindow::about()
{
  QMessageBox::about(this, tr("About CuteEdit"),
              tr("CuteEdit 1.0\nA Qt application example.\n"
                 "(c) 2006 Daniel Molkentin, Open Source Press"));
}
```

The first parameter is a pointer to the parent window towards which the info box should behave in a modal manner. If you pass 0 here, Qt generates a non-modal box.

Building a Project

Finally, to display the program, we generate the project file with qmake -project and build the program with qmake and make.

```
#cuteedit2/cuteedit2.pro

TEMPLATE  = app
SOURCES   = main.cpp mainwindow.cpp
HEADERS   = mainwindow.h
FORMS     = mainwindow.ui
RESOURCES = pics.qrc
```

4.4 Making the Most of the Status Bar

Qt Designer–generated main windows already have a status bar. This is used both to announce short-term responses, as we have already done in saveFile() (page 114) and loadFile() (page 113), as well as more persistent messages of an application. In this way, CuteEdit could display word statistics for the current document there, for example. We will discuss this and how to implement it in more detail from page 121.

Figure 4.6:
The size grip at the
bottom right

The bar also provides a *size grip* (outlined in bold in Figure 4.6) for the window. This is the serrated triangle at the lower right edge of the window, which changes its size. Even if you don't want to have any status messages displayed but only require this "size change handle," it is recommended that you display the status bar in the main window. If required, setSizeGripEnabled(false) can be used to hide the size grip.

The class that is responsible for the status bar, and which also contains the method just mentioned, is called QStatusBar. QMainWindow::statusBar() returns a pointer to the QStatusBar object used by the main window. If the window does not yet have any status bar, then this function generates one and adds it to the main window.

If, in an instance of QMainWindow not generated by Designer, we add the line

```
statusBar();
```

the application window is given a status bar that shows only the size grip. On the other hand, the line

```
statusBar->hide();
```

causes an undesired status bar (in this case: statusBar) to disappear again.

The status bar presents three different types of status messages:

Temporary messages
> These are used for information that should only be visible for a short time (Figure 4.7). This includes, for example, the URL of a link over which the mouse in the web browser is currently located, or progress details during a download.

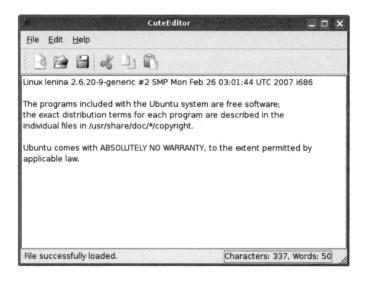

Figure 4.7:
The left side of the status bar is often used to briefly display messages to the user, as shown here in CuteEdit.

Normal messages
> These are always shown by an application unless a temporary message is

shown. This covers over normal messages which are used for general status information, such as the coordinates of the mouse in a CAD application.

Permanent messages
> These always monopolize the status bar and can never be covered by temporary messages. They are used for messages that should always be visible, such as the connection status of a network application.

Temporary and normal messages appear on the left in the status bar, permanent messages on the right. A status bar can display several normal and permanent messages at the same time, but it is not possible to display more than one temporary message: The new one always displaces the old one.

4.4.1   Temporary Messages

Temporary messages are activated with the QStatusBar::showMessage() slot and are deleted with QStatusBar::clearMessage(). The message text is passed to show-Message() as an argument in the form of a QString. In our example we add the line

```
statusBar()->message(tr("File successfully loaded."));
```

to the constructor so that the temporary message is displayed in the status bar.[8] The temporary message remains visible until we either set a new message with showMessage(), delete the current text with clearMessage(), or overwrite it by invoking showMessage() again.

If you want to display the temporary message only for a specific length of time, the showMessage() slot accepts an optional second parameter. If specified, the QStatusBar-Object automatically deletes the message after a specified time. So the call

```
statusBar()->message(tr("File successfully saved."), 3000);
```

displays the message *File successfully saved.* for 3,000 milliseconds (that is, three seconds). Then the normal messages take over again, provided any exist.

4.4.2   Normal Messages

Normal messages are not so easy to handle, unfortunately. You must use widgets for them. If you want to show a simple text as a normal message, for example,

---

[8] To compile the program successfully, you must also include the QStatusBar header with #include <QStatusBar>. The entire code is available from http://www.qt4-buch.de/examples.tar.gz.

then you generate a QLabel object and add this to the status bar, with the QStatus-Bar::addWidget() function. This is a bit more complicated, but it has the advantage that it is not restricted to text messages. You can also use icons, for example, or a progress bar for an operation that takes more than a brief amount of time.

In accordance with its signature, addWidget(QWidget* widget, int stretch=0), the addWidget() function requires two arguments, one of which is optional. First it is passed a pointer to the widget to be added. The QStatusBar destructor deletes this automatically; for this reason it must have been created on the heap with new.

The second argument does not have to be specified if you are satisfied with the default values. It determines how several widgets divide the space in the status bar among themselves. The value 0 means that the widget has as much space as necessary. Another value specifies the proportions of the widgets to each other. If, for example, you have a widget with a stretch value of 1 and the second one with a value of 2, then they jointly occupy the entire space in the status bar so that the second one is twice as wide as the first. In the example of Figure 4.8, whose five widgets have been assigned stretch values of 1, 2, 3, 4, and 5, the first widget is only allocated the space it requires. The other widgets occupy the remaining space so that the third one has twice as much space as the second, and so on.

Figure 4.8:
Different stretch values in the status bar

4.4.3   Permanent Messages

As with addWidget(), there is the addPermanentWidget() function for permanent messages. Widgets inserted with this method appear on the extreme right: These are appropriate for permanent status displays, for example. Permanent messages are guaranteed not to be interrupted, even for a short time, by messages that are displayed as described above via showMessage().

To expand our MainWindow class so that it displays word statistics in the status bar, we first insert a label into the status bar. Since we need to access this later, we create a member variable called mStatLabel in the class definition:

```
// cuteedit2/mainwindow.h (added)

...
class QLabel;

class MainWindow : public QMainWindow,
                   private Ui::MainWindow
{
...
  private:
```

```
        QString mFilePath;
        QLabel *mStatLabel;
}
```

The line class QLabel; is a *forward declaration* of the QLabel class—in this way we do not yet need to include the QLabel header file. Because of this, the parser needs less time for mainwindow.h and for the files that later include this file.

In a header file containing a forward declaration of a class, one can only declare variables of pointer and reference types derived from the class;[9] variables representing instances of the class can't be declared because the compiler doesn't know how much space they should occupy until it sees the class's definition.

However, the source text file needs to include the QLabel header file, of course, since the compiler would otherwise not recognize the interface of the class.

In the constructor we include code that generates a QLabel object and displays this in the status bar as a permanent message; the message should only take up as much space as it needs, so that we still have room for temporary messages. Since a stretch of 0, which would cause this, is the default, we can just leave out the second argument of addPermanentWidget() altogether in this case. We place the QLabel object on the heap with new, since the QStatusBar object will delete it in the destructor.[10]

```
// cuteedit2/mainwindow.cpp (continued)

#include <QtGui>
#include "mainwindow.h"

MainWindow::MainWindow(QWidget *parent)
  : QMainWindow(parent)
{
  setupUi(this);
  setupActions();

  mStatLabel = new QLabel;
  statusBar()->addPermanentWidget(mStatLabel);
  connect(textEdit, SIGNAL(textChanged()), this, SLOT(updateStats()));
  updateStats();
}
```

As mentioned before, statusBar() not only returns a pointer to the status bar, but also generates it if it does not yet exist.

To now update statistics each time whenever the edited document is changed, we listen to the textChanged() signal and connect it to the slot (still to be implemented)

---

[9] In this case the compiler knows the size of the memory to be reserved, since an address on each platform always has the same size, for example, four bytes on IA32 architectures.

[10] The QStatusBar object is deleted in turn by its parent object, the QMainWindow instance.

updateStats(), which is responsible for updating the word statistics label. In this way we ensure that Qt really does update statistics correctly. Finally, we call the new slot manually so that the label can obtain an initial status.

After we have entered updateStats() as a slot in the class declaration of MainWindow, we must now find a way of having the statistics delivered to the label in the status bar. The text, with all its many properties—QTextEdit can even handle simple HTML constructions and allows the user to precisely format texts—is stored in an instance of QTextDocument:

```
// cuteedit2/mainwindow.cpp (continued)

void MainWindow::updateStats()
{
  QString text = textEdit->document()->toPlainText();
  int chars = text.length();
  text = text.simplified();
  int words = 0;
  words = text.count(" ");
  if (!text.isEmpty()) words++;
  QString output = tr("Characters: %1, Words: %2").arg(chars).arg(words);
  mStatLabel->setText(output);
}
```

Each QTextEdit possesses exactly one document, which is encapsulated in the QText-Document class. What at first glance just seems to be an implementation detail is, in reality, a very powerful tool for displaying and manipulating text. But here we just use one method to access the current text of the document: With the call document()->toPlainText(), QTextDocument generates a QString from its currently saved text, but this is more than enough for our relatively simple analysis.

This searches the string for individual words and characters. To count the characters, we simply query its length, taking into account that line breaks are also counted as spaces. If you don't want this, you can remove the line breaks from the string beforehand using text.replace('\n', "").

When determining the number of words in the text, we also do not need a more complex parser, since our statistics are relatively simple (and even so can be quite slow, depending on the text length): It defines a word as a string separated by a space. Thus the number of words is one more than the number of spaces which lie between them. So that superfluous empty spaces do not get in the way, we use the QString method simplified(), which removes all whitespace (that is, spaces, word wraps, etc.) at the beginning and end of the string and reduces the white spaces between individual words to exactly one space. The string, which we are now examining for empty spaces, exactly matches our desired definition, and the number of spaces plus one results in the number of words. The only tricky detail is that because an empty text has no words, we may only increase the space count by one if text is not empty.

We construct the lettering for the label with tr("Characters: %1, Words: %2"). arg(chars).arg(words);. The tr() function returns the text *Characters: %1, Words: %2* as a QString, and if necessary translates this into a different language. The QString class has an arg() method, which searches for the strings %1, %2, …, %9, and from those it finds, replaces the one with the smallest number with the function argument. In our case we will thus obtain the desired result, because the contents of chars and words, converted into a string, replace the placeholders %1 and %2, in that order.

Using this method, you can create strings containing dynamic text. This has the advantage that the order of the strings in translations may change if this is necessary from a grammatical point of view.

Finally, we set the text of the label with the QLabel function setText(), so that the status bar displays *Characters: 0, Words: 0*, provided that the function for the variables chars and words returns the value 0. Our expanded application now looks like Figure 4.9.

Figure 4.9:
The editor program
CuteEdit, now with an
added status bar with
a permanent message

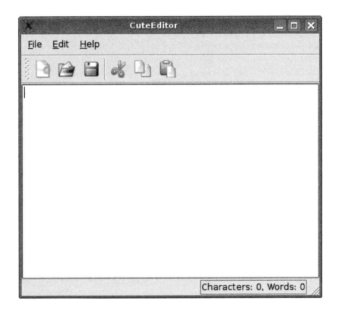

The status bar shows messages that do not interrupt the user's work, in contrast to notification dialogs, which obtain the keyboard focus and which the user must close explicitly. For messages that are not so important, you should weigh whether they really require a separate dialog, or whether a temporary message in the status bar is sufficient, and whether the message is indeed relevant enough to the user to be shown at all. An application that is too "talkative" can quickly get on your nerves.

4.5   Toolbars

Each toolbar has a so-called *handle* with which it can be moved (see Figure 4.10), so that a user can rearrange the toolbars in his application and move them to different positions in the window. If you want to prevent this, you should use setMovable(false);.

Figure 4.10:

A typical toolbar with a handle (on the left)

To locate a toolbar at a position other than horizontally beneath the menu bar, such as directly on the left margin of the window, we must make a slight change to our example. There is a second version of the addToolBar() method that requires positioning details as the first argument. We therefore change the call in this way:

```
QToolBar *mainToolBar = addToolBar(Qt::BottomToolBarArea,
                           tr("Main Toolbar"));
```

Now the main toolbar appears on the bottom margin; Table 4.1 specifies the possible positions. In practice, though, this only makes sense for toolbar selections in the style of Photoshop or GIMP, which are usually implemented anyway as dock windows (see page 130). Users are creatures of habit, and tend to look for toolbars in the upper section of the window.

Value	Position
Qt::LeftToolBarArea	Vertically, on the left side of the main window.
Qt::RightToolBarArea	Vertically, on the right side of the main window.
Qt::TopToolBarArea	Horizontally, as high up as possible but beneath the menu bar and above any dock windows.
Qt::BottomToolBarArea	Horizontally, as low down as possible, but above the status bar and beneath any dock windows.
Qt::AllToolBarAreas	All previous positions. Not permissible for ad-dToolBar().

Table 4.1:

The ToolBarAreas *enumerator*

Using setAllowedAreas(), it is also possible to allow toolbars only at certain positions. Table 4.1 provides the values valid for this, which can be linked with a logical OR operator. The following code restricts the placement of the mainToolBar toolbar to beneath the menu bar and above the status bar:

```
mainToolBar->setAllowedAreas(Qt::TopToolBarArea |
                       Qt::BottomToolBarArea);
```

Since the user can remove the tool selections, it is the duty of the programmer to ensure that they can be found again at any time. A suitable place for the toolbar retrieve instruction is the menu bar, since the user can normally not hide this. The toggleViewAction() method provides a pointer to a QAction and ensures that the toolbar reappears—or disappears, if that is what the user wants. The visible text of the action is oriented towards the windowTitle of the icon bar, which is why this should be set in the Designer. If you don't like it, you can define your own text for the action, using QAction::setText().

Menu entries which allow an option to be switched on or off, that is, to be *toggled*, are derived from *toggle actions*.

To make the toolbar in our example program disappear or reappear, we build an action like this into the (yet to be implemented) Settings→Toolbars submenu of the menu bar. To do this, we add the following code to the end of the setupActions() function on page 112:

```
QMenu *toolBarMenu = settingsMenu->addMenu(tr("&Toolbars"));

toolBarMenu->addAction(mainToolBar->toggleViewAction());
...
```

For the code to work, we must first insert an addtional menu with the title Settings in the Designer, which we will call settingsMenu. The Settings menu here belongs *in front of* the Help menu, since the latter should always be the last entry in the menu bar.

This results in a selectable entry being located in the tool bars submenu. All visible bars are prefixed with a checkmark. You can see here why toolbars should always be given a name.

4.6   How Do Actions Work?

We have already made contact with the QAction class. So far however, the Designer generated the appropriate code. So to get a better picture, we should not forget to mention how actions work and how you can use them "manually." Those not interested in these details can continue reading on page 130.

Each QAction object encapsulates information involving a user interface action.[11] All important properties are summarized in Table 4.2 on page 129.

[11]   In Qt 3, actions (also called QActions) were active objects that selected the matching display method themselves, dependent on the object in which they were included. In Qt 4 Trolltech has reversed this principle: Now widgets decide on the display form of the actions presented.

4.6.1   How to Instantiate QAction Manually

We do not have to use the Designer every time, of course, to create QAction objects. The following example demonstrates how you can create actions yourself in the constructor of a QMainWindow subclass.

First we instantiate the desired action with an icon and name, and assign it to the main window as a parent object. The QIcon() class encapsulates an icon:

```
QAction *action_open;
action_open = new QAction(QIcon(":/pics/fileopen.png"),
                          tr("&Open"), this);
action_open->setShortcut(tr("Ctrl+O"));
action_open->setStatusTip(tr("Opens an existing file."));
```

In contrast to QPixmap, an action can take in images for various states (normal, active, and grayed out) and stages (selected or not selected). If the class contains just one image—as in this case—it tries to calculate the icons for the other states and stages from the icon specified.

By means of setShortcut() we can set the corresponding key binding as a string. Together with the translation function tr(), this has the advantage that the translators can select an appropriate shortcut for the Open action *in the respective language*. setStatusTip() sets the text that appears in the status bar if the mouse is held over the action.

To integrate actions directly into the menu bar, the following code suffices:

```
menuBar()->addAction(action_open);
```

menuBar(), a method of QMainWindow returns the main windows menu bar. The procedure just shown is rather unusual, however. Normally menus are first inserted into the menu bar, and then the actions are integrated. The QMenu instance representing the menu can be generated via the addMenu() *Factory Method*. We insert the Open action into this as follows:

```
QMenu *menu_Datei = menuBar()->addMenu(tr("&File"));
menu_Datei->addAction(action_open);
```

For actions that are used as information carriers for various widgets simultaneously, you should particularly think about the parenthood in the object model of Qt. The main window, as the father of all other widgets, is always the last to be deleted. So that Qt will delete action objects as late as possible, it is best to turn them into direct descendants of the main window.

If actions are used in several windows simultaneously, there are basically two alternatives: Either you duplicate all actions for each window, or you turn them into children of QApplication. In this case you can simply pass qApp as a parent to the QAction constructor.

4.6.2   Selectable Actions

Some actions contain a binary state. A typical example of this is a word-wrap function in CuteEdit. So that the user can see whether this is active or not, we convert it to a selectable action with setCheckable():

```
QAction *action_linebreak;
action_linebreak = new QAction(tr("&Line break"), this);
action_linebreak->setCheckable(true);
```

Its status can be queried with isChecked(). Although a selectable action automatically changes its state every time it is selected, you can alternatively change it with setChecked() instead.

4.6.3   Grouped Actions

Several selectable actions can be grouped together so that the user can always activate only one of them. This function is particularly familiar from word processing programs, in which you can exclusively select from text alignment to the left, to the right, or centered. If you select one of these actions, the others are automatically deactivated.

To implement this in Qt, all states must be available as QAction instances. But first we create a QActionGroup object, which we pass to the QAction constructor as a parent widget. This causes the action to be automatically inserted into the action group. If we now make each individual element in the group selectable, the actions are linked to each other:

```
QAction *act_alignleft;
QAction *act_alignright;
QAction *act_aligncenter;
QActionGroup *aligngroup = new QActionGroup(this);
act_alignleft = new QAction(tr("Align &right"), aligngroup);
act_alignright = new QAction(tr("Align &left"), aligngroup);
act_aligncenter = new QAction(tr("&Center"), aligngroup);
act_alignleft->setCheckable(true);
act_alignright->setCheckable(true);
act_aligncenter->setCheckable(true);
```

Since QActionGroup is just an administration class, we must insert the individual actions manually, with addAction(), into the appropriate menu or toolbar. If the user now selects an action, the class emits the triggered() signal with the selected action as an argument. With this, a matching slot can decide how to react to the corresponding action, such as by comparing the pointer to the passed on QAction instance with the actions produced.

Property	Get method	Set method	Description
text	text()	setText(const QString&)	Short description of action, used as a menu text, for example
icon	icon()	setIcon(const QIcon&)	Icon that symbolizes the action
iconText	iconText()	setIconText(const QString&)	Text that fits in the icon or underneath the icon; if not set, text() is used
shortcut	shortcut()	setShortcut(const QKeySequence&)	Shortcut
statusTip	statusTip()	setStatusTip(const QString&)	Longer text that the status bar shows when the mouse passes over it
whatsThis	whatsThis()	setWhatsThis(const QString&)	Extensive help text that is displayed in the *What's This?* mode[12]
toolTip	toolTip()	setToolTip(const QString&)	Text displayed floating below the widget that has recorded the action
font	font()	setFont(const QFont&)	Specifies the font properties for menu entries
enabled	isEnabled()	setEnabled(bool)	If this is false, the action is grayed and cannot be selected
visible	isVisible()	setVisible(bool)	If this is false, the action is not displayed
checkable	isCheckable()	setCheckable(bool)	If this is true, the action can be switched on and off (*toggled*) (for example, bold typeface in a word processing program)

Table 4.2:
Important properties of QAction

[12] In the *What's This?* mode the application displays an information text for each selected entry, which can be defined for each widget and for each QAction with setWhatsThis(). Users can navigate to the What's This? mode via (Shift)+(F1) or via a QAction, which generates the call QWhatsThis().createAction(). It must be inserted explicitly into the Help menu.

continued

Property	Get method	Set method	Description
checked	isChecked()	setChecked(bool)	Defines whether a toggled action is on (true) or off

4.7 Dock Windows

In some cases it is useful, apart from simple actions, to also group together more complex widgets so that the user can place them either inside the main window or separate from this. Such so-called *dock windows* are also provided by Qt 4: The class responsible for this is called QDockWidget.

Users are especially aware of these in development environments such as Microsoft Visual C++ or the Qt Designer,[13] which arrange all their tools within the main window. As can be seen in the example of the Designer in Figure 4.11, the user can dock them in the same way as toolbars to side areas of the window, or position them floating over the main window. If they are docked, the latter have a *splitter* (see Chapter 5.3 on page 150), with which the user can fine-tune the size ratio of the dock window to the main window, if necessary. Dock windows also have a *handle* (similar to toolbars), with which the user can move them to another margin of the window or, if he pulls them out of the window, make them independent.

Figure 4.11:
The Designer with a
floating widget box.
All other dock
windows are stuck to
the right margin.

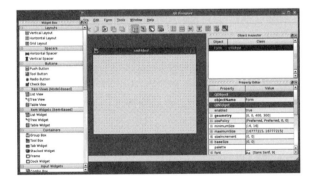

To the right of the handle there are two miniaturized buttons. The left one makes the window independent, while the right one closes it, whether or not it is currently docked to the main window. Closing it does not delete the QDockWindow instance though, but merely hides it, using hide() (inherited from QWidget). Two methods

---

[13]   For Designer, only while in the dock window mode, which can be set via Edit→ User Interface Mode→Docked Window.

are available to the programmer if he now wants to display them again: He can either make the widget itself visible at any time via show(), or he can use the toggleShowAction() method, as already used for toolbars, which then generates a corresponding entry in menus or toolbars.

The developer has the option of restricting a series of privileges that QDockWidget provides to the user. These privileges are described in the enumerator QDockWidget::DockWidgetFeatures. They can either be defined as a property in the Qt Designer or by passing a combination of enumerator elements to the setFeatures() method:

DockWidgetClosable
  Determines whether a dock window may be closed

DockWidgetMovable
  Specifies whether a dock window may be moved

DockWidgetFloatable
  Defines whether a dock window may float

If you want to restrict privileges, you must interpret these DockWidgetFeatures as *bit flags* that can be combined with a logical OR. This can be done because the enumerator has values that are based on the power of 2, which are referred to as "bit flags."[14]

To prevent the user from closing and removing the dock window, the following call is sufficient

```
dockWindow->setFeatures(QDockWidget::DockWidgetClosable|
                        QDockWidget::DockWidgetFloatable);
```

To remove or assign all freedoms, the Qt additionally provides the enumerated values QDockWidget::NoDockWidgetFeatures and QDockWidget::AllDockWidgetFeatures.

Enumerators that are used as bit flags are an elementary concept in Qt, and we will come across them frequently.

4.7.1   Positioning Dock Windows

Another important difference between toolbars and dock windows is their positioning. As can be seen in Figure 4.12, QMainWindow divides its margins into two

---

[14]   Unix users know this from the file permissions in the filesystem. Unix-based operating systems form the permissions for reading, writing, and executing (rwx) from the powers of two, using a single digit. A file with access permissions 5 is readable (4) and executable (1), but not writable (2).

rings; toolbars are always located directly on the window margin, but dock windows are always inside the margin.

Figure 4.12:
The main window
takes in toolbars and
dock windows in two
rings as decorations
on the margin.

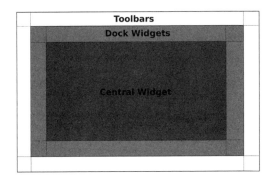

Dock windows have a title and a child widget, so their contents can be arranged in any way you like. With setWidget() we insert the widget created specifically for the dock window. The heading set with setWindowTitle() appears as the title of the dock window.

addDockWidget() then integrates the dock window into the main window. As the first parameter, the method expects the position of the tool window, because, in contrast to toolbars, Qt does not specify a standard position for dock widgets. Which one you choose depends heavily on the intended purpose. In the code example on page 133 we "stick" the window to the left main window frame, with Qt:LeftDockWidgetArea. The DockWidgetAreas enumerator is used to specify the location, and is described in Table 4.3.

Table 4.3:
The DockWidgetAreas
enumerator

Value	Position
Qt::LeftDockWidgetArea	Vertically, on the left side of the main window, but to the right of any possible menu bars
Qt::RightDockWidgetArea	Vertically, on the right side of the main window, but to the left of any possible menu bars
Qt::TopDockWidgetArea	Horizontally, as high up as possible but beneath the menu bar and any possible icon bars
Qt::BottomDockWidgetArea	Horizontally, as low down as possible, but above the status bar and any possible icon bars
Qt::AllDockWidgetAreas	All previous positions; not permissible for addDockWidget()

As the second argument, addDockWidget() expects a pointer to the QDockWidget to be inserted. During the instantiation of the dock window on page 133, we could leave out details of a parent, because addDockWidget() not only integrates the window graphically into the main window, but also transfers the parenthood for the dock window to the main window.

Since dock windows usually contain more complex widgets, horizontal docking is generally recommended—that is, positioning on the left or right side of the window. The upper and lower sides of the main window are only rarely suited to docking. The areas in which the dock window may reside are again summarized by the enumerator type Qt::DockWidgetAreas; which of them are actually permitted is determined by setAllowedAreas(). Members of the enumeration are used as an argument, and they are linked with a logical OR. To prevent docking on the upper and lower window margin, for example, we extend the constructor from the above example as follows:

```
dockWidget->setAllowedAreas(Qt::LeftDockWidgetArea |
                            Qt::RightDockWidgetArea);
```

Normally the user may also position the dock window as floating over the window, instead of docking it. The call setFloating(false) prevents this—the corresponding dock window then sticks only to the window sides allowed by setAllowedAreas().

As has already been indicated, dock windows can also be closed. Just like menu bars, they therefore have a method called toggleViewAction(). The example from page 126 works here in the same way: If it is included in the menu bar, the user can make the dock window reappear at any time through the entry generated with this.

4.7.2 A Dock Window for Our Editor

Now that we have had a good look at the theory of dock windows, we will turn our attention to a small example. Our editor should be given a list of templates which can be inserted by clicking the current cursor position.

To do this, we generate a new dock window in the Designer and give it, together with the text editor, a horizontal layout.[15] In the Property Editor we allow docking for it only on the right and left sides of the main window. Finally we give the object a name: TemplateDocker.

Alternatively, we can generate the dock window in the constructor of the Main-Window as follows:

```
QDockWidget *templateDocker = new QDockWidget;
templateDocker->setAllowedAreas(Qt::LeftDockWidgetArea|
```

---

[15] The Designer interprets dock windows in design mode as widgets in the central widget.

```
        Qt::RightDockWidgetArea);
templateDocker->setObjectName("TemplateDocker");
templateDocker->setWindowTitle(tr("Templates"));
addDockWidget(Qt::LeftDockWidgetArea, templateDocker);

QListView *view = new QListView();
templateDocker->setWidget(view);

new TemplateHandler(view, textEdit, this);
```

The main window requires the object name to save the window properties. We will discuss this topic at the end of Section 4.8. If the name is missing, Qt complains at runtime on the standard output. Unfortunately, it is not possible to set the windowTitle attribute of QDockWidget in the Designer, which is why it is important that this must be done separately in the constructor. windowTitle labels the window and also gives a name to the toggle action that is generated by toggleViewAction().

In the final step we breathe life into the widget by filling it with a list view. We will later find the templates in this view. The TemplateHandler class now instantiated is responsible for filling the list and for inserting templates at the current cursor position in the editor window:

```
// cuteedit2/templatehandler.cpp

TemplateHandler::TemplateHandler(QListView *view, QTextEdit *textEdit,
  QObject *parent) : QObject( parent ), mTextEdit(textEdit)
{
  mModel = new QStringListModel(this);
  QStringList templates;
  templates << "<html>" << "</html>" <<  "<body>" << "</body>";
  mModel->setStringList( templates );
  view->setModel(mModel);
  connect(view, SIGNAL(clicked(const QModelIndex&)),
               SLOT(insertText(const QModelIndex&)));
}
```

In Qt 4, list views work on the basis of the *model/view* principle introduced in Chapter 8: A *model* is responsible for obtaining data, while the **view** displays the data. In the case of our templates, one model is enough, which takes data directly from a QStringList. As before, these are fed with several templates, in this case for HTML.[16].

We pass the list created in this way to the model via setStringList() and turn this into the reference model for our view, the list view. The list view is now filled, and

---

[16] In a proper application the templates are not compiled statically, of course, but are loaded from a file.

we just need to include the selected template in the editor window. To do this, we connect the clicked() signal of the view and implement the insertText() method (which we must first declare in the class definition as a slot, of course):

```
// cuteedit2/templatehandler.cpp (continued)

void TemplateHandler::insertText( const QModelIndex& index )
{
  QString text = mModel->data(index, Qt::DisplayRole).toString();
  QTextCursor cursor = mTextEdit->textCursor();
  cursor.insertText(text);
  mTextEdit->setTextCursor(cursor);
}
```

The model index passed represents the selected line in our model. Using the data() method, we can obtain the data as QVariant from this, which we must still convert into a QString. QVariant works in a similar way to a union in C++. The class can also convert various types—both Qt-specific data types such as QString and QSize, as well as C++ types such as int or double—from one to another.

Figure 4.13:
The template dock window in docked condition: A click inserts the text into the corresponding line in the editor window.

The model/view concept of Qt has many different *roles* for a model index (see table 8.1 on page 209; for instance, many views can display an icon (Qt::DecorationRole), in addition to normal text (Qt::DisplayRole). At the moment, however, only Qt::DisplayRole is relevant to us.

The textCursor() method of the text window represents the current position of the writing cursor.[17] We pass the text, which it should insert at the cursor position, to the instance. Now we must insert the text cursor to the current cursor position again, using setTextCursor, to update the cursor.[18]

Our dock window is now completely implemented. Thanks to the QObject base class and the fact that we pass the main window as the parent object, we do not need to delete the instance of TemplateHandler manually. The result is shown in Figure 4.13.

4.8   Saving Preferences

Last but not least, our program should be able to keep the settings made by the user, even after the program is restarted. To this end, different conventions have become established on different operating systems.

Depending on the platform, application data may be stored in the Windows Registry (in the user scope HKEY_LOCAL_MACHINE\Software) or in the system scope HKEY_CURRENT_USER\Software), in an XML-based .plist file under Mac OS X, or in /etc/xdg,[19] (system-wide settings) or ~/.config (user-defined settings) under Unix.

Qt encapsulates access to these configuration storage systems with the help of theQSettings class. Every filing system in this is a *backend*. QSettings objects can be created either on the heap or on the stack. Since little work is needed to instantiate them, we recommend that you create them on the stack, if this is necessary.

In case two or more QSettings instances are working with the same data, the class ensures that data between different instances is always correctly synchronized, in case two or more QSettings objects are working with the same file. The same applies for two threads, both of which contain a QSettings object with the link to the same file, and even for two different processes, in case both are using QSettings linked to a common file. Qt uses internal locking mechanisms for this purpose.

The QSettings constructor normally requires two parameters for the instantiation in order to generate the appropriate entry in the configuration storage system: the name of the organization for which the programmer works, and the name of the program. In Windows,

---

[17] The QTextCursor class in general does not have to describe the currently visible cursor, but it can manipulate text at any position at all.

[18] This is necessary because QTextCursor works not in a pointer-based manner, but in a value-based one, and we therefore work with a copy created with the allocation to the cursor variable.

[19] The directory name stands for an abbreviation of *X Desktop Group* the now-obsolete generic term for the Freedesktop.org developers. See also http://www.redhat.com/archives/xdg-list/2003-March/msg00041.html.

```
QSettings settings("OpenSourcePress", "CuteEdit");
```

would reference the registry path

```
HKEY_CURRENT_USER\Software\OpenSourcePress\CuteEdit
```

If a programmer generates such QSettings instances at many locations in the code, it would be a good idea not to have to constantly pass the parameters. This is possible if we feed the application itself with program and organization details, preferably straight in the main() function:

```
QCoreApplication::setOrganizationName("OpenSourcePress");
QCoreApplication::setOrganizationDomain("OpenSourcePress.de");
QCoreApplication::setApplicationName("CuteEdit");
```

From now on, QSettings makes use of these details, so that an instance without parameters is all that is needed:

```
QSettings settings;
```

It is surprising that setOrganizationDomain() method exists, since we have just managed without it. But it is justified through the way that Mac OS X stores its settings: it tries to sort the organizations according to an inverted domain name pattern. If the domain details are missing, QSettings creates artificial details from the organization name. If setOrganizationDomain() is specified correctly, the file-names in OS X are as follows:

```
$HOME/Library/Preferences/de.OpenSourcePress.CuteEdit.plist
$HOME/Library/Preferences/de.OpenSourcePress.plist
/Library/Preferences/de.OpenSourcePress.CuteEdit.plist
/Library/Preferences/de.OpenSourcePress.plist
```

It is not absolutely essential to specify the domain, but it should not be left out in case the organization has a real domain name. The first two parts specify the user scope, and the last two specify the system scope, a distinction that—as hinted above—concerns all three platforms.

In the user scope (QSettings::UserScope) an application saves all the applications involving just that user, while in the system scope (QSettings::SystemScope) it saves data that are important for all users. Because writing in the system scope generally requires root or administrator rights, the following constructor is normally relevant only for installation programs:[20]

---

[20] *Never* assume that the user has administrator rights, even if this is standard practice in many Windows home installations.

```
QSettings settings(QSettings::SystemScope);
```

QSettings now ignores the user scope and reads and writes exclusively in the system scope. If you specify QSettings::UserScope instead, the class behaves as if it was called via the standard constructor. QSettings looks in this for a setting, first in the user scope. If the object is not found there, it then looks for it in the system scope.

To write the actual data, QSettings provides the setValue() call, which expects a key and the actual value. The value itself is of the QVariant type, with which we are already familiar. The following code first stores a value in the system-specific configuration backend and then reads it out:

```
// configtest/main.cpp

// manufacturer, product
QSettings settings("OpenSourcePress", "ConfigTest");
QString hello = "Hello, world!";
// store a value
settings.setValue("Greeting", hello);
// reset variable
hello = "";
// read value and assign to variable
hello = settings.value("Greeting").toString();
qDebug() << hello; // prints "Hello, world!"
```

The explicit conversion to a QString using toString() is necessary because C++ is not in a position to correctly convert the QVariant value returned by Qt because QString has no knowledge of QVariant, and thus it does not provide an assignment operator.

After it is run, the program generates a file in Unix called ~/.config/OpenSource Press/ConfigTest.conf with the contents

```
[General]
Greeting=Hello, world!
```

Since we have not specified any group, QSettings stores the key in the [General] standard group. There are generally two methods of naming a specific group. On one hand, we can specify the desired group before one or more setValue() calls, but we must remove this setting afterward if we want to continue using the object for other purposes:

```
settings.beginGroup("My Group");
settings.setValue("Greeting", hello);
settings.endGroup();
```

On the other hand, we can simply place the name of the group in front of the key, separated by a slash:

```
settings.setValue("My Group/Greeting", hello);
```

In both cases the result looks like this:

```
[My Group]
Greeting=Hello, world!
```

Under Windows, groups are subpaths of the current application path in the Registry, whereas Mac OS X structures them through XML tags.

4.8.1   Extending CuteEdit

To use QSettings in CuteEdit, we first set up two methods for reading and writing in MainWindow: readSettings() and writeSettings().

We call writeSettings() in the destructor. This generates a new QSettings object and saves the size of the current window in the Size key of the MainWindow group. In the next step we save all internal settings for the MainWindow; for instance, the positions of the toolbars and dock windows. To do this, QMainWindow provides the saveState() method, which converts these properties into a QByteArray:

```
// cuteedit2/mainwindow.cpp (continued)

void MainWindow::writeSettings()
{
  QSettings settings;
  settings.setValue("MainWindow/Size", size());
  settings.setValue("MainWindow/Properties", saveState());
}
```

We call its counterpart, readSettings(), as the final step in the constructor of the class. It reads the settings and applies them to the finished main window, using restoreState(). restoreState() restores the internal status of the main window, using the read-out QByteArray. But first we must convert the QVariant returned by value() into a QSize or QByteArray:

```
// cuteedit2/mainwindow.cpp (continued)

void MainWindow::readSettings()
{
  QSettings settings;
  resize(settings.value("MainWindow/Size", sizeHint()).toSize());
```

```
    restoreState(settings.value("MainWindow/Properties").toByteArray());
}
```

The second parameter that we pass to value()—sizeHint()—is also unusual. It is the default value if the backend cannot find the key. In specific cases it ensures that the editor window has an appropriate initial size.

5

Laying Out Widgets

Even if you leave it up to Qt to arrange the widgets in a dialog or main window (as we have done so far), there is nothing preventing you from doing the layout manually using the class library in special cases. In practice this is seldom done, but a closer look at manual layout provides an understanding of the Qt layout mechanism, which we will examine below.

5.1 Manual Layout

In the traditional version of GUI design, each widget is "attached by hand" to a point in the overlying window or widget (that is, the widget that has been specified as a parent object for the given GUI element) and fixed values for its height and width are defined. The QWidget class provides the setGeometry() method as a basis class for nearly all graphical elements. This expects four integer parameters: first the values for the x and y positions relative to the parent widget, followed by the height and width. At this point in time the parent widget does not have to display its own final size.

As an example, we can look at a window derived from QWidget (Figure 5.1):

```
// manually/window.cpp

#include <QtGui>
#include "window.h"

Window::Window(QWidget *parent) : QWidget(parent)
{
    setFixedSize(640, 480);

    QTextEdit *txt = new QTextEdit(this);
    txt->setGeometry(20, 20, 600, 400);

    QPushButton *btn = new QPushButton(tr("&Close"), this);
    btn->setGeometry(520, 440, 100, 20);
}
```

Figure 5.1:
A simple, manually
laid out widget

The setFixedSize() method instructs the window to accept a fixed, unchanged size. Then we position an editor window (a QTextEdit widget[1]) and a button.

From these setGeometry() calls it is already evident that it is quite difficult to guess the correct values. Getting a layout constructed in this manner to work is a continuous cycle of choosing candidate values, compiling, and then adjusting the values to improve the appearance. It can also be quite awkward if the widget or dialog

---

[1] For all those who have not (yet) read, or so far merely browsed through Chapter 4: The QTextEdit class provides a multiple-line input field for text, which can be formatted via the API. In addition to pure text, it can also load structured HTML.

changes: If you want to add a new button in the middle of an arrangement, for example, the position of all elements placed beneath the new element must be modified.

Now, it can be argued that none of this is a problem in practice, since the Qt Designer considerably simplifies the positioning work involved. But even a GUI designer cannot solve all problems without using automatic layouts.

One of these problems concerns widgets that would look better if they could shrink or grow: In an inflexible layout and without additional aids, such elements—like the editor window in the example—always retain the same size, although it would be nice if they would adjust to the available screen size or at least give the user the option of changing their dimensions.

To keep the size of the dialog flexible, we could replace the setFixedSize() call with the resize() method, which also expects two integer parameters or a QSize parameter. This only adjusts the size, and does not fix it. The user can now change the dimensions of the dialog with the mouse, although the widgets that it contains retain their dimensions.

Alternatively, you could reimplement the QWidget method resizeEvent(): Qt always invokes this method when the widget size changes. You could write code to compute the new sizes and positions of the window elements on each resize event. But this procedure is much too complex in most cases, and also requires manual calculation of the widget proportions.[2]

In addition, reimplementing resizeEvent() poses a particular problem in combination with internationalization: With localized software, the dimensions of a labeled widget may depend on the language in which it is displayed. A button called *Close* in English has a much longer label in the German translation (*Schließen*), and the text will be cut off unless special precautionary measures are taken.

Ultimately, we can only patch up the symptoms in this way. To actually solve the underlying problem, we cannot avoid using automatic layout.

5.2 Automatic Layout

The QLayout class and specialized layouts derived from it help the developer to position widgets dynamically. For this to succeed, each graphic element derived from QWidget has a sizeHint() method, which returns how much space the widget would like to occupy under normal circumstances. In the same way, there is a minimumSizeHint() method—a widget may under no circumstances be smaller than the value returned by minimumSizeHint(). Both sizeHint and minimumSizeHint are properties, which can be changed with the corresponding set method.

---

[2] In some cases this procedure is very useful, however. A number of KDE programs use resizeEvent() to display status windows on the current layout at the lower-right edge of the window.

Each widget also has a *size policy*, which the developer can set for the horizontal and vertical values using setSizePolicy(). The purpose of this can best be explained by means of an example: The QTextEdit object from Figure 5.1 should, if possible, use all of the space in the window not required by other widgets—that is, the fully available width and height. Since this applies not only here, but in general for editor windows, the standard setting for this widget type defines the size policy QSizePolicy::Expanding for both directions (that is, "windows for this widget type should expand as much as possible").

A button, on the other hand, should only take up as much space vertically as is specified in the sizeHint(). This is ensured by QSizePolicy::Preferred (that is, widgets of this type should occupy the ideal size, if possible). QPushButtons expand in width as far as possible, because for this direction Trolltech specifies QSizePolicy::Expanding.

Figure 5.2:
All layouts inherit
from the QLayout
base class.

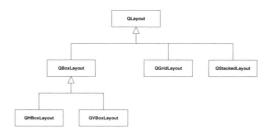

5.2.1 Horizontal and Vertical Layout

QLayout as an abstract base class only covers the basic functions for layouts. Specific strategies, such as the already familiar horizontal or vertical layout, are looked after by the special Qt clusters shown in Figure 5.2 inheriting from QLayout.

Thus the QVBoxLayout class, used in the example on page 29 and the following pages, arranges widgets among themselves, vertically. Here the order in which the widgets are included in the layout using addWidget() is crucial.

The example from page 142 now appears as follows:

```
// vertically/window.cpp

#include <QtGui>
#include "window.h"

Window::Window(QWidget *parent) : QWidget(parent)
{
    resize(640, 480);

    QVBoxLayout *lay = new QVBoxLayout(this);
```

```
QTextEdit *txt = new QTextEdit(this);
lay->addWidget(txt);

QPushButton *btn = new QPushButton(tr("&Close"), this);
lay->addWidget(btn);
}
```

The resize() instruction is not absolutely necessary. Without it, Qt adds the minimum sizes of the editor window and the button suggested by minimumSizeHint() to the *spacing* inserted by the layout, that is, the distance between two widgets in a layout. In addition it adds a *margin* for the layout and fixes the window size to the total.

Figure 5.3:
The widget with a
vertical layout

Figure 5.3 clearly shows the weaknesses of the vertical layout: The button takes over the full width, which is not what we had in mind.

There are two ways of overcoming this problem. In the first case we make use of something we are already familiar with, and take a look at the API documentation of QBoxLayout,[3] the class from which QVBoxLayout inherits: The addWidget() method actually has two other parameters, stretch and alignment. The latter looks after the horizontal alignment of a widget. It is now possible to arrange the button correctly, thanks to Qt::AlignRight.

To do this, we simply replace the last two lines of code above with the following:

```
QPushButton *btn = new QPushButton(tr("&Close"), this);
lay->addWidget(btn, 0, Qt::AlignRight);
```

You should try this method, particularly if you had trouble with the grid layout described in Chapter 5.2.2. Grid layouts remain the better choice, particularly for

---

[3] See http://doc.trolltech.com/4.1/qboxlayout.html.

more complex layouts, in which you can easily lose track of what is lined up where when using box layouts.

Box layouts have an additional property which we have so far ignored, the so-called *stretch* factor. If this does not equal 0, it determines the proportional space occupied by the widget in the overall layout, in the direction of the box layout. This assumes, of course, that the widget is interested in spreading out in this particular direction. It does not make any sense for a button, for example, to stretch out vertically above the height or below the depth of the text or the icon that it displays.

If this should still be necessary, however, the *size policy* can be adjusted using set-SizePolicy(). The method expects two parameters here from the QSizePolicy::Policy enumerator (see Table 5.1), which define the size guidelines for the horizontal and vertical stretches.

Table 5.1:
The Enumerator Policy

Value	Meaning
QSizePolicy::Fixed	The widget may never have a size other than sizeHint().
QSizePolicy::Minimum	sizeHint() is the smallest acceptable size for the widget, but the widget may be enlarged as much as you want.
QSizePolicy::Maximum	sizeHint() is the largest acceptable size for the widget, but the widget may be reduced in size as much as you want.
QSizePolicy::Preferred	sizeHint() is the optimal size, but the widget may be either larger or smaller than this value (default for QWidget).
QSizePolicy::Expanding	As Preferred, but the widget demands any available space in the layout.
QSizePolicy::MinimumExpanding	As Minimum, but the widget absolutely demands any available space in the layout.
QSizePolicy::Ignored	Ignore sizeHint()—the widget is given as much space as possible in the layout.

But let's return to the stretch factor: This is illustrated by the following code example, which places five stretchable text edits next to each other, but assigns a different stretch to each of them:

```
// stretchfactors/main.cpp

#include <QtGui>

int main(int argc, char *argv[])
{
  QApplication a(argc, argv);

  QWidget w;
  QHBoxLayout lay(&w);
  QTextEdit *txtEdit = 0;
  for (int stretch = 1; stretch <= 5; stretch++) {
    txtEdit = new QTextEdit(&w);
    lay.addWidget(txtEdit, stretch);
  }

  w.show();

  return a.exec();
}
```

We choose a horizontal layout in this example and insert dynamically generated text fields into it. These contain a stretch factor of 1 to 5, according to the status of the loop counter. As can be seen in Figure 5.4, the widgets now take up more space, increasing from left to right according to their factor. Thus the second text field has twice as much space as the first one, the third, three times as much, and so on.

The text edit behaves strangely as soon as the horizontal window size is reduced: Although all widgets become proportionately smaller, they always try to attain their smallest possible size (minimumSize()), which is always the same despite the stretch factor. Therefore, all the text fields in our example are the same size as soon as the window has reached its minimum size.

Figure 5.4:
Stretch factors
provide individual
widgets with more
space.

While horizontal stretches seldom cause problems, hardly any widget wants to be stretched vertically. However, if the user expands a dialog lengthways, the layouts insert ugly spaces between all the GUI elements contained in the dialog window. This can also be avoided using manually defined spaces. One approach is to define a stretch factor in one of the addWiget() calls for a single position, to define a pretetermined breaking point, so to speak. An alternative is to use addStretch() to add a stretch of any size to the end of the layout (that is, at the lower or right edge, depending on the layout type).

5.2.2 Grid Layout

The best way to describe the grid layout in Qt is probably as a kind of table, such as frequently encountered, for example, in HTML or spreadsheet calculations. In contrast to QBoxLayout derivatives, the grid layout class QGridLayout also requires information on the *column* and *row* in which the layout should insert a widget.

As can be seen in Figure 5.2 on page 144, QGridLayout inherits directly from QLayout, so it has properties differing from those of QBoxLayout-based layouts.

In particular, these include another addWidget() method that requires, in addition to the widget to be inserted, at least two more details, namely the row and the column of the insertion point. For widgets that should take up more space than one cell, an overloaded version of the method exists that expects four extra parameters: the coordinates of the first cell and the number of cells that the widget should cover in each direction.

In addition the setColumnStretch() and setRowStretch() methods allow stretch factors to be set for individual columns or rows. Here the first parameter specifies the row or column, and the second parameter specifies the relevant stretch factor.

The following example implements our input dialog using a grid layout. Through addWidget(), it positions the text field at the coordinates $(0, 0)$ and specifies for it a width of two columns and a height of one row.

The button is placed on the second row and in the second column, with coordinates $(1, 1)$, because we start from zero when counting positions, as is usual in information technology. Stretching the first column with addColumnStretch() then ensures that the second column, in which the button is located, is squashed up. Using this trick, the layout is restricted to the optimal width:

```
// grid/window.cpp

#include <QtGui>
#include "window.h"

Window::Window(QWidget *parent) : QWidget(parent)
{
    resize(640, 480);

    QGridLayout *lay = new QGridLayout(this);

    QTextEdit *txt = new QTextEdit(this);
    lay->addWidget(txt, 0, 0, 1, 2);
```

```
    QPushButton *btn = new QPushButton(tr("&Close"), this);
    lay->addWidget(btn, 1, 1);
    lay->setColumnStretch(0, 1);
}
```

5.2.3 Nested Layouts

Sometimes it is useful to nest layouts inside one another, for instance if you need to include a new layout, with all its widgets, in an existing one. For this reason, QLayout classes provide a way of including other layouts, with addLayout(). This method expects the same parameters as the addWidget() method of the same layout object.

For more complex layouts in particular, the clear hierarchy created in this way turns out to be very useful, especially if you want to arrange several buttons, as in the following code:

```
// nested/main.cpp

#include <QtGui>

int main(int argc, char* argv[])
{
  QApplication app(argc, argv);
  QWidget *w = new QWidget;
  QHBoxLayout *mainLayout = new QHBoxLayout(w);

  QTextEdit *txtEdit = new QTextEdit(w);
  mainLayout->addWidget(txtEdit);

  QVBoxLayout *buttonLayout = new QVBoxLayout;
  QPushButton *cancelBtn = new QPushButton(QObject::tr("&Cancel"), w);
  QPushButton *okBtn = new QPushButton(QObject::tr("&OK"), w);
  QPushButton *defaultBtn = new QPushButton(QObject::tr("&Default"), w);
  buttonLayout->addWidget(defaultBtn);
  buttonLayout->addWidget(cancelBtn);
  buttonLayout->addWidget(okBtn);
  buttonLayout->addStretch();

  mainLayout->addLayout(buttonLayout);
  w->show();
  return app.exec();
}
```

By placing the individual buttons in a separate layout (buttonLayout), they are made to appear as one unit to the overlying layout mainLayout. You can now use addLayout() to insert the buttonLayout into mainLayout.

Within buttonLayout, use is again made of addStretch(): The variable empty space created by this forces the buttons upwards and takes up the remaining space.

5.3 Splitter

Although horizontal and vertical layouts are dynamic, they cannot be changed directly by the user. But sometimes he should be able to adjust the spacing between two or more widgets interactively.

This need is fulfilled by the QSplitter class that, just like the standard layouts, have an addWidget() (but no addLayout()) method. The partial widgets inserted using this method are separated by a so-called *handle*, which can be picked up and moved by using the mouse (Figure 5.5).

Figure 5.5:
Two text fields moved
with the splitter

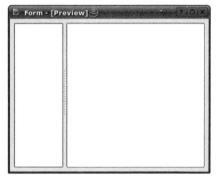

In contrast to the QBoxLayout class, there are no specialized classes for QSplitter that determine whether vertical or horizontal layout is used. Instead the orientation property determines the alignment. It can be set in the constructor, or set later on. If no orientation is specified, Qt creates horizontal splitters.

5.3.1 Behavior During Size Changes

The freedom of movement allowed the user by the splitter is restricted by the widgets involved: The smallest size is specified by the minimumSizeHint or (if set) the minimumSize property. If the user tries to shrink the widget more than this, the splitter is completely hidden by the widget. This is known as a *collapsible* widget. If you want to prevent the user from so "getting rid of the widgets," you can disable this behavior with setCollapsible(0, false), where 0 stands for the first widget from the left for a horizontal splitter, or, with vertical splitters, for the top widget in the splitter.

The isCollapsible() method, which takes one integer argument, provides information on whether the widget with the specified number is collapsible or not. Another property of the adjacent widget, maximumSize, ensures that the corresponding area above the splitter cannot be made any smaller once the neighboring widget has achieved its maximum size.

Splitters can react in two ways if the user pulls the handle in one direction while holding down the mouse button: They either draw a gray line at the point where the handle would come if the mouse button is released, or else actually move the handle to the corresponding location. This latter method is known as opaque resizing (that is, a size change that "lets no light in").

Normally opaque resizing is a better choice, since the user can directly see the results of his actions. Since this technique can often trigger a resizeEvent() under certain circumstances, however, ugly artifacts can appear if one of the widgets controlled by the splitter performs very complex drawing operations, or is not optimally programmed. In this case it is often better to disable opaque resizing, with setOpaqueResize(false).

5.3.2 Saving Splitter Positions and Determining the Widget Size

To save the positions of individual splitters beyond program sessions, the QSplitter API provides the methods saveState() and restoreState().

Since saveState() stores all values in a QByteArray, the method is ideally suited to saving the sizes of a splitter between one program session and the next. This is done using the class presented on page 136, QSettings. If we hadn't implemented the templates in CuteEdit as dock windows in Chapter 4, but separated them from the text field with a splitter, we could save the values of a splitter as a key/value pair called SplitterSizes in the configuration file, with the following code:

```
QSettings settings("OpenSourcePress", "CuteEdit");
settings.setValue("SplitterSizes", splitter->saveState());
```

Conversely, the following code extract resets the size of the splitters when the program is started:

```
QSettings settings("OpenSourcePress", "CuteEdit");
splitter->restoreState(settings.value("SplitterSizes").toByteArray());
```

For situations in which, depending on the alignment of the splitter, the widths or heights of individual widgets are required as individual integer values, the QSplitter API has the methods sizes() and setSizes(), which work with the list type QList<int>. This means that you can read out the sizes, for example by using the foreach macro defined by Qt:

```
foreach(int size, splitter->sizes())
  qDebug("Size: %i", size);
```

qDebug() is one of the debugging macros that works like the C function printf(), and returns the error message specified in the argument. We use it here to quickly produce output. Details on debugging with Qt are contained in Appendix A.

Analogous to reading out the current splitter sizes, it is also possible to change them by passing the new values with setSizes() in list form:

```
QList<int> sizes;
sizes << 20 << 60 << 20;
splitter->setSizes(sizes);
```

In this example, which assumes a splitter with three widgets, these are now 20, 60, and 20 pixels wide (for a horizontal splitter) or high (for a vertically arranged splitter).

5.3.3 Defining Relative Sizes

Just like a normal layout, QSplitter also provides a way of defining a stretch factor for each widget inserted. In contrast to layouts, these must be specified for splitters afterward using the setStretchFactor() method. Since this function also requires the position of the widget, apart from the stretch, you first have to define the position of the widget using the indexOf() method. This returns the correct position for a given widget or a handle.

The example below, documented in Figure 5.6, is derived from the stretch factor example on page 147, but now uses a splitter instead of a layout. Since splitters are aligned horizontally if no other details are given, the result more or less matches that of a QHBoxLayout—with the exception that the spaces between widgets now carry handles which can be used to define the size of the text edit.

```
// stretchfactorsplitter/main.cpp

#include <QtGui>

int main(int argc, char *argv[])
{
  QApplication a(argc, argv);

  QSplitter s;
  QTextEdit *txtEdit = 0;
  for (int stretch = 1; stretch <= 5; stretch++) {
    txtEdit = new QTextEdit(&s);
    s.addWidget(txtEdit);
    s.setStretchFactor(s.indexOf(txtEdit), stretch);
```

```
    }
    s.show();

    return a.exec();
}
```

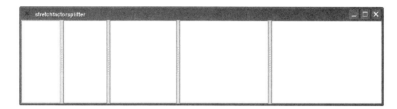

Figure 5.6:
The stretch factor
example from Figure
5.4 also works with
splitters.

Splitters are often used, for example, to separate a main widget from a page bar. With different-sized monitors, the relative size created here by the use of stretch factors can quickly become a nightmare: If the space on the the screen is too small, the page bar will appear too small, while on widescreen displays, currently very popular on laptops, they will take up too much space. In such cases it is better to specify a fixed initial size with setSizes() and to manage the sizes defined by the user with saveState() and restoreState().

5.3.4   Customizing Handles

The splitter handle itself is implemented in the QSplitterHandle class. But sometimes the standard implementation is not enough, for example, if you want to have the splitter collapse when it is double-clicked, similar to the way the page bar of the Mozilla browser reacts. Then you have to use your own implementation, derived from QSplitterHandle. We will call this ClickSplitterHandle.

Since we want to react to a double-click, we must also reimplement the mouseDoubleClickEvent() method, as well as the constructor. To be able to use this double-clickable handle in a splitter, the design of QSplitter also forces us to create a subclass of the actual splitter. A method that allows a QSplitterHandle instance to be set is not enough, since a splitter—as already explained—can have any number of handles.

Because the copy operators of QWidget-based widgets are disabled, the QSplitter API performs a trick: The class has a protected method called createHandle(), which is allowed to overwrite subclasses. The only purpose of this *factory method* consists of creating a new instance of QSplitterHandle or a subclass. QSplitter then uses this method when creating new handles.

In the following example we will therefore create, besides the subclass of QSplitter-Handle called ClickSplitterHandle, a class with the name of ClickSplitter, which inherits directly from QSplitter and which overwrites only the createHandle() method:

```
// clicksplitter/clicksplitter.h

#include <QSplitter>
#include <QSplitterHandle>

class ClickSplitterHandle : public QSplitterHandle
{
  Q_OBJECT
  public:
    ClickSplitterHandle(Qt::Orientation o, QSplitter *parent = 0);
    void mouseDoubleClickEvent(QMouseEvent *e);
  private:
    int lastUncollapsedSize;
};

class ClickSplitter : public QSplitter
{
  Q_OBJECT
  friend class ClickSplitterHandle;
  public:
    ClickSplitter(Qt::Orientation o, QSplitter *parent = 0)
      : QSplitter(o, parent) {}
    ClickSplitter(QSplitter *parent = 0)
      : QSplitter(parent) {}

  protected:
    QSplitterHandle * createHandle() {
      return new ClickSplitterHandle(orientation(), this);
    }
};
```

The implementation is centered on the mouseDoubleClickEvent() method. In the constructor we initialize only the class variable lastUncollapsedSize, which we later require in mouseDoubleClickEvent() so that we can remember how large the widget was before it was collapsed:

```
// clicksplitter/clicksplitter.cpp

#include "clicksplitter.h"
#include <QtGui>

ClickSplitterHandle::ClickSplitterHandle(Qt::Orientation o,
  QSplitter *parent) :QSplitterHandle(o, parent)
{
  lastUncollapsedSize = 0;
}

void ClickSplitterHandle::mouseDoubleClickEvent(QMouseEvent *e)
```

```
{
  QSplitter *s = splitter();
  Qt::Orientation o = s->orientation();
  int pos = s->indexOf(this);

  QWidget *w = s->widget(pos);

  if (lastUncollapsedSize == 0)
    if (o == Qt::Horizontal)
      lastUncollapsedSize = w->sizeHint().width();
    else
      lastUncollapsedSize = w->sizeHint().height();

  int currSize = s->sizes().value(pos-1);

  if (currSize == 0)
    moveSplitter(lastUncollapsedSize);
  else {
    lastUncollapsedSize = currSize;
    moveSplitter(0);
  }

}
```

In ClickSplitterHandle::mouseDoubleClickEvent() we first determine the alignment of the splitter. We obtain the position of the splitter, using the QSplitter::indexOf() method. This is also the position of the widget lying to the right of (or directly beneath) the splitter.

For reasons of symmetry, a zeroth handle exists in every splitter, which QSplitter never displays. This guarantees that indexOf() always delivers a sensible position. The function makes a distinction between general widgets and splitters when doing this, and is able to determine the number of a specific widget or splitter. Thus the splitter can be defined for a widget as follows,

```
...
QSplitter *splitter = new QSplitter;
splitter->addWidget(new QWidget);
QLabel *lbl = new QLabel;
splitter->addWidget(lbl);
splitter->handle(splitter->indexOf(lbl));
...
```

while in the mouseDoubleClickEvent() method on page 154, we look for the widget to go with a splitter.

The ClickSplitterHandle class variable lastUncollapsedSize remembers the last size of the widget in an uncollapsed state. If this is 0 for any reason, the implementation uses the value of the respective sizeHint(). The current position of our splitter depends on the size of the widget *in front of* the splitter, which is why the code detects the size of the widget that occupies the space up to the position pos-1, by accessing sizes().

If the left widget is currently collapsed, the last lines of code on page 154 open it again using the lastUncollapsedSize variable. Otherwise the widget "disappears" to the left of the handle, but not without remembering its current size in last-UncollapsedSize.

5.3.5 Layout for Languages Written from Right to Left

The way in which texts in some languages, such as Hebrew, are read differs fundamentally from European languages in one respect: They are read from right to left, and this must also be accounted for by software applications. For such texts, it is not the top left, but the top right edge of the screen that is the starting point for the eye when reading. Accordingly, a toolkit must be able to invert the layout horizontally. The KDE browser Konqueror in Figure 5.7 masters this task correctly, because Qt manages to mirror all layouts horizontally, largely without the help of the user, if the language configured is oriented from right to left, or if the program is passed the -reverse option. The Qt-internal equivalent for this option is the QApplication::setLayoutDirection(Qt::RightToLeft) call. This program option is mainly used for test purposes.

In the development of your own layouts and widgets, you must always make your own provisions in case inverted layout is used. Thus our example from above no longer works correctly in the case of a right-to-left configuration: It still collapses the widget to the left of the splitter, although the widget that should collapse is now on the right side.

Figure 5.7:
Because languages like Hebrew require a horizontally reflected layout, developers of widgets and layouts must take this case into account and test it.

To examine such special cases, QApplication has the static methods isLeftToRight() and isRightToLeft(), which developers can easily use to check the current layout.

5.4 Stacked Layouts

In *stacked layouts*, several widgets are placed on top of each other on the same area—in contrast to other layouts, which arrange widgets on a single level. This technique is usually applied when implementing complex configuration dialogs (see Figure 5.8, page 160).

The class that implements this functionality in Qt is called QStackedLayout. New widgets are also added in this form of layout with the addWidget() method. You should remember the ID returned when this is done: The widgets can be identified later on with its help. Alternatively, you can save the pointer to the inserted widget.

So that you can access one of the inserted widgets again, QStackedLayout has two slots: setCurrentIndex() expects a position of the widget as an integer value, whereas setCurrentWidget() accepts a pointer to an instance of a class derived from QWidget.

5.4.1 The Alternative: Stacked Widgets

A QStackedLayout, like all layouts, requires a widget that will manage it. In most cases this needs to be additionally created, and you have to equip this widget with a layout. To simplify this, Qt provides so-called *stacked widgets* with the QStackedWidget class, which have the same API as QStackedLayout. Internally, these are widgets equipped with a stacked layout.

5.4.2 When to Use Stacked Layouts and Widgets

Below we will develop a simple variation of such a configuration widget ourselves, which of course can also be implemented as a dialog.[4]

Configuration dialogs such as those in KDE provide a very good example of the use of a QStackedLayout: A standard KDE configuration dialog consists of a list or icon view, as well as a stacked layout or a stacked widget. Depending on which entry the user selects from the list, the stacked class ensures that the relevant widget comes to the front. List and icon views in Qt are normally based on the so-called *model/view concept*, which is covered separately in Chapter 8. For our purposes, a simplified list view that is provided by Qt with the QListWidget class will be sufficient. Each list entry is encapsulated in an instance of the lightweight

---

[4] Exactly how dialogs function is explained in Chapter 6.

QListWidgetItem class. Each QListWidgetItem contains the text belonging to the entry, as well as a definition for a possible icon. In our configuration dialog we associate a page in the stacked widget to each widget item.

The heart of our new class, which we derive directly from QWidget, is the addPage() method, which adds new pages to the stacked widget. In addition we require this very stacked widget and a list view as member variables:

```
// configwidget/configwidget.h

#include <QWidget>

class QListWidget;
class QStackedWidget;

class ConfigWidget : public QWidget
{
  Q_OBJECT
  public:
    ConfigWidget(QWidget *parent = 0);

    void addPage(const QString& title, const QIcon& icon, QWidget *page);

  private:
    QStackedWidget *widgetStack;
    QListWidget    *contentsWidget;
};
```

In the constructor we initially arrange the list view to the right of the stacked widget and restrict its width to 180 pixels so that it doesn't take up too much space.

The list view regards each widget item as a *row*. As soon as the user selects another item, it reports via the currentRowChanged(int) signal. It helps that stacked layouts and widgets save the positions of their widgets as integers, in which the number value corresponds to the number of the widget. These classes therefore have the setCurrentIndex(int) slot, which causes the widget with the number specified as an argument to be displayed. We connect this slot in the connect() instruction in the final lines of the constructor to the currentRowChanged(int) signal.

Now it is important to create the entry in the list view when the stacked widget incorporates the accompanying widget. Since both indices start at zero, and since only addPage() carries out changes to both widgets, it is guaranteed that the list view entry is associated with the correct widget.

```
// configwidget/configwidget.cpp

#include <QtGui>
#include "configwidget.h"
```

```
ConfigWidget::ConfigWidget(QWidget *parent)
 : QWidget(parent)
{
  QHBoxLayout *lay = new QHBoxLayout(this);

  contentsWidget = new QListWidget;
  widgetStack = new QStackedWidget;

  lay->addWidget(contentsWidget);
  lay->addWidget(widgetStack);

  contentsWidget->setMaximumWidth(180);

  connect(contentsWidget, SIGNAL(currentRowChanged(int)),
          widgetStack, SLOT(setCurrentIndex(int)));

}

void ConfigWidget::addPage(const QString& title, const QIcon& icon,
                           QWidget *page)
{
  QListWidgetItem *item = new QListWidgetItem;
  item->setText(title);
  item->setIcon(icon);
  contentsWidget->addItem(item);
  widgetStack->addWidget(page);
}
```

Using this new API, we insert only a few simple QLabels below, but widgets are possible, of course, in any combination and size:

```
// configwidget/main.cpp

...
    ConfigWidget *w = new ConfigWidget;
    w->addPage("First Page", icon,
               new QLabel("<center>first page</center>"));
    w->addPage("Second Page", icon,
               new QLabel("<center>second page</center>"));
    w->addPage("Third Page", icon,
               new QLabel("<center>third page</center>"));
...
```

Figure 5.8 shows the result. Instead of a stacked widget, we could just as well use a layout in this example. To do this only the member variable widgetStack needs to use the QStackedLayout type. We change the constructor as follows:

...

```
contentsWidget = new QListWidget;
QWidget *widget = new QWidget;
widgetStack = new QStackedLayout(widget);

lay->addWidget(contentsWidget);
lay->addWidget(widget);
...
```

All API calls in this example remain intact in the same way when changing to a stacked layout.

Figure 5.8:
With the selection widget on the left, Qt brings the relevant widget in the stacked widget or layout to the top.

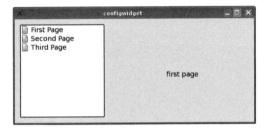

6

Dialogs

Dialogs and their base class, QDialog, which we have already briefly encountered in Chapter 2, are used in various contexts. These contexts determine the proper behavior of the dialog. For example, normally a configuration dialog should always remain in the foreground of the application until the user has made the desired changes to the settings. The interaction with a search dialog in a word processor is somewhat different, however—a user may have such a dialog window open during the editing of a document, but he will certainly not want to be prevented from making changes to the document at the same time. This chapter looks at the various dialog types and how they can be implemented with Qt.

6.1 Modal Dialogs

Some dialogs remain in the foreground until the user completes his interaction with them, and the rest of the application is blocked until the dialog window is closed. These dialogs normally implement operations that should be completed before the user can continue working. Such dialogs are known as *modal dialogs*.

This dialog type is specifically suited to configuration interfaces: If these do *not* block the application, this often means increased programming work, particularly if settings altered using this dialog influence other parts of the GUI. In such a case unexpected phenomena could occur for the user, but these can be elegantly avoided with the help of the modality.

A modal dialog represents a new *top level widget*. In Qt this means that the developer must make instances of this type of QDialog visible explicitly, since dialogs are always invisible after being instantiated.[1] For modal dialogs the exec() method is normally used for this, which generates a new event loop and displays the dialog at the same time. The similarity of the method name to QApplication::exec(), the function which starts the main event loop for the overall program, is thus intentional.

The following code fragment demonstrates how to proceed when instantiating a modal dialog, using the subclass QFileDialog of QDialog as an example, which we will get to know more closely in Section 6.5.3. First we instantiate a dialog and let it enter its own event loop, by invoking its exec() method:

```
QFileDialog dialog;
int status = dialog.exec(); // start dedicated Event-Loop
//execution continues here after the dialog has been closed
```

Only when the QFileDialog's exec() finishes and returns control to the application, for example because the user closes the dialog window, does the main event loop resume (i.e., the QApplication::exec() method). This behavior ensures the modality of the dialog internally, together with the Qt::WA_ShowModal flag (see page 164). It also means that modal dialogs started via exec() can return a success or failure code for the main event loop to examine, in a similar way to how the main() function of a C/C++ program returns a status code to the operating system.

The return value is determined by a slot: QDialog provides two predefined slots, accept() and reject(), that are normally triggered by clicking the OK or Cancel buttons, respectively, with the latter also triggered by pressing the (Esc) key. At the same time these slots close the dialog, but without deleting the dialog object. Supplied with the return value, the code that called the dialog can conveniently take over the processing logic.

Of course, if a subclass of QDialog implements the processing of its GUI elements internally, or if the return value is not relevant, as in the number converter example from Chapter 2, the programmer may ignore the return value.

---

[1] In general widgets are only invisible at first when they do not possess a parent window; for dialogs this rule does not apply.

6.2 Non-modal Dialogs

It is not always possible or sensible to use modal dialogs. A classic example is the dialogs provided by word processors for searching in an open document. Here, the user must be able to interact simultaneously with both the dialog and the document view, which is stored either in the main window or in another widget.

A QDialog implementing a non-modal dialog can be displayed using the show() method. As with the function of the same name possesed by "normal widgets," this call immediately returns a value. However, communication with the dialog is accomplished not through the return value, but through signals and slots.

We have already come across this type of behavior in the ByteConverterDialog example, which we discussed in Chapter 2.

```
int main(int argc, char *argv[])
{
  ByteConverterDialog bc;
  bc.setAttribute(Qt::WA_QuitOnClose);
  bc.show();
  return a.exec()
}
```

The show() call returns immediately. This is not a problem in the above example because bc is not deleted from the stack before the program quits, causing a.exec() to return. However, dialogs outside the main method must be allocated on the heap, since objects on the stack get deleted as soon as the method they are created in (e.g., the constructor) goes out of scope. Usually we can also manage without the setAttribute() call, which is used only to terminate the main event loop as soon as the dialog returns.

6.2.1 Usability Problems

A warning is appropriate at this point, particularly in view of the example of the search dialog just mentioned: Non-modal dialogs that are used together with the main application window frequently present the user with a visually impenetrable barrier. This is because dialogs are placed above the matching main window, so that the user knows which program they belong to. Unfortunately, it is almost impossible to prevent the dialog from covering over relevant information displayed in the application's main window.

In practice, two different approaches exist to get round this problem: On one hand, the application can ensure that the relevant part of the document or application window and the non-modal (search) dialog never overlap by moving the dialog if necessary.[2] KDE applications, at least in KDE 3, use this approach to a large extent.

On the other hand, it is often feasible to do without a separate dialog altogether and to display an additional search widget in the main window, as is the standard practice, for example, in the Firefox browser. But here there is a danger that the user, expecting a dialog, will not see the input widget.

6.3 Semi-modal Dialogs

A separate category of dialog is represented by the *semi-modal* dialogs. The term[3] is based on the fact that they are displayed, like non-modal dialogs, via show(). The application program therefore continues running. However, these dialogs are meant to be used in a modal fashion: The user should not continue working in the application, but in all cases turn his attention to the dialog. To enforce such a modal interaction, you must call setModal(true)[4] before calling show().

6.4 Avoiding Bloated Dialogs

A user-friendly dialog does not overwhelm its users with options. It is much more sensible to set reasonable default settings and to present the user only with choices for which he really must make a decision. He should be shown more options only if he explicitly demands to see them. This usability requirement can be set using the QDialog API extensions.

Figure 6.1:
Example of the use of
extensions: The Run
dialog of KDE usually
looks neat and tidy.

These provide a good service, for example in the KDE Run dialog. This dialog allows the user to type URLs or program names, and tries to either display the web page or start the correct program (Figure 6.1), as appropriate.

---

[2] QWidget::mapToGlobal() and QWidget::mapFromGlobal() are a great help here in transferring coordinates between widgets.

[3] Although the Qt documentation also refers to instances of this type of dialog as *modal dialogs*, the author considers the distinction to be relevant.

[4] This is a wrapper around the call setAttribute(Qt::WA_ShowModal, true), which can also be applied to every other top-level widget.

More advanced users will sometimes have extra wishes, such as specifying real-time priority, a different priority, or execution of a program as a user with restricted permissions. Since these options are only rarely required, they are not stored in the basic dialog but in another widget, which is displayed only if requested by the user via the Options button from Figure 6.1. Figure 6.2 shows the result.

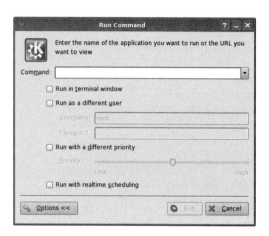

Figure 6.2:
Thanks to the
extension, it still
provides advanced
users with a wide
range of setting
options.

The following code example illustrates the state of affairs:

```cpp
// extensions/main.cpp

#include <QtGui>

int main(int argc, char* argv[])
{
  QApplication app(argc, argv);
  QDialog dlg;
  QPushButton *btn = new QPushButton(QObject::tr("Expand/Collapse"),
                                     &dlg);
  btn->setCheckable(true);
  QVBoxLayout *lay = new QVBoxLayout(&dlg);
  lay->addWidget(btn);
  QLabel *ext = new QLabel(QObject::tr("Extension"));
  dlg.setExtension(ext);
  QObject::connect(btn, SIGNAL(toggled(bool)),
                   &dlg, SLOT(showExtension(bool)));

  dlg.exec();
  return app.exec();
}
```

A button with the inscription Expand/Collapse allows the user to fold down a label with the inscription Extension (Figure 6.3). The extension itself is a QWidget in Qt 4, which we pass to the dialog via QDialog::setExtension(). If it should fold downward rather than sideways, which is the default, the call QDialog::setOrientation(Qt::Vertical) can be used; thus, in the example code above we would include the following line:

```
dlg.setOrientation(Qt::Vertical);
```

So that the button will display and hide the extension, we turn it into a toggle switch using setCheckable(true) and connect its toggled() signal to the showExtension() slot of QDialog.

Figure 6.3:
The example program
from page 165 with
and without a
horizontally folded
out extension

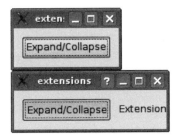

6.5 Ready-made Dialogs in Qt

Many dialogs are universal enough to justify a predefined class. One of these is the open file dialog implemented in QFileDialog, with which we became acquainted in Chapter 4.

In addition to this, Qt 4 has other such ready-to-use dialogs, which will be introduced below.

6.5.1 Message Dialogs

Very frequently, a program must forward information to the user. If it is essential that the user notices this or needs to make a decision based on it, a simple message in the status bar is not sufficient.

A possible alternative would be to derive a separate class from QDialog that displays the message in a label and additionally provides one or several buttons with actions. Luckily this is not necessary, since Qt provides the QMessageBox class for this purpose. Apart from the text to be displayed and the obligatory window title (also called a *caption*, which is set using the windowTitle property), a QMessageBox contains up to three buttons. Optionally, an icon can be defined that is displayed in the message dialog next to the text message. The text in the dialog can—as in all Qt dialogs—be formatted using HTML tags. This is demonstrated by the following code, visualized in Figure 6.4:

```
// messageboxmanually/main.cpp

...
QString text = QObject::tr("<qt>This is a <b>very</b> complicated way"
  "of showing message boxes. <i>Only use this in exceptional cases</i>! "
  "Do you want to continue?</qt>");
QMessageBox msg(QObject::tr("Academic Example Warning"), text,
  QMessageBox::Warning, QMessageBox::Yes|QMessageBox::Default,
  QMessageBox::No|QMessageBox::Escape, QMessageBox::NoButton);

if (msg.exec() == QMessageBox::Yes)
{
  qDebug() << "Keep on going!";
}
...
```

Figure 6.4:
A manually
instantiated
QMessageBox

The call to the message box's constructor seems to be quite complicated, but this is only due to the many arguments. After specifying the dialog heading and a message to be displayed in the first two parameters, we can choose from one of four predefined icons by passing one of the following values as the third argument:

QMessageBox::Question
    This is intended for the message dialogs that ask questions.

QMessageBox::Information
    This emphasizes general information.

QMessageBox::Warning
    This should be used for potentially dangerous actions.

QMessageBox::Critical
    This is the choice of preference to emphasize serious errors.

QMessageBox::NoIcon
    This displays no icon at all.

How the displayed icon will ultimately appear is determined by the currently selected style. If you do not like any of the predefined icons, you can instead define any QPixmap you want as an icon for the message dialog, using the setPixmapIcon() method.

The fourth to sixth arguments to the constructor are used to specify up to three different buttons. Possible values for these parameters are listed in Table 6.1. The value QMessageBox::NoButton has a special meaning: As in the example, it specifies that the corresponding button is not desired, and will therefore not be displayed.

Since the call to the message dialog's exec() method causes the application to enter a separate event loop and remain there for the duration of the display of the dialog, it is quite enough to instantiate the object on the stack. This way we do not specify a parent widget here. To make the dialog modal, you would, however, be required to specify a parent. The parent parameter follows the final button specification in the QMessageBox constructor.

Which button the user ultimately chooses is specified by the return value of exec(), which can be compared, in an if or switch statement, against the values from Table 6.1, as in the example.

Through an OR link with QMessageBox::Default and QMessageBox::Escape, we can also specify the actions that are triggered when the user presses the (Enter) or (Esc) key.

Table 6.1:

Possible button texts

Value	Button text
QMessageBox::Ok	Ok
QMessageBox::Cancel	Cancel
QMessageBox::Yes	Yes
QMessageBox::No	No
QMessageBox::Abort	Abort
QMessageBox::Retry	Retry
QMessageBox::Ignore	Ignore
QMessageBox::YesAll	Yes, all
QMessageBox::NoAll	No, all
QMessageBox::NoButton	—

The approach described here is unsatisfactory in one respect—namely, the programmer has to be careful that all of the sections of code implementing the message boxes for a given type of event are the same, or else the application's user interface will be inconsistent. So that we do not have to rely too much on the discipline of developers, QMessagebox provides a range of static methods that can be used to display finished message dialogs for different purposes. Only if these are not sufficient for your requirements should you try and assemble your own customized info box. We will present the static methods below, in order of importance of the message they transmit.

Asking Questions

The question dialog QMessageBox::question() (Figure 6.5) is one of the most frequently needed message dialogs. Apart from a parent widget, its constructor expects a caption, a short descriptive text, and the text for its buttons. According to Microsoft's style guide, the heading should match the name of the application. This is returned by qApp->applicationName(). Other style guides suggest using a combination of the program name and a short description of the operation currently being processed, for example "Overwrite file? – *application name*".

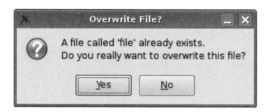

Figure 6.5:
QMessageBox::question()
takes decisions off
the user's hands.

In the example below we assign the buttons—as is normal for question dialogs—the text labels Yes and No, making the Yes button the default and allowing the No button to react to the (Esc) key. Since we do not need a third button, we leave it out by specifying QMessageBox::NoButton.

The status code returned by QMessageBox::question() corresponds to the value of the button chosen by the user. To check whether the user has answered the question with Yes, we compare the return value with QMessageBox::Yes:

```
bool checkOverwrite(const QString &filename)
{
    int status = QMessageBox::question( this,
                tr("Overwrite File?"),
                tr("A file called '%1' already exists. \n"
                  "Do you realy want to overwrite this file?")
                  .arg(filename),
                QMessageBox::Yes|QMessageBox::Default,
                QMessageBox::No|QMessageBox::Escape,
                QMessageBox::NoButton);

    if (status != QMessageBox::Yes)
            return false;
    return true;
}
```

Yes-No questions have one considerable disadvantage, however: The user needs to read through the entire text and understand it. It is possible, especially with complex user prompts, that the user will misunderstand the question and decide on the wrong answer.

This drawback can be avoided to a large extent by following two basic principles. First, a question should never be formulated in the negative. Words that negate the meaning of a phrase or clause are generally passed over in a quick reading: There is a high probability that questions such as "Are you sure that you do *not* want to overwrite the file?" will be misunderstood. For the sake of better usability, such negated phrases should absolutely be avoided in a GUI, even if they match the logic of the application code itself.

In addition, users can be more sure of their responses to a question dialog if instead of the simple button labels Yes and No, they can read a descriptive text that again emphasizes the options described in the description text.

QMessageBox provides programmatic support for this paradigm of GUI design: Trolltech has included another version of the static method question() for this purpose. The second variant takes the same first three parameters as the one just described, but after this there are differences.

Instead of three enumerator values, we now pass the strings that are to appear on the buttons. If a button is not required, this is signaled with an empty string, as shown in the following example (in the sixth parameter).[5] Finally, you again need to specify the buttons in turn that are "clicked" if the user operates the (Enter) or (Esc) key; this is done with the final two parameters. The numbering of the buttons corresponds to their position (in the code and in the order of reading, from the user's point of view), whereby 0 refers to the first button and 2 to the third one. The button with the Choose a different name inscription (Figure 6.6) thus becomes the default button with the code below—an additional feature that helps to prevent the user from losing data by accident:

```
bool checkOverwrite(const QString &filename)
{
  int status = QMessageBox::question( this,
      tr("Overwrite File?"),
      tr("<qt>A File called <i>%1</i> already exists. "
        "Do you want to overwrite the file or cancel "
        "the procedure to choose a different name?</qt>").arg(filename),
      tr("&Overwrite file"), tr("&Choose different name"),
        QString(), 1, 1);
  if (status == 1)
      return false;
  return true;
}
```

---

[5] The QString constructor called with no arguments always makes a QString that denotes the empty string.

QMessageBox processes the text enclosed in <qt> tags as HTML and line-wraps it automatically. We can take advantage of the fact that simple HTML formatting is possible within these tags and put the filename displayed to the user in italics.

The return value of this QMessageBox::question() variant is based on the position of the selected button—in contrast to the first variant, which returns the enumerator value for the selected button. This is an essential semantic difference that can easily lead to faulty code: Since enumerators can also be used as integer values, the compiler does *not* complain if the code you write to check the status is based on the return semantics of the opposing variant.

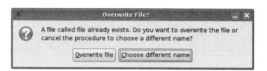

Figure 6.6:
QMessageBox::ques-
tion() *with individual*
responses to the
buttons

Conveying Information

If you want the program to inform the user about matters occurring during a work process that is proceeding normally, information dialogs are ideal and are provided by the QMessageBox::information() static method (Figure 6.7). Just like QMessageBox::question(), this is also overloaded twice and works identically, except that it merely displays a different icon: an exclamation mark instead of a question mark. Some style guides even suggest using normal information dialogs instead of the question dialog. But since Qt allows you to easily differentiate between question dialogs and information dialogs, it is recommended that you do so.

Figure 6.7:
QMessageBox::infor-
mation() *is used quite*
rarely as a
replacement for the
question dialog

In particular, you should not make use of the option of equipping an information dialog with more than one button (i.e., an OK button). If you require a second one for canceling, QMessageBox::question() is usually the better choice.

For example, to inform a user of the success of a search process, you can use an information box, as shown in Figure 6.7:

```
QMessageBox::information( this,
        tr("Search Failed"),
```

```
tr("No matches found!"),
QMessageBox::Ok|QMessageBox::Default,
QMessageBox::NoButton, QMessageBox::NoButton);
```

With OK as the only response, querying the return value in this case is not necessary.

Issuing Warnings

Warnings are encapsulated in Qt inside warning dialogs, represented by the QMessageBox::warning() static method. This works in the same way as QMessageBox::question(), but it should only be used for unusual problems that interrupt the normal program sequence.

Figure 6.8:
To report errors that
interrupt the course
of the program, use
QMessage-
Box::warning().

In the example from Figure 6.8, a program absolutely needs a server connection, without which it cannot start. The warning dialog allows the user to choose between trying again to establish a connection, or terminating the program, thus ensuring the availability of the network if the application continues:

```
int result = QMessageBox::warning(this, tr("Applicationname"),
    tr("Could not connect to server.\n This application requires"
       "a server to function correctly."),
    tr("&Retry"), tr("&Exit application"), QString(), 0, 1);

if (result == 1)
    qApp->quit();
else
    retryConnect();
```

Of the three buttons available, we label two and leave the third one empty. As in the QMessageBox::question() example, the third button is thus not displayed. The last two parameters link (Enter) to the first button (0) and (Esc) to the second one (1). If the user selects the second button, the result variable receives the button code 1, and the application terminates. Otherwise, the program tries again, via retryConnect(), to establish a connection to the server.

Passing on Critical Messages

A program should open a special dialog for critical messages reporting errors that the user himself cannot solve, or can solve only with great difficulty. This dialog is also available in the same two versions as discussed until now. It is normally used as follows (Figure 6.9):

```
QMessageBox::critical(this, qApp->applicationName(),
        tr( "A critical error has occurred. "
            "If the problem persists,\n"
            "please contact our support center"
            "at +01 555 12 34 56."),
        QMessageBox::Ok, QMessageBox::NoButton,
            QMessageBox::NoButton);
```

Here, as with the information dialog, we do not to check for a return value, since there is only one button. In a real situation the dialog should contain more information on the type of critical error that was encountered. It is recommended that you use critical messages very sparingly—they should be the exception rather than the rule.

Figure 6.9:
Only if nothing else works is it is time for QMessage-Box::critical().

Providing Your Own Information on the Application

The help area of an application usually contains a small dialog providing information on the application. We have already encountered one in Section 4.3.3 on page 117, without explaining it in more detail.

Like the other static methods listed here, QMessageBox::about() also first expects a parent widget and a window title. The third parameter is a free text that can also be HTML formatted. If an icon for the application was defined with QApplication::setWindowIcon(), it is displayed as an icon next to the free text. The dialog only has one button and has no return value.

If you also want to show that you have written your application with the Qt toolkit, you can include an additional help menu entry in your program that calls QMessageBox::aboutQt(). This notification dialog provides information on Qt.

6.5.2 Error Messages That Are Only Visible Once

Apart from QStatusBar::showMessage() (see page 114) and QMessageBox, there is a third possibility for supplying the user with information—namely, using the QErrorMessage class.

In contrast to QMessageBox, QErrorMessage does not provide static methods. It displays messages if its showMessage() slot is called, either directly or via the connection with a signal.

Figure 6.10:
Queuing with
QErrorMessage: Only
if the first error
message was
confirmed ...

Figure 6.11:
... does the second
message appear.

Two other features make this class very useful. First, if two messages are waiting, as in the following example, then QErrorMessage only shows the second one once the user has clicked the first one away:

```
QErrorMessage *msg = new QErrorMessage(this);
msg->showMessage(tr("This error message will only reoccur if you "
                    "don't uncheck the checkbox in this message box."));
msg->showMessage(tr("If you can see this message, you have closed the "
                    "previous message box."));
```

The effect of this code is shown in Figures 6.10 and 6.11. Second, each of these dialog boxes contains a "Show this message again" checkbox. If the user unchecks this, Qt suppresses the error message if the same situation arises in future.

6.5.3 File Selection Dialogs

Applications frequently use dialogs to prompt the user to select files or directories. For this reason nearly all platforms provide implementations of such selection dialogs. Each one has its own special features, to which the end users of applications quickly become accustomed.

As a platform-independent toolkit, Qt is in somewhat of a quandary here: On the one hand the user should be able to use his or her own system dialog, but on the other, these dialogs cannot be extended with the widgets you as a programmer have written.

The QFileDialog class, which implements the file and directory selector, is therefore split into two parts: If you instantiate the class via the constructor, then Qt displays a separate dialog. If you use the predefined static methods, on the other hand, which cover most needs of application developers, then Qt tries to use the file dialog for the appropriate operating system.[6]

If you explicitly want to use *no* native system dialogs, you notify static methods of this via the QFileDialog::DontUseNativeDialog flag. In this case Qt uses its own dialog at the corresponding position. This and other flags are documented in Table 6.2.

Value	Effect
QFileDialog::ShowDirsOnly	Show only directories.
QFileDialog::DontResolveSymlinks	Do *not* resolve symbolic links, but interpret them as regular files or directories.
QFileDialog::DontConfirmOverwrite	Do not confirm whether an existing file should be overwritten.
QFileDialog::DontUseSheet	Do not display the Open file dialog in Mac OS X as a sheet. Only works if DontUseNativeDialog is *not* set.
QFileDialog::DontUseNativeDialog	Always use Qt's own dialog.

Table 6.2: Options for QFileDialog

File Selection Dialogs

In an initial example, illustrated in Figure 6.12, we want to allow the user to select an image. To do this we use the static method getOpenFileName():

---

[6] An exception is provided by the X11 platform. Currently, the Portland project (http://portland.freedesktop.org/) is working on a solution in which applications can use the file dialogs of the currently running desktop environment (GNOME or KDE).

```
QString file = QFileDialog::getOpenFileName(
                    this,
                    tr("Pick a File"),
                    "/home",
                    tr("Images (*.png *.xpm *.jpg)"));
```

If successful, the method call returns a filename; otherwise, it returns a null QString (which can be checked with file.isNull()). As the first argument, the method expects a pointer to the dialog's parent widget. If a null pointer is given as the first argument, then the dialog will not be modal. The next two arguments are the dialog heading and the start directory.

The QDir class provides static methods for retrieving the paths to the most important directories, which can be used as the third argument instead of a fixed string:[7]

QDir::currentPath()
> This returns the current directory of the application.

QDir::homePath()
> Under Windows, this returns the contents of the HOME environment variable. If this does not exist, it tries to evaluate the USERPROFILE environment variable. If this also fails, Qt forms the directory from HOMEDRIVE and HOMEPATH. If these variables are also not set, the method calls rootPath(). In Unix systems, including OS X, the method uses the HOME environment variable. If this is not set, rootPath() is used.

QDir::rootPath()
> In Windows, this returns drive C:\; in Unix, the root directory /.

QDir::tempPath()
> This is /tmp in Unix, while in Windows it is based on the environment variables TEMP and TMP.

Finally, as the fourth argument, getOpenFileName() expects a file filter. It allows only files with specific endings to appear in the dialog. Here you must adhere to the following syntax:

```
"filetypedesignator(*.ex1 *.ex2 ... *.exn)"
```

The file type designator can be freely chosen. It explains to the user what sort of file is involved. The file extensions listed in the parentheses act as the actual filter for the filenames contained in the directory. The following filter, for example, finds all files that end in .png, .xpm, or .jpg:

---

[7] For an example see page 178.

```
"Images (*.png *.xpm *.jpg)"
```

Every filter should be made localizable, that is, enclosed by tr(). In this way, readers of other languages can still enjoy a file type description in their own language.

If the user himself should decide which filters are to be used, alternatives can be appended to the first filter, separated from it by two semicolons. For example, if the filter is

```
"Images (*.png *.xpm *.jpg);;Text files (*.txt)"
```

then a corresponding drop-down dialog appears in the Open file dialog, as in Figure 6.12.

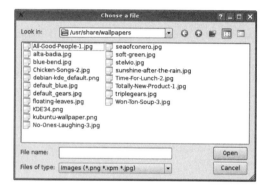

Figure 6.12:
The static methods of
QFileDialog *allow the*
use of standard
dialogs with their
own filters.

We can now choose from exactly those files that have either one of the three graphic file extensions or the extension .txt in this example. In general, the amount of filters is of course not limited.

Selecting Several Files Simultaneously

If a user needs to be able to select several files simultaneously, this possibility is covered by the getOpenFileNames() static method. In contrast to its little sister getOpenFileName(), it returns a QStringList, but the arguments are identical. Each entry in the returned list corresponds to a selected file.

This method of QFileDialog also makes use, in Windows and OS X, of the native dialogs of the corresponding operating system. The following example prints all the selected files, together with their paths, to the debug stream:

```
QStringList fileList = QFileDialog::getOpenFileNames(
                  this,
                  tr("Pick a File"),
                  "/home",
```

```
                        tr("Images (*.png *.xpm *.jpg)"));

foreach(QString file, fileList)
    qDebug() << file;
```

Selecting Existing Directories

Some programs require a base directory for their operations. When prompting the user for this path, the application must prevent the user from specifying a file target. A photo-manipulating program, for example, cannot store its gallery beneath a file.

To ensure that the user is shown only directories, you can call the file dialog class's getExistingDirectory() method. This does not expect a filter and displays only directories. Furthermore, it checks to see whether a specified directory really does exist—the user or another application could have deleted it in the meantime.

The following example queries the user for a directory, in which the program intends to store all its photos in future. As the base directory we will use the home directory of the current user:

```
QString directory = QFileDialog::getExistingDirectory(
        this,
        tr("Please pick the folder containing the photo gallery."),
        QDir::homePath());
```

Selecting a Filename

If a user wants to save a file, this file usually does not yet exist. getOpenFileName() tests whether the specified file exists, however, so it is of no use for saving files. We require a new static method that meets the requirements of storage semantics. In Qt this function is called getSaveFileName(), and it is analogous in its arguments and in its return value to getOpenFileName().

The following example requires the user to select the name of a file in which to save data. Here, if the user selects the name of an already existing file, the program does not question this, thanks to the DontConfirmOverwrite flag. This can be useful, for example, if the program wants to investigate the state of affairs outside the dialog.

```
QString file = QFileDialog::getSaveFileName(
                this,
                tr("Save File As..."),
                QDir::homePath(),
                tr("Images (*.png *.xpm *.jpg)"),
                QFileDialog::DontConfirmOverwrite );
```

6.5.4 Input Dialogs

For simple queries, Qt provides various template input dialogs, consisting of a suitable input widget and two buttons, OK and Cancel. The relevant QInputDialog class has only ready-made static methods that we will now look at in more detail.

Frequently, you are put in the position of having to ask the user to enter a value. Qt distinguishes here between whole number values and floating-point values, which it provides in double precision.

Accepting Integer Input Values

The following example (Figure 6.13) shows how the getInteger() method of QInputDialog is used:

```
bool ok;
int alter = QInputDialog::getInteger (this, tr("Enter Age"),
            tr("Please enter year of birth"), 1982,
            1850, QDate::currentDate().year(), 1, &ok);
if (ok)
{
  ...
}
```

Figure 6.13:
QInputDialog::getInteger() with preset
default value

The first two arguments of this are—as in other dialogs—a pointer to the parent widget and the heading of the dialog. Then getInteger() expects an explanatory text, which it displays above the input widget. This is followed by a default value and then the limits of the allowed input range. This example restricts the upper limit to the current year to avoid input that makes no sense (i.e., specifying a year of birth in the future). To do this we use QDate, a class for processing date details. The currentDate() static method provides the system time according to the current date, and in turn, year() extracts the year from this and returns it as an integer value. Also, instead of inserting a static lower limit (1850), as is done here, this can be formed dynamically (e.g., with an expression such as QDate::currentDate().year() - 200).

In the next-to-last parameter, getInteger() asks for the amount by which the integer value should be increased or decreased if the user clicks on one of the two buttons to the right of the input field to increment or decrement the value (a so-called *spin box*).

Since the return value provides no information on whether the user has canceled the dialog or has made a proper data entry, the method expects a pointer to a Boolean variable as the final parameter. If the user cancels the dialog, getInteger() stores the value false in the variable; otherwise, it is set to true.

Accepting Floating-point Numbers as Input Values

In the same way as with getInteger(), you can also prompt the user for real numbers with getDouble(). The dialog in the next example expects the price for a given product. getDouble() also expects the pointer to the parent widget, the dialog heading, and the description of the expected input as its first three parameters. This is again followed by the default, minimum, and maximum values.

However, for the next-to-last parameter, there is a difference between getInteger() and getDouble(): The floating-point variant here expects the number of places after the decimal point (see Figure 6.14). We use two of them in this example, in order to specify a price.

Figure 6.14:
QInputDialog::getDouble()
works here with only
two places after the
decimal point.

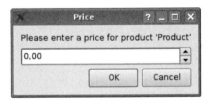

Once again, you can find out whether the dialog completed normally or was interrupted by using an auxilliary variable, the address of which is passed as the last parameter:

```
double getPrice(const QString& product, bool *ok)
{
return QInputDialog::getDouble(this, tr("Price"),
             tr("Please enter a price for product '%1.'").arg(product),
             0, 0, 2147483647, 2, &ok);
}
```

The value 2147483647 is the maximum number here that an integer can display.

Reading in Strings

The most frequent use of QInputDialog is to allow the user to select a string from several predefined strings. For this purpose the static method getItem() is used (Figure 6.15): This expects a QStringList and displays its contents in a drop-down widget.

Figure 6.15:
QInputDialog::getItem()
*returns the selected
string.*

Again, the first three parameters specify the pointer to the parent widget, the heading, and the user query. This is followed by the list of strings to be displayed. Then comes the index of the list element that the drop-down widget displays at the beginning. The next-to-last parameter specifies whether the user can add his own entries to the list. If this is this case, the return value does not have to match one of the predefined entries. The final parameter, as before, is the address of a variable that indicates whether the user has terminated the dialog with OK or Cancel:

```
QStringList languages;
bool ok;
languages << "English" << "German" << "French" << "Spanish";
QString language = QInputDialog::getItem(this, tr("Select Language"),
            tr("Please select your language"), languages,
            0, false, &ok);

if (ok) {
        ...
}
```

Reading in Free Text

Freely written texts are read in with the QInputDialog method getText(). The following example introduces probably the most frequent usage of this type of user input: entering a password.

The first three parameters specify the details of the parent widget, dialog heading, and dialog text, and are followed by the display form, which is specified by a value from the EchoMode enumerator of the QLineEdit input widget: QLine-Edit::NormalMode displays the text as it is entered; QLineEdit::NoEcho prints nothing at all, so that anybody watching cannot see how many characters getText() accepts; and the QInputDialog::Password value used here causes a placeholder to be printed for each character entered, usually stars or circular icons (Figure 6.16).

Figure 6.16:
QInputDialog::getText()
in password mode

Since a default value is normally not specified for input of a password, we pass an empty QString object as the next-to-last parameter.

```
QString getPassword(const QString& resource)
{
QString passwd = QInputDialog::getText(this, tr("Please Enter Password"),
        tr("Please enter a password for '%1'").arg(resource),
        QLineEdit::Password, QString(), 0);
}
```

Our final parameter in this example is a 0 (i.e., a null pointer) instead of a pointer to a bool variable, because in the case of the password it is sufficient to check the return value with QString::isEmpty() in order to see whether anything has been entered. Since these last two values match the default values for the fifth and sixth arguments of QInputDialog::getText(), you can shorten the method call in this case as follows:

```
QString getPassword(const QString& resource)
{
QString passwd = QInputDialog::getText(this, tr("Please Enter Password"),
        tr("Please enter a password for '%1'").arg(resource),
        QLineEdit::Password);
}
```

6.5.5 Font Selection Dialog

The QFont class is responsible for the description of a font type in Qt. Each widget has a font() method that returns the current font as a QFont object and a setFont() method that sets a new font type. QApplication knows these methods as well. It changes or reveals the standard font type for new widgets.

If you need to have the user select font types, you can make use of QFontDialog (Figure 6.17).

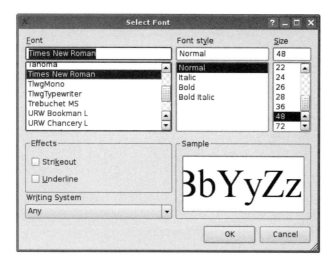

Figure 6.17:
QFontDialog::getFont()
displays the default
font.

This class offers a getFont() static method, which apart from a pointer to the parent widget requires a pointer to a Boolean value as its first argument: true.

```
bool ok;
QFont font = QFontDialog::getFont(&ok, this);
```

If the user has selected a font, this value is set to true. If you want to define a font type that deviates from the default font, you can define an appropriate QFont object and hand it over to getFont(). Note that the QFont object needs to be number two in the getFont() argument list:

```
bool ok;
QFont initial("Times New Roman", 48);
QFont font = QFontDialog::getFont(&ok, initial, this);
```

Here we select Times New Roman. If this font does not exist on the system, Qt tries to make an approximation by finding a similar font through the use of heuristics. The second parameter of the QFont constructor shown above gives the font size, in this example 48 points.

6.5.6 Color Selection and Printing Dialog

As well as the dialogs mentioned until now, Qt also provides a color selection and a printing dialog. It makes more sense to explain the use of these after we have introduced the color and painting system of Qt in more detail, so these dialogs will be introduced in Chapter 10 on pages 275 and 302.

7

Events, Drag and Drop, and the Clipboard

From Section 1.1, we know that all interactive Qt programs have *event loops*, because they work in an event-driven manner: GUI-based programs are influenced by application events such as mouse movements.

7.1 Event Loop and Event Handler

The event loop performs two kinds of tasks. First, it manages events that it obtains from the window system used, such as queries to redraw a window area. To do this it transforms them into Qt-specific events. Events are encapsulated in classes that are derived from the QEvent base class.

At the same time, Qt also generates its own events. An example of this is the QTimerEvent, which is triggered after a specific time has expired, set by the programmer. Such events are also based on QEvent and are processed by the event loop.

Each QEvent has a type. Subclasses of QEvent can contain arbitrary amounts of information; for example, QMouseEvent handles messages about buttons clicked and the position of the mouse cursor.

Qt passes events via QCoreApplication::postEvents() specifically to certain objects. These objects must inherit from QObject. The method expects the receiving object as the first parameter, followed by a QEvent.

To deliver it, postEvents() passes the event to the event() method of the target object. The task of the event() method is to either process or ignore the incoming events, depending on the requirements of the class of the receiving object. This method is therefore also referred to as an *event handler*. If an event cannot be processed immediately by the receiver, the event is put into a queue and scheduled for delivery. If another part of the application blocks the application by executing a syncronous long-winded operation,[1] the queue cannot be processed by the event loop during that time. User can easily confuse this behavior with an application "crashing."

The standard implementation of event() calls a separate virtual method for the most important event handlers, which already used the matching QEvent subclass as a parameter. This allows us to save code. We will now take a closer look at how this works.

7.2 Handling Events

We will implement a widget that displays the clock time in the local display format and the current date, also in the appropriate format, alternating every ten seconds (Figure 7.1 on page 189). The display itself should update every second.

7.2.1 Using Specialized Event Handlers

We implement the clock in a class called ClockWidget, which we derive from Q-LCDNumber, a Qt class that provides an imitation of an LCD display:

```
// clockwidget/clockwidget.h

#ifndef CLOCKWIDGET_H
#define CLOCKWIDGET_H

#include <QLCDNumber>
```

---

[1] You can use *threads* to avoid blocking. We will discuss this in Chapter 12.

```
class QTimerEvent;

class ClockWidget : public QLCDNumber
{
  Q_OBJECT
  public:
    ClockWidget(QWidget *parent = 0);

  protected:
    void timerEvent(QTimerEvent *e);

  private:
    int updateTimer, switchTimer;
    bool showClock;
};

#endif // CLOCKWIDGET_H
```

Here we are particularly interested in, besides the constructor, the specialized event handler timerEvent(), which will update the clock time. In the updateTimer and switchTimer member variables we save numbers that serve as identifiers for the timers. The showClock status flag determines whether the clock time (showClock= true) or the date (showClock=false) appears on the widget.

The implementation in clockwidget.cpp begins by specifying the form of the display. Usually QLCDNumber shows a frame around the digital display. This behavior, inherited from QFrame, is disabled by the QFrame::NoFrame frame style. In addition we dissuade the widget from drawing the LCD elements with shadows and a border, by passing on QLCDNumber::Flat to the widget's setSegmentStyle() method.

```
// clockwidget/clockwidget.cpp

#include <QtGui>
#include "clockwidget.h"

ClockWidget::ClockWidget(QWidget *parent)
  : QLCDNumber(parent), showClock(true)
{
  setFrameShape(QFrame::NoFrame);
  setSegmentStyle(QLCDNumber::Flat);

  updateTimer = startTimer(1000);
  switchTimer = startTimer(10000);

  QTimerEvent *e = new QTimerEvent(updateTimer);
  QCoreApplication::postEvent(this, e);
}
```

Now we need two timers. Each QObject can start a timer using the startTimer() method. As an argument startTimer() expects the number of seconds that must pass before it triggers a QTimerEvent, which is addressed to the current widget. Each QTimerEvent in turn contains an identification number, which is returned by the invocation of startTimer() that originates it. We can use this to distinguish between the two timers in timerEvent() later on.

So that we do not have to wait for a second to elapse before the time appears on the widget's display, we manually send a timer event with the ID of the update-Timer, using the postEvent() method of QCoreApplication. As the target we specify the current widget (in this case, this) as we do later on for the events generated by the timers themselves.

In the timerEvent() method we first check whether the pointer to the event really is valid—just to be on the safe side. Next, if the event contains the switchTimer ID, this only toggles the showClock variable. The actual work awaits in the last conditional statement, which is triggered by an event containing the updateTimer ID.

```
// clockwidget/clockwidget.cpp (continued)

void ClockWidget::timerEvent(QTimerEvent *e)
{
  if (!e) return;

  if (e->timerId() == switchTimer)
    showClock = !showClock;

  if (e->timerId() == updateTimer) {
    if (showClock) {
      QTime time = QTime::currentTime();
      QString str = time.toString(Qt::LocalDate);
      setNumDigits(str.length());
      display(str);
    } else {
      QDate date = QDate::currentDate();
      QString str = date.toString(Qt::LocalDate);
      setNumDigits(str.length());
      display(str);
    }
  }
}
```

If the widget is supposed to display the time, then we first determine the current time. In Qt, the QTime class is responsible for handling time. The currentTime() static method of this provides the current system time in a QTime object. This time is converted by toString() into a QString. Qt::LocalDate instructs the method to take into account the country settings (locales)of the user. Finally we must inform the display how many LCD digit positions are required. We deduce this from the string length and display the string with display().

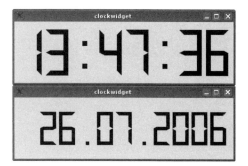

Figure 7.1:
Our ClockWidget
alternately displays
the time (above) and
the date (below).

Although QLCDNumber cannot display all alphanumerical characters, it does cope with all the characters required for the date and clock time (0–9, slash, colon, and dot). setNumDigits(), by the way, does not change the size of the widget, the text just gets smaller, the more numbers there are.

On the other hand, if showClock is set to false, which means that the widget should display just the date, we proceed in the same way with the QDate class, which in Qt is responsible for managing date specifications, and whose API corresponds almost exactly to that of QTime.

Now we can try out our widgets with the following test program (Figure 7.1 shows the result in the form of two screenshots recorded at an interval of ten seconds):

```cpp
// clockwidget/main.cpp

#include <QtGui>
#include "clockwidget.h"

int main(int argc, char* argv[])
{
  QApplication app(argc, argv);

  ClockWidget w;
  w.show();

  return app.exec();
}
```

7.2.2 Using the General Event Handler

Instead of treating the timer event specifically, we could also use the general event() event handler. Since this receives all types of events and we are only interested in timer events, we must first check the event type. Furthermore, in order to access the timerId() method of a timer event, a cast to QTimerEvent is necessary:

```
bool ClockWidget::event(QEvent *e)
{
  if (!e) return;

  if (e->type() == QEvent::Timer) {
    QTimerEvent *te = static_cast<QTimerEvent*>(e);
    if (te->timerId() == switchTimer) {
      showClock = !showClock;
      return true;
    }

    if (te->timerId() == updateTimer) {
      // handle event timer as before
      ...
      return true;
    }
  }
  return QObject::event(e);
}
```

Otherwise, we work with the te variable in the same manner as in the timerEvent()
method (see page 188). One peculiarity is that event(), in contrast to the specialized
event handlers, returns a Boolean value. This reveals whether an event has been
processed or not.

If we override the default event(), we must not forget to forward all events that
we do *not* handle to the event() method of the parent class. Otherwise, the event()
method of the parent class would never be called and the event handling of our
class would be lastingly disrupted. By calling QObject::event() unconditionally in
the end, we avoid a broken event handling.

Thus, whenever there is an appropriate specialized event handler, you should override it, rather than implement a general event handler. There is no need for a cast
because the input parameter is already of the correct event type, and no need to
forward unhandled events. In this way it can also be seen from just a glance at the
class declaration which event handlers are implemented by the class.

7.3   Using Event Filters

QObject-based classes have, in addition to the event handlers with which they react
to their own events, *event filters* that allow an object A to receive the events of
another object B. For each B event that A receives, A can then either forward it to
B or remove it from B's event stream.

Before you can filter events, the event filter must be installed. To do this we call
installEventFilter() in the constructor of the object A that is to monitor the events
of object B:

```
b->installEventFilter(this);
```

Here b is a pointer to B. Now B gives up all its events to A and leaves A with the decision whether it should filter out the event or let it through to B. For this purpose an eventFilter() method is used, which has the following signature:

```
bool QObject::eventFilter(QObject *watched, QEvent *e);
```

This must be reimplemented by A. The watched parameter allows events from several monitored objects to be distinguished from one another, and e is the event to be processed.

The return value tells the event system of Qt how it should proceed with the event. If false is returned, it is forwarded to the monitored object, whereas true causes it to be filtered out. This means that the event does not arrive at the object for which it was originally intended.

Classes with event filters can change the behavior of other QObject-based objects in this way. This is of particular benefit because you do not want to reimplement a widget just to make a minor modification to its event processing.

A classic example of the use of event handlers is in chat dialogs, in which QTextEdit is used. In contrast to the standard implementation of the class, here the (Return) and (Enter) keys should not start a new line, but send off what has been written.[2] The declaration in chatwindow.h appears as follows:

```
// chatwindow/chatwindow.h

#ifndef CHATWINDOW_H
#define CHATWINDOW_H

#include <QWidget>

class QTextBrowser;
class QTextEdit;
class QEvent;

class ChatWindow : public QWidget
{
  Q_OBJECT
  public:
    ChatWindow(QWidget *parent = 0);
    bool eventFilter(QObject *watched, QEvent *e);
    void submitChatText();

  private:
```

---

[2] Although (Return) and (Enter) are generally used synonymously, strictly speaking they are two different keys, which is reflected in the code.

```
      QTextBrowser *conversationView;
      QTextEdit *chatEdit;
};
#endif // CHATWINDOW_H
```

The submitChatText() method is responsible for sending the text. In this example its only task consists of including the written text from the QTextEdit instance chatEdit into the conversationView. Pointers to each of these widgets are saved in member variables.

In the chatwindow.cpp implementation, we first define the constructor: We place a vertical splitter into the widget with a QVBoxLayout. The conversation view comes into the splitter at the top, followed by the actual input widget, chatEdit:

```
// chatwindow/chatwindow.cpp

#include <QtGui>
#include "chatwindow.h"

ChatWindow::ChatWindow(QWidget *parent)
  : QWidget(parent)
{
  QVBoxLayout *lay = new QVBoxLayout(this);
  QSplitter *splitter = new QSplitter(Qt::Vertical, this);
  lay->addWidget(splitter);
  conversationView = new QTextBrowser;
  chatEdit = new QTextEdit;
  splitter->addWidget(conversationView);
  splitter->addWidget(chatEdit);
  chatEdit->installEventFilter(this);
  setWindowTitle(tr("Chat Window"));
  setTabOrder(chatEdit, conversationView);
};
```

Then we install the event filter in the input widget using installEventFilter(), as just described. The target is the ChatWindow object itself (this).

The ChatWindow will filter the keypress events of the chatEdit object and respond to them, so that we do not need to implement a specialized subclass of QTextEdit for this application.

Finally, we set the window title and use setTabOrder() to specify the order in which the widgets will be given focus inside the ChatWindow if the user presses the (Tab) key. The call in this case has the effect that chatEdit obtains the focus before conversationView, so that the user can begin typing immediately after the program starts. At the same time chatEdit obtains the focus as soon as the show() method of a ChatWindow instance is called.

Until now we have only learned how to specify the tab order with the help of the Qt Designer, in Chapter 3.1.5 on page 89. If you read the C++ code generated by uic, you will realize that the Designer also converts the tab order specified into a series of setTabOrder() calls.

We shall now turn to the core item of the example, the eventFilter() method:

```
// chatwindow/chatwindow.cpp (continued)

bool ChatWindow::eventFilter(QObject *watched, QEvent* e)
{
  if (watched == chatEdit && e->type() == QEvent::KeyPress) {
    QKeyEvent *ke = static_cast<QKeyEvent*>(e);
    if (ke->key() == Qt::Key_Enter ||
        ke->key() == Qt::Key_Return) {
      submitChatText();
      return true;
    }
  }
  return QWidget::eventFilter(watched, e);
}
```

We first use a pointer comparison to check whether the filter is currently handling chatEdit at all and whether the pressing of a key (QEvent::KeyPress) is involved. Once we are sure of this, we cast the generic event e into its actual event type, QKeyEvent, with a static_cast.

This is necessary to access the keypress event's key() method, which we now use to check whether the key pressed is either the (Enter) or (Return) key. If this is the case, we call submitChatText() and request Qt to filter the event with return true, that is, not to forward it to the chatWindow object. If the event is not a keypress event, we forward it to the parent class's event filter. We take this precaution since several Qt classes rely on event filters.

The submitChatText() method, which would also be responsible for forwarding text in a real chat client, in our example only attaches the typed text to the conversation view and empties the text window:

```
// chatwindow/chatwindow.cpp (continued)

void ChatWindow::submitChatText()
{
  // append text as new paragraph
  conversationView->append(chatEdit->toPlainText());
  // clear chat window
  chatEdit->setPlainText("");
}
```

We also check this class again for its functionality with a short test program, by starting an event loop via QApplication::exec(), after we have instantiated and displayed ChatWindow:

```
// chatwindow/main.cpp

#include <QtGui>
#include "chatwindow.h"

int main(int argc, char* argv[])
{
    QApplication app(argc, argv);
    ChatWindow win;
    win.show();
    return app.exec();
}
```

7.4   Drag and Drop

The *drag and drop* functionality, that is, the capability to transfer information with the mouse between two widgets within the same program, or between two applications, is also regulated in Qt via events (Figure 7.2 on page 196). Each event has its own event handler in QWidget-based classes.

7.4.1   MIME Types

The first question to arise here is how the information should be encoded so that it can be transferred at all between two widgets via drag and drop. This is solved by the QMimeData class: It serves as a container for data, whose type is specified as a MIME type.[3] A PNG image, for example, has the MIME type image/png, and a normal ASCII text file has the type text/plain.

It is also possible to use your own MIME types that are understood only by your own application. The names of these are defined according to the pattern application/x-*vendor.content designator* (page 242 shows an example).

In the following example we pack an image so that it can be "sent away" with a drag. To do this we write a QLabel-based widget that expects the path to a PNG image, displays it, and allows it to be included in other applications via drag and drop.

The following help function, called prepareImageDrag(), packs the image into a QMimeData object:

```
QMimeData* prepareImageDrag(const QString& path)
{
  QFile file(path);
```

---

[3] MIME stands for *Multipurpose Internet Mail Extensions* and is described in RFCs 2045, 2046, and 2047.

```
  if (!file.open()) return;
  QByteArray image = file.readAll();
  QMimeData *mimeData = new QMimeData;
  mimeData->setData("image/png", image);
  return mimeData;
}
```

Fortunately QMimeData already includes its own encoding methods for the most important data types, such as for colors, HTML, reformatted text, and URLs. In practice, the following code is therefore sufficient to encode an image:

```
QMimeData* prepareImageDrag(const QString& path)
{
  QImage image(path);
  QMimeData *mimeData = new QMimeData;
  mimeData->setImageData(image);
  return mimeData;
}
```

Qt even makes the image available in different formats with setImageData(). QMime-Data can save several MIME types together with their data in one object. When dragging, Qt offers all supported image formats, but it has a preference for PNG here, since this displays the best quality. The program that receives the drop then iterates through the list of MIME types and selects the data for the first MIME type that it can handle.

We make use of this property to include the path specification for the image: We pack it into a QUrl object, which converts it into an RFC-compliant URL, and we also include the normalized path specification as a text:

```
// draglabel/draglabel.cpp

#include <QtGui>

QMimeData* prepareImageDrag( const QString& path )
{
  QImage pic( path );
  QMimeData *mimeData = new QMimeData;
  mimeData->setImageData( pic );
  QList<QUrl> urls;
  QUrl imageUrl( path );
  urls.append( imageUrl );
  mimeData->setUrls( urls );
  mimeData->setText( imageUrl.path() );
  return mimeData;
}
```

We intentionally do not use the path variable here directly: If we are passed a relative path, this could become a problem with drag and drop between applications with different working directories. QUrl, however, resolves relative paths.

An application that obtains a drop originating from a drag with these MIME data first comes across the image data. If it cannot handle images, it then checks whether it can handle URLs, which would be the case for a file manager, for example. If these attempts are unsuccessful, the program can still access the path in text form, so that even an editor may act as a drop target. We will use this flexible variation in our example.

Figure 7.2:
A specific event
handler is responsible
for every
drag-and-drop step
in Qt.

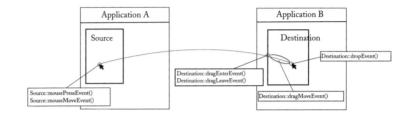

7.4.2 The Drag Side

We have seen how to encode data in MIME format. But how do the MIME data from a widget in one part of our program manage to get to another part—or even into a completely different application? To illustrate this, Figure 7.2 shows the sequence of a typical drag-and-drop operation.

The source widget defines when a drag begins. If the widget cannot be clicked, which is the case for labels, it is sufficient to reimplement the mousePressEvent() event handler in a way that a drag is triggered by clicking:

```
// draglabel/draglabel.cpp (continued)

void DragLabel::mousePressEvent(QMouseEvent *event)
{
  if (event->button() == Qt::LeftButton) {
    QMimeData* data = prepareImageDrag(picPath);
    QDrag *drag = new QDrag(this);
    drag->setMimeData(data);
    if (pixmap())
      drag->setPixmap(pixmap()->
        scaled(100,100, Qt::KeepAspectRatio));
    drag->start();
  }
}
```

First we check whether the user is holding down the left mouse button. Then we prepare the QMimeData object with the help function prepareImageDrag() (page 195). We obtain the path from the member variable picPath. The constructor

retrieves the image displayed by the label from the specified path, with the help of
the QLabel::setPixmap() method, as shown in the following code:

```
// draglabel/draglabel.cpp (continued)

#include "draglabel.h"

DragLabel::DragLabel(const QString& path, QWidget *parent)
  : QLabel(parent), picPath(path)
{
  setPixmap(QPixmap(path));
}
```

In order to start the actual drag, we need to instantiate a new QDrag object in the
mousePressEvent() and equip it with the MIME data using setMimeData().

In addition we assign the image from the label to the drag, for which we obtain a
pointer with pixmap(). The graphical interface links it to the mouse cursor so that
the content of the drag object is visualized. Therefore drags do not have to have
an image set, although this is recommended from a usability point of view, since
the user can then see what he is juggling with. We must ensure that the image
is presented in the preview size. To do this we specify a version scaled down, with
scaled(). KeepAspectRatio instructs the method to retain the page proportions, but
not to exceed the maximum size of 100 pixels in either direction.

drag->start() begins the actual drag action. In the pattern from Figure 7.2, the
source corresponds to our DragLabel.

To test the widget, we will write a small program that requires the path of an image
file that can be read by Qt as a command-line argument. If this is available, we pass
it to DragLabel during the instantiation:

```
// draglabel/main.cpp

#include <QtGui>
#include "draglabel.h"

int main( int argc, char* argv[] )
{
  QApplication app( argc, argv );

  if (argc < 2) return 1;

  DragLabel w(argv[1]);
  w.setWindowTitle(QObject::tr("Drag me!"));
  w.show();

  return app.exec();
}
```

The program then looks something like what is shown in Figure 7.3. We can drag the image into various programs, such as Gimp or Paint, and see what happens to it.

Figure 7.3:
The DragLabel *with
the Qt-4 logo*

7.4.3   The Drop Side

So that we can better understand the drag-and-drop process illustrated in Figure 7.2 on page 196, we will now implement a label widget complementary to the DragLabel, which we will call DropLabel.

Each widget that should accept drops must first activate this capability in its constructor, with setAcceptDrops(true):

```
// droplabel/droplabel.cpp

#include <QtGui>
#include "droplabel.h"

DropLabel::DropLabel(QWidget *parent)
  : QLabel(parent)
{
  setAcceptDrops(true);
}
```

Events to be Handled

The first drop event that the widget needs to process occurs as soon as the mouse cursor moves into the widget. Accordingly, the widget's dragEnterEvent() handler must check to see if the MIME types contained in the drag object are ones it can handle. For this purpose we access the the QMimeData object, via the mimeData() method:

```
// droplabel/droplabel.cpp (continued)


void DropLabel::dragEnterEvent(QDragEnterEvent *event)
{
  if (event && event->mimeData()) {
    const QMimeData* md = event->mimeData();
    if (md->hasImage() || md->hasUrls() || md->hasText())
        event->acceptProposedAction();
  }
}
```

We check the contents of the QMimeData object and accept the drop action, via acceptProposedAction(), as soon as we find that there is an image, some URLs, or a text. Otherwise the mouse cursor will display an *X*, signaling to the user that the widget will not accept the drop. If you want, you can carry out more precise checks here, but you should be aware that too much checking at this point may prevent the widget from signaling promptly that it can accept the drag.

If you want to perform additional checks within the widget, such as allowing drops only in specific areas, you can implement a dragMoveEvent() handler. The function takes a pointer to a QDragMoveEvent, with which the current position in the widget can be checked, using pos(). This method must also call acceptProposedAction(), passing it the event, if the widget should accept a drop at a particular point. Most widgets and applications usually do not need to handle this event, however.

For the sake of completeness, we should also give a mention to dragLeaveEvent(). This event handler is also normally not needed, but can be used in special cases to undo changes made to the current widget by dragEnterEvent() or dragMoveEvent().

The dropEvent() Handler

The core part of a drop operation is the dropEvent() handler; it is used to decode the mimeData() object and complete the drag-and-drop process:

```
// droplabel/droplabel.cpp (continued)

void DropLabel::dropEvent(QDropEvent *event)
{
  QPixmap pix;
  if(event && event->mimeData()) {
    const QMimeData *data = event->mimeData();
    if (data->hasImage())
      pix = data->imageData().value<QPixmap>();
    else if(data->hasUrls())
      foreach(QUrl url, data->urls()) {
        QFileInfo info(url.toLocalFile());
```

```
            if(info.exists() && info.isFile())
              pix = QPixmap(url.toLocalFile());
            if (pixmap() && !pixmap()->isNull())
              break;
        }
      else if(data->hasText()) {
        QUrl url(data->text());
        QFileInfo info(url.toLocalFile());
        if(info.exists() && info.isFile())
            pix = QPixmap(url.toLocalFile());
    }
  }
  if (!pix.isNull()) {
    setPixmap(pix);
    resize(pix.size());
  }
}
```

Because the QMimeData object is const (that is, write protected), we are not responsible for freeing its memory.

If the image exists as a data stream in the QMimeData instance (determined using hasImage()), we convert this to a pixmap. Since imageData() returns a QVariant and QPixmap is a component of the QtGui module, about which the QVariant "living" in QtCore has no knowledge, we will make use of the QVariant template method value<*type*>(), to which we pass QPixmap as a type parameter.

If the MIME data contain URLs instead, we first convert each of them to the corresponding local file path with toLocalFile(). If the path is not local, the method returns an empty string.

Using QFileInfo, we then check the path to see if it exists and also to see whether it really references a file. If this is the case, we try to read the file as an image file. If this doesn't work, pix becomes a null object, which will respond to isNull() with true. As soon as we have found a valid URL, we skip the other URLs, with break.

It may sometimes be the case that QMimeData contains several URLs for the same object. For example, the KDE desktop environment references files on external data media first with a media:/ URL, but also provides the matching traditional Unix path for non-KDE programs.

Finally, if all else fails, because a file locator can also be represented as unformatted text, we try to interpret any existing text part of the MIME data as an URL, so that we can try to obtain a pixmap from this.

If one of our extraction attempts is successful, the pix filled with data becomes the new label's pixmap, and we can adjust the label to the pixmap size.

We will also put this example to the test with a small test program. Instead of a DragLabel, we instantiate a DropLabel here and blow it up to an initial size of 100x100 pixels, so that there is enough space for objects to be dropped:

```
// droplabel/main.cpp

#include <QtGui>
#include "droplabel.h"

int main( int argc, char* argv[] )
{
  QApplication app( argc, argv );

  DropLabel w;
  w.setWindowTitle(QObject::tr("Drop here!"));
  w.resize(100,100);
  w.show();

  return app.exec();
}
```

If we pull the image from the DragLabel example on page 197 onto the DropLabel window, the widget accepts the drop. If you let go of the button the DropWidget accepts the graphics, as can be seen in Figure 7.4. The program can also process drops made from file managers, thanks to its ability to interpret URLs.

Figure 7.4:
The DropLabel, *after it has received the drop with the Qt-4 logo*

7.5   The Clipboard

The Qt QClipboard class is responsible for handling the "clipboard" provided by many operating systems. Interaction with the system clipboard requires no event handling, but like the Qt drag-and-drop functionality, it utilizes MIME data encoding.

You don't even need to define a QClipboard object, because every QApplication already provides one that you can use to read text from or write text to, as shown below.

```
QClipboard *clipboard = QApplication::clipboard();
```

```
qDebug() << clipboard->text();
clipboard->setText(newText);
```

But the clipboard can also store and retrieve more complex data, and it is able to do so based on a MIME type. The methods mimeData() and setMimeData() transfer the MIME data in existing QMimeData objects to and from the clipboard.

To demonstrate how closely the clipboard and the drag-and-drop system are related, we shall write a small test application called drag2clip. The core of this is a label widget named D2cLabel, which copies data received from a drop to the clipboard. Conversely, the clipboard data can be retrieved by dragging from the D2cLabel object.

Apart from the constructor and the three events handlers necessary for drag and drop, mousePressEvent(), dragEnterEvent() and dropEvent(), there is also the clone-MimeData() method. This creates an identical copy of a write-protected QMimeData object, as is obtained by QClipboard or QDropEvent:

```
// drag2clip/d2clabel.h

#ifndef D2CWIDGET_H
#define D2CWIDGET_H

#include <QLabel>
class QMimeData;

class D2cLabel : public QLabel
{
  Q_OBJECT
  public:
    D2cLabel(QWidget *parent = 0);

    void mousePressEvent(QMouseEvent *event);
    void dragEnterEvent(QDragEnterEvent *event);
    void dropEvent(QDropEvent *event);

  protected:
    QMimeData* cloneMimeData(const QMimeData *data);
};

#endif // D2CWIDGET_H
```

In the constructor we add an inscription to the new label and enable drops into it. Thanks to setWordWrap(true), the label line-wraps the text the moment it is longer than the widget is wide. By enclosing the text inside <center> tags, we cause it to appear centered:

```
// drag2clip/d2clabel.cpp
```

```
#include <QtGui>
#include "d2clabel.h"

D2cLabel::D2cLabel(QWidget *parent)
  : QLabel(parent)
{
  setWordWrap(true);
  setText(tr("<center>Drag from here to retrieve the text currently "
             "located in the clipboard or fill the clipboard by "
             "dragging text from abitrary places and dropping it here."
             "</center"));
  setAcceptDrops(true);
}
```

In the mousePressEvent() we retrieve the MIME data from the clipboard and check the pointer to it for its validity. If everything is in order, we generate a QDrag object and transfer the MIME data there:

```
// drag2clip/d2clabel.cpp (continued)

void D2cLabel::mousePressEvent(QMouseEvent *event)
{
  if (event->button() == Qt::LeftButton) {
    const QMimeData *mimeData = QApplication::clipboard()->mimeData();
    if (!mimeData) return;
    QDrag *drag = new QDrag(this);
    drag->setMimeData(cloneMimeData(
                             QApplication::clipboard()->mimeData()));
    drag->start();
  }
}
```

At this point we require cloneMimeData(), as we have no information on the MIME types from the clipboard and their lifespans, which also has a bearing on the validity of the mimeData() pointer from the QApplication::clipboard(). We can pass the cloned QMimeData instance, on the other hand, with a free conscience to the QDrag object, and initiate the drag process with start().

Next, we implement dragEnterEvent(). This accepts everything, and after all, we want to leave all the data in the clipboard:

```
// drag2clip/d2clabel.cpp (continued)

void D2cLabel::dragEnterEvent(QDragEnterEvent *event)
{
  event->acceptProposedAction();
}
```

Next, dropEvent() does exactly the opposite of mousePressEvent(). It clones the MIME data from the MIME data from the QDropEvent, after it has first checked the validity of the pointer, so that it can forward them on to the QClipboard instance:

```
// drag2clip/d2clabel.cpp (continued)

void D2cLabel::dropEvent(QDropEvent *event)
{
  if(event && event->mimeData()) {
    QApplication::clipboard()->setMimeData(cloneMimeData
                                    (event->mimeData()));
  }
}
```

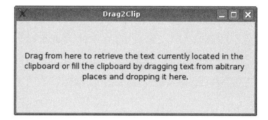

Figure 7.5:
Drag2Clip mediates
between the
drag-and-drop
system and the
clipboard.

Finally, cloneMimeData() uses the formats() method, which contains all MIME types as a list of strings. We use this list to read out the data of an entry, together with its MIME type, using the data() method. This we copy to a new QMimeData object with the help of setData(). In this way we obtain an exact copy of the contents:

```
// drag2clip/d2clabel.cpp (continued)

QMimeData* D2cLabel::cloneMimeData(const QMimeData *data)
{
  if (!data)
    return 0;

  QMimeData *newData = new QMimeData;
  foreach(QString format, data->formats())
    newData->setData(format, data->data(format));

  return newData;
}
```

The test application with which we want to verify the functionality of this instantiates the D2cLabel and sets it to a size of 400x150 pixels, as before with the DropLabel, so that there is enough space available as a "drop space":

```
// drag2clip/main.cpp

#include <QtGui>
#include "d2clabel.h"

int main( int argc, char* argv[] )
{
  QApplication app( argc, argv );

  D2cLabel w;
  w.resize(400, 150);
  w.setWindowTitle(QObject::tr("Drag2Clip"));
  w.show();

  return app.exec();
}
```

The visual result of our work is shown in Figure 7.5. However, the application is only of interest if you can pull data onto the widget and then retrieve it from the clipboard or copy data to the clipboard, remove it from the widget via drag and drop, and place it somewhere else.

8

Displaying Data Using "Interview"

In GUI-based applications, data is often presented in list and table views, which can be nested within one another. When using list views, programmers often take a very simple approach: They simply add values, such as strings, to lists. However, this raises the possibility that what should be distinct items in the list view cannot be distinguished from one another, particularly if duplicate labels are allowed or if the user can manipulate the strings used to label the list items. Qt 4 therefore does not support purely string-based list views.

A second approach to data visualization is to represent each of the list entries as a separate object. On page 157 we already tackled such *item-based* lists, which encapsulate each entry as a lightweight *item*. These items can be extended to contain references to data denoted by the corresponding list entries, or to incorporate this data directly in the item object itself.

Although this concept stands out because of its simplicity, it is not always the best solution. Why should you pack the results of SQL queries into items, thus storing the data of the original query a second time? In addition, certain advantages of SQL would be lost, such as incremental delivery of queried data to the application: The user has to wait until all data are available, or the programmer is faced with much more work to display the data from the source in an item-based view.

For this reason Qt 4 has a model/view concept called *Interview*. This is much more flexible than item-based programming, but it is also more complex, so that even professionals need a while to fully understand it. We will therefore first look at the underlying ideas, and then take a closer look at some simple examples of model/view programming. Starting on page 222 we will develop our own models, and we will briefly discuss item-based views on page 251.

8.1 Underlying Concepts

The model/view architecture is based on the idea of separating data from its display. By doing so, the same data can easily be represented in a variety of forms, such as lists or tables. Since the data source ideally knows nothing about the view that displays it, and a view knows nothing about the internal organization of the source, an element in between is required—the *model*. Figure 8.1 illustrates this relationship.

Figure 8.1:
In Interview, the
views display data
fetched via a model
from any data source
at all. For writable
models, changes flow
back to the source.

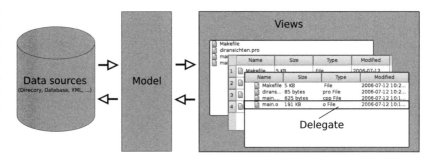

So that models and views can understand one another, the model has knowledge of the basic properties of the views: Each entry occupies one row and one column in the model, and if necessary has a link to a parent object. The latter is of importance only for nested lists, not for normal lists and tables. Interview describes these basic properties with the QModelIndex class.

With the help of the QModelIndex class, a model can reference the data to which it refers and thereby supply it to a view in the format that the view demands.

In order to display data on the screen correctly, a view queries the data source, via a QModelIndex, in various *roles*. In the DisplayRole the view expects to receive text to be displayed; in the DecorationRole, an icon; in the FontRole, the font type for some displayed text; and in the ToolTipRole, the text to be shown in a tooltip. There are more than a dozen predefined roles in total, as Table 8.1 shows.

Value	Effect (typical content)
Qt::DisplayRole	Main data to be displayed (usually text)
Qt::DecorationRole	Additional decoration (usually icons)
Qt::EditRole	Data in a form suitable for an editor (e.g., the file path if the DisplayRole data is an image)
Qt::ToolTipRole	Data that should be displayed by a tooltip (text, HTML)
Qt::StatusTipRole	Data to be displayed in the status line (text)
Qt::WhatsThisRole	Data that the widgets should return in the "What's This?" mode (text, HTML)
Qt::SizeHintRole	Size hint for the element; is forwarded to the views (QSizeHint)
Qt::FontRole	Font type for rendering the DisplayRole
Qt::TextAlignmentRole	Alignment of the text of the DisplayRole
Qt::BackgroundColorRole	Background color (QColor)
Qt::TextColorRole	Color for the DisplayRole text (QColor)
Qt::CheckStateRole	Defines whether an element is completely, partially, or not at all selected; the values from the Qt::CheckState enumerator are valid: Qt::Unchecked, Qt::PartiallyChecked,[1] or Qt::Checked
Qt::AccessibleTextRole	Screenreader or other accessibility tools output this text; an example for the Accessible-Role is the text description of an icon, which a blind person could not understand
Qt::AccessibleDescriptionRole	A description of the item for accessibility purposes
Qt::UserRole	Offset for your own roles that may be required in the development of your own delegates

Table 8.1:

Roles in models

The data() method of a model is responsible for delivering data and therefore needs to react accordingly when it is passed each type of role, together with a model

---

[1] In a tree view, Qt::PartiallyChecked is useful for items with children of which only a few can be selected, that is, those that have the Qt::CheckState status.

index. It returns data to the view in the form of a QVariant. This enables the view to interpret the data it receives in accordance with the role it adopted to make the request. If, given a role and a model index, there is no data available to return, the model signals this by returning an empty QVariant object as the result of the call to data(). This procedure also enables the view to present different data types in accordance with the various roles. Figure 8.2 illustrates the use of roles in an example of a list view.

If the predefined roles are not sufficient, you can define your own roles and make them available in the model. The predefined views, however, can't use them yet. But there is an easier way to use your self-defined roles than inheriting your own view class from the pre-defined view class. This is because a so-called *delegate* is in charge of drawing list or table entries (see Figure 8.1).

The delegate provided by Qt that is implemented in the QItemDelegate class will be sufficient in most cases. It also provides an editor function for modifying data elements displayed in the view. For this to be useful, however, the model must support writing back to the data source, which is not always the case: Many models only make information available for reading and do not provide write access.

Figure 8.2:
Roles define the
space entries can
take up in a view.

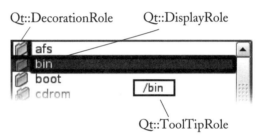

8.1.1 The View Classes

For the data visualization itself, Interview provides three ready-to-use classes that we can admire in use in Figure 8.5 on page 213:

QListView

>This class displays one-dimensional lists (Figure 8.5 at the top left) and also has an icon mode in which it shows all of its entries arranged as icons (Figure 8.5 at the top right).

QTreeView

>This class displays lists in tree form (Figure 8.5 at the bottom left) and is thus more elaborate than QListView. In addition this class can display several columns, which QListView is not capable of doing.

QTableView

This class displays data in a table (Figure 8.5, bottom right). At the top and side are the row and column headings, which can be individually customized.

In addition, QHeaderView provides header lines for QTreeView as well as header columns and lines for QTableView. This class is not used as a separate view, but it can be adjusted to your own requirements and then used in instances of QTreeView and QTableView.

These views inherit from QAbstractItemView, the base class of all views in Interview. If you look more closely at the inheritance structure in Figure 8.3, you will realize that QAbstractItemView does not inherit from QWidget directly. Rather, the view classes are based on QAbstractScrollArea, a class that provides a widget with an embedded widget.

The embedded widget, called the *viewport*, can be many times larger than the widget that encloses it. The frame widget displays vertical or horizontal scrollbars where appropriate. In this way the view can make available much more space for the data than was actually allocated for it in the layout in question; of course, the user must then navigate through the viewport using the scrollbars.

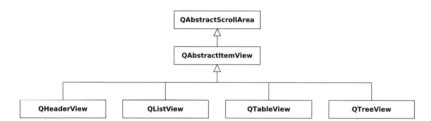

Figure 8.3:
All view classes are
derived from
QAbstractItemView.

8.1.2   The Model Classes

All the models that are included in Qt also inherit from a common abstract base class called QAbstractItemModel. *Abstract* here means that the class cannot be instantiated directly, because it contains unimplemented methods. The programmer can create objects only from a subclass that is tailored for a specific purpose and implements the missing methods. As can be seen in Figure 8.4, every model is also a QObject, and thus benefits from automatic memory management.

QAbstractItemModel is not the only abstract class in the inheritance model. If you look more closely at the inheritance structures, you will see two additional classes derived from QAbstractItemModel, called QAbstractListModel and QAbstractTableModel, whose APIs further specialize that of QAbstractItemModel with list or table views. These abstract subclasses also cannot have objects directly instantiated from them.

Figure 8.4:
The inheritance
hierarchy of models
in Interview

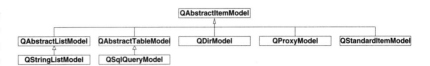

For compatibility reasons, classes based on QAbstractListModel and QAbstractTable-Model can be used in tables, nested lists, and one-dimensional lists. The practical benefits of doing so, however, are strictly limited if you try to use them in QListView and QTableView, respectively. QAbstractListModel, for example, reduces the number of usable columns to one single one—which makes little sense in a table view.

With QStringListModel, Interview also provides a specific implementation of QAbstractListModel, an editable model, the data source of which is a string list. If the user changes a string in the view, the model adjusts the corresponding entry in the string list.

QStandardItemModel allows data to be stored directly in the model. Although this contradicts the basic idea that a model only provides a pure mediation service between the data source and views, it turns out to be very practical in certain application cases with modest data-handling requirements. For large applications, however, QStandardItemModel is usually too inflexible.

QAbstractProxyModel replaces the QProxyModel class in Qt 4.1, which was intended to extract data from a model, manipulate them, and return them to a new model, for example, to filter the data. But the class turned out to be too inflexible, and was therefore replaced. Trolltech advises against using it in new projects. QAbstractProxyModel is powerful, but again it is an abstract class, and so it relies on subclasses to implement the functionality it offers.

In order that the effort in using the new class is not larger than that required for the directly usable QProxyModel, Trolltech provides the QSortFilterProxyModel subclass. It allows you to perform the most frequently performed tasks of a proxy model, mainly filtering and sorting, without the need to first derive further subclasses.

Finally, Interview provides a model in QDirModel that can be used, if required, to project a directory hierarchy in QListView, QTreeView, and QtableView.

8.2 Displaying Directory Hierarchies

We are now ready to acquire our first practical experience with Interview and create a small program, using QDirModel and the three ready-to-use views, which displays the home directory in four different views (Figure 8.5). In the source code we first instantiate, in addition to the obligatory QApplication object, a QDirModel. You again have to remember that here, as an exception, we allocate the model not on the heap but on the stack, because our entire code is located in the main() method.[2]

In the next step we create a widget with a table layout, into which we insert two list views at the top and a tree view and table view at the bottom. In doing so, we switch the second list view to icon mode. For each of the views we use the instance of QDirModel that was just created as the model, which we pass on to the view's setModel() method as a pointer. This way we bind the views to the model.

Before we can work with the views, we have a chicken-and-egg problem to solve: The views have to know the path to the directory that they should initially display. But strictly speaking, they cannot learn this path, as they themselves only work on the directory model.

For this reason, QDirModel provides an overloaded version of the index() method. This function usually expects a triplet of indices (column, row, and parent) as an argument, a representation which is of no help to us here. The overloaded version, on the other hand, accepts a path description encoded as a QString.

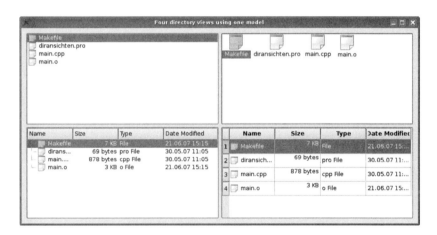

Figure 8.5:
Four views, one model as the source: Here the Qt QDirModel is used to display the contents of the current directory.

Then we specify the directory beneath which the views should operate. Since all views access the model independently of each other, we must also set the index separately for each view. After that, we only need to display the widget and start the event loop. The code for the application is shown below:

```
// diransichten/main.cpp

#include <QtGui>

int main(int argc, char* argv[])
{
```

---

[2] See Section 1.2.2 on page 31.

```
QApplication app(argc, argv);

QDirModel dirModel;
QWidget w;
w.setWindowTitle(QObject::tr("Four "
    "directory views using one model"));
QGridLayout *lay = new QGridLayout(&w);

QListView  *lv = new QListView;
lay->addWidget(lv, 0, 0);
lv->setModel(&dirModel);

QListView  *lvi = new QListView;
lay->addWidget(lvi, 0, 1);
lvi->setViewMode(QListView::IconMode);
lvi->setModel(&dirModel);

QTreeView *trv = new QTreeView;
lay->addWidget(trv, 1, 0);
trv->setModel(&dirModel);

QTableView *tav = new QTableView;
tav->setModel(&dirModel);
lay->addWidget(tav, 1, 1);

QModelIndex cwdIndex = dirModel.index(QDir::currentPath());
lv->setRootIndex(cwdIndex);
lvi->setRootIndex(cwdIndex);
trv->setRootIndex(cwdIndex);
tav->setRootIndex(cwdIndex);

w.show();

return app.exec();
}
```

8.2.1 Using View Classes in the Designer

Unfortunately, QDirModel has one significant restriction: Because the views do not react to mouse clicks, we have to build this functionality in ourselves. In addition, only one element can be selected in each of the views. If you want to allow several items to be selected, then you will also have to go it alone. We can correct these shortcomings by designing our own file dialog, such as can be seen in Figure 8.6. As a nice side-effect, we will get acquainted with how to use view classes in the Designer.

Our file selection dialog is based on the Designer template Dialog with Buttons and consists of a combo box with the available drives, a button (Tool Button) to the right of this, and a stacked widget.[3] The two small triangles in the upper-right corner of the stacked widget also allow us to move through the stack in the Designer. As the first widget, we place a list view on the stack.

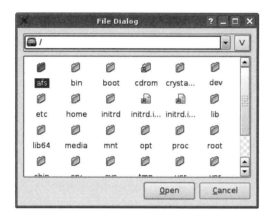

Figure 8.6:
The file dialog in the icon mode

The Insert page entry located in the context menu[4] (Figure 8.7) makes it possible to add new pages in which there is space for further widgets, if required. In this way we can extend the stack by adding another list view and a tree view.

Figure 8.7:
Quickly clicked together: combo box, button, and stacked widget with list view

Later we want to use the button—the object name of which we set to switchButton in the Property Editor, and whose text property we change to V (for *View*; if you want something else, you can select a suitable icon in the icon property)—to switch back and forth between the different views. We place the combo box with a tool button into a frame. To do this we must first position the frame and then place the combo box and tool button inside it. If the frame becomes colored before the drop, then it will accept the widgets as children. We arrange both of them horizontally

---

[3] Figure 8.8 shows all the required widgets at a glance.
[4] The context menu of the stacked widget only opens if you right-click while hovering directly above the two small triangles.

via the Lay out menu in the context menu. We also rename the OK button: After a right-click and the subsequent selection of Change text..., we can type in the new text label Open, replacing OK.

Figure 8.8:
The dialog in the
draft view with the
required tools from
the toolbox

Finally we use a layout to integrate the label, the stacked widget, and the horizontal button layout (using the Lay out entry in the context menu). So that the views can take up as much space as possible in their stacked widget, we select the three page objects beneath the stacked widget in the object inspector and set the value for margin in the Property Editor in the Layout section of the stacked widget to 0. Finally we assign the object name iconView to one of the two list views and change the viewMode property of the iconView list view to iconMode. It should then display the directory contents as shown in Figure 8.6, while the other list view displays the information for each file in a separate row of the view.

In this basic framework it is appropriate to enable multiple selections. This is done via the selectionMode property. In all three views we switch this property to ExtendedSelection so that the user may select several entries at the same time.

The dialog itself we call FileDialog by setting the objectName property accordingly. Then we save the file as filedialog.ui in a separate dialog called filedialog.

8.2.2 Implementing the Functionality of the File Selection Dialog

After giving the standard include guards in the header file filedialog.h, which contains the declaration of the FileDialog class, we #include each class definition that uic generates from the UI file created by the Designer. The forward class declarations prevent the need to read in the corresponding header files for those classes at this point:

```
// filedialog/filedialog.h

#ifndef FILEDIALOG_H
#define FILEDIALOG_H
```

```
#include "ui_filedialog.h"

class QModelIndex;
class QDirModel;
class QItemSelectionModel;

class FileDialog: public QDialog, private Ui::FileDialog {
  Q_OBJECT
  public:
    FileDialog(QWidget *parent = 0);
...
  private:
    QItemSelectionModel *selModel;
    QDirModel *dirModel;
};

#endif // FILEDIALOG_H
```

As well as QDirModel, we now require a *selection model*, which manages and compares the selections for the views assigned to it. Accordingly we create a QItemSelectionModel in addition to the directory model in the FileDialog constructor, after we have called setupUi() to initialize the Designer-generated widgets. To do this we assign the directory model to the QItemSelectionModel constructor. This way, the selection model knows the data source, and as such can manage the entries.

Now we assign all views the same model, via setModel() and the same selection model via setSelectionModel(). The latter step ensures that the same selections are switched on for all three views: If you select several files in one view, these automatically appear highlighted in the other two views as well:

```
// filedialog/filedialog.cpp

#include <QtGui>
#include "filedialog.h"

FileDialog::FileDialog(QWidget *parent)
  : QDialog(parent)
{
  setupUi(this);

  dirModel = new QDirModel;
  selModel = new QItemSelectionModel(dirModel);

  listView->setModel(dirModel);
  treeView->setModel(dirModel);
  iconView->setModel(dirModel);

  listView->setSelectionModel(selModel);
  treeView->setSelectionModel(selModel);
```

```
iconView->setSelectionModel(selModel);

QModelIndex cwdIndex =
    dirModel->index(QDir::rootPath());

listView->setRootIndex(cwdIndex);
treeView->setRootIndex(cwdIndex);
iconView->setRootIndex(cwdIndex);
```

The views still require an entry point for the model, however, which we set using setRootIndex(). This function expects a QModelIndex as an argument, but we are using the semantics of the filesystem here. To mediate between these two "worlds" we use the overloaded index() method from QDirModel as a "translator": This accepts a path, searches for the matching index in the model, and returns it.

Then we fill the combo box generated in the Designer with the base directories (Windows) or the root directory (Linux). Because QDir::rootPath() consists of drive C: in Windows, the question arises, how do we obtain a list of all available drives? As an answer, we recommend a brief digression on the way models function in general and how QDirModel functions in particular.

Figure 8.9:
The structure of a
model using the
example of QDirModel

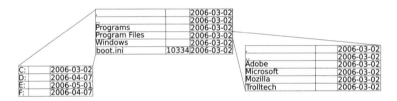

A model basically has two dimensions: In a QDirModel each row corresponds to one file entry, whereas each of the columns contains one file property (name, size, date of creation). If a file entry also points to a valid QModelIndex, this corresponds to a subdirectory. As can be seen in Figure 8.9, this forms a third dimension, as it were. Although the list and table views cannot display this additional level of structure, the tree views visually represent data items from the source (i.e., the filesystem) that are themselves valid QModelIndex objects as subtrees. This explains the code that appears next in the constructor of the file dialog:

```
// filedialog/filedialog.cpp (continued)

for (int r = 0; r < dirModel->rowCount(QModelIndex()); ++r) {
  QModelIndex index = dirModel->index(r, 0, QModelIndex());
  if (index.isValid())
    comboBox->addItem(dirModel->fileIcon(index),
      dirModel->filePath(index));
}
```

An invalid (i.e., empty) QModelIndex means that the model should select the root level in the filesystem as the start index. In our case this level contains all the drives in Windows, and only the directory tree root in Linux. We determine the number of drive entries via rowCount(), so that with this knowledge we can iterate through all entries. For this purpose we use the zeroth column, since QModelIndex provides us with the desired information at these positions. To be on the safe side, we check whether the index really is valid. In this case we add an entry for the corresponding drive to the combo box.

To be able to work with the models, we require a number of slots, which we declare in the header following the declaration of the constructor:

```
// filedialog/filedialog.h (replenished)
...
  protected slots:
    void switchToDir(const QModelIndex& index);
    void syncActive(const QModelIndex& index);
    void switchView();
...
```

switchToDir() should react to clicks and update the other list views so that they also show the directory selected. syncActive() compares the *active* entry, that is, the one highlighted in color in all three views, and opens at the corresponding branch in the tree view, while switchView() reacts to the toggle button and runs through the views stacked on top of each other in the stacked widget.

We now need to connect each of these new slots in the constructor with the activated() signal of all three views. switchToDir() and syncActive() require the QModelIndex as an argument, which references the new directory. Finally we instruct Qt to call the switchView() slot if there is a click on the switchButton defined in the Designer:

```
// filedialog/filedialog.cpp (continued)

  connect(listView, SIGNAL(activated(const QModelIndex&)),
            SLOT(switchToDir(const QModelIndex&)));
  connect(treeView, SIGNAL(activated(const QModelIndex&)),
            SLOT(switchToDir(const QModelIndex&)));
  connect(iconView, SIGNAL(activated(const QModelIndex&)),
            SLOT(switchToDir(const QModelIndex&)));

  connect(listView, SIGNAL(clicked(const QModelIndex&)),
            SLOT(syncActive(const QModelIndex&)));
  connect(treeView, SIGNAL(clicked(const QModelIndex&)),
            SLOT(syncActive(const QModelIndex&)));
  connect(iconView, SIGNAL(clicked(const QModelIndex&)),
            SLOT(syncActive(const QModelIndex&)));
```

```
    connect(switchButton, SIGNAL(clicked()), SLOT(switchView()));
}
```

The constructor is now finished, and we can turn our attention to the implementation of the slots: In switchToDir() we first check to see whether the index passed really is a directory. The appropriate method is contained in QDirModel itself. If this is the case, we set the start index in the model to the new directory. Note: We do not need to switch over to the tree view, since this type of view should always display the entire drive contents. Since the tree view uses the same selection model as the other views, it automatically shows the selected entries:

```
// filedialog/filedialog.cpp (continued)

void FileDialog::switchToDir(const QModelIndex& index)
{
    if (dirModel->isDir(index)) {
        listView->setRootIndex(index);
        iconView->setRootIndex(index);
    }
}
```

syncActive() compares the active entry in all three views. The corresponding API call in QAbstractItemView is setCurrentIndex():

```
// filedialog/filedialog.cpp (continued)

void FileDialog::syncActive(const QModelIndex& index)
{
    listView->setCurrentIndex(index);
    treeView->setCurrentIndex(index);
    iconView->setCurrentIndex(index);
}
```

The slot to switch through the views is just one line in length: It queries the index of the current widget and increases this by one. To ensure that the index does not become larger than the number of views, we insert a modulo operation (when the value becomes greater than the index of the last view, we should land back in the first view, which has index zero):

```
// filedialog/filedialog.cpp (continued)

void FileDialog::switchView()
{
    stackedWidget->setCurrentIndex(
        (stackedWidget->currentIndex()+1)%stackedWidget->count());
}
```

Finally, we make the selected files available to the user. To do this we define a method called selectedFiles(). After the dialog ends—when the user clicks Open (the Designer has already linked the corresponding signal to the accept() slot)—you can read out the selected filenames (together with their paths) as a QStringList using this FileDialog method:

```
// filedialog/filedialog.cpp (continued)

QStringList FileDialog::selectedFiles()
{
  QStringList fileNames;
  QModelIndexList indexes = selModel->selectedIndexes();
  foreach( QModelIndex index, indexes )
    fileNames.append( dirModel->filePath(index) );
  return fileNames;
}
```

Which entries are returned is revealed by the selection model: selectedIndexes() returns the selected QModelIndex entries from the QDirModel instance. With the filePath() method provided by the model, we can obtain the file paths.

8.3 The String Lists Model

Simple, text-based lists are presented in Interview via the QStringListModel class. This operates on a string list that it displays in a column. Each entry in the list thus corresponds to a row in the model.

The following example deposits a shopping list into a string list and passes it to the model. As soon as we assign the string list model to the list view, it displays the list entries:

```
// stringlistenmodell/main.cpp

#include <QtGui>

int main(int argc, char* argv[])
{
  QApplication app(argc, argv);
  QStringListModel model;
  QStringList toBuy;
  toBuy << "butter" << "milk"
       << "cherries" << "bananas";
  model.setStringList(toBuy);
  QListView view;
  view.setModel(&model);
  view.show();
  return app.exec();
}
```

The model also has write access to the data source: If the user changes an entry in the view (perhaps by clicking an entry and typing something in the editor that then appears), the model writes the changes back to the string list, which can be read out again at any time with the stringList() method.

8.4   Implementing Your Own Models

The best way to understand how models are constructed is to create your own model. Initially, it should only read data from a source and display this in a view. Later we will make it writable, so that changes to the view will cause the data source to be updated.

8.4.1   An Address Book Model

Our example model should read an address book from a CSV file. Such a data source is formatted as follows:

```
''title (column 1)'', ''title (column 2)'', ...,''title (column n)''
''value'', ''value'', ..., ''value''
''value'', ''value'', ..., ''value''
''value'', ''value'', ..., ''value''
```

We regard this data as specifying a table, where the first line reveals the column headings, and all subsequent lines contain the entries in each of the rows. Because a two-dimensional table should be formed from this file, we use QAbstractTable-Model as the base class, since, in contrast to QAbstractItemModel, it implements an index() method that is suitable for a list whose items have several columns.

The constructor in our model, defined in addressbookmodel.cpp, receives the entire address book as a QString. In order to work with this, we split it up into the individual lines of data (using QString::split(), specifying the newline character, n, as a field separator). Our model will represent the address book internally as a QList<QStringList> called addressBook, in which each string list in the QList is a dataset corresponding to one address. Given a line of address book data, the help function splitCSVLine() separates the line into the components of the address, removes the quote characters, and returns the resulting dataset. The constructor uses this helper function to turn each of the lines of address book data into a dataset and packs them into a QList, thus producing the data structure we desire:

```
// addressbook/addressbookmodel.cpp

#include <QtGui>
#include "addressbookmodel.h"
```

```
QStringList splitCSVLine(const QString& line)
{
  bool inItem = false;
  QStringList items;
  QString item;

  for (int pos = 0; pos < line.length(); pos++)
  {
    QChar c = line.at(pos);
    if ( c == '\'') {
      if (inItem) {
        items.append(item);
        item = "";
      }
      inItem = !inItem;
    }
    else
      if (inItem) {
          item += c;
      }
  }
  return items;
}

AddressbookModel::AddressbookModel(const QString& addresses,
 QObject *parent): QAbstractTableModel(parent)
{
  QStringList records = addresses.split('\n');
  QStringList line;
  foreach(QString record, records)
      addressBook.append(splitCSVLine(record));
}
```

We know that our model manages $n - 1$ datasets, where n is the number of rows of actual data in the CSV file, since the first line of the CSV file contains the column names. In addition, CSV files finish with an unused empty line. The number of data lines (*rows*) is therefore exactly two less than the total number of lines in the CSV file.

A view can use the rowCount() method to find out the number of rows of data contained in the model. Since the reference to the parent QModelIndex passed via the parent parameter variable is not needed—after all, this is just a flat two-dimensional model—we can suppress any irritating compiler warnings using the Q_UNUSED macro, which in addition serves to explicitly document that we do not want to use the variable:

```
// addressbook/addressbookmodel.cpp (continued)

int AddressbookModel::rowCount(const QModelIndex &parent ) const
{
```

```
    Q_UNUSED(parent);
    return addressBook.count() - 2;
}
```

To determine the number of columns, we look at the dataset from the first line of the CSV file. The QStringList::count() method is used to determine the number of strings in the string list that contains the dataset corresponding to the first line of the file, obtained from addressBook by invoking at(0):

```
// addressbook/addressbookmodel.cpp (continued)

int AddressbookModel::columnCount(const QModelIndex &parent ) const
{
    Q_UNUSED(parent);
    return addressBook.at(0).count();
}
```

Views that use our address book model can discover the labeling of the rows and columns via the headerData() method. To do so, they must specify the numeric position of the *section* of data for which the heading is desired, where a section is either a row or a column—whether the desired heading is a row heading or a column heading is decided by the value given for the orientation. This is of the enumeration type Qt::Orientation and has the possible values Qt::Vertical or Qt::Horizontal.

When it comes to roles, in this example we are interested only in supporting the DisplayRole, which is used when the view needs the text to be displayed. Everything else we pass on to the implementation of the overclass. QAbstractTableModel does more than just return empty QVariants: If we had not reimplemented headerData(), it would number all the rows and columns. In order to ensure that we can use the model later with a QTableView that also queries row descriptions, we call the headerData() function of the overclass, particularly in case the orientation is *not* horizontal. This means that by default, a label to the left of the datasets will denote the dataset number. For horizontal orientation we use the entries from the first dataset in the list, which as we know contains the column names:

```
// addressbook/addressbookmodel.cpp (continued)

QVariant AddressbookModel::headerData(int section,
                        Qt::Orientation orientation, int role) const
{
  if (orientation == Qt::Horizontal) {
    if (role == Qt::DisplayRole) {
      return addressBook.at(0).at(section);
    }
  }
  return QAbstractTableModel::headerData(section, orientation, role);
}
```

Finally, the model delivers actual data to a view via the data() method. As arguments we pass a QModelIndex, which contains the position requested by the view, and the requested role:

```
// addressbook/addressbookmodel.cpp (continued)

QVariant AddressbookModel::data(const QModelIndex &index,
                                              int role) const
{
  if (!index.isValid()) return QVariant();
  QStringList addressRecord = addressBook.at(index.row()+1);
  if (role == Qt::DisplayRole || role == Qt::EditRole) {
    return addressRecord.at(index.column());
  }
  if (role == Qt::ToolTipRole) {
    QString tip, key, value;
    tip = "<table>";
    int maxLines = addressRecord.count();
    for (int i = 0; i < maxLines; i++) {
        key = headerData(i, Qt::Horizontal, Qt::DisplayRole)
                                        .toString();
        value = addressRecord.at(i);
        if (!value.isEmpty())
            tip += QString("<tr><td><b>%1</b>: %2</td></tr>")
                                        .arg(key, value);
    }
    tip += "</table>";
    return tip;
  }
  return QVariant();
}
```

First we check that the index passed is valid—a good practice that prevents nasty crashes in Interview programming, since out-of-range indices can always occur.

Then we retrieve the desired dataset from the list. In doing this we access the dataset following the one in the row specified by the index—after all, the column headings are in the first row.

We deliver an address dataset ourselves if the view asks for data in the DisplayRole. To extract this, we proceed in almost exactly the same way as before when reading out the headings, with one difference: We localize the dataset via the row() detail of the index.

Since the model is supposed to be editable, we must also handle the situation in which the view asks for data in the EditRole: Because the same text should appear later on in the editor as in the DisplayRole, we handle the EditRole- and Qt::DisplayRole queries in one go.

To make the example a little more interesting, we will also implement the ToolTip-Role at this point. A *tooltip* is a yellow box that contains a description of a view element and appears if you linger over it with the mouse. In the tooltip for a list entry, our address book view will show the components of the dataset corresponding to that entry, as depicted in Figure 8.10. It is our aim to display only the nonempty components in the dataset.

Figure 8.10:
Thanks to the
treatment of the
ToolTipRole, *the views*
now show an
individual tooltip
when the mouse
lingers over an entry.

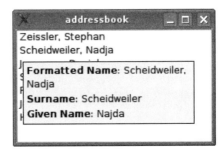

HTML formatting can be used in tooltip texts, and we construct the description of the address book entry using the <table> tag. Each row of the table consists of two cells, one of which contains the name of the address book field (the key) and the other, the matching value. Both of them will be shown in the tooltip only if the value is not the empty string. We obtain the key by calling the headerData() method just implemented, and we obtain the value by reading it out of the current dataset. We format the cells using the <tr> and <td> tags and append the resulting HTML phrase to the string that we started previously with the table tag. Finally, when all of the fields of the dataset have been processed, we complete the tooltip text string by appending the closing </table> tag, and return the finished string.

We will now write a program to test our model. This reads in the CSV file, allocates a model, and passes the file's contents to the model as a QString. We then bind the model to a list view, a table view, and a tree view. The result is shown in Figure 8.11.

```cpp
// addressbook/main.cpp

#include <QtGui>
#include "addressbookmodel.h"

int main( int argc, char* argv[] )
{
  QApplication app( argc, argv );

  // Open the addressbook file in the working directory
  QFile file("addressbook.csv");
  if ( !file.open(QIODevice::ReadOnly|QIODevice::Text) )
        return 1;

  // Read its content into a string
  QString addresses = QString::fromUtf8(file.readAll());
```

```
AddressbookModel model(addresses);

QListView listView;
listView.setModel(&model);
listView.setModelColumn(0);
listView.show();

QTreeView treeView;
treeView.setModel(&model);
treeView.show();

QTableView tableView;
tableView.setModel(&model);
tableView.show();

return app.exec();
}
```

The column to be displayed by the list view can be selected from the model with a setModelColumn() instruction; for example, setModelColumn(2) would display all first names instead of the formatted name.

Figure 8.11:
These three views use
our address book
model.

If a model you have written yourself does not turn out to work as you wished, you should first check whether the overridden const methods have been declared properly. Since they should merely provide information about the model, Interview does not give them any write access to the class. If the const keyword is missing, the correct method will not be available, because the inheritance mechanism of C++ makes a distinction between const and non-const versions of a method.

8.4.2   Making Your Own Models Writable

Just outputting data in the EditRole is not enough if you want to modify the data source via the model. In order to be able do this, we need to overwrite the flags() and setData() methods.

flags() returns specific properties of an index entry, so-called *flags* (see Table 8.2). Views use this method to check whether operations are allowed for a specific item.

Table 8.2:	Value	Effect
ItemFlags for models	Qt::ItemIsSelectable	Element can be selected
	Qt::ItemIsEditable	Element can be modified
	Qt::ItemIsDragEnabled	Element can be used as a starting point for drag-and-drop operations
	Qt::ItemIsDropEnabled	Element can be used as a target for drag-and-drop operations
	Qt::ItemIsUserCheckable	Element has a selection status with two states (selected, deselected); requires the implementation of Qt::CheckStateRole in the model
	Qt::ItemIsEnabled	Element reacts to user requests
	Qt::ItemIsTristate	Element has a selection status with three states (selected, not selected, partially selected); useful in hierarchical models where several child entries are selected and others not selected; requires the implementation of Qt::CheckStateRole in the model in advance

We will come back to the services of this method on page 241, when we equip our model with drag-and-drop capability for data. Here we must first make all the cells editable:

```
// addressbook/addressbookmodel.cpp (continued)

Qt::ItemFlags AddressbookModel::flags(const QModelIndex &index) const
{
    if (!index.isValid())
        return 0;

    return QAbstractItemModel::flags(index) | Qt::ItemIsEditable;
}
```

Now the user can edit every position. To do this, the views use a QItemDelegate by default, just as for the display. Once it has finished its work, it calls the setData() method to store the new data in the model. As soon as this has stored the data successfully in the model, it returns true.

setData() is the counterpart to data(): Both functions must work together. Since the standard implementation of setData() does nothing more than return false, we need to reimplement it as follows:

```
// addressbook/addressbookmodel.cpp (continued)
```

```
bool AddressbookModel::setData(const QModelIndex & index,
                               const QVariant& value, int role)
{
  if (index.isValid() && (role == Qt::EditRole ||
                          role == Qt::DisplayRole)) {
    // add 1 to the row index to skip over the header
    addressBook[index.row()+1][index.column()] = value.toString();
    emit dataChanged(index, index);
    return true;
  }
  return false;
}
```

First we check, as always, whether the index is valid. This time we also ensure that we are located in the editing or in the display role. We do not have to make a distinction between these two roles for our address book model, because in both cases the same string is involved. Other models may need to make a distinction between the two roles; for example, when delivering or updating image data, a model may need to work with actual pixmaps for the DisplayRole, but with paths to pixmaps when in the EditRole.

If these conditions apply, we set the new value, passed via value, at the appropriate point. Here we use the index operator [], instead of at() as usual, in order to avoid the normally desirable behavior of at(): The method provides only a const reference to the string, whereas the index operator provides a simple reference.[5]

After successfully changing the data, it is important that the dataChanged() signal is emitted so that the views linked to the model update the data. This demands two indices as parameters, of which the row and column properties should form a rectangle. Because usually only one value is being changed at a time, we pass the same index twice in order to indicate the position of the corrected data item. Finally we signal the successful completion of the process with return true. In all other cases, in which we have not saved anything, we consequently return false.

Inserting and Removing Rows

So that the model will be completely flexible, we implement the insertion and removal of rows. To do this we overwrite the insertRows() and removeRows() methods. The equivalent removeColumns() and addColumns() methods also exist to remove or insert columns, but we are not concerned with these at this point. As parameters we pass an index to the row beneath which we wish to insert empty rows, as well as the number of rows to be inserted. We can safely ignore the parent argument.

To insert an empty row, we first need to create an empty dataset. To do this we fill a string list with as many empty strings as there are columns in the model. Then we

---

[5] On this subject, see also page 400 in Appendix B.

inform the model, with beginInsertRows(), that we want to insert rows. If we do not do this, existing selections in this model could get mixed up. Next, we insert the empty dataset—again incrementing the row by 1 because of the header—and end the insert mode. Finally, we signal that the data have been successfully inserted, by returning true:

```
// addressbook/addressbookmodel.cpp (continued)

bool AddressbookModel::insertRows(int row, int count,
                                      const QModelIndex & parent)
{
  Q_UNUSED(parent);
  QStringList emptyRecord;
  for (int i=0; i<columnCount(QModelIndex()); i++)
    emptyRecord.append(QString());
  beginInsertRows(QModelIndex(), row, row+count-1);
  for (int i=0; i<count; i++)
    addressBook.insert(row+1, emptyRecord);
  endInsertRows();

  return true;
}
```

We implement removeRows() in the same way, but with a safety check in this case: If there are more lines to be removed than there are datasets in the address book, we return false—otherwise, we would run the risk of the application crashing. We also need to announce the removal of lines and signal the end of the action. If everything was successful, we return true to the caller as a confirmation:

```
// addressbook/addressbookmodel.cpp (continued)

bool AddressbookModel::removeRows(int row, int count,
                                      const QModelIndex& parent)
{
  Q_UNUSED(parent);
  if (row-count-1 > addressBook.count()-1) return false;
  beginRemoveRows(QModelIndex(), row, row+count-1);
  for(int i=0; i<count; i++)
    addressBook.removeAt(row+1);
  endRemoveRows();
  return true;
}
```

With these changes, a program that accesses the model can delete datasets by calling removeRows() or add them by inserting empty datasets with insertRows() and filling them via setData()—the method is not reserved just for delegates.

Outputting the Contents of the Model

In order to round off our model and to complete our tour through the world of writable models, we construct a method called toString(), which converts the contents of the model back into CSV form and outputs this as a string.

To do this we go through all the datasets and use the QStringList method join to combine each string list into a single line in which the individual strings are separated from one another with commas (,). We terminate each line with a newline character before beginning the next line, which ensures that the desired empty line at the end of the CSV file is created:

```
// addressbook/addressbookmodel.cpp (continued)

QString AddressbookModel::toString() const
{
    QString ab;
    foreach (QStringList record, addressBook) {
      ab += "\"";
      record.join("\",\"");
      ab += "\"\n";
    }
    return ab;
}
```

To save the current status of the model, you now only need to save the return value from toString().

8.5 Sorting and Filtering Data with Proxy Models

Our model up until now has lacked the capability to return its entries to a view in a sorted form. This is because there is no sorting criterion in this model for any of the columns. It is also practically impossible to filter out specific entries from the model.

To address this shortcoming, Interview has provided, starting from Qt version 4.1, the QSortFilterProxyModel class, after its predecessor QProxyModel proved to be too unwieldy. It is based on the QAbstractProxyModel base class, which represents so-called *proxy models*. These lie somewhere between a model and view, obtaining their data from the model and returning it to the view in modified form (see Figure 8.14 on page 237). The proxy model therefore becomes the source model for the view. On page 237 we will look in more detail at how proxy models function and implement our own proxy model. For the moment, we will just look at what QSortFilterProxyModel can do: sort and filter.

During filtering, the model returns the model indices for those rows in which the text in a column matches the search filter. During sorting, the row order is arranged according to the values in a specified column, whereby you can sort in ascending or descending order.

We will demonstrate both capabilities of QSortFilterProxyModel with a small example, the FilteringView. This consists of a tree view, above which is a line edit that accepts a filter term. Next to this we place a combo box containing all the column names. Figure 8.12 shows how you can use this to select the column that is to act as the search column.

Figure 8.12:
QSortFilterProxyModel
helps in sorting and
filtering models.

8.5.1 Adjustments to the User Interface

Simplifying Sorting

Since our view will use a QSortFilterProxyModel instance, which can already sort, we need only to adjust the viewer accordingly. The work necessary for this is done by the constructor of the class:

```cpp
// addressbook/filteringview.cpp

#include <QtGui>
#include "filteringview.h"

FilteringView::FilteringView(QAbstractItemModel *model, QWidget *parent)
    : QWidget(parent)
{
    setWindowTitle(tr("Filter View"));
    proxyModel = new QSortFilterProxyModel(this);
    proxyModel->setSourceModel(model);

    QVBoxLayout *lay = new QVBoxLayout(this);
    QHBoxLayout *hlay = new QHBoxLayout;
    QLineEdit *edit = new QLineEdit;
    QComboBox *comboBox = new QComboBox;

    int modelIndex = model->columnCount(QModelIndex());
    for(int i=0; i < modelIndex; i++)
```

```
comboBox->addItem(model->headerData(i, Qt::Horizontal,
                            Qt::DisplayRole).toString()));


hlay->addWidget(edit);
hlay->addWidget(comboBox);

QTreeView *view = new QTreeView;
view->setModel(proxyModel);
view->setAlternatingRowColors(true);

// Make the header "clickable"
view->header()->setClickable(true);
// Sort Indicator festlegen
view->header()->setSortIndicator(0, Qt::AscendingOrder);
// Sort Indicator anzeigen
view->header()->setSortIndicatorShown(true);
// Initial sortieren
view->sortByColumn(0);

lay->addLayout(hlay);
lay->addWidget(view);

connect(edit, SIGNAL(textChanged(const QString&)),
    proxyModel, SLOT(setFilterWildcard(const QString&)));

connect(comboBox, SIGNAL(activated(int)),
            SLOT(setFilterKeyColumn(int)));
}
```

First we create a proxy model and save it in a member variable called proxyModel. Then we create both a vertical and a horizontal layout used later to enclose the widgets: We group the line edit and the combo box together in one line with the horizontal layout. With the help of the vertical layout, we position this above the view to which we pass the proxy model as the source.

To make reading easier, every other line in the tree view is displayed with a second background color. We activate this feature with setAlternatingRowColors(true).

To obtain the widget containing the column headers in tree views, we use header(). So that it can react to clicks, we set setClickable(true). In addition we provide it with a *sorting indicator*, usually this is a triangle that charts whether data is shown sorted in ascending or descending order. In this case we sort column 0 in ascending order (Qt::AscendingOrder) and display the indicator via setSortIndicatorShown(true). To make sure that the list is already sorted before the user clicks the header for the first time, we prearrange the datasets sorted by the first column, with sortByColumn(0).

Restricting the View to Specific Datasets

In order to restrict the data shown in the view to datasets matching a filter string specified in the line edit widget, two connect() instructions are needed: The first one informs the proxy model as soon as the text changes in the line edit. The proxy model then uses this text as the new filter.

There are three slots in the proxy model to which the textChanged() signal can be linked. setFilterFixedString() delivers all rows where the search column contains the specified filter string as a substring, whereas setFilterWildcard()—which we use in the example—also accepts * as a wildcard in the filter string. For example, when setFilterWildcard() is used, the search term Hel*ld would match a dataset in the model with "Hello world" in the search column. A search for Hel*ld using setFilter-FixedString() will return only datasets that contain the exact six-character string Hel*ld.

setFilterRegExp() accepts filter strings that are regular expressions. Using Hel*ld as a search string, it will return rows of which the search column contains one of the following substrings: Held, Helld, Hellld, Helllld and so on.

The second signal/slot connection is used to select the field which the proxy model should compare against the filter string. For this purpose the proxy model has the setFilterKeyColumn() method, which expects the search column as the argument. Since this method is unfortunately not implemented as a slot, we must implement our own slot in the view, which will call the function:

```
// addressbook/filteringview.cpp (continued)

void FilteringView::setFilterKeyColumn(int col) {
  proxyModel->setFilterKeyColumn(col);
}
```

The slot is also the reason we created the proxyModel member variable: We require access to the proxy model outside the constructor.

8.6   Making Entries Selectable with Checkboxes

If it is intended that the user should make a selection from a list, Interview places a box in front of the corresponding entries that can be checked via the QItemDelegate used by default, a *checkbox*. We make use of this property in a new subclass of our address book model, the CheckableAddressbookModel subclass.

To implement selectable entries, we need to reimplement only three methods, apart from the constructor: In flags() we inform the view that specific entries can be selected. In order for the delegate to draw the checkbox, we need to use a new role in data() and setData()—the CheckStateRole.

```
// addressbook/checkableaddressbookmodel.h

class CheckableAddressbookModel : public AddressbookModel
{
  Q_OBJECT
  public:
    CheckableAddressbookModel(const QString& addresses,
                              QObject *parent = 0);
    virtual QVariant data ( const QModelIndex & index,
                            int role = Qt::DisplayRole ) const;
    virtual bool setData(const QModelIndex & index,
                      const QVariant & value, int role = Qt::EditRole);
    virtual Qt::ItemFlags flags(const QModelIndex &index) const;
  private:
    QList<bool> checkedStates;
};
```

In the constructor we first call the constructor of the overclass, passing it the complete dataset as a string (addresses), as well as the parent widget. We then have to find out how many datasets the passed string contains. Equipped with this value, we can keep track of the selection status of the respective line in the checkedStates list.

We can find out the number of datasets through the number of newline characters. Only those datasets should be selectable that really contain address data—so not the first line with the headers:

```
// addressbook/checkableaddressbookmodel.cpp

CheckableAddressbookModel::CheckableAddressbookModel(
                    const QString& addresses, QObject *parent)
 : AddressbookModel(addresses, parent)
{
  // Contrary to what we've done in the AddressbookModel,
  // we don't add 1 to the index here
  // since the headers can't be checked by the user
  int rows = addresses.count('\n');
  for ( int i = 0; i < rows; i++) {
    checkedStates.append(false);
  }
}
```

In the reimplementation of flags() we first catch invalid indices again. So that there is not a checkbox in front of every single column entry, only the entries in the first column are selectable, standing for the whole line. For this reason we check the index and allow the additional status only in column 0. It is important here to consult the base implementation, AddressbookModel::flags(index), because this, among other things, ensures that it is editable. Provided that we are in the first column, we apply a bitwise logical OR operation with Qt::ItemIsUserCheckable to the existing flags. This operation combines the flags with each other:

```
// addressbook/checkableaddressbookmodel.cpp (continued)

Qt::ItemFlags CheckableAddressbookModel::flags
                               (const QModelIndex &index) const {
    if (!index.isValid())
       return 0;

    if (index.column() == 0)
      return AddressbookModel::flags(index)| Qt::ItemIsUserCheckable;
    else
      return AddressbookModel::flags(index);
}
```

Then we implement data(). If the caller is located in the first column and queries the model while in the CheckStateRole, we look up the status of the current row (index.row()) in the checkedStates list. If the checkbox is selected, the corresponding element is true, which we signal by returning Qt::Checked; otherwise, if it is false, we return Qt::Unchecked. In all other cases we retrieve the return value from the overclass:

```
// addressbook/checkableaddressbookmodel.cpp (continued)

QVariant CheckableAddressbookModel::data(
                      const QModelIndex &index, int role) const
{
    if (!index.isValid()) return QVariant();

    if (role == Qt::CheckStateRole && index.column() == 0) {
      if (checkedStates[index.row()] == true)
        return Qt::Checked;
      else
        return Qt::Unchecked;
    }
    return AddressbookModel::data(index,role);
}
```

Although QItemDelegate now draws a checkbox for every row, the user can still not change its status. This only works if setData() has been implemented accordingly:

```
// addressbook/checkableaddressbookmodel.cpp (continued)

bool CheckableAddressbookModel::setData(const QModelIndex & index,
                                 const QVariant& value, int role)
{
    if (!index.isValid()) return false;

    if (role == Qt::CheckStateRole && index.column() == 0) {
      checkedStates[index.row()] = !checkedStates[index.row()];
      emit dataChanged(index, index);
```

```
        return true;
    }

    return AddressbookModel::setData(index, value, role);
}
```

Here we also check whether the role is correct and whether we are located in the first column. If everything is all right, we negate the status of the list element at the relevant position. In order for the views to display the changed value, we trigger the dataChanged() signal for the index when we are finished, just as we did in the overclass. We forward all other calls to the overclass, as we did for the other two methods.

To try out the model we have just completed, we change the main() program so that it instantiates our new model instead of the AddressbookModel overclass, and adjust the #include compiler directive accordingly. The results can be seen in Figure 8.13.

Figure 8.13:
CheckableAddress-bookModel *inserts a checkbox for each row.*

8.7 Designing Your Own Proxy Models

With QSortFilterProxyModel we have already gotten to know one class that inherits from QAbstractProxyModel. But proxy models can also display the original models in very different ways. To demonstrate this we will write our own proxy model that swaps the columns and rows of the original model in a way similar to the matrix transpose operation in mathematics.

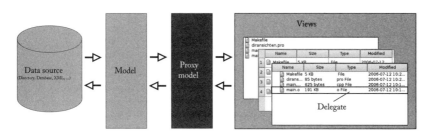

Figure 8.14:
Proxy models lie between the original model and the view.

First we will start with the constructor: Since we are not using additional data structures of our own, it remains empty and merely initializes the overclass:

```
// addressbook/transposeproxymodel.cpp

TransposeProxyModel::TransposeProxyModel(QObject *parent)
  : QAbstractProxyModel(parent)
{
}
```

The two methods that follow define how the data from the source model are arranged in the proxy model: mapFromSource() converts an index from the source model to an index for the proxy model, while mapToSource() converts an index from the proxy model to an index for the source model. In the mapFromSource() implementation we fetch the index using the method of the same name, but pass column() as the row number and row() as the column number. mapToSource() works in exactly the same way, but calls the index() method of the source model, in case the source model index has been manipulated:

```
// addressbook/transposeproxymodel.cpp (continued)

QModelIndex TransposeProxyModel::mapFromSource(
                        const QModelIndex& sourceIndex) const
{
  return index(sourceIndex.column(), sourceIndex.row());
}

QModelIndex TransposeProxyModel::mapToSource(
                        const QModelIndex& proxyIndex) const
{
  return sourceModel()->index(proxyIndex.column(), proxyIndex.row());
}
```

But we are still not finished, because QAbstractProxyModel inherits directly from QAbstractItemModel. This means that we must also implement all of its methods. Take index(), for example. Since we are planning a normal, two-dimensional model, we use the createIndex() function to generate the index. Columns and rows must not be swapped here, since the this would undo the mappings to and from the source:

```
// addressbook/transposeproxymodel.cpp (continued)

QModelIndex TransposeProxyModel::index(int row, int column,
                        const QModelIndex& parent) const
{
  Q_UNUSED(parent);
  return createIndex(row, column);
}
```

We also have to implement the parent() method. But since our proxy model only supports two-dimensional models, and therefore does not support parent relations, we return an invalid index here:

```
// addressbook/transposeproxymodel.cpp (continued)

QModelIndex TransposeProxyModel::parent(
                            const QModelIndex& index) const
{
  Q_UNUSED(index);
  return QModelIndex();
}
```

Next we reimplement rowCount() and columnCount(). The view uses these functions to determine which indices it should query. For our purposes, rowCount() should call the source model's columnCount(), and vice versa.

```
// addressbook/transposeproxymodel.cpp (continued)

int TransposeProxyModel::rowCount(const QModelIndex& parent) const
{
  return sourceModel()->columnCount(parent);
}

int TransposeProxyModel::columnCount(const QModelIndex& parent) const
{
  return sourceModel()->rowCount(parent);
}
```

In addition, data() must deliver the correct data. We also fetch this directly from the source model. It is important here that you convert the index correctly, using the previously created mapping methods. Since the passed index originates from the proxy model, we use mapToSource():

```
// addressbook/transposeproxymodel.cpp (continued)

QVariant TransposeProxyModel::data(const QModelIndex& index,
                                      int role) const
{
  if (!index.isValid()) return QVariant();
  return sourceModel()->data(mapToSource(index), role);
}
```

Even if not required (the headerData() method is not completely virtual), it is recommended that you swap the column and row headers. To do this we simply pass the other value of the Orientation enumerator in each case:

```
// addressbook/transposeproxymodel.cpp (continued)

QVariant TransposeProxyModel::headerData(int section,
                        Qt::Orientation orientation, int role) const
{
  if (orientation == Qt::Horizontal)
    return sourceModel()->headerData(section, Qt::Vertical, role);
  else
    return sourceModel()->headerData(section, Qt::Horizontal, role);
}
```

We can now place this model as a proxy model between a table view and our address book model, for example. To do this we first modify the main() program from the original address book example on page 226 by including the header file transposeproxymodel.h, displayed below:

```
// addressbook/transposeproxymodel.h

#ifndef TRANSPOSEPROXYMODEL_H
#define TRANSPOSEPROXYMODEL_H

#include <QAbstractProxyModel>

class TransposeProxyModel : public QAbstractProxyModel {
Q_OBJECT
  public:
    TransposeProxyModel(QObject *parent = 0);

    virtual QModelIndex      mapFromSource(
                        const QModelIndex& sourceIndex) const;
    virtual QModelIndex mapToSource(
                        const QModelIndex& proxyIndex) const;

    virtual QModelIndex index(int, int,
            const QModelIndex& parent = QModelIndex()) const;
    virtual QModelIndex parent(const QModelIndex& index) const;
    virtual int rowCount(const QModelIndex& parent) const;
    virtual int columnCount(const QModelIndex& parent) const;
    virtual QVariant data(const QModelIndex& index,
                        int role = Qt::DisplayRole) const;

    virtual QVariant headerData(int section,
                        Qt::Orientation orientation,
                        int role = Qt::DisplayRole) const;
};
#endif // TRANSPOSEPROXYMODEL_H
```

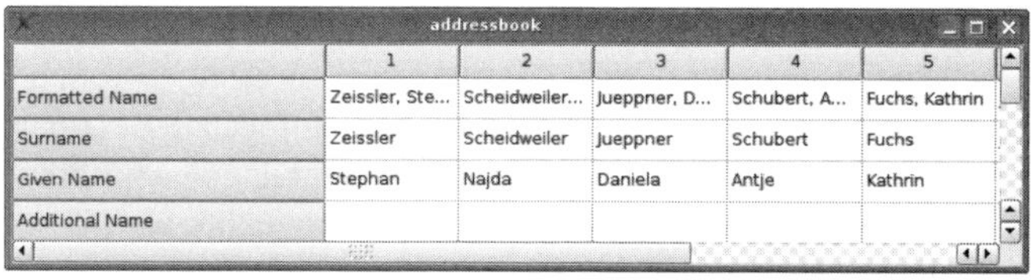

Figure 8.15:
Our proxy model
transposes the
original model.

Then we instantiate the proxy, invoke its setSourceModel() method, passing this a pointer to the original model, and make the proxy model be the source for the view. Figure 8.15 shows the result.

8.8 Implementing Drag and Drop in Models

So far our model is not able to move or copy individual rows via drag and drop. In Section 7.4 we got to know how drag and drop can be implemented for any widgets you like, and Interview also offers the possibility of using elements from views as drag objects. But in contrast to the previous examples, it is *not* necessary here to use inheritance and adjust one of the view classes in this manner. It is sufficient to modify the model.

To demonstrate this we will use a subclass of the already-implemented Address-bookModel class, called DndAddressbookModel.[6] To provide it with drag-and-drop capability, we must now overwrite the following methods:

```
// addressbook/dndaddressbookmodel.h

#ifndef DNDADDRESSBOOKMODEL_H
#define DNDADDRESSBOOKMODEL_H

#include "addressbookmodel.h"

class DndAddressbookModel : public AddressbookModel
{
  public:
    DndAddressbookModel(const QString& addresses, QObject *parent = 0);
    virtual Qt::ItemFlags flags(const QModelIndex &index) const;
    QStringList mimeTypes() const;
    QMimeData *mimeData( const QModelIndexList &indexes ) const;
    bool dropMimeData( const QMimeData *data, Qt::DropAction action,
                int row, int column, const QModelIndex &parent );
```

---

[6] Of course, we could also inherit from CheckableAddressbookModel and extend its functionality, but that would be more complex, and is therefore less suitable for didactic purposes.

```
};
#endif //ADDRESSBOOKMODEL_H
```

In our example implementation, if the user touches any element from a row with the mouse, the entire row will always be copied, so that the dataset remains intact. For this reason the DndAddressbookModel is useless for table views. (Although with a bit more work, it is possible to copy only individual elements, we will not go into this here, to avoid things becoming too complicated.)

In the constructor we do nothing more than forward the arguments to the overclass. Calls such as setDropEnabled() are not necessary here:

```
// addressbook/dndaddressbookmodel.cpp

#include <QtGui>
#include "dndaddressbookmodel.h"

DndAddressbookModel::DndAddressbookModel(const QString& addresses,
                                         QObject *parent)
  : AddressbookModel(addresses, parent)
{
}

Qt::ItemFlags DndAddressbookModel::flags(const QModelIndex &index) const
{
  Qt::ItemFlags defaultFlags = AddressbookModel::flags( index );

  if (index.isValid())
    return Qt::ItemIsDragEnabled | Qt::ItemIsDropEnabled | defaultFlags;
  else
    return Qt::ItemIsDropEnabled | defaultFlags;
}
```

If we want to allow drops, we must signal this for each model index in the flags() method. Whereas we only allow drags from valid model indices, dropping is also possible on invalid ones: If the user releases a drag after the last entry in a list, this position is invalid as a model index, although it can be used to signify that a new element should be appended to the list.

In the next step we define which MIME types can be handled by our model. Here we use our own format called application/x-osp.text.csv, which will save us some work on the next page when copying the entries between two model/view instances:

```
// addressbook/dndaddressbookmodel.cpp (continued)

QStringList DndAddressbookModel::mimeTypes() const
{
  QStringList types;
  types << "application/x-osp.text.csv";
```

```
  return types;
}
```

The mimeData() method comes into play if the user pulls a selection away from the view, thus initiating a drag. We are given a list with the model indices involved. The method should pack them into a QMimeData object, and the instantiation of a QDrag object is taken over by Interview:

```
// addressbook/dndaddressbookmodel.cpp (continued)

QMimeData *DndAddressbookModel::mimeData(
                        const QModelIndexList &indexes) const
{
  QMimeData *mimeData = new QMimeData();

  QList<int> rows;
  foreach (QModelIndex index, indexes)
    if (index.isValid())
      if (!rows.contains(index.row()))
        rows += index.row();

  QByteArray encodedData;
  QDataStream stream(&encodedData, QIODevice::WriteOnly);

  foreach(int row, rows)
      stream << addressBook.at(row+1);

  mimeData->setData("application/x-osp.text.csv", encodedData);
  return mimeData;
}
```

Since we are interested only in complete rows, we extract the respective row numbers from the model indices passed and save them in a list.

In the second step we must find a suitable way of storing our datasets in a QByteArray. Here the QDataStream class is of help, which we will get to know better in Chapter 11 on page 317. It can serialize all primitive data types in Qt via the << operator, including QStringList objects. The byte array encodedData is used here as an output medium, because although QDataStream is intended for output into files and for real output devices, thanks to an overloaded constructor the class can also write to QByteArray objects or read from them. Corresponding to the file semantics, the second parameter QIODevice::WriteOnly indicates that the QDataStream instance stream may only write to the byte array.

Now we go through the just-created rows list and access the corresponding entry of the addressBook structure. To get to the position we really want, we must again access one entry beyond that position.

Each entry found in this way is read via a QDataStream into the byte array encodedData. We pass the finished byte array to the mimeData object. The fact that the contents no longer have to be pure ASCII text after transformation through QDataStream is another reason we cannot use text/plain as MIME types, in addition to the issue of distinguishability during the drop procedure.

The other side of the drag-and-drop procedure is handled by the dropMimeData() method. Apart from the MIME data, it also contains the type of drop: Should the data be copied (CopyAction), moved (MoveAction), linked (LinkAction), or ignored (IgnoreAction)?

Furthermore, we are given both the row and column in which the user released the mouse, thus triggering the drop. Via parent we learn whether the current item is a child of another item. Since this cannot be the case in our childless model, we can ignore parent as well as column, since we are only dragging and dropping entire rows at a time. The method returns true if the drop procedure is successful, otherwise false:

```
// addressbook/dndaddressbookmodel.cpp (continued)

bool DndAddressbookModel::dropMimeData(const QMimeData *data,
                                       Qt::DropAction action, int row,
                                       int column, const QModelIndex &parent)
{

  Q_UNUSED(column);
  Q_UNUSED(parent);

  if (action == Qt::IgnoreAction)
    return true;

  if (!data->hasFormat("application/x-osp.text.csv"))
    return false;

  // workaround for Qt 4.1.2 bug
  if (row == -1)
    row = rowCount();

  QByteArray encodedData = data->data("application/x-osp.text.csv");
  QDataStream stream(&encodedData, QIODevice::ReadOnly);
  QList<QStringList> lines;
  while (!stream.atEnd())
    stream >> lines;


  int rows = lines.count();
  insertRows(row, rows, QModelIndex());
  foreach(QStringList line, lines) {
    addressBook.replace(row+1, line);
    row++;
  }
  return true;
}
```

We react to all actions, but to be on the safe side we catch IgnoreAction. We shouldn't really accept this action. If this happens, though, we announce a successful completion of the drop operation—after all, we successfully ignored the drop. In addition we must ensure that our drag contains the application/x-osp.text.csv MIME type, otherwise we terminate with return false, since the drop action was not successful.

In several Qt versions, including 4.1.2, the problem occurs that row returns the value -1 if the drop target lies beneath the last entry in a list or tree view. For this reason we will intercept this case and return the number of columns in the model so that the new dataset(s) can be inserted after the last row, as intended.

Now we read out the QByteArray for our MIME types. This is the data we obtained by combining the various string list entries. We now reverse that process by reading out the lines list from encodedData, string list by string list, but this time marked as read-only. The use of the atEnd() method demonstrates that we have treated the byte array, through QDataStream, like a file.

Now we can calculate the number of rows to be inserted with count and add them to the model with insertRows(). row provides us with the offset here. Finally we replace the empty string lists created by insertRows() with the real contents. The drag operation is now completed, which we will announce to the caller of the method with return true.

To test our modified model, we replace AddressbookModel with DndAddressbook-Model in the main() function of the address program on page 226 and start two instances of the application. Drag and drop is now possible between them, and also within the same view.

8.9   Your Own Delegates

Until now we have accepted that views display their entries themselves. We will now reveal the secret of the *delegates*, which are responsible for the display of individual elements and for providing an editor for writable models. Each model has exactly one delegate.

All delegates inherit from QAbstractItemDelegate, in the manner of Figure 8.16. By default, all views use the QItemDelegate class derived directly from this, which provides a standard editor and contains the character logic for the entries. We will get to know a similar SQL-specific class called QSqlRelationalDelegate in Chapter 9.

Below we will write a delegate that not only provides an editor like QItemDelegate but also has tab completion and an overview of all existing entries. The current column serves as the data source. In the case of our address book model, this can save the user a great deal of typing work, for example, for frequently occurring first names and family names.

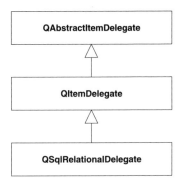

Figure 8.16:
The inheritance
pattern of delegates
in Interview

First we shall look at the constructor: All this has to do is call the constructor of the overclass, because for this model we don't need any member variables that we would have to initialize:

```
// addressbook/completiondelegate.cpp

#include <QtGui>
#include "completiondelegate.h"

CompletionDelegate::CompletionDelegate(QObject *parent)
  : QItemDelegate(parent)
{
}
```

The view calls the createEditor() method when the user launches an editor for the first time from any index position at all, by double-clicking or pressing (F2):

```
// addressbook/completiondelegate.cpp (continued)

QWidget *CompletionDelegate::createEditor(QWidget* parent,
                         const QStyleOptionViewItem& option,
                         const QModelIndex& index ) const
{
  const QAbstractItemModel *model = index.model();
  if (!model)
    return QItemDelegate::createEditor(parent, option, index);

  QComboBox *box = new QComboBox(parent);
  box->setEditable(true);
  box->setAutoCompletion(true);
  box->setModel(const_cast<QAbstractItemModel*>(model));
  box->setModelColumn(index.column());
  box->installEventFilter(const_cast<CompletionDelegate*>(this));
  return box;
}
```

As the processing widget we display a combo box, which can be edited like a line edit, and in addition it should be able to perform tab completion. We use the parent pointer passed as the father for the constructor; as a result, the view, and not the delegate, controls the widget.

To fill the combo box with data, it is sufficient to pass the combo box the current model, because QComboBox, although not an official view class, can handle the QAbstractItemModel-based models as a source. Just as with QListView, here we must also specify the column from the model for which the selection box should look, using setModelColumn().

The const_cast is necessary here because we are in a const method and our model pointer is a const pointer. This means that we must prevent any write operations to the model. In addition we must ensure that certain keys, such as (Enter) or (Esc), close the editor and signal to the delegate that it should write the data back to the model.

This is done by the event filter that we install on the combo box. It diverts all the keystrokes to the delegate. Now we would have to overwrite the eventFilter() method to intercept the keystrokes. In practice, however, QComboBox has such an event filter in the private (that is, internally hidden) QComboBoxPrivateContainer class,[7] which is undocumented, however.

This means that in theory, the filter may disappear in each new Qt release. If you want to be completely sure, you should write your own event filter, based on the implementation of this Qt class.

Figure 8.17:
Our
CompletionDelegate
completes the entry
on the basis of other
entries in the same
column of the source
model.

The editor is now available, but it is possible that the user may want to use it again later on at the same index position. To supply it with current data every time it is used, the setEditorData() method exists. Our combo box serves as an editor widget, which is why we convert the object via qobject_cast:

```
// addressbook/completiondelegate.cpp (continued)

void CompletionDelegate::setEditorData(QWidget* editor,
                           const QModelIndex & index ) const
{
  QComboBox* box = qobject_cast<QComboBox*>(editor);
```

[7] See qcombobox_p.h/qcombobox.cpp in the Qt source code.

```
const QAbstractItemModel *model = index.model();

if (!box || !model)
  QItemDelegate::setEditorData(editor, index);
box->setCurrentIndex(index.row());
}
```

qobject_cast functions like a dynamic_cast but does not require any RTTI support,[8] which many people like to disable for reasons of space, particularly on embedded platforms. In addition it works beyond the borders of dynamic libraries—normally dynamic_cast will not work here. The only consolation: It can only be used for QObject-based classes.

Exactly like a dynamic_cast, qobject_cast also returns a zero pointer if the conversion fails. Although the conversion should never fail, we will intercept this scenario and busy ourselves instead with the base implementation. If everything goes according to plan, we pass the row coordinates of our current position in the model to the combo box. It uses this information at this point as the standard text. Our final task now consists of implementing setModelData(). After a few security checks, we simply set the current contents of the combo box as the new value for the current model index. If you want to be really sure, you should do this both for the DisplayRole and for the EditRole:

```
// addressbook/completiondelegate.cpp (continued)

void CompletionDelegate::setModelData(QWidget *editor,
                                      QAbstractItemModel *model,
                                      const QModelIndex &index) const
{
  if (!index.isValid())
    return;

  QComboBox* box = qobject_cast<QComboBox*>(editor);
  if (!box)
    return QItemDelegate::setModelData(editor, model, index);

  model->setData(index, box->currentText(), Qt::DisplayRole);
  model->setData(index, box->currentText(), Qt::EditRole);
}
```

We can now insert our own delegates into whatever views we want (into our address book as well, or course) using setItemDelegate(). What this looks like is shown in Figure 8.17.

---

[8] RTTI stands for *Runtime Type Information*. It allows the type of a method to be determined in C++. Since RTTI support heavily inflates the size of the object file created, and moc obtains the corresponding information anyway at compile time, you can manage without RTTI support in Qt programs.

8.10 Without Your Own Data Source: The Standard Model

For many purposes, creating your own model would seem to be excessive, as well as quite inconvenient. If you just want to display a few numbers, for example, that do not change or change very little, QStandardItemModel is the right choice. This class has the advantage that it manages without inheritance in most cases, so we can use it directly.

For a small example we will again use our address book model, which we now implement with the help of QStandardItemModel. To demonstrate that the model manages without inheritance, will carry out all tasks in the main() function.

First we again require the splitCSVLine() help function from page 222, which converts a row from the CSV file into a string list:

```
// stdmodeladdressbook/main.cpp

#include <QtGui>

QStringList splitCSVLine(const QString& line)
{
  ...
}
```

The first part of the main() function also appears to be as before: We open the file, read the complete contents into a string, chop off the line ends, and store the result in a string list. We remove the first line of this, with takeAt()—in contrast to removeAt(), takeAt() returns the removed string directly:

```
// stdmodeladdressbook/main.cpp (continued)

int main(int argc, char* argv[])
{
  QApplication app(argc, argv);

  // Open file
  QFile file("addressbook.csv");
  if ( !file.open(QIODevice::ReadOnly|QIODevice::Text) )
        return 1;
  // Read addresses line for line into a stringlist
  QString addresses = QString::fromUtf8(file.readAll());
  QStringList records = addresses.split('\n');

  // Take the first row with the headers and split them
  QString header = records.takeAt(0);
  QStringList headers = splitCSVLine(header);
```

```
// Create a model using the number of rows and columns as arguments
QStandardItemModel model(records.count(), headers.count());

// Add headers
for (int col=0;col<headers.count(); col++) {
   model.setHeaderData(col, Qt::Horizontal, headers.at(col));
}

// Add contents
for (int recNo=0;recNo<records.count(); recNo++) {
   QStringList cells = splitCSVLine(records.at(recNo));
   for (int col=0;col<cells.count(); col++) {
      QModelIndex index = model.index(recNo, col, QModelIndex());
      model.setData(index, cells.at(col));
   }
}

// Create, set and show model
QTreeView treeView;
treeView.setWindowTitle(QObject::tr("Addressbook
                    via QStandardItemModel"));
treeView.setModel(&model);
treeView.show();

return app.exec();
}
```

After we have split the headers, with splitCSVLine(), it is time to instantiate QStandardItemModel with the number of rows and columns as arguments. At this point we have collected enough data to know the maximum number of rows and columns, but we still have to insert the data into the model. This is the next step.

First the headers are included in the model, via setHeaderData(), followed by the actual data. For each element of the model we must create a separate model index. Because we know both the current row and also the current column, this is not a problem. The only disadvantage: We have to manage without the more convenient foreach() loop.

In the final segment of code, we instantiate a tree view, set the model and display the view. Last of all, we start the event loop.

This example demonstrates that Interview can also be used via QStandardItemModel without the need for time-intensive reimplementation of models. In doing this you save all the data in the model, however. For the user, the result is identical. But the procedure does have some disadvantages: With reimplemented models, we can use complex data structures in the background, whereas in this case we must get by with duplicated data in the model, only addressable via QModelIndex.

Writable models thus become very complex, so that in this case you should always choose reimplemented models. If this still seems too time consuming, you should take a look at the element-based views.

8.11 Element-based Views Without Model Access

Qt 3 programmers are used to every element in a view being represented by a separate object. Although this concept is no longer up to date in Qt 4, there is still a use for it in some areas, but usually it serves as a porting aid for Qt 3-based applications that are converted only at a later stage to model/view programming. For this reason Trolltech has developed an element-based class for each of the Interview views that manages without an external model. To distinguish these from normal views, we will call them *view widgets* from now on. We will discuss them only briefly here, because for most purposes a standard model is just as suitable.

Internally, view widgets are based on the respective view classes, but they provide an extended API. Because this makes them completely autonomous, and they require no further classes, they are called widgets.

In this way the QListView list view becomes the QListWidget, the counterpart to the QTreeView list view is QTreeWidget, and the table view QTableView is called QTableWidget in the independent version.

8.11.1 Items

Each entry in these view widgets is an instance of an *element* or *item*. For each of the three widgets there are separate item classes that do not have a common parent class. This also means that the data in a view widget in each case cannot be used in the other two widget types without additional processing.

In order that the item classes remain lightweight, they do not inherit from QObject, and, if they are not controlled by a view widget, they are therefore not part of the automatic Qt memory management.

The item classes are each named according to the view widget to which they belong: QListWidgetItem is used as an entry in a list view, QTreeWidgetItem represents an entry in a tree view, and QTableWidgetItem is responsible for displaying entries in a table.

Each item has certain properties that can be selectively modified via its API. These can be compared with roles, which we used to make distinctions in the data() method of QAbstractItemModel (see Table 8.1). The setFont() method allows another font to be used, so it corresponds to the Qt::FontRole, whereas setToolTip() corresponds to the Qt::ToolTipRole. The items are basically pointer-based so they must always be created on the heap.

8.11.2 The List View

Below we will insert a few names into a list widget. We create the view widget as before when doing this, but we create the entries via QListWidgetItem. By passing this to the view widget as the second argument, it takes over control of the item and inserts it. For this reason we do not need to intercept the pointer returned by new:

```
// listwidgetexample/main.cpp

#include <QtGui>

int main(int argc, char* argv[])
{
  QApplication app(argc, argv);
  QListWidget listWidget;
  new QListWidgetItem(QObject::tr("Antje"), &listWidget);
  new QListWidgetItem(QObject::tr("Barbara"), &listWidget);
  new QListWidgetItem(QObject::tr("Daniel"), &listWidget);
  listWidget.show();
  return app.exec();
}
```

There are two ways of instantiating a QListWidgetItem. You can call the item constructor, which expects a string or an icon, followed by a string as a parameter. A suitable view widget can be passed optionally as the third parameter, into which the item is inserted. The example uses an alternative constructor that gets by without specifying an icon.

A more direct way is to use the addItem() method, which every view widget possesses. It expects a string, generates the item automatically, and inserts the item into the view widget.

8.11.3 The Tree View

If you want to have a tree structure as a view widget, the QTreeWidget is used as a base class, in which the number of columns is fixed from the beginning. We specify this with setColumnCount(). Then we define the header, with setHeaderLabels().

We now insert the first item into the widget, as before, but we save the pointer. In this way we can insert three child entries with the addChild() method of the item:

```
// treewidgetexample/main.cpp

#include <QtGui>

int main(int argc, char* argv[])
{
  QApplication app(argc, argv);
  QTreeWidget treeWidget;
  treeWidget.setColumnCount(1);
  QStringList headerLabels;
  headerLabels << "Namen";
```

```
treeWidget.setHeaderLabels(headerLabels);
QTreeWidgetItem *parent =
  new QTreeWidgetItem(&treeWidget,
                      QStringList(QObject::tr("Otto+Margit")));
parent->addChild(new QTreeWidgetItem
                      (QStringList(QObject::tr("Daniel"))));
parent->addChild(new QTreeWidgetItem
                      (QStringList(QObject::tr("Moritz"))));
parent->addChild(new QTreeWidgetItem
                      (QStringList(QObject::tr("Philipp"))));
treeWidget.expandItem(parent);
treeWidget.show();
return app.exec();
}
```

Before we display the widget, we first expand the parent item Otto+Margit by calling the expandItem() slot. Otherwise the user would have to do this with the + icon in front of the item. Now the view appears as shown in Figure 8.18.

Figure 8.18:
A simple tree view is
quickly implemented
with QTreeWidget.

Since tree views may have more than one column, most set methods expect the column as the first argument from QTreeWidgetItem. The following instruction fills the second column of an item called item with (new) text:

```
item->setText(1, tr("Text"));
```

In the same way, setIcon() inserts an icon and setFont() determines the font type of the text. An exception is setFlags(), with which the properties listed in Table 8.2 on page 228 can be set. They refer to the entire row. It is therefore not possible to provide individual columns with checkboxes: setFlags(Qt::ItemIsUserCheckable) sets the box in the first column.

8.11.4 The Table View

The third and last ready-to-use view widget, QTableWidget, is based on QTableView and uses QTableWidgetItem as an item class. The size of the table can be conveniently specified in the constructor. Items are inserted here with the setItem() method, which expects a column and row number and the item itself as arguments.

The following example creates a 3x3 table, in which each cell contains the product of its column and row coordinates:

```
// tablewidgetexample/main.cpp

#include <QtGui>

int main(int argc, char* argv[])
{
  QApplication app(argc, argv);
  QTableWidget tableWidget(3,3);
  for (int row=0;row<tableWidget.rowCount(); row++)
    for (int col=0;col<tableWidget.columnCount(); col++)
      tableWidget.setItem(row, col,
        new QTableWidgetItem(QString::number(row*col)));
  tableWidget.show();
  return app.exec();
}
```

8.11.5   Cloning Items

Often, you want to have items that are identical up to a certain point: the same font type, the same icons, and so on, with only the text different each time. In such cases the clone() method, contained in all item classes, is very useful. It allows an item to be put together into a prototype, from which new items can then be cloned. Then all you need to do is give the clone separate text and insert it into the view widget:

```
// listwidgetexample2/main.cpp

#include <QtGui>

int main(int argc, char* argv[])
{
  QApplication app(argc, argv);
  QListWidget listWidget;

  // Setup a prototype
  QListWidgetItem *proto = new QListWidgetItem;
  proto->setFont(QFont("Times"));
  proto->setTextColor(Qt::blue);
  proto->setBackgroundColor(Qt::yellow);


  // Clone and modify object, insert it
```

```
// before everything else
QListWidgetItem *name = proto->clone();
name->setText("Antje");
listWidget.insertItem(0, name);

// Same procedure...
name = proto->clone();
name->setText("Daniel");
listWidget.insertItem(0, name);

// Use proto itself
name = proto;
name->setText("Barbara");
listWidget.insertItem(0, name);

// Sort the list
listWidget.sortItems();

listWidget.show();
return app.exec();
}
```

The sortItems() method sorts the already inserted items in descending order, so that the names appear below each other, sorted in alphabetical order in the list widget.

The QtSql Module

Nowadays, it is difficult to imagine many applications being able to function without relational databases to back them up. For this reason Qt provides a range of classes in the QtSql module that work with various relational database management systems (DBMS). Relational tables and queries can also be used as the basis of Interview models.

9.1 Structure of the QtSql Module

The QtSql module is an independent library that can load additional plugins if required. In contrast to QtCore and QtGui, its contents are not integrated by default (with qmake -project) into the generated projects. In order to use the library, the following entry is therefore necessary in the .pro file:

```
QT += sql
```

To be able to work with the classes of the module, Qt provides a meta-include for this package as well, which contains all the class definitions from the module. The command to integrate it into a source file is as follows:

```
#include <QtSql>
```

Each of the classes of the module belong to one of three layers. The *driver layer* implements the interface between the drivers for various databases and the *API layer* (see Table 9.1). This provides application developers with access to the databases and enables typical SQL operations, such as browsing or modifying tables or querying data.

In order to include the results of queries in Interview views, the *user interface layer* provides models that are based on SQL tables or queries. Figure 9.1 provides an overview of the layers and the classes belonging to them.

Figure 9.1:
The structure of the
QtSql module

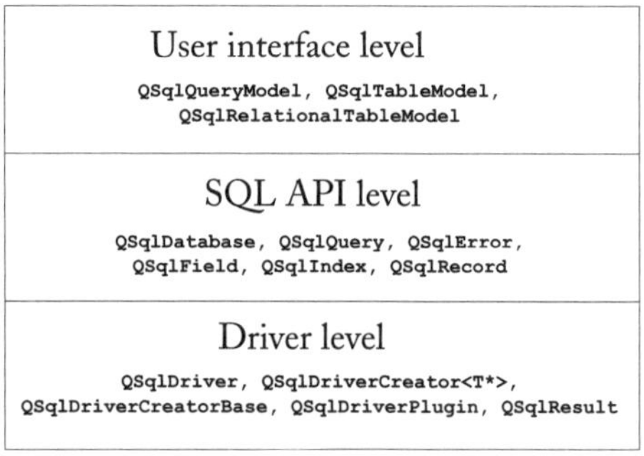

```
┌─────────────────────────────────────────────┐
│          User interface level                │
│   QSqlQueryModel, QSqlTableModel,            │
│        QSqlRelationalTableModel              │
├─────────────────────────────────────────────┤
│             SQL API level                    │
│   QSqlDatabase, QSqlQuery, QSqlError,        │
│     QSqlField, QSqlIndex, QSqlRecord         │
├─────────────────────────────────────────────┤
│              Driver level                    │
│     QSqlDriver, QSqlDriverCreator<T*>,       │
│ QSqlDriverCreatorBase, QSqlDriverPlugin, QSqlResult │
└─────────────────────────────────────────────┘
```

9.2 Selecting the Appropriate Driver

Since the license of the client API for some database systems is not GPL-compatible, a number of drivers are missing (marked in Table 9.1 with *[*]) in the open source edition.

Table 9.1:
Drivers for QtSql

Driver name	Database system
QDB2	IBM DB2 (Version 7.1 and newer)[*]
QIBASE	Borland InterBase
QMYSQL	MySQL
QOCI	Oracle Call Interface driver (versions 8, 9, and 10)[*]
QODBC	Open Database Connectivity (ODBC), used by Microsoft SQL server and other ODBC-capable databases

continued

Driver name	Database system
QPSQL	PostgreSQL (version 7.3 and newer)
QSQLITE2	SQLite (version 2)
QSQLITE	SQLite (version 3)
QTDS	Sybase Adaptive Server[*]

If the Qt version originates from packages of a Linux distribution, you may need to install additional packages. Ubuntu stores the SQL library in the package libqt4-sql, whereas OpenSUSE, in addition to installing qt-sql, requires a DBMS-specific database package, such as qt-sql-mysql for MySQL.

If you build Qt from the sources, you should take a look at the output of ./configure --help:

```
...
-Istring ........... Add an explicit include path.
...
-qt-sql-<driver> ...... Enable a SQL <driver> in the Qt Library, by
                        default none are turned on.
-plugin-sql-<driver> .. Enable SQL <driver> as a plugin to be linked
                        to at run time.
-no-sql-<driver> ...... Disable SQL <driver> entirely.

                        Possible values for <driver>:
                        [ db2 ibase mysql oci odbc psql sqlite
                          sqlite2 tds ]

                        Auto-Detected on this system:
                        [ sqlite ]
...
```

By default Qt builds the driver modules as *plugins* for all systems found automatically—in this case for SQLite. If you do not want to compile one of these explicitly, the -no-sql-*driver* switch is used; for example, in the case of SQLite the switch would be -no-sql-sqlite. Qt also includes its own SQLite version. If you want to use a version of SQLite installed on the system instead, you must also specify the -system-sqlite switch.

If ./configure cannot find an installed database system, despite the development packages installed, then you can specify the include directory of the database system with the -I switch, for example -I/usr/include/mysql, in the case of MySQL. It is left to each user to decide whether a driver is built separately as a plugin (-plugin-sql-*driver*) or compiled permanently into the library (-qt-sql-*driver*). Plugins are more flexible, whereas compiled-in drivers are simpler to handle if the Qt library is to be included in the program.

9.3 Making a Connection

The QSqlDatabase class is used to manage contact with the database server, and its addDatabase() static method returns an instance of QSqlDatabase:

```
QSqlDatabase db = QSqlDatabase::addDatabase("QPSQL");
```

As an argument, addDatabase() expects at least the name of the database driver in string form, thus something like "QPSQL" for the Postgres driver. A QSqlDatabase instance generated in this manner serves as the standard connection. If the program needs to establish contact with more than one database, the addDatabase() method additionally requires a connection name:

```
QSqlDatabase webdb =
        QSqlDatabase::addDatabase("QMYSQL", "WebServerDB");
QSqlDatabase personaldb =
        QSqlDatabase::addDatabase("QOCI", "PersonalDB");
QSqlDatabase embeddeddb =
        QSqlDatabase::addDatabase("QSQLITE", "EmbeddedDB");
```

If this argument had been omitted in the variable definitions above, all three QSql-Database instances would end up pointing to the SQLite database, since each addDatabase() call without additional parameters modifies the standard connection.

In the following example we set up a connection to a single MySQL server. We establish a connection to a database on this server using a QSqlDatabase object initialized with the relevant driver. To do this we declare the server name, the name of the database, the username, and the password:

```
// sqlexample/main.cpp

#include <QtGui>
#include <QtSql>
#include <QDebug>

int main(int argc, char* argv[])
{
  QApplication app(argc, argv);

  QSqlDatabase db = QSqlDatabase::addDatabase("QMYSQL");
  db.setHostName("datenbankserver.example.com");
  db.setDatabaseName("firma");
  db.setUserName("user");
  db.setPassword("pass");

  if (!db.open()) {
     qDebug() << db.lastError();
     return 1;
  }
```

The open() method establishes the connection to the database with this access data. Whether the attempt to connect was successful or not is indicated by its Boolean return value. In case of error, we can determine the reason for the connection failure by using lastError(). The method returns an object of type QSqlError, which qDebug() can read out. If you want to reuse this error object elsewhere, the QSqlError class method text() can be used.

9.4   Making Queries

In the following examples we will work with two tables: The employees table holds information on the employees in a company (Table 9.2), and the departments table (Table 9.3) describes the various organizational units in the company.

id	last name	first name	department
1	Werner	Max	1
2	Lehmann	Daniel	2
3	Roetzel	David	1
4	Scherfgen	David	2
5	Scheidweiler	Najda	2
6	Jueppner	Daniela	4
7	Hasse	Peter	4
8	Siebigteroth	Jennifer	3

Table 9.2:
The employees *table from the example database*

id	name
1	Management
2	Development
3	Marketing
4	Accounting

Table 9.3:
The departments *table from the example database*

For database operations we use the QSqlQuery class. If a class used in the constructor is given an SQL command as a string, the instanced object immediately carries out this statement. You can re-run the command stored in the query object later on using exec() (for example, after modification to the database). If there are several open connections, the QSqlQuery class accepts a QSqlDatabase instance as a second parameter.

If the SQL operation was successful, the QSqlQuery object is regarded as active, which can be checked with isActive(). If it has collected datasets, for example through a SELECT query, you can navigate through them: first() jumps to the first dataset, last() to the last one, next() to the next one, and previous() to the previous one. With seek() you can address a specific dataset by specifying an integer index. The number of datasets contained in the query object is revealed with size().

The QSqlQuery::record() method returns a QSqlRecord object. It contains information on the response to a SELECT query. Using it we can learn, for example, the numerical index of a specified column in the query result via QSqlRecord::indexOf(). We can use this index to read the value in that column of a dataset (row) in the result with QSqlQuery::value(). The row is determined by the current position in the query object, which we can retrieve using QSqlQuery::at() and change using QSqlQuery::next().

```
// sqlexample/main.cpp (continued)
```

```cpp
QSqlQuery query("SELECT firstname, lastname FROM employees");
QSqlRecord record = query.record();
while (query.next()) {
  QString  firstname =
    query.value(record.indexOf("firstname")).toString();
  QString  lastname =
    query.value(record.indexOf("lastname")).toString();
  qDebug() << query.at() << ":" << lastname << "," << firstname;
}
```

For operations that change the contents of the database (such as UPDATE or DELETE), numRowsAffected() returns the number of datasets involved:

```
// sqlexample/main.cpp (continued)
```

```cpp
query.exec("DELETE FROM employees WHERE lastname = 'Hasse'");
qDebug() << query.numRowsAffected(); // "1"
```

Things are a little more complicated for INSERT instructions. Since these are used to write values from the program's own data structures to the database, it can be quite complicated to construct a string containing the corresponding SQL instruction. For this reason we take a different path: Using prepare() we save a template for the desired command, equipped with placeholders, in the QSqlQuery object:

```
// sqlexample/main.cpp (continued)
```

```cpp
query.prepare("INSERT INTO employees (lastname, firstname, department)"
              "VALUES(:lastname, :firstname, :department)");
query.bindValue(":lastname", "Hasse");
query.bindValue(":firstname", "Peter");
query.bindValue(":department", 3);
query.exec();
```

The *named wildcards* in the VALUES part of the SQL command, originating from the Oracle world, each begin with a colon. Using the bindValue() command we can replace them with the specific values.

QSqlQuery can also handle the *unknown parameters* familiar from the ODBC using addBindValue() . Each call to this method replaces one of the question marks in the VALUES clause, in the order in which they appear:

```
// sqlexample/main.cpp (continued)

  query.prepare("INSERT INTO employees (lastname, firstname, department)"
              "VALUES(?, ?, ?)");
  query.addBindValue("Schwan");
  query.addBindValue("Waldemar");
  query.addBindValue(3);
  query.exec();
```

If you don't want to specify the unknown values according to the sequence of occurrence, you can use the following overloaded variant:

```
  query.bindValue(2, 3);
  query.bindValue(0, "Schwan");
  query.bindValue(1, "Waldemar");
```

Here the first parameter specifies the position of the question mark to be replaced in the prepare() string.

bindValue() also plays a central role in the use of *stored procedures*, because the parameters of these procedures can be declared both as IN and as OUT. Parameters declared as cmdOUT function as return values.

In order to access a return value, we must adjust the bindValue() method: The value passed does not matter here, as it will be overwritten by the OUT value later. But the QSql::Out specification, which tells QSqlQuery to overwrite the value, is important here. After we have executed exec(), the value lies at the corresponding position. We can check this with boundValue():

```
// sqlexample/main.cpp (continued)

  query.prepare("CALL countEmployees(?)");
  query.bindValue(0, 0, QSql::Out);
  query.exec();
  qDebug() << query.boundValue(0).toInt()
```

Unfortunately, this approach does not work correctly in MySQL 5, due to API limitations. In order to access the OUT values under MySQL 5, we must make two queries manually: First we run the stored procedure with CALL, and then we read in the value produced, using SELECT. In order to refer to the value, in each case we use a wildcard with @ as a MySQL-specific prefix, so that we can read out the return value of the stored procedure as a dataset:

```
// sqlexample/main.cpp (continued)

  query.exec("CALL countEmployees(@outwert)");
  query.exec("SELECT @outwert");
  query.next();
  qDebug() << query.value(0);
  return 0;
}
```

9.5   Transactions

Not all database systems support transactions, which combine several SQL operations into an atomic operation. To help the Qt programmer keep the code portable, QSqlDriver can therefore be asked about its transaction capabilities with hasFeature():

```
if (db.driver()->hasFeature(QSqlDriver::Transactions)) ... ;
```

If the driver supports transactions, you can introduce them with the QSqlDatabase method transaction(). If all operations are completed, the transaction is closed with commit(). If an error occurs, rollback() undoes all the operations of the current transaction.

9.6   Embedded Databases

Qt's SQLite driver enables data to be stored in a relational database and queried, without an external database server. There are restrictions, of course, but the demands made of embedded databases are usually less severe than those for databases residing on dedicated servers, and SQLite is intended for just such situations. This means that SQLite cannot handle stored procedures and does not scale as well as its big brothers. It is well suited, however, to applications that need a basic relational data store. A perfect example is the KDE music player Amarok, which stores metadata about pieces of music in a SQLite database.

To open a connection to a SQLite database, you only need to specify a database name. The SQLite driver expects a filename in this case:

```
QSqlDatabase db = QSqlDatabase::addDatabase("QSQLITE");
db.setDatabaseName("firma.db");
```

If the database should only remain in memory while the program is running, a temporary database can be generated by enclosing the database name within colons, as shown below. The :results: database will not not be saved as a file when the program terminates:

```
QSqlDatabase db = QSqlDatabase::addDatabase("QSQLITE");
db.setDatabaseName(":results:");
```

You can work with this database as normal, with the understanding that any changes made to it will later be lost. A temporary database does not need its own data structures if the data is already of a relational nature.

9.7 Using SQL Model Classes with Interview

In order to display the contents of databases, table views are usually appropriate, and in some cases, list views are as well. This is why the QtSql module has a range of models for Interview (see Chapter 8 on page 207).

9.7.1 Displaying SQL Tables Without Foreign Keys in Table and Tree Views

QSqlTableModel enables complete tables to be displayed directly in a table or tree view. The column headers correspond to the field names (attributes, columns) of the SQL table. In our personnel database from Table 9.2 on page 261, these are id, first name, last name, and department. Each line corresponds to a dataset. To illustrate this better, we will look at the following example, which assumes an open standard connection:

```
// sqlmvd/main.cpp

...
  QTableView tableView;
  QSqlTableModel tableModel;
  tableModel.setTable("employees");
  tableModel.select();
  tableModel.removeColumn(0);
  tableView.setModel(&tableModel);
  tableView.setWindowTitle("'employees' table");
  tableView.show();
```

First we create a table view and then the model. We allocate a table to it from the current database and order it to fetch data with select(). Then we remove the id column from the view using removeColumn() (Figure 9.2). This method originates from QAbstractItemModel, the ultimate base class of all models. Finally, we bind the model to the table view, give the table a name, and display it.

Figure 9.2:
QTableModel is
responsible for SQL
tables in Interview.

	lastname	firstname	department
1	Werner	Max	1
2	Lehmann	Daniel	2
3	Roetzel	David	1
4	Scherfgen	David	2
5	Kupfer	Andreas	2
6	Scheidweiler	Najda	2

9.7.2 Resolving Foreign Key Relations

QSqlRelationalTableModel extends the functionality of the table model for use with relational databases. In addition, objects in this class set off foreign key relations. We can use these to replace the uninformative number shown in the department field with the name of the department, by making use of the departments table (see Table 9.3 on page 261).

Figure 9.3:
QSqlRelationalTa-
bleModel records the
foreign key field id
with the help of a
second table.

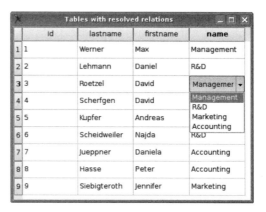

	id	lastname	firstname	name
1	1	Werner	Max	Management
2	2	Lehmann	Daniel	R&D
3	3	Roetzel	David	Managemer
4	4	Scherfgen	David	Management / R&D
5	5	Kupfer	Andreas	Marketing / Accounting
6	6	Scheidweiler	Najda	R&D
7	7	Jueppner	Daniela	Accounting
8	8	Hasse	Peter	Accounting
9	9	Siebigteroth	Jennifer	Marketing

To describe this relation, the setRelation() method is used: It expects the number of the column containing the foreign key as the first argument. In our example, the value in the name field from the departments table should appear in the third column instead of the value in the foreign key field (that is, the id field) of the departments table. This information is encapsulated in the instance rel of the QSqlRelation help class, which we pass to setRelation() as the second argument.

Now we can start the query via select(), bind the model to the view, and display the results, as in the previous example:

```
// sqlmvd/main.cpp (continued)

  QTableView tableRelationalView;
  QSqlRelationalTableModel tableRelationalModel;
  tableRelationalModel.setTable("employees");
  QSqlRelation rel("departments", "id", "name");
  tableRelationalModel.setRelation(3, rel);
  tableRelationalModel.select();
  tableRelationalView.setModel(&tableRelationalModel);
  tableRelationalView.setItemDelegate(
              new QSqlRelationalDelegate(&tableRelationalView));
  tableRelationalView.setWindowTitle(
              "Tables with resolved relations");
  tableRelationalView.show();
```

This is now followed by a peculiarity that only functions in combination with QRelationalTableModel: A special delegate called QSqlRelationalDelegate allows the user to select the value from a list when editing columns for which a relation is defined (Figure 9.3). It compiles these independently from the QSqlRelation used. In the example it takes suggestions from the name column; the value written back to the table, on the other hand, comes from the id column.

9.7.3 Displaying Query Results

To display the results of particularly complex SELECT queries that cannot simply be modeled on a QSqlTableModel with a filter, make use of the QSqlQueryModel. The following example evaluates how many employees the company has in each department. In addition the columns should bear descriptive names, as can be seen in Figure 9.4.

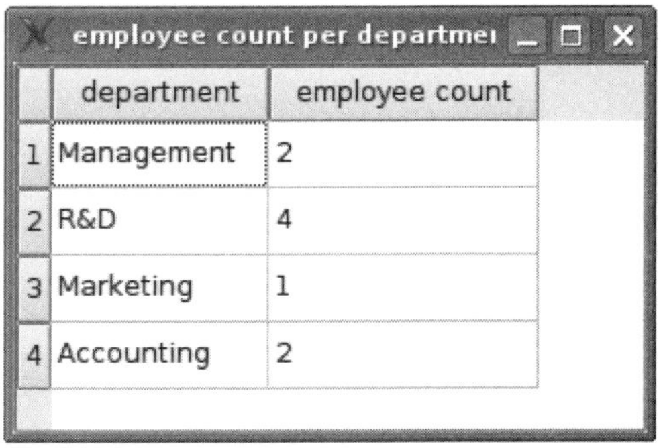

Figure 9.4:
QSqlQueryModel is used as a source for queries of all types in Interview.

After instantiating the model, we pass the query as a string to setQuery(). Alternatively, we could use a QSqlQuery object.

Since errors can occur in more complex queries, we should introduce an error check immediately after the query executes. lastError() returns the last error announced by the SQL server in an QSqlError object. If this is valid, an error has occurred, which we can display with qDebug():

```
// sqlmvd/main.cpp (continued)

  QTableView queryView;
  QSqlQueryModel queryModel;
  queryModel.setQuery("SELECT departments.name, "
        "COALESCE(COUNT(employees.lastname),0) "
        "FROM departments LEFT JOIN employees "
        "ON employees.department = departments.id "
        "GROUP BY employees.department");

  if (queryModel.lastError().isValid())
    qDebug() << queryModel.lastError();

  queryModel.setHeaderData(0, Qt::Horizontal,
                                QObject::tr("department"));
  queryModel.setHeaderData(1, Qt::Horizontal,
                                QObject::tr("employee count"));
  queryView.setModel(&queryModel);
  queryView.setWindowTitle("employee count per department");
  queryView.show();
```

We can achieve user-friendly column headers by replacing the first two column headers withsetHeaderData().[1] Then we bind the model to the view and display the view, as before, with a customized heading.

9.7.4 Editing Strategies

All of these table models are writable. However, we have not yet looked closely at the point in time when the model writes the data back to the database.

QSqlTableModel and QSqlRelationalTableModel know three *editing strategies*, which are allocated to models using setEditStrategy(). They are as follows:

SqlTableModel::OnRowChange
      This is the default in all models. If this strategy is active, the model sends an

---

[1] This can also be done with the SQL instruction AS, of course, but then you would have to ensure, via tr(), that the query can be internationalized; otherwise, the column headers cannot be transferred to other languages.

UPDATE for the dataset as soon as the user selects another dataset—that is, another row in the view.

SqlTableModel::OnFieldChange

This transfers every change to the database directly after the user has changed a value in a field.

SqlTableModel::OnManualSubmit

This temporarily saves all changes in the model until either the submitAll() slot, which transfers all changes to the database, or the revertAll() slot is triggered. The latter rejects all cached data and restores the status from the database (see Chapter 9.7.5 on page 270 for more on the revertAll() slot).

We will illustrate this last scenario by modifying the example from page 265 so that it additionally contains two buttons that are arranged in a layout beneath the table view. All other commands are left as they are.

```
// sqlmvd/main.cpp (continued)

  QWidget w;
  QPushButton *submitPb = new QPushButton(
              QObject::tr("Save Changes"));
  QPushButton *revertPb = new QPushButton(
              QObject::tr("Roll back changes"));
  QGridLayout *lay = new QGridLayout(&w);
  QTableView *manualTableView = new QTableView;
  lay->addWidget(manualTableView, 0, 0, 1, 2);
  lay->addWidget(submitPb, 1, 0);
  lay->addWidget(revertPb, 1, 1);
  QSqlTableModel manualTableModel;
  manualTableModel.setTable("employees");
  manualTableModel.select();
  manualTableModel.setEditStrategy(
              QSqlTableModel::OnManualSubmit);
  manualTableView->setModel(&manualTableModel);
  QObject::connect(submitPb, SIGNAL(clicked(bool)),
              &manualTableModel, SLOT(submitAll()) );
  QObject::connect(revertPb, SIGNAL(clicked(bool)),
              &manualTableModel, SLOT(revertAll()) );
  w.setWindowTitle("manually revertable table");
  w.show();

  return app.exec();
}
```

After converting the editing strategy to OnManualSubmit, we insert two signal/slot connections: A click on the submitPb button calls the submitAll() slot, whereas revertPb triggers revertAll().

Figure 9.5:
With the
OnManualSubmit
editing strategy, local
changes can be
transferred at any
time you want to the
database.

Now we must not forget to display the main widget w as the new top-level widget. The result is illustrated in Figure 9.5.

9.7.5 Errors in the Table Model

Several problems that occur in connection with the table models in Qt 4.1 should not be left unaddressed at this point. One is that editor operations do not always function reliably after columns have been removed. The QSqlRelationalTableModel even ignores the removeColumn() instruction entirely. As a workaround, a proxy model that filters out the unwanted datasets is recommended here. If the data should only be displayed, you can instead simply place an SQL query above the QSqlQueryModel.

Another problem involves the revertAll() slot, which is intended to undo all changes in relational tables with the OnManualSubmit editing strategy. However, in the columns in which a foreign key relation was previously defined with setRelation(), revertAll() does not revert back to the old values. The only solution until now was to connect the slot of the button with a custom-developed slot that replaces the current model with a new one that has the same properties. Since the model temporarily saves the data, it will be lost in this way, and the new model will display the original data from the database.

The Graphics Library "Arthur"

This chapter looks at the drawing methods of the class library that Trolltech has baptized "Arthur," presumably as a reference to Microsoft's "Avalon" technology. In this chapter we will work with examples that let us observe how Qt "paints" on buffers in the graphics and main memory as well as on widgets and other devices, and we will introduce in detail the classes belonging to Arthur, together with their classic fields of application. But first we must explain more precisely how drawing really works in Qt. First we will look at the color specifications used by Qt.

10.1 Colors

Color specifications are of central importance in graphic interfaces, including the issues of how colors are generated and how known colors are named so that you can work with them efficiently. The following section is devoted to the question of how developers can manage colors.

10.1.1 The RGB Color Space

Qt encapsulates colors in the QColor class. This is based on the RGB model, in which 8 bits, representing a range of values from 0 to 255, are allocated to a color. In addition, QColor specifies another value, the so-called *alpha value*, also referred to as the *alpha channel*. This defines the transparency of a pixel.

QColor can also work with values other than integers. For each color command that accepts an integer, there exists a floating-point variation that allows colors to be specified more precisely. Whenever a QColor method that expects integer color information is discussed below, you can always substitute an associated floating-point variant instead, which accepts qreal values. For example, the setRgb() method, which expects three integer values for the red, green, and blue color components and takes an optional alpha value, has a corresponding floating-point equivalent called setRgbF().

There are several ways to generate a new QColor object. The basic QColor() constructor creates an object with an invalid color. Furthermore, there is a constructor that accepts colors described using integers. The semantics here correspond to those of setRgb(). There is no separate constructor that takes floating-point numbers as arguments, since this would be ambiguous, as C++ automatically converts integer values to floating-point values. To initialize a color with floating-point values, you first create an empty (and initially invalid) QColor object, and then set color via setRgbF().

Earlier examples often used yet another constructor that accepts a color chosen from 20 predefined colors that are defined in the GlobalColor enumerator. This enumeration also includes values describing a number of special cases: The "color" Qt::transparent, for example, corresponds to QColor(0, 0, 0, 0) and allows a background color to show through.

In addition, QColor can deduce the desired color from a name, as defined in the SVG-1.0 specification.[1] For this purpose the class has a constructor that accepts a QString or a string. The setNamedColor() method works in the same way. This option permits a named color to be set later on, as illustrated in the following example:

```
QColor color("navy"); // sets a dark blue
color.setNamedColor("royalblue"); // sets a light blue
```

The names of all available named colors are returned by QColor with the colorNames() method.

Finally, QColor has a constructor that accepts a QRgb value. QRgb in this case is not a class name, but a name, given by a type definition, for a 32-bit integer. Given such a value as an argument, this constructor sets the RGB values and the alpha

---

[1] See http://www.w3.org/TR/SVG/types.html#ColorKeywords.

value of the new QColor instance to the values encoded in the QRgb variable. The advantage of QRgb as a lightweight alternative for transporting RGB color information is particularly evident whenever large amounts of pixel data from an image need to be read in.

QRgb divides the available bits in the 32-bit integer into four integer color values, each consisting of eight bits representing values from 0 to 255. This is done as follows, in hexadecimal notation ("A" = alpha value, "R" = red, "G" = green, "B" = bluc):

```
0xAARRGGBB
```

You do not have to construct your own QRgb values, however: The help functions qRgb() and qRgba() take on this task and expect the color details to be provided in three integer arguments, as values between 0 and 255. qRgba() expects the alpha channel as the fourth argument. qRgb() omits the specification of the alpha channel, and sets this component of the constructed QRgb value to 255 (corresponding to an opaque, that is, a nontransparent, color). You can then access the individual QRgb components via QRgb::qRed(), QRgb::qGreen(), QRgb::qBlue(), and QRgb::qAlpha(). These functions return values from 0 to 255.

The following example creates a red, semitransparent QRgb value and passes it to a QColor object, from which we read out the colors and the alpha channel with the rgba() function and write it back to the QRgb variable:

```
QRgb rgba = qRgba(255, 0, 0, 127); // A=127, R=255, G=0, B=0
QColor color = QColor::fromRgba(rgba);
rgba = 0; // A=0, R=0, G=0, B=0
rgba = color.rgba();  // A=127, R=255, G=0, B=0
```

It is important here to use the fromRgba() static method because the standard constructor, which accepts a QRgb value, ignores the alpha channel.

10.1.2   Other Color Spaces

In addition to RGB, QColor can also use the HSV model, which defines a color through *hue*, *saturation*, and brightness (or *value*) parameters. (HSV is therefore sometimes also referred to as HSB, where the B stands for *brightness*, which is actually a more precise term for the third parameter.) The HSV model corresponds most closely to the human perception of color composition.

To make use of it, we must accordingly convert the color, via toHsv(). Then we can read out the HSV parameters, either componentwise via hue(), saturation(), value(), and alpha(), or all at the same time, using getHsv():

```
QColor red(Qt::red);
QColor red = red.toHsv();
int h, s, v, a;
red.getHsv(&h, &s, &v, &a);
// HSV values now in h, s, v, a
```

To specify a color in the HSV model, we have the setHsv() method, which expects the three HSV components as integers and, optionally, the alpha channel. If the alpha value is missing, QColor assumes it to be 255, that is, *opaque*.

QColor is also able to accept CMYK specifications and to display colors specified in CMYK format. Since there are differences between the color spaces of the RGB and CMYK models, however, and CMYK is a subtractive color model whereas RGB is an additive one, not all colors can be represented in both color models. In cases where there is no exact equivalent for a desired conversion from one system to the other, Qt tries to approximate the color as closely as possible.

To obtain the CMYK representation of a color, it is sufficient to read out the four color components and the alpha channel, with getCmyk():

```
QColor red(Qt::red);
int c, m, y, k, a;
red.getCmyk(&c,&m,&y,&k,&a);
// CMYK values now in c, m, y, k, a
```

Here Qt calculates the matching four-color values in getCmyk() from the QColor's internally stored RGB parameters. If a routine of an application program requires the color to be specified in a color model other than RGB particularly often, QColor can also represent it internally in CMYK or HSV. In these cases, no resources are used for conversion when the color is accessed via getCmyk() or getHsv(), respectively, but their interpretation as RGB colors is resource intensive. To convert to another color model, the methods toHsv(), toCmyk(), and toRgb() are used. The conversion can be done at any time before the corresponding color is accessed:

```
QColor red(Qt::red);
// convert to CMYK internally
QColor red = red.toCmyk();
int c, m, y, k, a;
// no conversion required, already converted
red.getCmyk(&c,&m,&y,&k,&a);
// CMYK colors now in c, m, y, k, a
```

You should only convert permanently to another color model, however, if you have good reason to do so—internally, Qt uses the RGB model nearly everywhere, which explains why a class is slower in operation after the internal representation of the colors it uses is changed from RGB to another color model.

The setCmyk() method defines a color with CYMK details, and, in the same way as getCmyk(), reads in four colors and, optionally, the alpha channel.

10.1.3   Color Selection Dialog

The color selection dialog QColorDialog (Figure 10.1, left) is specialized for the selection of colors described using the RGB model.[2] Its API has static methods only. To read out an RGB value, getColor() is used:

```
QColor color = QColorDialog::getColor(Qt::red, this);
```

The first parameter defines the color that the dialog initially selects, and the second describes the obligatory parent widget, which can also be 0 if the modality of the dialog does not play any role. If the user interrupts the dialog, the method returns an invalid color, which in this case can be checked with !color.isValid().

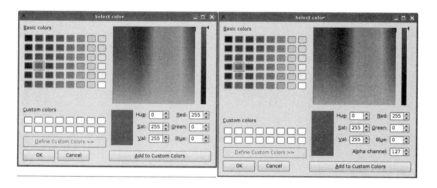

Figure 10.1:
QColorDialog::
getRgba() *(right)*
differs from QColor-
Dialog::getColor() *(left)*
only in the input field
for the alpha channel.

Another method called getRgba() can be used to define the alpha channel for a color (Figure 10.1, on the right):

```
bool ok;
QRgb rgb = QColorDialog::getRgba(qRgba(255,0,0,127), &ok, this);
QColor color(rgb);
```

In contrast to getColor(), this method expects a QRgb value. Since QRgb has no dedicated value for "invalid," getRgba() again has an ok parameter, which is set to false if Cancel is clicked. In this case getRgba() returns the default value passed. The last line shows how you can store a QRgb value (together with its alpha channel) in a QColor object.

```
bool ok;
QColor color = Qt::red;
color.setAlpha(127);
color = QColorDialog::getRgba(color.toRgba(), &ok, this);
```

---

[2] An HSV selection dialog is available as a commercial Qt solution.

QColorDialog allows a number of your own colors, in addition to the default color, to be stored in a separate palette. The number of fields available is defined by the QColorDialog::customCount() static method.

To set a color in this palette, the setCustomColor() is used. This method expects the palette position and the color as a QRgb value. The following call loads the first position of the palette with a semitransparent red tone:

```
QColorDialog::setCustomColor(0, qRgba(255, 0, 0, 127));
```

customColor() calls up the color in your custom palette at a particular position. This method returns the QRgb value set for the index specified:

```
QRgb QColorDialog::customColor(0);
```

Once they are set, the colors apply for the entire lifetime of the application for all QColorDialog calls.

10.2   Painting with Qt

We will now take a look at the classes that paint colors in specific shapes. As in real life, painting tools and a drawing board are necessary.

Figure 10.2:
The base class
QPaintDevice *and its*
specializations

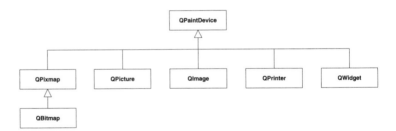

Painting tools are bundled by Qt into the QPainter class. This can be used to both draw simple brushstrokes and handle more complex geometric forms, as well as bitmaps. A wide range of classes are eligible for use as the drawing areas targeted by QPainter operations. They are descendants of the QPaintDevice class. Each QPaintDevice can therefore be a recipient for QPainter operations. These include, among others, all widgets and pixmaps, as well as the print interface, QPrinter. An extensive overview is shown in Figure 10.2.

To start, here is a small program that draws a filled-in circle:

```
// pixmap/main.cpp

#include <QtGui>
```

```
int main(int argc, char* argv[])
{
  QApplication app(argc, argv);
  QPixmap pm(100,100);
  pm.fill();

  QPainter p(&pm);
  p.setRenderHint(QPainter::Antialiasing, true);
  QPen pen(Qt::blue, 2);
  p.setPen(pen);
  QBrush brush(Qt::green);
  p.setBrush(brush);
  p.drawEllipse(10, 10, 80,80);
  QLabel l;
  l.setPixmap(pm);
  l.show();
  return app.exec();
}
```

First we create an empty QPixmap object. The contents of this are initially undefined, which is why we fill it with a basic color; when it is called Without a fill color as an argument, fill() uses white.

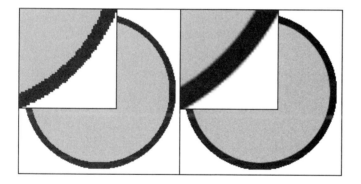

Figure 10.3:
Anti-aliasing
minimizes formation
of staircase artifacts.

Now it is the painter's turn: It performs the actual drawing operations. So that the circle looks really round, and not square-edged, we switch on anti-aliasing. This technique smooths the edges through color gradients, thus minimizing the formation of steps (Figure 10.3). Before setting the QPainter::Antialiasing flag to true, you should bear in mind that this can lead to significant loss of performance, particularly under X11.

Two significant properties of a painter are contained in additional classes. The QPen defines how the painter draws lines. In contrast to this, the paintbrush, in the form of a QBrush, describes how an area is filled, together with patterns and textures.

In our case we will use a blue pen, two pixels wide. We define the paintbrush color as green, without a pattern or texture. We can already define these properties via the constructors. Then we bind these new definitions to the painter with setPen() and setBrush().

Finally we use a QPainter drawing method to actually draw the circle. drawEllipse() draws a circle, starting from the coordinates $(10, 10)$, in a square of 80×80 pixels. Since we have set the size of the whole image to 100×100 pixels, the circle is right at the center of the picture. Qt adheres to the standard programming convention in which the coordinates $(0, 0)$ specify the top left corner of the current reference system. In our case this is the top left corner of the pixmap defined.

Figure 10.4:
Our pixmap in a
simple label

We display the resulting image in a QLabel, which can display pixmaps as well as text if you use the setPixmap() method instead of setText(). (This method expects a reference to a QPixmap.) The result is shown in Figure 10.4.

10.3 Geometrical Helper Classes

In the examples just mentioned, we have placed the circle, using

```
p.drawEllipse(10, 10, 80, 80);
```

in a square with the side lengths of 80×80 pixels, the left top corner of which is at the point $(10, 10)$. If we had chosen two different values for height and width, this would have resulted in a bounding rectangle instead of a bounding square—and drawEllipse() would have drawn an ellipse. To describe other geometric objects, Qt provides the classes QPoint, QSize, QRect, and QPolygon.

The QPoint class saves two coordinates, without reference to an external system. QSize, on the other hand, also combines two parameters passed in the constructor, but interpreted as a height and a width instead of as coordinates, again without defining a reference point. These object types are united by the QRect class, which generates a rectangle: When passed a QPoint and a QSize as arguments, the QRect constructor instantiates a corresponding rectangle. Alternatively, you may use an overloaded constructor and specify the (x, y) position for the top left corner of the rectangle and the height and the width of the rectangle, in the form of four integers.

In case a rectangle is to be defined not via its attachment point and details of its length and width, but by specifying a top left and bottom right point, QRect provides another constructor that expects this pair of coordinates in the form of two QPoints.

The QPolygon constructor takes a number of points and sketches out a polygon, edge by edge, as determined by the pairs of consecutive points. This class is a special case of QVector<QPoint> and includes a series of useful methods. For example, QPolygon::boundingRect() defines the smallest possible rectangle that contains all the points of the polygon.

There are also floating-point variants of all these classes: QPointF, QSizeF, QRectF, and QPolygonF, which provide for increased precision.

Instead of supplying drawEllipse() with rectangle parameters, as above, you can use an alternative version of the method that accepts a QRect as an argument:

```
QRect rect(10, 10, 80, 80)
p.drawEllipse(rect);
```

The advantage of this notation becomes clear as soon as several actions take place within the same coordinates, for example, if another geometric figure is to be added. Practical use of the classes discussed so far is illustrated by the following, slightly modified example:

```
// pixmap2/main.cpp

#include <QtGui>

int main(int argc, char* argv[])
{
    QApplication app(argc, argv);
    QRect r(0,0, 100, 100);
    QPixmap pm(r.size());
    pm.fill();

    QPainter p(&pm);
    p.setRenderHint(QPainter::Antialiasing, true);
    QPen pen(Qt::red, 2);
    p.setPen(pen);
    QBrush brush(Qt::blue);
    p.setBrush(brush);
    QRect ri = r.adjusted(10,10,-10,-10)
    p.drawEllipse(ri);
    QLabel l;
    l.setPixmap(pm);
```

```
    l.show();
    return app.exec();
}
```

Here the rectangle r forms the global reference system to which everything else is aligned. The constructor of the corresponding pixmap stretched out by this expects merely a size detail. Accordingly, we pass the size of the rectangle, with r.size(), as QSize.

To draw the ellipse, we generate a rectangle shrunk by 10 pixels on each edge, which we can use for other drawing operations.[3] The adjusted() function, with r as the reference system, generates the coordinates for a new rectangle: This is done by moving from the top left corner 10 pixels to the right and 10 pixels down, from the lower right corner 10 pixels to the left (since this is a negative value) and 10 pixels upwards, and moving the edges in parallel with r until they lie on these points.

Qt stores drawing paths in instances of the QPainterPath class; they are provided for creating more complex geometric objects, for which several of these primitives are necessary. A QPainter object can use these paths to fill a described area, to cut that shape out of some other area,[4] or to simply draw a corresponding outline.

10.4   How to Paint on Widgets

As can be seen in the inheritance diagram in Figure 10.2, QWidget, and therefore all widgets, are also QPaintDevices. This brings us to the most important question in this chapter: How can you paint on widgets?

To explain this, we recommend a brief tour of event handling in Qt. If the user starts a program, calls a dialog, alters the interface, or terminates a program in the current window, the graphics subsystem of the operating system requests the application to redraw the corresponding window or regions. For this purpose it sets off a *paint event.*

Qt then calls the paintEvent() method for the widgets involved. This method describes how the widget is drawn. The paintEvent() expects a QPaintEvent object as an argument. This object is only relevant for more complex widgets: With a complex widget it can often be worthwhile to redraw only the parts that need to be updated. To do this, the class has two methods: region() reveals which region of the widget needs to be redrawn, and rect() returns a rectangle that encloses this region.

---

[3] Scaling would also be possible via a matrix transformation. Qt enables this via the QMatrix class, which we will introduce on page 290.

[4] We will look at this process, also known as *clipping*, on page 307.

For our simple example, we do not need these details. The declaration part of the code appears as follows:

```
// widgetpaint/paintwidget.h

#include <QWidget>

class PaintWidget : public QWidget
{
    Q_OBJECT
    public:
    PaintWidget(QWidget* parent = 0);
    ~PaintWidget() {};

    virtual void paintEvent(QPaintEvent*);
    virtual QSize sizeHint() const {return QSize(200,200);}
};
```

Here we first override paintEvent(). In addition we redefine the return value of the sizeHint() method. This ensures that we have a square, at least when the program starts, in which drawEllipse() then draws a circle. Otherwise, sizeHint() would be oriented according to the layout into which the widget is inserted, or else return an invalid size if no layout is responsible for the widget. In these cases we would thus not have ensured that height and width were identical.

Qt uses the size hint supplied by sizeHint() when displaying the widget, unless another layout forces a different size. In the current example we will force neither a permanent fixed size nor a fixed page ratio, so that the circle may turn into an ellipse if the widget is enlarged or if it is fitted into a layout.

If you can manage with just a widget of a fixed size, you can simply use the QWidget method setFixedSize(), which accepts either a QSize container object or integers specifying the details of height and width. If you call setFixedSize() in a widget's constructor, you don't need to reimplement sizeHint(). In this case even layouts cannot change the size of the widget in this case.

The problem can also be solved more flexibly with a separate layout class, which guarantees a fixed page ratio.

From the above example it soon becomes clear what an advantage it is to define the circle relative to a fixed reference system, in this case the frame of our widget: The circle now grows and shrinks automatically, relative to the widget's size.

If overriding sizeHint() does not work, for whatever reason, it is essential that you check whether you may have forgotten the keyword const. The compiler will otherwise generate a nonconstant variant of the method, which is also valid in C++, but is something different, which is why it does not issue a warning.

In the implementation part of our example's code, we are only interested in the definition of the paintEvent() method:

```
// widgetpaint/paintwidget.cpp

void PaintWidget::paintEvent(QPaintEvent* ev)
{
  QWidget::paintEvent(ev);
  QPainter p(this);
  p.setRenderHint(QPainter::Antialiasing, true);
  QPen pen(Qt::blue, 2);
  p.setPen(pen);
  QBrush brush(Qt::green);
  brush.setStyle(Qt::Dense4Pattern);
  p.setBrush(brush);
  QRect ri = rect().adjusted(10,10,-10,-10);
  p.drawEllipse(ri);
}
```

We first forward the paint event ev, passed in the call to PaintWidget::paintEvent(), to the corresponding method of the parent class in the inheritance line, which in this case is QWidget::paintEvent(). This is the first thing to be drawn.

Then we instantiate a Painter on the stack and treat this as discussed in Section 10.2. The only difference consists in the selection of our reference system. Now this is no longer chosen artificially, but depends dynamically on the environment dimensions of the widget, which QWidget::rect() returns to us as a rectangle.

Figure 10.5:
Drawing directly: Our
example uses a
QPainter to paint
directly on a widget.

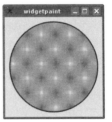

We now redraw our circle, but this time on the PaintWidget instead of on a pixmap. The result can be viewed in Figure 10.5. As a further detail, this time our paintbrush is not completely green, but displays a pattern (Qt::Dense4Pattern). Paintbrushes can generate patterns, tiles, and gradients; the examples to come will further illustrate this.

In this context we should mention that it is worthwhile to store the actual character code in helper methods: From our experience, paintEvent() can grow rapidly, so you can quickly lose track of what's happening there.

10.4.1 How to Prevent Monitor Flicker

To display the graphics drawn with QPainter without flicker on the monitor, Qt 4 uses a technique called *double buffering*. During this procedure, all QPainter operations first land in a memory buffer that is not displayed. Only when all painting operations are finished does Qt copy the buffer's contents to the screen. Double buffering thus elegantly prevents the user from seeing an unpleasant flicker on the screen caused by the multiple steps needed to update the screen as objects are redrawn.

If, under X11, you want to implement double buffering yourself, you can switch off automatic double buffering by Qt with the following instructions:

```
extern void qt_x11_set_global_double_buffer(bool);
qt_x11_set_global_double_buffer(false);
```

This is only useful in specific cases, for example, if part of the program uses a different rendering library. Otherwise, double buffering is always switched on, on all platforms, and should be left that way.

10.5 Using QPainter in Practice

As we have now become familiar with the geometry classes and the underlying capabilities of QPainter, it is time to put them to the test in a practical example.

We will write a PieWidget class, which paints a pie chart together with its legend on a widget and calculates the size required for both parts (Figure 10.6). It uses the sizeHint() and minimumSizeHint() methods to do this.

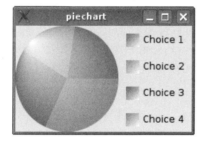

Figure 10.6:
A pie chart with
legend

We implement the actual drawing process in paintEvent(), and the widget obtains the data necessary for this from a QHash. This is an associative data structure that connects a key to a value.

In the values associative hash, the name (a QString) serves as the key and the integer as the corresponding value. From a semantic point of view, the key is the legend entry, and the integer value is the associated number:

```
// piechart/piewidget.h

#ifndef PIEWIDGET_H
```

```
#define PIEWIDGET_H

#include <QWidget>
#include <QHash>

class PieWidget : public QWidget {
  Q_OBJECT
  public:
    PieWidget(QWidget *parent=0);

    QSize sizeHint() const;
    QSize minimumSizeHint () const;
    void addEntry(const QString& key, int val);

  protected:
    void paintEvent(QPaintEvent *ev);

  private:
    QHash<QString, int> values;
};

#endif // PIEWIDGET_H
```

10.5.1 Drawing a Pie Chart

In this specific case we will populate the values hash table with data from a fictitious survey on the most important goals in life, as can be seen in Figure 10.6. Questions here serve as the key, and the associated values are the number of people who made the corresponding choice.

In the constructor we only perform the initializations for the parent class. The addEntry() method allows new values to be entered into the hash table:

```
// piechart/piewidget.cpp

#include <QtGui>
#include "piewidget.h"

PieWidget::PieWidget(QWidget *parent)
 : QWidget(parent)
{
}

void PieWidget::addEntry(const QString& key, int val) {
  values.insert(key, val);
}
```

Before we take a look at the details of paintEvent(), we must think about how to divide up the widget. The pie charts must always be round, so here the height should be the same as the width. The legend part should always be as wide as the longest text in the hash. The minimum height is calculated from the number of legend entries and their vertical spacing. The handler for the paint event and the reimplemented methods sizeHint() and minimumSizeHint() must take these conditions into account.

Before we can start painting, we first calculate the sum of all the values. We'll need this later on to calculate (using a rule of three calculation) how much of the pie the current segment should take up:

```
// piechart/piewidget.cpp (continued)

void PieWidget::paintEvent(QPaintEvent * /*ev*/)
{
  // calculate total
  QHash<QString, int>::const_iterator it;
  int total = 0;
  for(it = values.begin(); it != values.end(); ++it)
    total += it.value();

  // prepare painter
  QPainter p(this);
  p.setRenderHint(QPainter::Antialiasing, true);
```

We now instantiate the Painter and assign it the current widget (this) as the paint device. We also enable anti-aliasing.

Drawing Segments of the Pie

We also need to have a series of colors for the different pie segments in the diagram. To do this we access the colorNames() method, which gives us all the colors predefined in QColor. We also introduce the colorPos variable, which will later be used to select an element from the list. We initialize it with 13, because from this point onward there are several pleasant pastel colors in succession (in practice you would probably define a list with your own colors):

```
// piechart/piewidget.cpp (continued)

  // prepare colors
  QStringList colorNames = QColor::colorNames();
  int colorPos = 13; // pastel colors

  int height = rect().height();
  QRect pieRect(0, 0, height, height);
```

Then we define the dimensions of the chart. These should exactly match the height of the widget. We obtain this height value from the current size of the widget:

rect() returns the size in the form of a QRect(), and we can extract the height from this with height().

pieRect is now initialized to contain the rectangle in which we will later draw our pie chart. We reserve the space remaining in the width for the key. We obtain the corresponding rectangle by first copying the measurements of the widget, with rect(), and then subtracting the width of pieRect from this square on the left side, with setLeft():

```
// piechart/piewidget.cpp (continued)

  // dedicate right half to legend
  QRect legendRect = rect();
  legendRect.setLeft(pieRect.width());
  legendRect.adjust(10,10,-10,-10);
```

With the adjust() call we move ten pixels further inward from all sides, so the rectangle becomes smaller. This has the effect that we obtain ten pixels of space from the outer edges and from the right side of the pie graphics.

This causes the geometries for both parts of the widget to be dependent on the current widget size, and we proceed to draw the segments of the pie and the legend entries belonging to it, entry for entry. We need two help variables to do this. lastAngleOffset specifies the angle in the circle where we previously stopped drawing. We also require currentPos later to draw the key entry at the correct position:

```
// piechart/piewidget.cpp (continued)

  int lastAngleOffset = 0;
  int currentPos = 0;

  // create an entry for every piece of the pie
  for(it = values.begin(); it != values.end(); ++it) {
    int value = it.value();
    QString text = it.key();

    int angle = (int)(16*360*(value/(double)total));
    QColor col(colorNames.at(colorPos%colorNames.count()));
    colorPos++;

    // gradient for the pie pieces
    QRadialGradient rg(pieRect.center(), pieRect.width()/2,
                       pieRect.topLeft());
    rg.setColorAt(0, Qt::white);
    rg.setColorAt(1, col);
    p.setBrush(rg);
    QPen pen = p.pen();
    p.setPen(Qt::NoPen);
```

```
p.drawPie(pieRect, lastAngleOffset, angle);
lastAngleOffset += angle;
```

We again iterate through the hash and remember the keys and values. For each entry in the hash table we can determine how many degrees of the circle are to be apportioned to the current segment of pie. The value stored in the current key, divided by the total sum, results in the fraction that this value represents. Multiplied by 360, this reveals how many degrees the segment of pie to be drawn takes up. It only remains to be explained from where the additional factor of 16 comes. This is due to a peculiarity of the drawPie() method, which expects its details in parts of $\frac{1}{16}$ th of a degree, for reasons of precision. angle therefore contains the actual number of degrees, multiplied by 16.

We then select the current color using the colorPos variable from the colorNames list. With a modulo calculation (%), we ensure that under no circumstances do we overwrite the end of the list, which means that if we were to run out of colors, we would just start assigning the current color from the beginning of the list again.

The next step is to define the form and color of the paintbrush and pen. Whereas we always used a continuous color for the paintbrush, we will now change to a gradient. Qt has several predefined gradient types. Here we will use a radial one.

This gradient has a center, a diameter, and a focus. We specify the center as the real center of pieRect, and we also determine the diameter via pieRect(). So that the gradient later "creases" the edge of the pie chart circle, thus creating the impression of spatial depth, we place the focus to the edge of the upper left region. We achieve this by specifying a region, with pieRect.topLeft(), which actually lies outside the pie. Between the center and the outer edge, we must also define at least two values for the course of the gradient. We do this using setColorAt(), which accepts colors for any floating-point numbers between 0 and 1. Instead of a color, we pass the gradients obtained in this way with setBrush().

Since we do not want any borders, we set the pen to NoPen, but not before saving the current pen—we still need it to draw the legend text, where it is used to define the font colors.

Now we can illustrate the current hash entry. drawPie() stretches out a rectangle in pieRect and draws an angle/16-degree large segment of pie, starting at lastAngleOffset.

Drawing Key Icons

The matching legend entry is still missing in the legendRect. We make this association clear with a square in the color of the corresponding segment of pie, which we store in the legendEntryRect variable:

```
// piechart/piewidget.cpp (continued)

    // calculate the squares for the legend
    int fh = fontMetrics().height();
    QRect legendEntryRect(0,(fh*2)*currentPos,fh,fh);
    currentPos++;
    legendEntryRect.translate(legendRect.topLeft());

    // define gradient for the legend squares
    QLinearGradient lg(legendEntryRect.topLeft(),
                    legendEntryRect.bottomRight());
    lg.setColorAt(0, col);
    lg.setColorAt(1, Qt::white);
    p.setBrush(QBrush(lg));
    p.drawRect(legendEntryRect);
```

Since this square should match the height and width of the type size, its size must be based on the nature of the current font. The QFontMetrics class is of help to us here, as it calculates the size of letters and strings in a specific font. The font metrics for the current widget are obtained via fontMetrics(). If you just want to change the font temporarily within the Painter, you should read out the font metrics via the method of the same name from QPainter.

Here we just require information on the maximum height of a letter, which we read out with height(). If we now plan as much space between the entries as is necessary for one entry, then we can calculate the position of the square: On the X-axis it lies directly at the zero point, while on the Y-axis it wanders two font heights down for each position ((fh*2)*currentPos). Width and height are also specified by fh in each case.

Now we still have to move legendEntryRect to the legendRect, because so far it is at the zero point of the X-axis. This is done using the translate method, to which we pass the upper left point, that is, our desired offset.

We redraw the square itself with a gradient, but this time with a linear gradient running from the top right to the bottom left, ending in the color white. Since the pen is still defined with NoPen, the drawRect() method now called with the rectangle also draws the square without the edge.

Inserting Legend Text

It is now time to draw the legend text next to the square. So that the distance from the square to the text is adjusted to the size of the font used, we select the width of the letter x in the respective font as the spacing. For this purpose we add the corresponding width to the x component of the textStart point. This variable now contains the top left point of our text. The lower left point is determined by combining the right edge of legendRect and the lower side of the current entry rectangle legendEntryRect into a new point. Together with textStart, this now opens up the textEntryRect in which space should be made for our text:

```
// piechart/piewidget.cpp (continued)

    // draw text behind squares
    QPoint textStart = legendEntryRect.topRight();
    textStart = textStart + QPoint(fontMetrics().width('x'), 0);
    QPoint textEnd(legendRect.right(), legendEntryRect.bottom());
    QRect textEntryRect(textStart, textEnd);
    p.setPen(pen);
    p.drawText(textEntryRect, Qt::AlignVCenter, text);
  }
}
```

After restoring our paintbrush, we insert the legend text precisely into the rectangle spcified, using the drawText() method. The AlignVCenter option ensures that the text is centered in its vertical alignment.

We repeat this procedure for each entry in the list until the circle is completely full.

10.5.2   Defining the Widget Size

In the minimumSizeHint() and sizeHint() methods, we need to determine only sensible minimum and default sizes for the widget. We specify that the widget must not be smaller than the default size, thus bringing both methods into line. But the widget may inflate at any time.

The height is the decisive factor for vertical expansion, which results from the total of all legend entries, together with the intervals between them. For the horizontal spread, we must first calculate the length of the longest entry in pixels. To do this we again iterate through the hash and look for the longest string in it:

```
// piechart/piewidget.cpp (continued)

QSize PieWidget::minimumSizeHint() const
{
  int fh = fontMetrics().height();
  int height = fh*2*values.count();
  int longest = 0;
  QHash<QString, int>::const_iterator it;
  QFontMetrics fm = fontMetrics();
  for(it = values.begin(); it != values.end(); ++it)
    longest = qMax(fm.width(it.key()), longest);
  int width = height+longest+fontMetrics().width('x')+fm+(2*10);
  QSize minSize(width, height);
  return minSize;
}
```

```
QSize PieWidget::sizeHint() const
{
  return minimumSizeHint();
}
```

The template function qMax() helps us in doing this. It is able to compare two objects of the same type, provided they both have the smaller-than operator, and it returns the larger element. In the same way, qMin() also exists.

The width is determined by the following parameters: the widget height of the square of the pie,[5] the longest entry in the hash table, the width of an x, the width of the legend square (fm) and the width of the 2×10 pixel–wide margin on both sides of the legend square. We pack the height and width into an instance of QSize and return this.

10.5.3   The Diagram Application

In order to use the class, we instantiate the widget, add a few entries with values, and display it. We have already seen the result in Figure 10.6:

```
// piechart/main.cpp

#include <QtGui>
#include "piewidget.h"

int main(int argc, char* argv[])
{
  QApplication app(argc, argv);
  PieWidget w;
  w.addEntry("Choice 1", 50);
  w.addEntry("Choice 2", 40);
  w.addEntry("Choice 3", 60);
  w.addEntry("Choice 4", 70);
  w.show();
  return app.exec();
}
```

10.6   Transformations of the Coordinate System

Normally a QPainter draws in a neutral, two-dimensional coordinate system. But sometimes it is necessary to manipulate this. Qt includes the QMatrix class for this purpose, which we will first approach theoretically. A QMatrix makes available a 3×3 matrix in the form

[5] With squares, length and width are equal.

$$\begin{pmatrix} m_{11} & m_{12} & 0 \\ m_{21} & m_{22} & 0 \\ dx & dy & 1 \end{pmatrix}$$

To understand how it functions, a short mathematics lesson is recommended: To transport a point (x, y) in a two-dimensional space to a new point (x', y'), it applies that:

$$x' = m_{11} * x + m_{21} * y + dx$$
$$y' = m_{22} * y + m_{12} * x + dy$$

The constructor of QMatrix has the form

```
QMatrix(qreal m11, qreal m12, qreal m21, qreal m22, qreal dx, qreal dy);
```

It therefore takes the individual matrix components as floating-point numbers and instantiates the corresponding 3×3 matrix.[6]

For matrices that are invertible, the corresponding *inverse* matrix undoes the operations carried out by the original matrix. QMatrix objects have a method by the name of inverted() that calculates the appropriate inverse matrix. This method expects as one of its parameters the address of a Boolean variable, and it returns a QMatrix. If the value stored in the variable after the method has been called is true, then the QMatrix object that inverted() returns is the inverse matrix of the specified matrix. If inverted() sets the Boolean variable to false, however, the original matrix is *singular*, meaning that no inverse matrix exists. In this case the method returns a *unit* or *identy matrix*, whose application results in no transformation taking place; that is, the unit matrix maps each point to itself. Whether a matrix can be inverted can be checked, when necessary, with isInvertible().

In the unit matrix, all the elements on the main diagonal (m_{11}, m_{22}, and the lower right-hand 1) have the value 1, and the others have the value 0. Whether a matrix is a unit matrix or not is revealed by the Boolean return value of the isIdentity() method.

To move points by a specific displacement using a transformation matrix, dx and dy are allocated values for the x and y offsets, in the following example 10 each, and the other values are like those of a unit matrix:

$$x' = 1 * x + 0 * y + 10$$
$$y' = 1 * y + 0 * x + 10$$

---

[6] qreal is a data type defined by Qt, corresponding to the C++ double type. Section B.6 in Appendix B lists all type definitions defined by Qt and explains their benefits.

This matrix transformation, called a *translation,* moves the point (x, y) so that the new x-coordinate x' is the value of x shifted by dx (here: 10) units. In the same way, you obtain y' by moving y by dy (in this example, also 10) units.

Instead of determining yourself what the corresponding QMatrix will look like, you can apply the translate() function to a unit matrix:

```
QMatrix matrix; // yields a unit matrix
matrix.translate(10.0, 10.0);
```

From now on, matrix moves all points by 10 units.[7]

The decisive variables when scaling (that is, when enlarging or decreasing in size) are m_{11} and m_{22}, each set to 10 in the following example:

$$x' = 10 * x + 0 * y + 0$$
$$y' = 10 * y + 0 * x + 0$$

The corresponding matrix transformation enlarges the points in the figure by a factor of 10 in each direction, thus scaling the coordinate system. The corresponding QMatrix can be obtained through the call

```
QMatrix matrix; // yields a unit matrix
matrix.scale(10.0, 10.0);
```

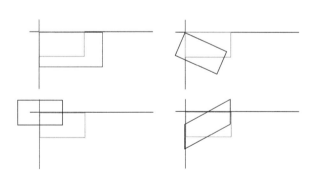

Figure 10.7: All four transformations at a glance: scaling and rotation (above), moving and shearing (below)

So far we have not seen the effects of m_{21} and m_{12}. These values in a transformation matrix cause the upper and lower sides of a rectangle to move apart from each other in a horizontal direction, and the sides to come closer together accordingly.

---

[7] The units themselves are specified by the class used by the matrix. At the moment we are using the term abstractly.

This effect, which can be seen in Figure 10.7 at the bottom right, is referred to as *shearing*:

$$x' = 1 * x + 10 * y + 0$$
$$y' = 1 * y + 10 * x + 0$$

Rotation uses the factors for shearing and scaling. The theory behind this is rather complicated, however; a more detailed treatment of this, together with derivations, would go beyond the scope of this book. At this point, we can only ascertain that rotation around the origin of the coordinate system can be represented as follows:

$$x' = \cos a * x - \sin a * y + 0$$
$$y' = \sin a * y + \sin a * x + 0$$

a stands for the degree of rotation in radian form; the rotational direction is counterclockwise. The rotate() method implements this rotation. As a parameter it demands the angle in degrees, which can be specified in floating-point precision.

10.6.1 Transformations in Practice

To achieve a better understanding of transformations with Qt, we shall look at the following example, which draws a circle filled with pattern onto a widget. A click on the widget starts it turning; the second click stops it again. In addition we allow the user to change the direction of rotation with the mouse wheel.

In addition to the sizeHint() method, which defines the initial size of the widget, we reimplement paintEvent() for drawing, mousePressEvent() for catching mouse clicks, wheelEvent() for reacting to the scroll wheel, and timerEvent(), which helps us to implement automatic rotation. rotate() performs the actual rotation work. We also need the variable timerId to be able to handle a timer. With degree we note by how many degrees the circle has just rotated:

```
// rotationwidget/rotationwidget.h

#ifndef ROTATIONWIDGET_H
#define ROTATIONWIDGET_H
#include <QWidget>
#include <QSize>

class RotationWidget : public QWidget {
  Q_OBJECT
  public:
    RotationWidget(QWidget *parent=0);

    QSize sizeHint() const {return QSize(200,200);}
```

```
    protected:
      void paintEvent(QPaintEvent *ev);
      void mousePressEvent(QMouseEvent *ev);
      void timerEvent(QTimerEvent *ev);
      void wheelEvent(QWheelEvent *ev);

      void rotate(int degree);

    private:
      int timerId;
      int degree;
};
#endif // ROTATIONWIDGET_H
```

The constructor initializes the parent class and ensures that the two member variables are preset to zero:

```
// rotationwidget/rotationwidget.cpp

#include <QtGui>
#include "rotationwidget.h"

RotationWidget::RotationWidget(QWidget *parent)
  : QWidget(parent)
{
  degree = 0;
  timerId = 0;
}
```

In paintEvent() we first determine the geometry of the widget. So that our drawEllipse() call immediately results in a circle, we match the width of the rectangle to its height. Then we adjust the rectangle. Specifically, QPainter from version 4.0 onward no longer includes the line that we draw with the pen into dimensions of the figures. Accordingly, we must reduce the rectangle in which we are about to draw the circle by the width of the pen, which in this case is two pixels:

```
// rotationwidget/rotationwidget.cpp (continued)

void RotationWidget::paintEvent(QPaintEvent* /*ev*/)
{
  QRect paintRect = rect();
  paintRect.setWidth(paintRect.height());
  paintRect.adjust(2,2,-2,-2);
  QPainter p(this);
  p.setRenderHint(QPainter::Antialiasing, true);

  QMatrix m;
  m.translate(center.x(), center.y());
```

```
    m.rotate(degree);
    m.translate(-center.x(), -center.y());
    p.setMatrix(m);

    QPoint center = paintRect.center();
    p.setBrush(QPixmap("qt.png"));
    p.setPen(QPen(Qt::black, 2, Qt::DashLine));
    p.drawEllipse(paintRect);
}
```

After we have instantiated the QPainter and have taught it to handle anti-aliasing, it is now time to create a transformation matrix that allows the coordinate system to rotate around the midpoint of the circle. To do this we create a new matrix. Since the center of the desired rotation is not the current zero point (origin) of the coordinate system, but the point at the center of the square, we first move the center of our square to the zero point of our coordinate system. Then we rotate the matrix and move the point back to its original location.

We then pass the matrix generated in this manner to the Painter. Everything that it now paints is rotated by the number of degrees specified in degree.

We select an ellipse as a drawing object. To fill it with a tiled pattern, we pass an image to the paintbrush, which then turns it into tiles placed next to each other, provided there is sufficient space.

This time we also select the pen slightly differently: It is black, has a thickness of two pixels (as mentioned), and forms a dashed line (Qt::DashLine). Finally, we draw an ellipse into the square, thus forcing a circle to be drawn.

As soon as the user clicks the widget with one of his mouse buttons, the widget obtains a mousePressEvent(). We first check whether the user pressed the left mouse button, and whether the timer is 0. If it is, then the timer is not running, and we can now start it. If, however, it contains a number not equal to 0, then it is active and we delete it, but not before resetting the timerId:

```
// rotationwidget/rotationwidget.cpp (continued)

void RotationWidget::mousePressEvent(QMouseEvent* ev)
{
  if (ev->button() != Qt::LeftButton)
    return;
  if ( timerId == 0 )
    timerId = startTimer(20);
  else {
    killTimer(timerId);
    timerId = 0;
  }
}

void RotationWidget::timerEvent(QTimerEvent *ev)
{
```

```
      if (ev->timerId() == timerId)
        rotate(1);

  }
```

We set the timer interval to 20 milliseconds, which corresponds to 50 timer events and therefore, ideally, 50 frames per second, since for each timerEvent() triggered, the program calls rotate(). The parameter in this call (here: 1) specifies by how many degrees the circle should turn.

With most mice, a scroll wheel movement corresponds to 15 degrees. Qt multiplies this by a factor of 8, so in this case we divide it again by 8. A scroll wheel movement therefore rotates the circle by 15 degrees clockwise or counterclockwise—depending on which direction the wheel is moved:

```
// rotationwidget/rotationwidget.cpp (continued)

void RotationWidget::wheelEvent(QWheelEvent *ev)
{
  rotate(ev->delta()/8);
}

void RotationWidget::rotate(int deg)
{
  degree = degree + deg % 360;
  update();
}
```

rotate now manages the degree value that we use in the paint event. As soon as it exceeds 359, the modulo operator ensures that the counter is reset to zero. In wheelEvent(), the delta() method from QWheelEvent holds the movement value.

To force a paint event, we must now call update(). update() sends a repaintEvent() via the event system to the widget. This in turn causes the repaintEvent() handler to be called, and the widget to be redrawn.

To demonstrate this behavior, it is sufficient to instantiate the widget, together with a QApplication, display it, and then enter the event loop, with app.exec():

```
// rotationwidget/main.cpp

#include <QtGui>
#include "rotationwidget.h"

int main(int argc, char* argv[])
{
  QApplication app(argc, argv);
  RotationWidget w;
  w.show();
  return app.exec();
}
```

10.7 QImage

If image points are to be manipulated directly, the QImage, which is optimized for this purpose, is ideal as a "screen." Qt carries out corresponding operations on the processor, whereas the graphic card is normally responsible for QPixmap operations.

Under X11 in particular, another difference between the two classes is of some significance: The X client is responsible for rendering QImages, whereas pixmaps are drawn by the server. Every conversion between classes is therefore slow, and possibly bandwidth intensive,[8] but nevertheless generally possible with QPixmap::convertToImage() and QPixmap::convertFromImage(). An advantage of QImage is its platform independence, a property that QPixmap does not have.

If a program should only be based on QCoreApplication, but should still process graphics, QPixmap is not available, but it is still possible to work with QImage.[9]

10.7.1 Storage Formats, Transparency, and Color Palettes

A QImage is capable of storing images in various ways in the main memory. The developer can specify the image format when calling the class constructor by passing it the matching value of the Format enumerator. The format() method accordingly returns the format of the current QImage.

Normally Qt stores images in a quality requiring 32 bits for each pixel. In doing this, QImage uses 8 bits each for the colors red, green, and blue, so that only 24 bits are used up. The remaining byte either remains unused,[10] or specifies the "transparency" (the *alpha channel*) of each pixel. The former option is specified using QImage::Format_RGB32, whereas the format with the predefined transparency value is referred to by Trolltech as *ARGB32* (QImage::Format_ARGB32).

It is relatively resource intensive to use an alpha channel when drawing, because a series of calculations must precede each drawing operation: For each pixel, the processor multiplies each color channel with the value of the corresponding alpha channel, and divides the result by 255. The obvious consideration, of performing these calculations when the pixel is set and saving the results in the color values, has been put into practice by Trolltech with the *ARGB32-Premultiplied* format (QImage::Format_ARGB32_Premultiplied). Here the alpha channel is still stored as an additional value. The disadvantage of this format is that when the alpha channel is recalculated, this does not result in exactly the same color. Since the deviation is very small, however, it can often be ignored. However, if you constantly con-

---

[8] Remember that any conversion is expensive, even in a local X-session—that is, even if you do not use the network capability of the X server.

[9] Nevertheless, QImage remains a part of the QtGui library. This must therefore be included in the project, whatever the case, even though you do not use a graphical interface.

[10] The obvious idea of reducing the size to 24 bits is a bad one, because modern processors usually process at least 32-bit words anyway. In the worst case, speed would be reduced by corresponding special adjustments.

vert colors that have already been converted back from the RGB32-Premultiplied format, the color deviation will become clearly visible at some stage. Because of its advantages in speed, the ARGB32-Premultiplied is nevertheless the preferred format of the RGB32 family supported by QImage.

Alternatively, you can use a color palette. In a similar way to the palette of a Painter, only selected colors are available here. With the QImage-*Indexed8* format (QImage::Format_Indexed8), an 8-bit index is available for colors, which means that there is space for a maximum of 256 colors on the palette simultaneously. Before you can work with this format, you must specify the number of colors in the palette, using setNumColors(), with a number between 1 and 256. The corresponding query method, numColors(), returns a valid value only for color palette-based formats; otherwise, it returns 0.

To set the color palette, the API provides two possibilities. setColorTable() allows the complete palette to be covered with a vector consisting of RGB color details (QVector<QRgb>). In addition to this, setColor() allows individual palette colors to be defined. This method expects the position as an integer and the color as QRgb as its parameters.

Monochrome images are saved by using QImage::Format_Mono. When this happens, each bit represents a pixel, whereby the *most significant bit* comes first. In contrast, QImage::Format_Mono_LSB saves monochrome images with the *least significant bit* first.

A QImage can be converted to another format via the convertToFormat() method. This method expects a first parameter specifying the new format, and for the second parameter it requires more details on the conversion, which may sometimes result in losses.

If a QImage becomes invalid, its form is also invalid, and format() returns QImage::Format_Invalid.

10.7.2   Reading out Pixels Line by Line

If you want to perform complex operations on images, you must have access to every single pixel. For this purpose, QImage provides the scanLine() method, which returns color information of the line pixel by pixel, as an array of unsigned chars. Since an unsigned char is eight bits in size, each individual pixel is represented by four array entries.

When this is done, however, the *byte order* gets in the developer's way: Some systems arrange bytes from left to right so that the byte with the lowest value lies at the lowest memory address. These architectures, which include the Intel x86 family, are referred to as *little endian*. For other systems the opposite is the case: They store the byte with the highest value at the lowest memory address. This species, the *big endian* system,[11] includes the PowerPC processor, which is used in a wide range of IBM Linux servers and in many Macintosh computers and laptops.

The color details of an image four pixels in size can therefore be arranged in two variations, depending on architecture on which the image is stored as a QImage:

BBGGRRAABBGGRRAA**BBGGRRAA**BBGGRRAA (little endian)

AARRGGBBAARRGGBB**AARRGGBB**AARRGGBB (big endian)

In order to implement color details without taking into account the byte order, Qt uses a small trick: It defines the type QRgb. This is nothing more than a 32-bit integer that stores the alpha channel and the three color channels in the form 0xAARRBBGG. When converting via reinterpret_cast<QRgb*>, Qt takes up the unsigned chars in the byte order of the platform. The individual components of the color can now be safely accessed via QRgb::qRed(), QRgb::qGreen(), QRgb::qBlue() and QRgb::qAlpha(), which also return values from 0 to 255.

The following example reads out an image line by line and runs through the RGB values. The result is also saved to a QImage.

The core of the program is the rotateRgb() method. This creates a new QImage object of identical size and identical color format. Then it opens the same array in both files and reinterprets the characters as a QRgb array. The number of rows are defined by the height of the image, the number of columns by the width. For each pixel we can now read out all color values separately, and recombine them as we please. The image processed in this way is then returned:

```
// rotatergb/main.cpp

#include <QtGui>

QImage rotateRgb(const QImage &in)
{
  QImage out(in.size(), in.format());
  for(int line = 0; line < in.height(); line++) {
    const QRgb* inPixels = reinterpret_cast<const QRgb*>
                                            (in.scanLine(line));
    QRgb* outPixels = reinterpret_cast<QRgb*>(out.scanLine(line));
    for(int pos = 0; pos < in.width(); pos++) {
      int red = qRed(inPixels[pos]);
      int green = qGreen(inPixels[pos]);
      int blue = qBlue(inPixels[pos]);
      int alpha = qAlpha(inPixels[pos]);
      outPixels[pos] = qRgba(blue, red, green, alpha);
    }
  }
```

[11] The terms *big endian* and *little endian* owe their origin to an analogy in a story from *Gulliver's Travels*, in which two states are at war over which end of a boiled egg should be chopped off. The similarly heated discussions on what is the best byte order now seem to be running in favor of big endian architectures. Big endian is is also known as *Network Byte Order*, as it is used to transport data across the Internet.

```
    return out;
}
```

In the main() function we load the reference image, have it rotated, and then display the distorted image in a label. Then we repeat the procedure and obtain an image that is still distorted. Only after the third swap are the colors again in order. All three labels are shown next to each other in Figure 10.8.

```
// rotatergb/main.cpp (continued)

int main(int argc, char* argv[])
{
  QApplication app(argc, argv);
  QImage img("qt.png");
  QLabel rgb;
  img = rotateRgb(img);
  QLabel brg;
  brg.setPixmap(QPixmap::fromImage(img));
  img = rotateRgb(img);
  QLabel grb;
  grb.setPixmap(QPixmap::fromImage(img));
  img = rotateRgb(img);
  rgb.setPixmap(QPixmap::fromImage(img));
  rgb.show();
  brg.show();
  grb.show();
  return app.exec();
}
```

Figure 10.8:
One image, three
color arrangements:
Our test application
has swapped the RGB
channels around.

10.8   SVG Support

Since version 4.1, Qt 4 has supported the *scalable vector graphics* format, in short, SVG. It is being officially published by the W3 consortium, which is also responsible for the HTML and CSS standards. SVG describes two-dimensional vector graphics and is based on XML, in contrast to many established vector graphics standards. The last SVG version to be published by the W3C was version 1.1, and the SVG working committee of the W3C is preparing version 1.2, which currently has the status of a working draft.

To guarantee its use on mobile platforms, the W3C additionally published so-called profiles with a reduced functionality, *SVG Basic* and *SVG Tiny*.[12]

Qt 4 implements SVG-Tiny and SVG-Basic in versions 1.1 and 1.2, but currently supports neither ECMA script (often referred to as JavaScript) nor other graphic manipulations via the *Document Object Model* (DOM).

Qt combines the SVG classes in a separate library called QtSvg. To use them, you must first extend the .pro file as follows:

```
QT += svg
```

The include instruction corresponds to the library name:

```
#include <QtSvg>
```

So far, Qt has not handled SVG files via QPixmap. Instead it makes the rendering API directly available, under the name QSvgRenderer. In addition there is a widget, QSvgWidget, which can directly display SVG images (below we create an instance that displays the file file.svg):

```
QSvgWidget *svgw = new QSvgWidget("file.svg");
```

QSvgWidget knows the load() slot in two variations. The first one expects a filename as a QString, similar to the constructor in the above example. The second one is passed the contents of an SVG file as a QByteArray. No corresponding constructor exists for this.

Another method that distinguishes QSvgWidget from a normal QWidget is the access function renderer(), which returns a pointer to the QSvgRenderer object used for the widget. QSvgRenderer is the class responsible for actual rendering.

If QSvgWidget has loaded an image, it finds out about its sizeHint(), which matches the image size proposed in the SVG file, with QSvgRenderer::defaultSize(). Without a loaded image, it inherits its behavior from QWidget::size().

The QSvgRenderer itself provides an extensive API for checking images and animations. In addition to the load() slot (which is available in QSvgWidget and QSvgRenderer), there is an additional render() slot, which expects a QPainter object as a parameter. This enables the redrawing of the widget by the Painter passed on,

---

[12] See http://www.w3.org/TR/SVGMobile/.

if you want to use the render object directly. This is always necessary for widgets, for example, if a paint event occurs. QSvgWidget reacts to this something like as follows:

```
void QSvgWidget::paintEvent(QPaintEvent *)
{
  ...
  QPainter p(this);
  renderer->render(&p);
}
```

renderer here is the QSvgRenderer instance. The QSvgRenderer::animate() method checks whether the loaded SVG file contains animated elements. If this is the case, animationDuration() returns the length of the animation as an integer value in seconds. In Qt 4.1, however, this method is not fully implemented: It always returns 0. framesPerSecond() reveals the number of frames per second. The standard playback speed is 30 frames per second. setFramesPerSecond() changes this value, thus slowing down or speeding up the animation.

If load() loads an SVG file with animated elements, QSvgRenderer emits the signal repaintNeeded() according to the details specified in framesPerSecond(). The current frame of an animation is revealed by currentFrame(). It is defined with setCurrentFrame().

10.9   Printing with QPrinter

The QPrinter class is responsible for printing in Qt. Like QPixmap or QImage, it is a QPaintDevice, but has several interesting special features.

So that the printing process can begin, the current Painter must explicitly confirm that it has finished its work, with end(). In addition you must call the QPrinter method newPage() for each new page, including the first one. The Painter, which works on the QPrinter instance, will then have a free page available again. Some parameters, such as the page orientation (portrait or landscape mode), can only be changed *before* the Painter registers with the QPrinter object, that is, back in the QPainter constructor.

There is also the QPrintDialog class, enabling a variety of settings to be made at the printer. Under Windows and Mac OS X the class shows the print dialog of the system; otherwise, it uses a separate dialog. The user can manipulate all the settings in the dialog.

We want to take a closer look at these classes, using as an example a small program to create screenshots (Figure 10.9 on page 307). This has a slot that prepares the acquisition of the screenshot, another slot that retrieves the screenshot, and a third one to print it out.

In addition it has the previewLabel member variable, pointing to a QLabel which displays the last screenshot in preview size, as well as a screenshot member, specifying a QPixmap with the screenshot in full resolution:

```
// screenshot/grabdialog.h

#ifndef GRABDIALOG_H
#define GRABDIALOG_H
#include <QDialog>
#include <QPixmap>

class QLabel;

class GrabDialog : public QDialog
{

  Q_OBJECT
  public:
    GrabDialog(QWidget *parent=0);

  protected slots:
    void prepareGrabDesktop();
    void grabDesktop();
    void printScreenshot();

  private:
    QLabel *previewLabel;
    QPixmap screenshot;
};
#endif // GRABDIALOG_H
```

In the constructor we set up a table layout into which we place the previewLabel so that it takes up two columns. Two buttons, one to start the screenshot and one to print it out, are placed one row beneath this, each in their own column. So that the preview label is always visible, we fix it to 300×200 pixels:

```
// screenshot/grabdialog.cpp

#include <QtGui>
#include "grabdialog.h"

GrabDialog::GrabDialog(QWidget *parent)
  : QDialog(parent)
{
  QGridLayout *lay = new QGridLayout(this);
  previewLabel = new QLabel;
  previewLabel->setFixedSize(300,200);
  lay->addWidget(previewLabel, 0, 0, 1, 2);
  QPushButton *screenshotBtn = new QPushButton(tr("&Screenshot!"));
  QPushButton *printBtn= new QPushButton(tr("&Print"));
```

```
lay->addWidget(screenshotBtn, 1, 0);
lay->addWidget(printBtn, 1, 1);
connect(screenshotBtn, SIGNAL(clicked()), SLOT(prepareGrabDesktop()));
connect(printBtn, SIGNAL(clicked()), SLOT(printScreenshot()));
grabDesktop();
setWindowTitle(tr("Screenshot"));
}
```

We now connect the clicked() signal of the Screenshot! button to the slot that prepares the screenshot, and the signal of the Print button to the slot that enables the configuration of the printing parameters. Then we call grabDesktop(), which retrieves a screenshot from the current screen at the time the program is started. It is intended merely as a substitute image for the previewLabel.

10.9.1   Digression: Making Screenshots

Because screenshot programs are normally not intended to record themselves, they should be hidden as much as possible during the screenshot itself. To do this we call hide(), directly followed by a *singleshot timer*,[13] which starts grabDesktop():

```
// screenshot/grabdialog.cpp (continued)

void GrabDialog::prepareGrabDesktop()
{
  hide();
  QTimer::singleShot(500, this, SLOT(grabDesktop()));
}
```

The 500-millisecond delay is intended to give the operating system a chance, before the actual screenshot is made, to adjust any possible artifacts that may have been caused by the window suddenly disappearing.

But how do we access a copy of the entire screen? Although QPixmap provides the static method grabWidget(), it can record only individual widgets in the current application. Luckily there is also the grabWindow() static method, which expects not a pointer to a widget, but a window ID. The use of these IDs is portable in principle; nevertheless, the documentation strongly warns against making certain assumptions about the IDs.

Information on the current desktop is provided by the QDesktopWidget class. The QApplication instance already provides an object of this class, which we can immediately access. The window ID for the entire current desktop can be obtained via the QWidget method winId(), applied to the current screen, which is returned

---

[13] In contrast to normal timers, a singleshot timer announces itself only once, not at fixed intervals.

byQDesktopWidget::screen(). screen() returns a QWidget, which you can unfortunately not scan directly using grabWidget(), but which instead has the sizes of the current desktop as well as its window ID.

But with grabWindow() we can obtain the screenshot and store it in screenshot. A pixmap scaled down to the size of the label is also included in the previewLabel. In addition we save the screenshot on the hard drive, to be more precise, in the current working directory of the application, and then display the window again:

```
// screenshot/grabdialog.cpp (continued)

void GrabDialog::grabDesktop()
{
  QDesktopWidget *w = qApp->desktop();
  screenshot= QPixmap::grabWindow(w->screen()->winId());
  previewLabel->setPixmap(screenshot.scaled(previewLabel->size()));
  screenshot.save("screenshot.png", "PNG");
  show();
}
```

10.9.2   Printing an Image File

Now we are ready to print: To do this we first instantiate a QPrinter object. Since we want to print an image, we require a high resolution. For this purpose it would be good to pass the QPrinter::HighResolution parameter to the constructor. But due to the immense amount of memory needed, this precautionary measure will be of no help to us under Linux. This is less the fault of Qt than that of the Linux memory management system. For such images, even on systems with 512 MB of main memory, it continues swapping until the system simply hangs. For this reason we will stick to the standard resolution, even if it produces somewhat poorer results:

```
// screenshot/grabdialog.cpp (continued)

void GrabDialog::printScreenshot()
{
  QPrinter printer;
  printer.setOrientation(QPrinter::Landscape);
  QPrintDialog dlg(&printer, this);
  if (dlg.exec() == QDialog::Accepted) {
    printer.newPage();
    QPainter p(&printer);
    QPixmap resized = screenshot.scaledToWidth(
                           printer.pageRect().width());
    p.drawPixmap(0,0, resized);
    p.end();
  }
}
```

In the next step we instantiate a print dialog and start it with exec(). In this way the user has the opportunity to change nearly all previously set printing options as he pleases. The dialog is based on the current QPrinter settings: the orientation is already set to Landscape, for example.

If the user has ended the dialog by clicking Ok, the actual printing process begins: We instantiate a new QPainter, which operates the printer. Then we scale the screenshot so that it fits exactly onto the page—normally it is slightly larger—depending on the resolution. As a help in orientation, we use pageRect() to do this: This value already takes into account any possible page margins already set. We now draw the resized pixmap matching in size, with drawPixmap(), to draw on the printer. With p.end(), we signal that our work is complete, and QPrinter sends our job to a printer.

10.9.3   Generating PDFs

Since Qt 4.1, QPrinter has also been able to generate PDF files. To write our image to a PDF file, just the following code is needed:

```
QPrinter printer;
printer.setOutputFormat(QPrinter::PdfFormat);
printer.setOutputFileName("out.pdf");
printer.newPage();
QPainter p(&printer);
QPixmap resized = screenshot.scaledToWidth(
                    printer.pageRect().width());
p.drawPixmap(0,0, resized);
p.end();
```

10.9.4   The Test Application

The test routine for the dialog instantiates a QApplication object and a dialog. Instead of sending it into a separate event loop with exec(), we display it normally with show() (Figure 10.9), and afterward enter the global event loop.

This way is ideal if you need neither a return value nor a dialog that behaves modally:

```
// screenshot/main.cpp

#include <QtGui>
#include "grabdialog.h"

int main(int argc, char* argv[])
{
  QApplication app(argc,argv);
```

```
    GrabDialog dialog;
    dialog.show();
    return app.exec();
}
```

Figure 10.9:
The screenshot
program after it
starts

10.10   Complex Graphics

The possibilities that are offered by QPainter can be skillfully combined, essentially using three techniques: clipping, Painter paths, and the composition modes.

10.10.1   Clipping

With clipping, a QPaintDevice is cut off, with the help of a figure, so that it can be seen only inside the boundary of the figure. This technique is demonstrated in Figure 10.10, in which the tiled pattern is restricted by a triangle.

In the corresponding code we create a QWidget subclass called PaintWidget. Apart from the empty constructor, this just has a static sizeHint():

```
// clipping/paintwidget.h

#include <QWidget>

class PaintWidget : public QWidget
{
    Q_OBJECT
    public:
    PaintWidget(QWidget* parent = 0);

    virtual void paintEvent(QPaintEvent*);
    virtual QSize sizeHint() const {return QSize(200,200);}
};
```

Figure 10.10:
A triangular polygon
restricts the Painter.

In the constructor we initialize the parent class, whereas in paintEvent() we instantiate a QPainter on the widget. There we then construct a QPolygon with three points:

```
// clipping/paintwidget.cpp

#include <QtGui>
#include "paintwidget.h"

PaintWidget::PaintWidget(QWidget *parent)
    : QWidget(parent)
{
}

void PaintWidget::paintEvent(QPaintEvent* /*ev*/)
{
  QPainter p(this);
  QPolygon poly;
  poly << rect().topLeft();
  poly << QRect(rect().center().x(), rect().bottom());
  poly << rect().topRight();
  p.setClipRegion(poly);
  painter.drawTiledPixmap(rect(), QPixmap("qt.png"));
}
```

The QPolygon class is based on QVector<QPoint> so that we can add new points with the streaming operators. We select them so that they open up a triangle between the two top corner points and the lower midpoint, and set the polygon created in this way as a *clip region*.

We now paint a tiled pattern over the entire widget background. But only the part inside the triangle is visible, as shown in Figure 10.10.

10.10.2 Painter Paths

The second technique that plays a role in connection with complex graphics is Painter paths. The QPainterPath class can combine instances of all primitive geometry classes into a figure that can be as complex as you want, and it can also include Bezier curves.

Figure 10.11:
Painter paths allow
flexible forms with
gradients.

With this technique, figures can be implemented as shown in Figure 10.11. These are created with the following source code:

```
// painterpath/paintwidget.cpp

#include <QtGui>
#include "paintwidget.h"

PaintWidget::PaintWidget(QWidget *parent)
    : QWidget(parent)
{
}

void PaintWidget::paintEvent(QPaintEvent* /*ev*/)
{
  QLinearGradient gradient(rect().topLeft(), rect().bottomRight());
  gradient.setColorAt(0, Qt::yellow);
  gradient.setColorAt(1, Qt::white);

  QPainterPath path;
  path.cubicTo(rect().topLeft(), rect().bottomLeft(),
    rect().bottomRight());
  path.cubicTo(rect().topRight(), rect().bottomRight(),
    rect().bottomLeft());
```

```
QPainter p(this);
p.setRenderHint(QPainter::Antialiasing, true);
p.drawTiledPixmap(rect(), QPixmap("qt.png"));
p.setBrush(gradient);
p.drawPath(path);
}
```

The class declaration and constructor match those from the previous example. The differences can be found in the paintEvent() method.

There we first instantiate a QLinearGradient object, the color gradation of which should run from yellow to white across the widget along the main diagonal. With this gradient we want to fill a Painter path consisting of two cubic Bezier curves. We fix the shapes of these to the corner points of the widget geometry.

After we have completed these preparations, we instantiate a QPainter here as well. In the next step we activate anti-aliasing, draw the background, and pass the gradient to the paintbrush. This now fills the pixels painted over by it according to the specifications of the gradient. If we draw the path, it contains the color gradient. Thus elegant figures can also be implemented via Painter paths.

10.10.3   Composition Modes

Finally, QPainter supports the so-called *composition modes* for pixels, according to Porter and Duff.[14]

In Porter-Duff compositing, a pixel is combined from two sources that each have color details with an alpha channel. So-called *composition operators* combine these sources into a new pixel.

In Qt these operators always refer to the current Painter operation (the *source*) as well as the current target pixel on the drawing device (target, or *destination*). The composition mode can be changed before every drawing operation. A new ARGB32 pixel is created according to the formula

$$\text{result color}_{\text{pixels}} = \text{source color}_{\text{pixels}} *_{\text{pdo}} \text{destination color}_{\text{pixels}}$$

Here the operator $*_{\text{pdo}}$ is not a normal multiplication, but stands for one of the Porter-Duff operators that combine both values with each other. If such an operator is set, this changes the composition mode in the QPainter.

For this to function, the QImage must use the Format_ARGB32_Premultiplied or the Format_ARGB32. If this is not the case, it is converted accordingly using convertToFormat().

---

[14] Named after Thomas Porter and Tom Duff, who developed this technique at Lucasfilm and went public at the SIGGRAPH conference (Thomas Porter and Tom Duff, "Compositing Digital Images," SIGGRAPH Vol. 88, 1984, pages 253–59). The term *Porter-Duff algebra* is also used.

Compositing Operators

A number of composition modes, such as *SourceOver* and *DestinationOver*, only reveal their full efects for images with Alpha channels. The SourceOver mode (QPainter::CompositionMode_SourceOver) is also known as *alpha blending*: Here the Painter paints the source pixel over the destination pixel. If transparency is switched on, parts of the destination pixel still shine through (Figure 10.12 links).

The opposite is the case with DestinationOver (QPainter::CompositionMode_DestinationOver): Here the source pixel becomes the background, and the destination pixel accordingly remains in the foreground (Figure 10.12 on the right).

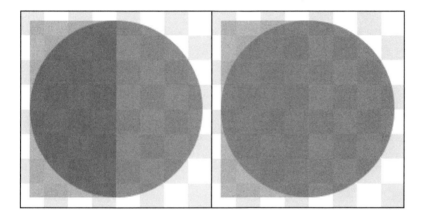

Figure 10.12:
A comparison of the SourceOver *and* DestinationOver *operators*

The *source* and *destination* operators also behave in a complementary manner: In the source mode (QPainter::CompositionMode_Source), the new pixel results directly from the source pixel. Its contents overwrite the previous contents of this pixel.

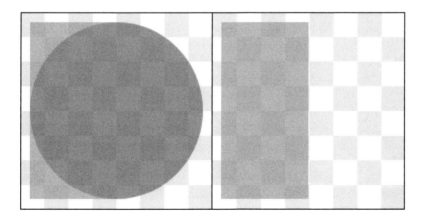

Figure 10.13:
The source and destination operators let only one color through, instead of combining them as their brothers SourceOver *or* DestinationOver *do.*

In QPainter::CompositionMode_Destination, the destination operator ignores the newly drawn pixel and takes into account only the already existing image content. This is illustrated in Figure 10.13: the left circle, drawn in source mode, completely covers over the rectangle and the transparent area. On the right, on the other hand, no circle is visible, because the transparent destination pixels themselves dominate the source pixels.

Both procedures behave in the same way, as SourceOver and DestinationOver if source and destination colors are opaque, that is, if they have an alpha value of 255.

Figure 10.14:
A comparison of the
complementary
SourceIn and
DestinationIn
operators

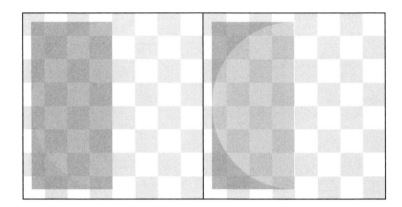

With the operators discussed below, the alpha channel plays an important role. With the *SourceIn* procedure (QPainter::CompositionMode_SourceIn), the color of the new pixel can be derived from the source, reduced by the alpha value of the destination. The reduction of the alpha channel here means a higher transparency,[15] as can be seen on the left in Figure 10.14. Conversely, the new color can be derived in the *DestinationIn* procedure (QPainter::CompositionMode_DestinationIn) from the destination, reduced by the alpha value of the source. The result of this mode can be seen on the right in the figure.

The *SourceOut* and *DestinationOut* modes function in the same way as SourceIn and DestinationIn, by using the alpha channel. The only difference consists in the value to be subtracted: With SourceOut (QPainter::CompositionMode_SourceOut), the inverse of the source is subtracted, and with DestinationOut (QPainter::CompositionMode_DestinationOut), the inverse alpha value of the destination is subtracted. Each of these is defined as follows:

$$\text{inverseAlpha} = 255 - \text{alpha}$$

Figure 10.15 shows the circle and the rectangle from the previous examples, painted in SourceOut mode (on the left) and in DestinationOut mode (on the right). There

---

[15] An alpha value of 0 makes a pixel fully transparent; 255 makes it fully visible.

the right half of the circle is invisible, since the alpha value for these positions amounts to 0.

Of course, the SourceOver and SourceIn modes and their counterparts DestinationOver and DestinationIn can be combined. These are given the names *SourceAtop* and *DestinationAtop*.

In the SourceAtop mode (QPainter::CompositionMode_SourceAtop), the source is overlayed on the destination, and the alpha value of the source is reduced by the alpha value of the destination.

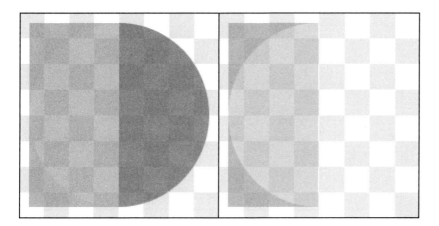

Figure 10.15:
The SourceOut and DestinationOut operators work like SourceIn and DestinationIn, but use an inverse alpha value.

In the inverse DestinationAtop mode (QPainter::CompositionMode_DestinationAtop) the source overlays the destination. The difference from SourceAtop becomes clear in Figure 10.16 from the dominance of the fill color for circle and rectangle. In addition, this mode subtracts the alpha value of the destination pixel from that of the source pixel.

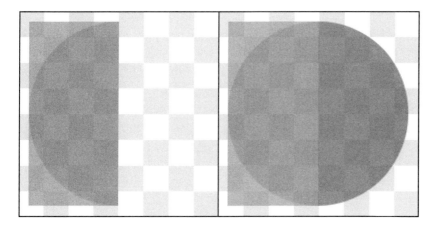

Figure 10.16:
SourceAtop and DestinationAtop combine SourceOver and SourceIn as well as DestinationOver and DestinationIn.

In *XOR* mode (QPainter::CompositionMode_Xor), the Painter links the alpha value of the source (subtracted from the inverse of the destination) to the destination, the alpha value of which it subtracts from the inverse of the source. The result of this operation is shown on the left side of Figure 10.17.

The *clear* mode displayed on the right (QPainter::CompositionMode_Clear) is used, for example, to stencil out masks from figures. For each pixel in the source in which the alpha channel has a value other than 0, the Painter in clear mode sets the alpha value of the destination pixel to 0, thus making the corresponding pixel transparent.

Figure 10.17: The XOR operator links source and destination with an exclusive OR; Clear enables complete figures to be stencilled out of images.

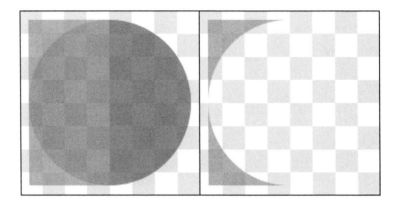

Using the DestinationOut Operator on a Painter Path

We will adjust the example from Section 10.10.2 (page 309) so that a compositing operator covers the area in a dark color. The result should match that shown in Figure 10.18.

The Painter path in paintEvent() remains the same; we again instantiate the Painter and activate anti-aliasing. Then we draw the background. For the paintbrush, we select black with a semitransparent alpha channel. With the DestinationOut operator, the Painter path thus acquires its black and semitransparent coloring:

```
// composition/paintwidget.cpp

#include <QtGui>
#include "paintwidget.h"

PaintWidget::PaintWidget(QWidget *parent)
    : QWidget(parent)
{
}
```

```
void PaintWidget::paintEvent(QPaintEvent* /*ev*/)
{
  QPainterPath path;
  path.cubicTo(rect().topLeft(), rect().bottomLeft(),
    rect().bottomRight());
  path.cubicTo(rect().topRight(), rect().bottomRight(),
    rect().bottomLeft());

  QPainter p(this);
  p.setRenderHint(QPainter::Antialiasing, true);
  p.drawTiledPixmap(rect(), QPixmap("qt.png"));
  p.setBrush(QColor::fromRgba(qRgba(0,0,0,128)));
  p.setCompositionMode(QPainter::CompositionMode_DestinationOut);
  p.drawPath(path);
}
```

The fact that the widget itself is opaque means that most of the compositing operators in this example are not very exciting, as they only reveal their full effects if a source and destination have a non-opaque alpha channel.

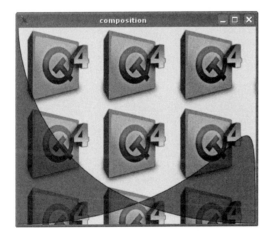

Figure 10.18: DestinationOut darkens the Painter path.

Nevertheless, compositing is an interesting alternative to clipping, which cannot offer capabilities such as alpha transparency or anti-aliasing. This advantage is offset at times, however, particularly under X11, by programs that run considerably more slowly.

11

Input/Output Interfaces

You can hardly imagine any application today that does not access files, networks, or external processes. Consequently, Qt 4 provides interfaces for communicating with the environment that are independent of the operating system.

Although each of the operating systems supported by Qt provides interfaces to deal with the various kinds of I/O, there is sadly no uniform standard for managing this functionality. These circumstances often force programmers to completely redesign the code if they want to, for example, send a datastream across a network instead of saving it to a file. Qt 4 gets around this problem by providing a base class called QIODevice, which provides a platform for all I/O interfaces.

11.1   The QIODevice Class Hierarchy

QIODevice implements operations such as reading and writing on one device. Qt also considers a network connection to be a device. Of course, there are some restrictions, because stream-oriented connections (also called *sequential connections*), such as those implemented via TCP, are not available for limitless access.

Figure 11.1:
The base class
QIODevice *and its*
specializations

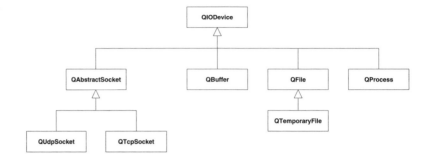

QIODevice is an abstract class, so the developer only ever instantiates its subclasses. It represents the lowest common denominator of all types of input and output operations. Figure 11.1 provides an overview of the input/output classes that are based on QIODevice.

11.1.1 Derived Classes

QAbstractSocket cannot be used directly as the base class for socket-based communication, in contrast to its subclasses QUdpSocket and QTcpSocket. QUdpSocket enables communications via the *User Datagram Protocol* (UDP). This works without a connection and provides no guarantee that the data sent will arrive intact or in the correct order. Due to the lack of corrective measures, however, it is considerably faster than the *Transmission Control Protocol* (TCP), via which the QTcpSocket class sends data.

In contrast to UDP, TCP connections are connection oriented and ensure a reliable transfer of data. Many of the protocols popular today, such as HTTP, which is used commonly in the World Wide Web for transmitting web pages and downloads, are based on TCP.

The QBuffer class allows you to write to QByteArray instances as if they were QIODevice-based devices. We were already introduced to this procedure in Section 8.8 on page 243, and we will take a further look at it on page 322 in connection with QDataStream.

Probably the most frequently used subclass of QIODevice is the QFile subclass. We learned about its ability to read and write files on the local filesystem for the first time on page 113.

In case there is not enough memory to store temporary data via QBuffer in a QByteArray, QTemporaryFile is available. In contrast to QFile, this class generates a filename independently and ensures that this name is unique, so that it will not overwrite other files by mistake. The temporary file is stored by QTemporaryFile beneath the temporary directory used by Qt. This directory's location is revealed by the static method QDir::tempPath(). As soon as the QTemporaryFile object is deleted, the temporary file associated with it is also automatically deleted.

QProcess is also based on QIODevice. This class enables processes to be started with additional arguments and permits communication with them via the QIODevice methods. In addition the class can selectively manipulate the environment variables of the process.

11.1.2 Opening I/O Devices

Every QIODevice must first be opened before it can be used. The open() method is available for this purpose, and its arguments describe in detail how the device in question is to be accessed, for example, whether the program (and thus the end user as well) should have only write or only read permissions. This method is therefore similar to the POSIX function open().

Flag	Value	Description
QIODevice::NotOpen	0x0000	Device is not open (not a useful detail for open())
QIODevice::ReadOnly	0x0001	Device is opened for reading
QIODevice::WriteOnly	0x0002	Device is opened for writing
QIODevice::ReadWrite	ReadOnly | WriteOnly	Device is opened for reading and writing
QIODevice::Append	0x0004	Device is opened in append mode and all data added to the end
QIODevice::Truncate	0x0008	If possible, all previous contents are deleted when device is opened
QIODevice::Text	0x0010	When reading text, line breaks are converted to the system-specific end-of-line indicators (Windows: \r\f, Unix/OS X: \r) and vice-versa when writing
QIODevice::Unbuffered	0x0020	Direct access, all buffers under device are ignored

Table 11.1: Parameters of the QIODevices::open() method

Table 11.1 shows the possible access flags represented as powers of base 2, so that they can be combined in any way you like (at least theoretically) by using a logical OR operator (|). With ReadWrite, Qt does this itself: This flag combines ReadOnly and WriteOnly. Since each device may ignore individual flags that do not apply to it, there is little risk that the device does not behave exactly to the programmer's expectations. In this case, you should check the API docs for exceptions.

This means that there is no reason *not* to make use of the very finely structured access methods. In plain language, if you only want to read from a file, then you should open the file with ReadOnly. The operating system can under certain circumstances manage without resource-intensive locking, and the program will get the files it wants much more quickly. In addition the application does not run any danger of overwriting files by accident when reading.

11.2   Access to Local Files

The QFile class was used to open files a number of times in the preceding chapters. When doing this we passed the file to be opened as an argument in the constructor and then opened the file. Below we have a new situation, in which we open traditional FILE pointers with QFile.

To demonstrate this we will write a small program that removes all the empty lines and comment lines from a file. The hash symbol (#) at the beginning of a line is assumed to be the comment sign.

Our program is invoked from the command line and expects the name of the file to be analyzed as the first argument. If there is a second argument, it writes the output to the file named there. Otherwise, the modified file appears on the console via the standard output, stdout.

It is remarkable that we do not even require a QCoreApplication object for this example, since QFile is not dependent on an event loop.

In the main() function we first check whether there is at least one argument apart from the name of the executable. Then we try to open the file for reading. If it does not exist, open() announces an error due to the ReadOnly access, which we catch with an error message. Thanks to the Text Flag, QFile converts the line endings when reading to the corresponding Unix conventions if necessary, for example, under Windows (see Table 11.1):

```
// extractessentials/main.cpp

#include <QtCore>
#include <iostream>
#include <stdio.h>
using namespace std;

int main(int argc, char* argv[])
{
  if (argc < 2) {
```

```
      cout << "Usage: " << argv[0] << " infile [outfile]" << endl;
      return 1;
  }

  QFile in(argv[1]);
  if(!in.open(QIODevice::ReadOnly|QIODevice::Text)) {
    cerr << "File " << argv[1] << " does not exist" << endl;
  }

  QFile out;
  if (argc >= 3) {
    out.setFileName(argv[2]);
    if (out.exists()) {
      cerr << "File" << argv[2] << " already exists" << endl;
      return 1;
    }
    if(!out.open(QIODevice::WriteOnly|QIODevice::Text)) {
      cerr << "Failed to open file " << argv[2] <<
        " for writing" << endl;
      return 1;
    }
  }
  else
    if(!out.open(stdout, QIODevice::WriteOnly|QIODevice::Text)) {
      cerr << "Failed to open standard output for writing" << endl;
      return 1;
    }

  while (!in.atEnd()) {
   QByteArray line = in.readLine();
   if (!line.trimmed().isEmpty() &&
       !line.trimmed().startsWith('#'))
     out.write(line);
  }

  in.close();
  out.close();

  return 0;
}
```

Then we check whether there is at least one more parameter supplied on the command line. Whether or not there is one, we require a second QFile instance, which we allocate on the stack without passing an argument to the constructor. If the second parameter exists, then we pass it to the QFile object, via setFileName(), as a filename. Before we overwrite the file, using the QIODevice::WriteOnly parameter, we use the exists() method to warn the user and exit the program. Only now do we open the file.

If the user has not passed a second parameter to the program, we direct the output to the standard output. To do this we use an overloaded variation of open(), which apart from the access permissions, expects a FILE pointer as the first argument. The

C Include stdio.h defines a series of FILE pointers, including stdout, which points to the standard output.

In the following loop we read out the contents of the file named by the first command-line argument, line by line. For each line, we check whether the line is empty or if it begins with a comment sign. trimmed() additionally removes all whitespaces at the beginning and end of a line so that the program will also recognize lines consisting of forgotten empty spaces as empty lines and indented comments as comment lines.

All lines that do not match the criteria for exclusion land in out, which is either the standard output or a new file, depending on the parameters.

Finally we close both files, to be on the safe side. However, as long as we place the QFile object on the stack or ensure that objects located on the heap are deleted before the program terminates, an explicit close() is not necessary, because the QFile destructor does this for us.

11.3   Serializing Objects

In C++, data is usually represented as an object. When data is in this form, programs cannot save it in files or send it across the network directly. Instead, the developer must first specify which properties of an object he wants to save and in what sequence he wants to send them.

What is involved is taking the objects apart and placing their basic components "on a conveyor belt." To restore them, data is taken from the conveyor belt and packed back into an object. These procedures are referred to as *serializing* and *deserializing*. (In interprocess communication, where this procedure is also applied, the terms *marshalling* and *demarshalling* are also used.)

The QDataStream class is responsible in Qt for the serialization of all data types. It therefore works on all QIODevice classes. On page 243 we used the class to pack a list of string lists into a QByteArray used for a drag-and-drop operation:

```
QByteArray encodedData;
QDataStream stream(&encodedData, QIODevice::WriteOnly);
```

The alternative QDataStream constructor used here simplifies handling the QByteArray, whereas the main constructor demands, as an argument, a pointer to the QIODevice with which it is to operate. The above code therefore corresponds to the following code that uses the standard constructor:

```
QByteArray encodedData;
QBuffer buffer(&encodedData);
buffer.open(QBuffer::WriteOnly);
QDataStream stream(&buffer);
```

To serialize the data of a QByteArray, therefore, you essentially use a QBuffer. We already know one application of this from Section 8.8: sending data between programs via drag and drop.

So that this can also function across network connections, for example, the format of QDataStream is platform independent. Thus, a stream serialized on a PowerPC can therefore be transferred back to an object on an Intel computer without any problem.

The QDataStream format has changed several times throughout the development of Qt, however, and will continue to do so in the future. This is why the class has different version types: If you try to bind a QDataStream to a specific version using setVersion(), then it will be sent correctly in this format, even in later Qt versions, and will be readable on the other side.

In order to read data into a datastream you use its << operator:

```
QByteArray encodedData;
QDataStream stream(&encodedData, QIODevice::WriteOnly);
QString text = "Now comes a timestamp";
QTime currentTime = QTime::currentTime();
stream << text << currentTime;
```

We can observe how QDataStream is used in practice to save data to a file in the following example, in which datasets are represented by a Dataset class defined as follows:

```
// record/record.h

#ifndef RECORD_H
#define RECORD_H

#include <QString>
#include <QDataStream>
#include <QDebug>

class Dataset
{
  private:
    QString m_surname;
    QString m_name;
    QString m_street;
    int m_streetnumber;
    int m_zip;
    QString m_locality;

  public:
    Dataset(QString name, QString surname, QString street,
      int streetnumber, int zip, QString locality)
```

```
    {
      m_name= name;
      m_surname = surname;
      m_street = street;
      m_streetnumber = streetnumber;
      m_zip = zip;
      m_locality = locality;
    }

    Dataset() {}

    QString name() const { return m_name; }
    QString surname() const { return m_surname; }
    QString street() const { return m_street; }
    int streetnumber() const { return m_streetnumber; }
    int zip() const { return m_zip; }
    QString locality() const { return m_locality; }

    void setName(const QString& name) { m_name = name; }
    void setSurname(const QString& surname) { m_surname = surname; }
    void setStreet(const QString& street) { m_street = street; }
    void setStreetnumber(int streetnumber) { m_streetnumber =
streetnumber; }
    void setZip(int zip) { m_zip = zip; }
    void setLocality(const QString& locality) { m_locality = locality; }

    Record(const Record& r) {
      m_surname = r.m_surname;
      m_name = r.m_name;
      m_street = r.m_street;
      m_streetnumber = r.m_streetnumber;
      m_zip = r.m_zip;
      m_locality = r.m_locality;
    }

    Record& operator=(const Record& that) {
      m_name = that.m_name;
      m_surname = that.m_surname;
      m_street = that.m_street;
      m_streetnumber = that.m_streetnumber;
      m_zip = that.m_zip;
      m_locality = that.m_locality;
      return *this;
    }
};
```

Each field in the dataset has a get method and a corresponding set method. It is important that the get methods are always declared as const. This is not only better for the compiler, but it also helps us when serializing data. In addition we require the copy operator dataset(const dataset& ds) and the assignment operator operator=, since we must copy the class in a value-based manner.

11.3.1 Defining Serialization Operators

Finally, we define operator<<() for serializing, which transfers a dataset into a QDataStream. The code shows the reason the get methods name(), surname(), and so on must be declared as const: The dataset instance is declared to be const:

```
// record/record.h (continued)

QDataStream& operator<<(QDataStream &s, const Record &r)
{
  s << r.name() << r.surname() << r.street()
    << (qint32)r.streetnumber() << (qint32)r.zip() << r.streetnumber();
  return s;
}
```

In the operator definition we now only need to specify the order of the data elements in the stream. In addition, we must cast primitive data types (PODs), such as integers, to a platform-independent type definition here, at the latest. An overview of all these type definitions can be found in Section B.6 in Appendix B on page 422.

We now define the opposite operator>>(), which converts data from a QDataStream into a dataset object. To do this we instantiate a QString and a qint32 and use these to read data in the order in which they were read in by operator<<(). Then we fill the respective property of the passed dataset instance using the corresponding set method. Finally we pass on the datastream using return, even though we have not changed it in this method:

```
// record/record.h (continued)

QDataStream& operator>>(QDataStream &s, Record(&r))
{
  QString data;
  qint32 number;
  s >> data;
  r.setName(data);
  s >> data;
  r.setSurname(data);
  s >> data;
  r.setStreet(data);
  s >> number;
  r.setStreetnumber(number);
  s >> number;
  r.setZip(number);
  s >> data;
  r.setLocality(data);

  return s;
}

#endif // RECORD_H
```

11.3.2 Saving Serialized Data to a File and Reading from It

Now that we have defined the dataset data structure and its serialization operators, we can write a small example program to work with them: It provides the saveData() and readData() functions so that suitable data can be stored to a file or read out from it.

saveData() opens the output file initially in write mode, installs the QDataStream instance ds on top of this, and sets the version to the most current version (at press time, QDataStream version 4.0). To ensure that the file has been written by our program, we reserve the first 32 bits for a so-called *Magic Number*. We also include information on the version in a second field (here, 1). Then we serialize each data set in the list, write it to the file, and then close it:

```cpp
// record/main.cpp

#include <QtCore>
#include <iostream>
#include "record.h"

using namespace std;

void saveData(const QList<Record> &data, const QString &filename) {
    QFile file(filename);
    if (!file.open(QIODevice::WriteOnly)) return;
    QDataStream ds(&file);
    ds.setVersion(QDataStream::Qt_4_0);
    // Magic number
    ds << (quint32)0xDEADBEEF;
    // Version
    ds << (qint32)1;
    foreach(Record r, data)
      ds << r;
    file.close();
}
```

The readData() function has the task of opening a file (the name of which it is given as a string), analyzing the contents, and reading them out. In this case we again open the file, but this time in read mode, and we again install theQDataStream and set the desired datastream version. Now we check, using the Magic Number, whether the file really does originate from us, and we also check the self-defined version. If everything is correct, we can now read out the information in the file dataset by dataset, to its end, close it, and provide the data structure we obtained to the requester:

```cpp
// record/main.cpp (continued)

QList<Record> readData(const QString &filename) {
```

```
QFile file(filename);
file.open(QIODevice::ReadOnly);
QDataStream ds(&file);
ds.setVersion(QDataStream::Qt_4_0);
// Magic number
quint32 magic;
ds >> magic;
if (magic != 0xDEADBEEF) {
  qWarning("Wrong magic!\n");
  return QList<Record>();
}
// Version
qint32 version;
ds >> version;
if (version != 1) {
  qWarning("Wrong version!\n");
  return QList<Record>();
}
QList<Record> recordList;
Record record;
while (!ds.atEnd()) {
  ds >> record;
  recordList.append(record);
}
file.close();
return recordList;
}
```

Now we have everything we need for a main program that we can use to try out the functionality of our methods. We first create two datasets, which we will insert into a typed QList. We pass this, with a filename, to saveData(). Then we delete all the entries in the list, so that afterward it can be refilled with the results from readData():

```
// record/main.cpp (continued)

int main()
{
  QList<Record> data;
  data.append(Datensatz("Tilda", "Tilli", "Rosenweg", 4, 20095,
    "Hamburg"));
  data.append(Datensatz("Lara", "Lila", "Lilienweg", 14, 80799,
    "Munich"));
  saveData(data, "file.db");
  data.clear();
  data = readData("file.db");
  foreach(Record record, data)
    cout << qPrintable(record.surname()) << endl;

  return 0;
}
```

If we now output the last names from each dataset read, the standard output will display the strings Tilli and Lila on the screen.

The helper function qPrintable() provides support in outputting QString objects, making use of the toLocal8Bit() method internally.

11.4   Starting and Controlling Processes

Now and again you may want to make use of the services of command-line based programs, particularly on Unix-based operating systems. QProcess is responsible for executing and controlling such external processes. Because it inherits from QIODevice, this class is in a position to read the output of processes and to create inputs. In addition it has methods for manipulating the environment variables of a process.

QProcess belongs to the group of asynchronous devices: As soon as data is waiting or other events occur, the class sets off a signal. The corresponding call returns immediately. You can use QProcess for operations that are short enough not to block the GUI, or even use them synchronously in threads. This behavior applies in the same way for all asynchronous, QIODevice-based classes.

11.4.1   Synchronous Use of QProcess

In the following example we can look at the contents of archive files, created using the system tool tar, in a QListWidget (Figure 11.2). Each file in the tarfile should form a separate entry in the list. We pass the archive to the program as a command-line argument; if this argument is missing, we terminate the program immediately:

```
// showtar/main.cpp

#include <QtGui>

int main(int argc, char* argv[])
{
  if (argc < 2)
    return 1;

  QApplication app(argc, argv);

  QProcess tar;
  QStringList env = QProcess::systemEnvironment();
  env.replaceInStrings(QRegExp("^LANG=(.*)"),"LANG=C");
  tar.setEnvironment(env);
  QStringList args;
  args << "tf" << argv[1];
```

Otherwise, we instantiate QApplication and QProcess. Then we ensure that tar displays its output in English—localized output would irritate our parser. For this purpose we look for the LANG variable in the environment variables of the process, which we can obtain from the systemEnvironment() method as a string list, and replace it with LANG=C, the standard locale.

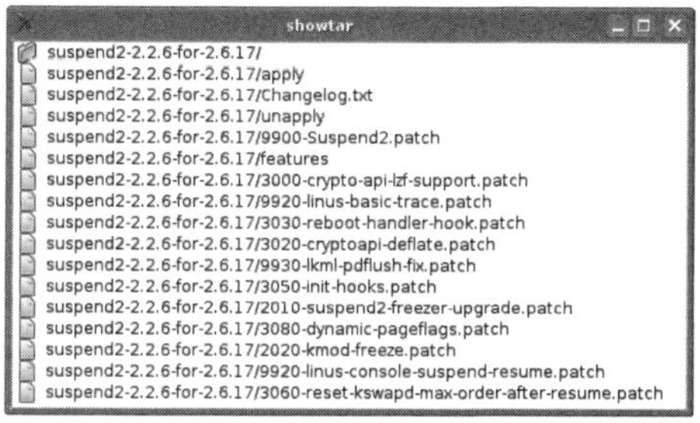

Figure 11.2:
showtar *displays the contents of a* .tar *archive.*

Once we have passed the new environment to the process with setEnvironment(), we collect the arguments with which we want to invoke tar into a string list: Given the flags tf, the tar program lists the contents of an archive file, which we also include here as the second argument to tar.

We pass on the finished argument list, together with the program name tar, to the start() method, which now runs the command tar tf *filename*:

```
// showtar/main.cpp (continued)

  tar.start("tar", args);
  QByteArray output;
  while ( tar.waitForReadyRead() )
    output += tar.readAll();
```

Since this method returns immediately, yet we want to work synchronously, we use waitForReadyRead() to wait until the first data arrives. We collect this in a QByteArray and continue waiting until the process is finished delivering data.

We now begin to parse the output by chopping up the line ends and putting them first into a string list:

```
// showtar/main.cpp (continued)

  QStringList entries = QString::fromLocal8Bit(output).split('\n');
  entries.removeLast();

  QListWidget w;

  QIcon fileIcon = app.style()->standardIcon(QStyle::SP_FileIcon);
  QIcon dirIcon = app.style()->standardIcon(QStyle::SP_DirClosedIcon);
```

```
foreach(QString entry, entries) {
  if (entry.endsWith('/'))
    new QListWidgetItem(dirIcon, entry, &w);
  else
    new QListWidgetItem(fileIcon, entry, &w);
}

w.show();
return app.exec();
}
```

The 8-bit encoded data is converted by the fromLocal8Bit() method to Unicode, as it can be understood by QString. We remove the final entry, as it is empty, because the final line of the tar output also ends with a \n.

We now instantiate the QListWidget in which we want to display the contents of the tar archive. We pack each entry into a QListWidgetItem in such a way that we can distinguish between directories and files: We embellish them with different icons, which we can take from the Style used. This has a series of standard icons, especially for input/output operations. We can access the current QStyle object via the QApplication method style(). All we have to do now is display the list widget and pass on control to the event loop.

The result should look similar to that shown in Figure 11.2. If you try out this example, you will realize that you hardly notice the delay at the beginning, particularly with smaller archives. Things are different with processes that perform more complex operations, such as searching directories, which can take a while even on very modern hard drives.

11.4.2 Asynchronous Use of QProcess

The following example demonstrates the asynchronous use of QProcess: The Line-ParserProcess class reads out the output of a process asynchronously and stores it, just as in the previous example, as items in a QListWidget. We implement it as a subclass of QProcess. The only slot we require here is called readData(). In this we must access the instance of QListWidget, which is why we make provision for a corresponding member variable:

```
// lineparserprocess/lineparserprocess.h

#ifndef LINEPARSERPROCESS_H
#define LINEPARSERPROCESS_H

#include <QProcess>

class QListWidget;
```

```
class LineParserProcess : public QProcess
{
  Q_OBJECT
  public:
    LineParserProcess(QListWidget*w, QObject *parent=0);

  protected slots:
    void readData();

  protected:
    QListWidget *listWidget;
};
#endif // LINEPARSERPROCESS_H
```

In the constructor we first connect the readyRead() signal to our new slot. Then we again ensure that the output of the process is not in localized form:

```
// lineparserprocess/lineparserprocess.cpp

#include <QtGui>
#include <QDebug>
#include "lineparserprocess.h"

LineParserProcess::LineParserProcess(QListWidget *w, QObject *parent)
  : QProcess(parent), listWidget(w)
{
  connect(this, SIGNAL(readyRead()), SLOT(readData()));
  QStringList env = systemEnvironment();
  env.replaceInStrings(QRegExp("^LANG=(.*)"),"LANG=C");
  setEnvironment(env);
}

void LineParserProcess::readData()
{
  QByteArray line;
  while (!(line = readLine()).isEmpty())
    new QListWidgetItem(QString::fromLocal8Bit(line), listWidget);
}
```

In readData() we read in all data to the final line break in the datastream, with readLine(), line by line. This procedure is safe, because we know that \n is the last character to be read in the output, and sooner or later we have read all the characters anyway. When there is no more new data, line remains empty and the program returns for the time being to the event loop, until readyRead() signals that new data is arriving.

Now we convert the 8-bit encoded lines, as in the previous example, with from-Local8Bit() to a QString and insert the contents into a QListWidgetItem. Since we specify the parent widget as the second argument, this is immediately included in the list widget.

Now we can use the class, for example, to list a directory tree recursively with ls. As before, we expect to receive the starting directory as a command-line argument. After we have ensured that an argument has been passed, we instantiate a QList-Widget (apart from the obligatory QApplication object) and a LineParserProcess (which contains a pointer to the instance of the QListWidget):

```
// lineparserprocess/main.cpp

#include <QtGui>
#include "lineparserprocess.h"

int main(int argc, char* argv[])
{
  if (argc < 2) return 1;
  QApplication app(argc, argv);
  QListWidget w;
  LineParserProcess process(&w);
  process.setWorkingDirectory(QString::fromLocal8Bit(argv[1]));
  process.start("ls", QStringList() << "-Rl" );
  w.show();
  return app.exec();
}
```

Instead of passing the original directory as an argument to ls, we change the process's current working directory to the corresponding directory with setWorkingDirectory(). Then we start the process; the argument -Rl ensures a recursive and detailed listing of all filenames beneath the current path. Finally we display the widget and enter the event loop.

If you try out this example, you will notice that the GUI does not lock while it is receiving new data from the process started. This type of asynchronous programming is also referred to as *event loop programming*.

11.5   Communication in the Network

Network functionality in Qt is also based to a large extent on QIODevice. This is not a component of the QtCore package but is stored in a library called QtNetwork. To make this accessible to a Qt application, the .pro file must contain the following line:

```
QT += network
```

There is also a separate meta-include file for the QtNetwork library that contains all the other headers. The following line is sufficient to integrate this into the application source code:

```
#include <QtNetwork>
```

The module consists of the QIODevice subclasses QAbstractSocket, QTcpSocket, and QUdpSocket, and also contains a class QTcpServer that enables the implementation of TCP-based services. In addition the QtNetwork also contains full implementations, in the classes QHttp (see page 361) and QFtp, two of the most common Internet protocols. In additon, the QHostAddress class, which encapsulates host names and IP addresses, is already IPv6-capable.

Thanks to the QNetworkProxy class, the module has had a Socks-5 proxy implementation for UDP and TCP as well as proxy support on the user layer for HTTP and FTP since Qt 4.1. The classes QHttp and QTcp thus contain methods for specifying an application proxy, without the need to instantiate QNetworkProxy manually.

11.5.1 Name Resolution with QHostInfo

The QHostInfo class is responsible for simple name resolution. The static method QHostInfo::fromName() provides information on the specified address as an instance of QHostAddress, but in doing so blocks the event loop. If you want to avoid this, you should make use of the static method lookupHost(), which expects a slot as an argument that operates further on the QHostAddress object passed. The following code ...

```
QHostInfo::lookupHost("www.example.com",
                      this, SLOT(doSomething(const QHostInfo&)));
```

... therefore looks up the host www.example.com in the DNS and delivers the result to a slot called doSomething().

11.5.2 Using QTcpServer and QTcpSocket

To become familiar with the way the network classes work, we shall implement a small service that binds itself to a port and returns the current time in ISO format to every inquirer. The client should acknowledge that it has processed the string, with ACK (not to be confused with the ACK packet of TCP).

The server uses the event loop of the system to do this: Each call, therefore, returns immediately, and results are delivered via signals, which we have to match up to slots accordingly.

As can be seen in the declaration, we only require one additional slot for this example, since the remaining functionality can be inherited from QTcpServer:

```
// timeserver/timeserver.h

#ifndef TIMESERVER_H
#define TIMESERVER_H
#include <QTcpServer>

class TimeServer : public QTcpServer
{
  Q_OBJECT
  public:
    TimeServer(QObject *parent = 0);

  protected slots:
    void serveConnection();
};
#endif // TIMESERVER_H
```

In the constructor we connect the newConnection() signal to this slot, called serve-Connection(). With nextPendingConnection() the slot retrieves the client connection closest to the socket. Each active connection is represented by a QTcpSocket object.

As a subclass of QIODevice, QTcpSocket() is able to send data to the client or to receive data from it. We delegate the socket to a helper class called Connection-Handler, which looks after everything else:

```
// timeserver/timeserver.cpp

#include <QtCore>
#include <QtNetwork>

#include "timeserver.h"

TimeServer::TimeServer(QObject *parent)
  : QTcpServer(parent)
{
  connect(this, SIGNAL(newConnection()),
                SLOT(serveConnection()));
}

void TimeServer::serveConnection()
{
   QTcpSocket *socket = nextPendingConnection();
   if (!socket)
     return;
   new ConnectionHandler(socket);
}
```

The ConnectionHandler first sends off the date and then waits for new data, which it checks in the confirm() slot. We use a QTimer, in case the client doesn't respond.

This class provides a timekeeper which—in contrast to the timerEvent() procedure from Chapter 7—calls calls a signal when its timeout expires.

If it is intended to set the timeout off once, as in this case, the static method singleShot() is sufficient; it expects the time to the timeout in milliseconds, as well as the object and the slots calling it, as arguments. Finally, we save the slot in the private member variable socket. After a timout we inform the client that we are no longer waiting and terminate the connection:

```
// timeserver/connectionhandler.h

#ifndef CONNECTIONHANDLER_H
#define CONNECTIONHANDLER_H

#include <QtCore>
#include <QtNetwork>
#include <QDebug>
class ConnectionHandler : public QObject
{
  Q_OBJECT
  private:
    QTcpSocket *socket;
  public:
    ConnectionHandler(QTcpSocket *socket, QObject *parent=0)
      : QObject(parent)
    {
      QString dt = QDateTime::currentDateTime().toString(Qt::ISODate);
      socket->write(dt.toUtf8());
      connect(socket, SIGNAL(readyRead()), SLOT(confirm()));
      QTimer::singleShot(10000, this, SLOT(timeout()));
      this->socket = socket;
    }

  protected:
    void closeConnection() {
      socket->close();
      delete socket;
      deleteLater();
    }

  protected slots:
    void timeout() {
      socket->write("ERROR: Timeout while waiting for
        acknowledgement\n");
      closeConnection();
    }
    void confirm()
    {
      QByteArray reply = socket->readAll();
      if(reply == "ACK\n")
        closeConnection();
```

```
      else
        socket->write("ERROR: Unknown command\n");
    }

};

#endif // CONNECTIONHANDLER_H
```

In the confirm() slot we check whether the client has sent an ACK followed by a line break. If this is not the case, we send the client an error message, and otherwise we close the connection without comment. Closing in both cases is taken over by the closeConnection() method. It simply closes the socket.

So that the ConnectionHandler is also deleted, we call deleteLater(). QObject-based objects must never be deleted directly with delete. deleteLater() ensures that the application, as it enters the event loop again, deletes the object.

We could have passed the QTcpServer object here as the parent object and then waited for the class to be deleted when the program ends. For an application that oversees several thousand connections, and therefore just as many Connection-Handler objects, memory usage would be enormous. For this reason, we first delete the QTcpSocket, which is no longer needed.

To try out our new program, we instantiate a TimeServer object, set it to listen to port 4711, and bind it to all network interfaces. If you just want to bind your service to the loopback interface, you would just use the address QHostAddress::LocalHost instead of QHostAddress::Any. Finally we enter the event loop, and our server is ready:

```
// timeserver/main.cpp

#include <QtCore>
#include "timeserver.h"

int main(int argc, char* argv[])
{
  QCoreApplication app(argc, argv);
  TimeServer ts;
  ts.listen(QHostAddress::Any, 4711);
  return app.exec();
}
```

12

Threading with QThread

If a program needs to use parallel processes or perform resource-intensive jobs without blocking the GUI, there are only two alternatives: forking or threading.

With *forking*, the operating system creates an exact copy of the current process. The new process can execute along a separate code path, for example, to make calculations while its parent performs some other task. Some form of interprocess communication is also required between the original process and its fork. Although this procedure is quite normal on Unix-based operating systems, support for forking under Windows is not so good, and it is very time consuming to carry out there.

Since Qt places an emphasis on platform-independent programming, threading is seen here as the means of choice. Here several threads, also called *lightweight processes*, run simultaneously within a process. It is a relatively simple matter to create new threads and to switch between them, since a thread merely has a stack and a copy of the processor registers. As can be seen in Figure 12.1, the threads in a process must share all other resources, such as the heap.

12.1 Using Threads

The QThread class represents threads in Qt. Even if you do not explicitly create any lightweight processes, QCoreApplication always creates a main thread internally. In connection with QApplication, we also talk about the *GUI thread*. This is entrusted with a very special task: Only the GUI thread can create widgets or draw with QPainter.

Figure 12.1:
Threads in a process
have their own
register set and a
separate stack, but
they share everything
else.

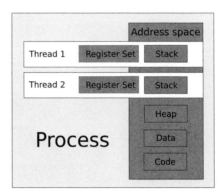

In the first example we will modify the timeserver from Section 11.5.2 (page 333) from asynchronously handling requests by using the event loop to using QThread. To do this we reimplement QTcpServer, but instead of connecting signals to slots in the constructor, which this time remains empty, we override the incomingConnection() method. This accepts an argument, socketDescriptor, which is a number identifying a TCP socket. QTcpServer makes a call to the incomingConnection() method for each incoming connection, in which socketDescriptor references the socket for the connection:

```
// threadedtimeserver/timeserver.h

#ifndef TIMESERVER_H
#define TIMESERVER_H
#include <QTcpServer>

class TimeServer : public QTcpServer
{
  Q_OBJECT
  public:
    TimeServer(QObject *parent = 0)
      : QTcpServer(parent) {}
  protected:
    void incomingConnection(int socketDescriptor);
};
#endif // TIMESERVER_H
```

In the implementation we create a separate thread for each incoming connection. After this thread has done its work, it should delete itself, which we implement by connecting the finished() signal to the deleteLater() slot. Once it is started, the thread prepared in this way alternates with the other existing threads at regular intervals:

```cpp
// threadedtimeserver/timeserver.cpp

#include <QtCore>
#include <QtNetwork>

#include "timeserver.h"
#include "connectionthread.h"

void TimeServer::incomingConnection(int socketDescriptor)
{
  ConnectionThread *thread = new ConnectionThread(socketDescriptor);
  connect(thread, SIGNAL(finished()), thread, SLOT(deleteLater()));
  thread->start();
}
```

The actual work is done by the ConnectionThread class. As a Qt thread, it inherits from QThread and must therefore implement, in addition to the constructor, the purely abstract run() method. run() is a protected method that is called by start(), so it must implement the functionality of the thread:

```cpp
// threadedtimeserver/connectionthread.h

#ifndef CONNECTIONTHREAD_H
#define CONNECTIONTHREAD_H

#include <QThread>
#include <QTcpSocket>

class ConnectionThread : public QThread
{
  Q_OBJECT
  public:
    ConnectionThread(int socketDescriptor, QObject *parent = 0);
    void run();

  private:
    int socketDescriptor;
};
#endif // CONNECTIONTHREAD_H
```

The constructor also remains empty here, and we only initialize the socketDescriptor and initialize the QThread base class with parent:

```
// threadedtimeserver/connectionthread.cpp

#include <QtCore>
#include <QtNetwork>
#include "connectionthread.h"

ConnectionThread::ConnectionThread(int socketDescriptor, QObject* parent)
  : QThread(parent), socketDescriptor(socketDescriptor)
{
}
```

In run() we generate a QTcpSocket object and pass the descriptor to it. If something should go wrong during this step, we issue a warning and cancel the procedure:

```
// threadedtimeserver/connectionthread.cpp (continued)

void ConnectionThread::run()
{
  QTcpSocket tcpSocket;
  if (!tcpSocket.setSocketDescriptor(socketDescriptor)) {
    qWarning("ERROR: %s", qPrintable(tcpSocket.errorString()));
    return;
  }
  QDateTime time = QDateTime::currentDateTime();
  tcpSocket.write(time.toString(Qt::ISODate).toUtf8());

  forever {
    if (!tcpSocket.waitForReadyRead(10*1000)) {
      tcpSocket.write("ERROR: Timeout while waiting for ACK\n");
      break;
    }
    QString reply = tcpSocket.readAll();
    if (reply.isEmpty()) {
      qWarning("ERROR: %s", qPrintable(tcpSocket.errorString()));
      break;
    }
    else if ( reply == "ACK\n")
      break;
    else
      tcpSocket.write("ERROR: Invalid command\n");
  }

  tcpSocket.disconnectFromHost();
  if (!tcpSocket.waitForDisconnected(1000))
    qWarning("WARNING: Could not disconnect");

}
```

If you need more precise information at this point about the error, you can call the QTcpSocket method error(), which returns a member of the SocketError enumerator.

As in the example from Section 11.5.2, we now obtain the current date and time and write both as a QString to the socket. The write() call immediately returns. However, since we want to process one call after another in the thread, we use the waitFor* methods, which we already used on page 329 for blocking calls.

Directly after the write() we enter into an infinite loop. Just like foreach(), forever is a keyword defined by Qt, and it corresponds to while(true). In the loop we first wait for data with waitForReadyRead(). In the argument we can specify a timeout in milliseconds, which we set here to 10 seconds. If the method returns false, the timeout has been exceeded. In this case we notify the client that we will no longer wait and leave the loop with break.

Otherwise, data has been received from the client and we read it out. If the returned byte array is empty, that means an error has occurred, and we close the connection to be on the safe side. If its contents correspond to the ACK string, we close the connection. Otherwise, we complain to the client about receiving an invalid command and wait for another reply.

After issuing the call to close the connection with disconnectFromHost(), we wait a second for possible errors and give a warning if one occurs. However, the run() method then terminates, so tcpSocket is deleted and the connection is closed automatically at this point anyway.

The main() method of this threaded TimeServer is no different from the one on page 336. We again create a QCoreApplication and a server object, get it to listen to a port, and start the event loop:

```
// threadedtimeserver/main.cpp

#include <QtCore>
#include "timeserver.h"

int main(int argc, char* argv[])
{
  QCoreApplication app(argc, argv);
  TimeServer ts;
  if (!ts.listen(QHostAddress::Any, 4711))
    qWarning("Server cannot listen on this port!\n");
  return app.exec();
}
```

12.2 Synchronizing Threads

In the example just displayed, each thread only manipulates the data on its stack (i.e., its local variables). If threads need to share data, problems can arise because the operating system can put one running process to sleep and execute another in its place at any time. For instance, a thread might be in the middle of chaging shared data when being sent to sleep. In this case, the next thread would operate on that inconsistent data, leading to unpredictable results.

To master this situation we must protect each critical section in the code to ensure that only one thread can execute it at any given time. A *critical section* is a portion of code that needs to run consecutively without being interrupted.

Other threads that want to run though this code section will just have to wait. This exclusive access is guaranteed by the QMutex class. The name *mutex* stands for *mutual exclusion*, and, as its name suggests, if a thread is executing a section of code protected by a mutex, then any other thread wanting to enter the critical section must wait until that thread leaves the critical section and releases the mutex.

A thread that has to wait for access to shared resources should be able to put itself to sleep for a while, without the system having to continually keep track of its status (*busy-waiting*). For this purpose, there is the QWaitCondition class: It can be used to put a thread to sleep until a certain condition occurs.

12.2.1   The Consumer/Producer Pattern

The two principles described above are put to good use in the so-called *consumer/producer use-case*, in which a producer thread makes data available for processing by a consumer thread. To move data from one thread to the other, the producer places it in a queue, from which the consumer takes them out.

As a shared resource, the queue must be protected by a mutex before it is accessed by either the producer or the consumer. If the consumer works more quickly than the producer, it is possible that the queue will become empty. If the producer works faster than the consumer, the queue may fill up. In either case, one of the two threads has to sleep: the consumer until more data are available, or the producer until the queue has free space.

We implement this scenario below using only Qt tools. To do this we first declare a few global variables: As the data structure for the g_queue queue in which we save integer data, we use the QQueue class, explained in more detail in Appendix B on page 404. This contains the methods enqueue(), which places a datum into the queue, and dequeue(), which reads out the oldest datum.

The integer g_maxlen specifies the maximum number of elements in the queue, and the mutex g_mutex will protect the code sections that access the queue. The *wait condition* g_queueNotFull should wake the sleeping producer thread when the queue has free space. Likewise, g_queueNotEmpty wakes the sleeping consumer when there are elements available in the queue:

```
// producerconsumer/producerconsumer.cpp

#include <QtCore>
```

```
#include <QDebug>

QQueue<int> g_queue;
int g_maxlen;
QMutex g_mutex;
QWaitCondition g_queueNotFull;
QWaitCondition g_queueNotEmpty;
```

First, we will look at the producer. The run() method enters an infinite loop in which it alternates between producing a message and then going to sleep for three seconds. The actual functionality is implemented here in produceMessage(). We use the mutex to protect sections of code that access g_queue by calling the mutex's lock() method immediately prior to the section and its unlock() method immediately after:

```
// producerconsumer/producerconsumer.cpp (continued)

class Producer : public QThread
{
  public:
    Producer(QObject *parent=0)
      : QThread(parent) {}

  protected:
    void produceMessage()
    {
      qDebug() << "Producing...";
      g_mutex.lock();
      if (g_queue.size() == g_maxlen) {
        qDebug() << "g_queue is full, waiting!";
        g_queueNotFull.wait(&g_mutex);
      }

      g_queue.enqueue((rand()%100)+1);
      g_queueNotEmpty.wakeAll();
      g_mutex.unlock();
    }

    void Producer::run()
    {
      forever {
        produceMessage();
        msleep((rand()%3000)+1);
      };
    }
};
```

In the critical section we check whether there is still room in the queue. If this is not the case, the wait condition comes into force. Since the mutex must not be blocked during the waiting period, we hand it to be looked after by the g_mutex method. This unlocks the mutex, provided the thread is waiting. In consequence, you need to ensure that there is room in the queue if you want to wake up the thread, and then wake up the consumer thread via the relevant wait condition object.

If the thread has been woken, or if the queue in this cycle was not full, we add a random number between 1 and 100. Since there is now at least one element in the queue, we can wake Consumer threads that have gone to sleep if the key was empty before the enqueue() call, and wait for a change in the wait condition g_queueNotEmpty. Now we no longer need to access g_queue, so we can unlock the mutex.

We leave the other side, the consumer, to sleep a little longer in run() than the producer, to obtain a full queue. To lock the mutex in this case we use a QMu-texLocker, which simplifies this task. The constructor of the class calls up lock(), while its destructor releases the mutex with unlock(). In this way it is out of the question that you could forget an unlock(), thus provoking a *deadlock*. In such a case, neither thread can any longer get through to the critical sections protected by the mutex—then the program hangs.

Now the consumer first tests to see if any entries have been stored in the queue. If this is not the case it goes to sleep, but in contrast to the producer thread, it uses the wait condition g_queueNotEmpty. If the thread is woken up again after this or if the queue was previously not empty, we remove an element from the queue and then wake any producer threads that might be sleeping and waiting for data:

```
// producerconsumer/producerconsumer.cpp (continued)

class Consumer : public QThread
{
  public:
    Consumer(QObject *parent=0)
      : QThread(parent) {}

  protected:
    int consumeMessage()
    {
      qDebug() << "Consuming...";
      QMutexLocker locker(&g_mutex);
      if (g_queue.isEmpty()) {
        qDebug() << "g_queue empty, waiting!";
        g_queueNotEmpty.wait(&g_mutex);
      }
      int val = g_queue.dequeue();
      g_queueNotFull.wakeAll();
      return val;
    }

    void run()
    {
```

```
      forever {
        qDebug() << consumeMessage();
        msleep(( rand()%4000 )+1);
      }
    }
};
```

To test the consumer/producer scenario, we will write a small main() function in which we restrict the number of elements in the queue to ten, create a producer and a consumer, and start them both:

```
// producerconsumer/producerconsumer.cpp (continued)

int main()
{
  g_maxlen = 10;
  Producer producer;
  Consumer consumer;
  producer.start();
  consumer.start();
  producer.wait();
  consumer.wait();
  return 0;
}
```

Since start() returns immediately, but we do not enter into any event loop, we wait for the end of the respective thread, with wait(). Since both threads never return from run(), the program must be ended at this point from the outside, using (Strg)+(C), because the return statement will never reach the program.

12.3   Thread-dependent Data Structures

If you want to store data in a thread context, the solution is to be found in the QThreadStorage template class. Because of compiler limitations it can only take in pointer-based objects, which is why data structures stored in it must be allocated using new.

A small example should explain the common usage of this class: Assume we want each thread to maintain its own list with timestamps. Since the content of QThreadStorage has to be a pointer, we declare the class as QThreadStorage<QList< QTime>*>:

```
// threadstorage/storingthread.cpp

#include <QtCore>
#include <stdlib.h>
```

```cpp
#include <QDebug>

class StoringThread : public QThread
{

  private:
    QThreadStorage<QList<QTime>*> storage;

  public:
    StoringThread(QObject *parent=0)
     : QThread(parent) {}

  protected:
    void StoringThread::run()
    {
      forever {
        if (!storage.hasLocalData()) {
          storage.setLocalData(new QList<QTime>);
          qDebug() << objectName() << ": Creating list."
                   << "Pointer:" << storage.localData();
        }
        storage.localData()->append(QTime::currentTime());
        qDebug() << objectName() << ":"
                 << storage.localData()->count() << "dates collected";
        msleep((rand()%2000)+1);
      };
    }
};
```

In run() we check in each thread, first with hasLocalData(), whether QThreadStorage has already been initialized here. If this is not the case, we create the list.

Now we can insert the current time in each loop pass. The debug output shows the amount of data currently collected by this thread. To be able to differentiate between the results of the threads, we select a random waiting time between 1 and 2,000 milliseconds before we again enter the loop. Now the execution sequence of the threads has been moved to a random one.

Now we will write a small test program with three threads. They are all given names—also a way to distinguish them in the debug output. Then we start them and ensure, with wait(), that they remain in their infinite loop:

```cpp
// threadstorage/storingthread.cpp (continued)

int main()
{
  StoringThread thread1;
  StoringThread thread2;
  StoringThread thread3;
  thread1.setObjectName("thread1");
  thread2.setObjectName("thread2");
```

```
thread3.setObjectName("thread3");
thread1.start();
thread2.start();
thread3.start();
thread1.wait();
thread2.wait();
thread3.wait();
return 0;
}
```

The debug output on the console shows that each thread in the QThreadStorage instants really does find a different data structure. We can see this from the different address for the respective pointer each time:

```
"thread3" : Creating list. Pointer: 0x8051b80
"thread2" : Creating list. Pointer: 0x8052090
"thread1" : Creating list. Pointer: 0x80573f0
```

Even after a few seconds there are also differences in the amount of data collected:

```
"thread2" : 4 dates collected
"thread1" : 7 dates collected
"thread3" : 6 dates collected
```

For each process, Qt allows a maximum of 256 QThreadStorage objects. In most cases this is not a problem. It is more important to know that the class automatically deletes the data for a thread as soon as this thread is ended.

12.4   Using Signals and Slots Between Threads

In Qt 4 it is possible to connect signals and slots across threads. This can be done thanks to so-called *queued connections*, which exist in Qt 4 in addition to the traditional *direct connections*.

By direct connections we mean connections within a thread or process, as you learned in Chapter 7. With queued connections, possible arguments of signals are copied, and these are handed over to the recipient thread on the next thread change. Usually, *worker threads* emit signals containing messages in the form of the arguments, which are taken up by a slot in the main thread. The reverse is also possible, but then the worker thread requires its own event loop (see Section 12.5 on page 350).

We can demonstrate this principle by extending the thread variation of the Time-Server example from Chapter 12.1 (page 338) so that the worker threads emit messages that arrive in a window in the GUI thread.

To do this we insert the following signal into the two declarations of the worker thread class ConnectionThread and the TimeServer class:

```
void message(const QString& message);
```

Now we adjust the ConnectionThread so that it triggers the message() signal with an error description for every possible error. In order to identify the connection, we obtain the host name of the client, using peerAddress():

```
// threadedtimeserverslots/connectionthread.cpp

void ConnectionThread::run()
{
  QTcpSocket tcpSocket;
  if (!tcpSocket.setSocketDescriptor(socketDescriptor)) {
    emit message("ERROR: "+ tcpSocket.errorString());
    return;
  }
  QByteArray error;
  QString peerHostName = tcpSocket.peerAddress().toString();
  emit message("INFO: "+ peerHostName + " connected.");
  QDateTime time = QDateTime::currentDateTime();
  tcpSocket.write(time.toString(Qt::ISODate).toUtf8());

  forever {
    if (!tcpSocket.waitForReadyRead(10*1000)) {
      error = "ERROR: Timeout while waiting for ACK";
      tcpSocket.write(error+"\n");
      emit message(peerHostName+": " + error);
      break;
    }
    QByteArray reply = tcpSocket.readAll();
    if ( reply != "ACK\n") {
      error = "ERROR: Invalid command: " + reply.simplified() ;
      tcpSocket.write(error+"\n");
      emit message(peerHostName+": " + error);
    }
    else
      break;
  }

  tcpSocket.disconnectFromHost();
}
```

We now extend the TimeServer class so that it forwards the message of each thread via its own message() signal: Since this connection crosses thread boundaries, it is a queued connection:

```
// threadedtimeserverslots/timeserver.cpp

#include <QtCore>
#include <QtNetwork>

#include "timeserver.h"
#include "connectionthread.h"

TimeServer::TimeServer(QObject *parent)
  : QTcpServer(parent)
{
}

void TimeServer::incomingConnection(int socketDescriptor)
{
  ConnectionThread *thread = new ConnectionThread(socketDescriptor);
  connect(thread, SIGNAL(message(const QString&)),
                  SIGNAL(message(const QString&)));
  connect(thread, SIGNAL(finished()), thread, SLOT(deleteLater()));
  thread->start();
}
```

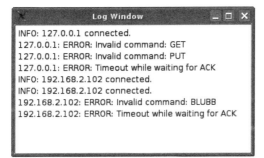

Figure 12.2:
Signals overcome the
thread barrier: The
log window receives
its messages via a
queued connection
from the connection
threads.

We modify the main() function so that it now instantiates a QApplication—we want
to have a graphical log window, after all. We implement this as a QTextBrowser and
give it a window name:

```
// threadedtimeserverslots/main.cpp

#include <QtGui>
#include <QDebug>
#include "timeserver.h"

int main(int argc, char* argv[])
{
  QApplication app(argc, argv);
  QTextBrowser logWindow;
  logWindow.setWindowTitle(QTextBrowser::tr("Log window"));
```

```
TimeServer ts;
QObject::connect(&ts, SIGNAL(message(const QString&)),
    &logWindow, SLOT(append(const QString&)));
if (!ts.listen(QHostAddress::Any, 4711))
  qWarning("Server cannot listen on port 4711!\n");
logWindow.show();
return app.exec();
}
```

After we have instantiated the server we connect its message() signal to the append() slot. This involves a direct connection, since the TimeServer is in the same thread as the log window. Now we can start the server with listen() and display the log window. The result after a few connections is shown in Figure 12.2.

12.5   Your Own Event Loops for Threads

Each thread can have its own event loop and thus make use of classes that can only work in an event loop, such as QTimer or QHttp. Threads with event loops may have slots, which function as recipients of queued signals. Furthermore, direct connections also function within such a thread-dependent event loop.

To start an event loop in a thread, the last method in run() must be exec(). The loop is therefore started with the same blocking call as in the case of QApplication. The event loop of threads can also be terminated by the quit() slot or the exit() function. These function calls correspond exactly to those in QApplication.

Below we will create a thread that writes the messages coming from the individual ConnectionThread instances to a file. This thread receives a public slot for this purpose, called append(), which we later connect in the main() method to the message() signal:

```
// threadedtimeserverslots/loggerthread.h

#ifndef LOGGERTHREAD_H
#define LOGGERTHREAD_H

#include <QThread>
#include <QFile>

class LoggerThread : public QThread
{
  Q_OBJECT
  public:
    LoggerThread(const QString& fileName, QObject *parent = 0);
    void run();
```

```
  public slots:
    void append(const QString& message);

  private:
    QFile file;
};
#endif // LOGGERTHREAD_H
```

In the constructor we specify the filename for the file but do not open it. In run() we only start the event loop of the thread via exec(). append() opens the file for each incoming message, writes the contents of message, together with a line wrap, and closes the file again. Although this is not very efficient, we can assume that our output will immediately appear in the log file:

```
// threadedtimeserverslots/loggerthread.cpp

#include <QtCore>
#include <QtNetwork>
#include <QDebug>
#include "loggerthread.h"

LoggerThread::LoggerThread(const QString& fileName, QObject* parent)
  : QThread(parent)
{
  file.setFileName(fileName);
}

void LoggerThread::run()
{
  exec();
}

void LoggerThread::append(const QString& message)
{
  file.open(QIODevice::WriteOnly|QIODevice::Append);
  file.write(message.toUtf8()+'\n');
  file.close();
}
```

Then we insert the following lines in front of the ts.listen() call in the main() method from page 349:

```
LoggerThread logger("timeserver.log");
QObject::connect(&ts, SIGNAL(message(const QString&)),
  &logger, SLOT(append(const QString&)));
QObject::connect(&app, SIGNAL(lastWindowClosed()),
  &logger, SLOT(quit()));
```

The first line creates a logger instance, while the second one forwards the message() signal to the append() slot. This also is a queued connection that accepts the recipient thread, thanks to the event loop.

12.5.1 Communication via Events Without a Thread-based Event Loop

It is still possible to use the method employed in Qt 3 to send messages to objects in other threads via events. In this process the QCoreApplication::postEvents() method unloads the event in the correct thread, because it is generally risky to call a QObject-based object from another thread than the one in which it was created.

To avoid problems, you should establish a connection to another thread only via postEvent(), via queued signal/slot connections, or via mutex-protected buffers. How postEvent() functions is described in Chapter 7 on page 185.

13

Handling XML with QtXml

File formats based on the Extensible Markup Language (XML) are becoming more and more common. In the QtXml module, Qt provides not one, but two APIs for handling XML files, each of which makes use of a different approach: the Simple API for XML (SAX) and the Document Object Model (DOM).

DOM, probably the more well-known representative of XML APIs, is a standard of the W3C. Here the contents of an XML document are transferred to an object model, a tree-like structure, which precisely mirrors the structure of the document. All modern web browsers use the Document Object Model internally, for example, because they can access any element whatsoever of the XML tree and read it out. But other applications also use DOM because a DOM tree in memory can be transferred back to an XML document. But this also means that the DOM is not suitable for large XML documents, due to its not inconsiderable memory memory needs. DOM is specified at various levels, whereby the Qt implementation complies with the standards of DOM level 2.[1]

---

[1] See http://www.w3.org/DOM/.

When parsing an XML document, on the other hand, SAX sets off various events, for example, each time it comes across an opening or closing tag. Each event is represented by a method. The programmer has to reimplement the methods and can decide which tags or attributes he or she wants to save. The fact that the results in this case lie in data structures defined by the user means that SAX is by design a purely reading API, in contrast to DOM. Its strengths come to the fore in its efficient analysis of large documents. The specification of SAX has now been taken over by the SAX Project.[2]

If you want to use the functionality of either of these two APIs, you must instruct qmake, with the following directive, to link the QtXml module to the current project:

```
QT += xml
```

Class implementations and declarations in which classes from the QtXml module are to be used can either use the class names as includes, or instead use the meta-include QtXml:

```
#include <QtXml>
```

This chapter will explain both APIs in detail and will look at important differences between the guidelines of the W3C and the SAX Project. A more in-depth treatment of the two standards is not possible at this point, however, due to the high complexity of the subject.

13.1   The SAX2 API

We shall first turn our attention to the SAX API. It corresponds as far as possible to the reference implementation of the SAX Project, which is in Java. The name conventions have been slightly adjusted by Trolltech, however, to fit in with the names given by Qt.

13.1.1   How It Works

The SAX API parses XML source text on an event basis. For example, the parser sets off events when it comes across a tag or text. As a practical example we will look at the following extract from an XML-based XHTML document:

```
<a href="http://www.example.com">
  <img src="http://www.example.com/example.png" />
```

[2] See http://www.saxproject.org/.

```
  <p>Click here</p>
</a>
```

The SAX parser triggers the following events from this extract:

- Start tag found (<a>)

- Start tag found (<img />)

- End tag found (<img />)

- Start tag found (<p>)

- Text found (Click here)

- End tag found (</p>)

- End tag found (</a>)

The parse results are caught by implementing certain methods in *handler classes*. We are interested here in two of the most frequently used classes: the QXmlContentHandler, which operates on tag and text events, and the QXmlErrorHandler, which goes to work as soon as the parser finds syntactical errors in the XML.

You need the QXmlDTDHandler and QXmlDeclHandler classes less often. Both treat (different) events that trigger the Document Type Definition (DTD) of an XML document. In addition you can operate on XML entities with the QXmlEntityResolver class, whereas the methods of the QXmlLexicalHandler class are triggered by lexical events. These are not discussed here. The homepage of the SAX Project does have a detailed interface documentation, however.

All methods of the handler classes are designed as interfaces, that is, they are purely virtual. To spare programmers the burden of implementing each method and each handler individually, QXmlDefaultHandler exists. It inherits from all handlers and implements their methods in such a way that all events are ignored. It is now the task of the programmer to intercept the events he or she requires and to process them.

13.1.2 Reimplementing a Default Handler to Read RSS Feeds

How you reimplement a default handler and use it for your own purposes is demonstrated in the following example, in which we will write a parser for the well-known RSS format.[3] We deliberately do not evaluate all the tags. A typical RSS file looks something like this:

[3] The abbreviation stands for *Really Simple Syndication*. This format has been used for some time to publish blog entries or news articles in XML.

```
<?xml version="1.0" encoding="utf-8"?>
<rss version="2.0">
  <channel>
    <title>Feed title</title>
    <link>Web link</link>
    <description>Short feed description</description>
    <language>en-en</language>
    <copyright>copyright information</copyright>
    <pubDate>creation date</pubDate>
    <image>
      <url>image link</url>
      <title>image title</title>
      <link>Blog URL or link to news.</link>
    </image>
    <item>
      <pubDate>Creation time</pubDate>
      <title>Title of first article</title>
      <link>Link to to article on the web page</link>
      <author>Author of article &lt;email address&gt;</author>
      <description>A short article summary</description>
    </item>
    <item>
    ...
    </item>
  </channel>
</rss>
```

The root tag <rss> can consist of one or several *channels*, specified by the <channel> tag. The channel is seen as the actual newsfeed.

In addition to its content, a channel contains a series of descriptive details, such as its title or an image. The actual blog or news entries in the channel are wrapped in <item> tags. Each item in turn contains the time of publication, a title, a link to the complete content, the name of the authors, and a *teaser* (specified with the <description> tag), which can contain either a summary or the entire entry.

Our RssHandler will fill a QStandardItemModel (see page 249) with data on the current feed. It inherits from QXmlDefaultHandler and intercepts the events startElement(), endElement(), and characters(), which originate from QXmlContentHandler, as well as fatalError() from QXmlErrorHandler. The errorString() function also originates from the error handler, but this does not represent any event:

```
// rssreader/rsshandler.h

#ifndef RSSHANDLER_H
#define RSSHANDLER_H

#include <QXmlDefaultHandler>
#include <QString>
#include <QModelIndex>
```

```
class QDocumentModel;
class QStandardItemModel;
class QXmlParseException;

class RssHandler : public QXmlDefaultHandler
{
  public:
    RssHandler(QStandardItemModel *model);

    bool startElement(const QString &namespaceURI,
        const QString &localName, const QString &qName,
        const QXmlAttributes &attributes);
    bool endElement(const QString &namespaceURI,
        const QString &localName, const QString &qName);
    bool characters(const QString &str);
    bool fatalError(const QXmlParseException &exception);
    QString errorString() const;

  private:
    bool rssTagParsed, inItem;
    QStandardItemModel *itemModel;
    QString errString;
    QString currentText;
};

#endif // RSSHANDLER_H
```

We require the Boolean variables rssTagParsed and inItem so that we can remember states: If you look at the RSS format, you will see that it uses some tag names in multiple contexts; for example, title is used both to describe the feed (i.e., the <rss> root) and to describe a news entry (i.e., an <item>). We use the status variables to differentiate the two functions.

currentText helps here to collect the text between a pair of opening and closing tags, and errString saves an error message. The implementation of errorString() will return this value if one of the methods returns false.

In the constructor we initialize the member variable itemModel with the standard model passed and all status variables with false. In addition we add headers to the first two columns in the model: The contents of the <title> tag should later be found in the first one, and the second one is reserved for the contents of <pub-Date>.

```
// rssreader/rsshandler.cpp

#include <QtXml>
#include <QtGui>
#include <QDebug>
#include "rsshandler.h"
```

```
RssHandler::RssHandler(QStandardItemModel *model)
{
  itemModel = model;
  rssTagParsed = false;
  inItem = false;
  model->setHeaderData(0, Qt::Horizontal, QObject::tr("Title"));
  model->setHeaderData(1, Qt::Horizontal, QObject::tr("Date"));
}
```

Plausibility checks take place in particular in the startElement() method, which is called as soon as an opening tag is being hit by the SAX parser. This is also responsible for appropriately setting status variables, together with endElement(), which runs as soon as the parser arrives at closing tags:

```
// rssreader/rsshandler.cpp (continued)

bool RssHandler::startElement(const QString & /* namespaceURI */,
                              const QString & /* localName */,
                              const QString &qName,
                              const QXmlAttributes &attributes )
{
  if (!rssTagParsed && qName != "rss") {
    errString = QObject::tr("This file is not an RSS source.");
    return false;
  }

  if (qName == "rss") {
    QString version = attributes.value("version");
    if (!version.isEmpty() && version != "2.0") {
      errorStr = QObject::tr("Can only handle RSS 2.0.");
      return false;
      rssTagParsed = true;
  } else if (qName == "item") {
    inItem = true;
    itemModel->insertRow(0);
  }
  currentText = "";
  return true;
}
```

The first two arguments involve the treatment of the namespace. Since RSS does not use any namespaces, we can ignore this. qName contains the name of the tag, and the QXmlAttributes class encapsulates any existing attributes.

The first lines of the method contain a plausibility check: If the variable rssTag-Parsed still has the value false, as set in the constructor, and the current tag is *not* <rss>, there must be an error, because the root tag in the document must be <rss>. Once we can find the <rss> tag, we set rssTagParsed to true later in the code. In this way we have formulated the condition "the root node must be <rss>," using a status and two comparisons. If this is not the case we set an error message and return from the method with false.

If, on the other hand, we come across <rss>, we first check the version number. We only support RSS version 2.0 (or a subset of this). We therefore reject other versions as a preventive measure. Now it is also time to set rssTagParsed to true so that we are not wrongly rejected by the first check on elements that we parse later.

If we come across <item>, then we change the status of inItem to true to distinguish the context of the tags, as described above. We also add a new line to the model, which we will then fill with values.

If a new tag starts, we should also empty currentText, since this variable should only contain the text between a pair of start and end tags.

Next, the characters method is used to read in the data that lies between a pair of start and end tags. If the parser interprets this text as several consecutive texts, for example, a normal text and a CDATA section in which data may be enclosed in diamond operators, without it being interpreted as XML, we combine all the texts into one. Since no error can arise here from our perspective, we return true in all circumstances:

```
// rssreader/rsshandler.cpp (continued)

bool RssHandler::characters( const QString &str )
{
  currentText += str;
  return true;
}
```

We insert the text collected in this way in endElement() into the ready-to-use line of the model. Again we are not interested in namespaces, but merely in the current tag, which is waiting in the qName variable:

```
// rssreader/rsshandler.cpp (continued)

bool RssHandler::endElement( const QString & /* namespaceURI */,
                             const QString & /* localName */,
                             const QString &qName )
{
  if ( qName == "item" ) {
    inItem = false;
  } else if ( qName == "title" ) {
    if (inItem) {
     QModelIndex idx = itemModel->index(0,0);
     itemModel->setData(idx, currentText);
    }
  } else if ( qName == "pubDate" ) {
    if (inItem) {
     QModelIndex idx = itemModel->index(0,1);
```

```
        itemModel->setData(idx, currentText);
      }
    } else if ( qName == "description" ) {
      if (inItem) {
      QModelIndex idx = itemModel->index(0,0);
      QString preview;
      if (preview.length() >= 300 )
        preview = currentText.left(300)+"...";
      else
        preivew = currentText;
      itemModel->setData(idx, preview, Qt::ToolTipRole);
      itemModel->setData(idx, currentText, Qt::UserRole);
      }
    }
    return true;
}
```

If we come across an <item> tag, we leave the context of an item, and we therefore set <inItem> back to false. If we are currently looking at the contents of the tags <title>, <pubDate>, or <description>, we must be sure in each case that we are located within an item, which is why we also need to check inItem in these cases.

Since we insert the data into line zero—after all, we inserted the new element into this line as well—we will specify the model index in column zero as the title. There we set currentText, that is the text read in, as the content between the tags. The same is done with pubDate, except that we select the first column here.

We proceed in two ways with the description from <description></description>. On one hand, we arbitrarily cut off the first 300 characters to provide a text preview in the tooltip. To indicate that the text continues, we attach an ellipsis (…) to it.[4]

In addition, we place data for the first time in the UserRole, in this case the complete contents of <description>. We will use this later to display the contents of the current entry in a QTextBrowser.

In the final part of the RssHandler implementation, we take a look at error handling. On page 357 it was briefly mentioned that errors that trigger the implementation of our class is retrievable for the parser via errorString(). This is why this method simply returns the last error description, written to the variable errorString:

```
// rssreader/rsshandler.cpp (continued)

QString RssHandler::errorString() const
{
  return errString;
}
```

---

[4] Since we are in the middle of an HTML tag, there is no guarantee that the user will actually see the three dots. A proper feed reader would have to use a better algorithm to cut the text.

This error, as well as fatal errors that originate from the parser itself, and which prevent the continued processing of the document, sets off a call to the fatalError() method, but only on the first parser error, unless we return true. Events are not processed further after an error has occurred:

```cpp
// rssreader/rsshandler.cpp (continued)

bool RssHandler::fatalError( const QXmlParseException &exception )
{
  QMessageBox::information( 0, QObject::tr( "RSS-Reader" ),
          QObject::tr( "Parse error in line %1, column %2:\n %3" )
                      .arg( exception.lineNumber() )
                      .arg( exception.columnNumber() )
                      .arg( exception.message() ) );
  return false;
}
```

We pass the error on to the user by means of QMessageBox. The parameter exception provides details on the error that has occurred.

13.1.3 Digression: Equipping the RSS Reader with a GUI and Network Capability

Now our parser can be built into a feed reader that uses an HTTP address to download an RSS feed, parse it, and display it. Figure 13.1 shows how the application is constructed: The line edit waits for the address of the feed, the contents of which are displayed by a QTextView on the left-hand page. On the right we see the article selected from the list in a QTextBrowser.

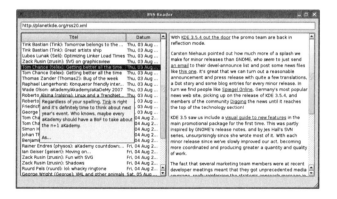

Figure 13.1:
The SAX-based RSS reader displays the blogs of KDE developers.

To download the file from a webserver, we use the QHttp class, which enables asynchronous communication with webservers. This is one of the network classes introduced in Chapter 11, but we have not yet discussed it in more detail. We also come across the QBuffer class again, where we temporarily store the contents of the RSS file. Later on we need the integer jobId in connection with QHttp. Our window is based on QMainWindow, among other things, because we will use its status bar:

```
// rssreader/mainwindow.h

#ifndef MAINWINDOW_H
#define MAINWINDOW_H

#include <QMainWindow>

class QLineEdit;
class QTextBrowser;
class QTreeView;
class QHttp;
class QBuffer;
class QModelIndex;

class MainWindow : public QMainWindow
{
  Q_OBJECT
  public:
    MainWindow(QWidget *parent=0);

  protected slots:
    void readResponse(int id, bool error);
    void retrieveRss();
    void showArticle(const QModelIndex& index);
    void showRss();

  private:
    QHttp *http;
    QLineEdit *lineEdit;
    QTextBrowser *textBrowser;
    QTreeView *treeView;
    QBuffer *rssBuffer;
    int jobId;
};

#endif // MAINWINDOW_H
```

In the constructor we give the window a name and arrange the subwindow in a table layout. Here we drag the line edit over one line and two columns, which can be seen in the fourth and fifth parameters of the first addWidget() details. We insert the tree view and the text browser in the second line, in the first and second columns respectively:

```
// rssreader/mainwindow.cpp

#include <QtGui>
```

```
#include <QtXml>
#include <QtNetwork>
#include "mainwindow.h"
#include "rsshandler.h"

MainWindow::MainWindow(QWidget *parent)
  : QMainWindow(parent), jobId(0)
{
  setWindowTitle(tr("RSS Reader"));
  QWidget *cw = new QWidget;
  QGridLayout *lay = new QGridLayout(cw);
  lineEdit = new QLineEdit;
  lay->addWidget(lineEdit, 0,0,1,2);
  treeView = new QTreeView;
  treeView->setRootIsDecorated(false);
  lay->addWidget(treeView, 1,0);
  textBrowser = new QTextBrowser;
  lay->addWidget(textBrowser, 1,1);
  setCentralWidget(cw);

  rssBuffer = new QBuffer(this);
  rssBuffer->open(QIODevice::ReadWrite);

  http = new QHttp(this);

  connect(lineEdit, SIGNAL(returnPressed()), SLOT(retrieveRss()));
  connect(treeView, SIGNAL(activated(const QModelIndex&)),
                    SLOT(showArticle(const QModelIndex&)));
  connect(treeView, SIGNAL(doubleClicked(const QModelIndex&)),
                    SLOT(showArticle(const QModelIndex&)));
  connect(http, SIGNAL(requestFinished(int, bool)),
                    SLOT(readResponse(int, bool)));

  statusBar()->showMessage(tr("Welcome to RSS Reader!"));
}
```

The entire layout lies on a simple QWidget by the name of cw, which we insert into the main window as the central widget. Finally, we generate a buffer and open it for read and write access.

In addition we create the QHttp object. This class works in a purely asynchronous manner, so there is not even the theoretical possibility of placing the object on the stack, which would block processing until an event is present. Instead, all calls immediately return. When the QHttp object has treated the request, it sends out a signal.

For this reason, we create signal/slot connections at the end, the last one of which is connected with the QHttp instance. As soon as the user sets off the inputs in the line edit with (Enter), retrieveRss() begins downloading the file. The second and third connect() calls connect a key action or a double-click to an entry in the list view with the showArticle() method, which displays the corresponding article. Finally, we connect the requestFinished() signal, which triggers QHttp after an operation has been completed, with the slot we have written ourselves, readResponse().

In retrieveRss() we transfer the text from the line edit into a QUrl object. It tries automatically to parse a URL from the text passed to it:

```
// rssreader/mainwindow.cpp (continued)

void MainWindow::retrieveRss()
{
  QUrl url(lineEdit->text());
  if(!url.isValid || url.schema() != "http") {
    statusBar()->showMessage(tr("Invalid URL: '%1'")
                                  .arg(lineEdit->text()));
    return;
  }
  http->setHost(url.host());
  jobId = http->get(url.path(), rssBuffer);
  statusBar()->showMessage(tr("Getting RSS Feed '%1'...")
                                .arg(url.toString()));
}
```

If the text does not yield a valid URL (i.e., isValid() returns false) or if the *scheme* (i.e., the protocol) is *not* http://, we do not need to continue, and return without leaving behind an error message. We now set the name of the server from which we want to obtain the RSS feed, using setHost(). The matching hostname is already stored for us by url.host().

Because of the asynchronous nature of QHttp, all method calls that work on the server are arranged into the queue and performed one after the other. Each method call returns a job ID. As soon as a job has been processed, QHttp emits the requestFinished() signal, the first argument of which is the job ID.

For this reason we make a note of the job ID (in the member variable jobId) for the Get request to the server. As arguments, the get() method demands the path to the file and a pointer to a QIODevice where it can store the retrieved file. Finally, we inform the user that we are downloading the RSS feed.

In the readResponse() slot we fetch only the result of the Get job. The second parameter specifies whether an error occurred during the file download, perhaps because the server was not available or the path was incorrect. If this is not the case, we process the data via showRss() and issue a three-second success message in the status bar. Otherwise, an error message will appear for the same length of time:

```
// rssreader/mainwindow.cpp (continued)

void MainWindow::readResponse(int id, bool error)
{
```

```
  if (id == jobId) {
    if (!error) {
      showRss();
      statusBar()->showMessage(
              tr("RSS-Feed loaded successfully"), 3000);
    }
    else
      statusBar()->showMessage(
              tr("Fehler while fetching RSS feed!"), 3000);
  }
}
```

showRss() does the actual work. Here we create a standard model with two columns that we later pass on to RssHandler:

```
// rssreader/mainwindow.cpp (continued)

void MainWindow::showRss()
{
  QStandardItemModel *model = new QStandardItemModel(0, 2);
  RssHandler handler(model);
  QXmlSimpleReader reader;
  reader.setContentHandler(&handler);
  reader.setErrorHandler(&handler);
  rssBuffer->reset();
  QXmlInputSource source(rssBuffer);
  if (!reader.parse(source))
    return;
  delete treeView->model();
  treeView->setModel(model);
}
```

QXmlSimpleReader is responsible for parsing the file using the RssHandlers. Since RssHandler inherits from QXmlDefaultHandler, and thus from all handlers, but we have implemented only the functionality of QXmlContentHandler and QXmlErrorHandler, we must register the RssHandler as both a content and error handler with the reader object.

As the document source for QXmlSimpleReader, the QXmlInputSource class is used, which obtains its data from a QIODevice. But before we instantiate such an input source, passing on the buffer as an argument at the same time, we must set the read position in the buffer to the beginning of the internal QByteArray with reset(), so that the content just written can be read out. reader.parse() now starts the actual parsing process.

If this runs successfully, we first delete any already existing model linked to the tree view, and then pass our model, equipped with fresh content, to the view.

In the final step we now need to implement the showArticle() slot to display the entry selected in the tree view in the text browser. To do this we access the data()

method of the active model. We obtain the index of the current entry from the argument of the slot. As the role we select UserRole, where we previously stored the complete contents of the<description> tag. We now convert this, using toString(), from a QVariant back to a QString and pass this to the text browser as HTML:

```
// rssreader/mainwindow.cpp (continued)

void MainWindow::showArticle(const QModelIndex& index)
{
  QVariant tmp = treeView->model()->data(index, Qt::UserRole);
  QString content = tmp.toString();
  textBrowser->setHtml(content);
}
```

Now our rudimentary RSS reader is finished. The obligatory main() method instantiates QApplication, and the MainWindow object displays the window and sets it to an initial size of 640×480 pixels. The application then enters the event loop:

```
// rssreader/main.cpp

#include <QtGui>
#include "mainwindow.h"

int main(int argc, char *argv[])
{
  QApplication app(argc, argv);
  MainWindow mw;
  mw.show();
  mw.resize(640, 480);
  return app.exec();
}
```

This simple example already demonstrates that SAX2 allows you to parse documents with comparatively small outlay. But the more exact the checks become, the more complex the code. If you want to avoid this complexity, and you only process small documents anyway, you should take a look at the Document Object Model, which follows a completely different approach.

13.2   The DOM API

QDom, the DOM API of Qt, is a very convenient way of accessing XML files. The QDomDocument class here represents a complete XML file. Its setContent() method is capable of generating DOM trees out of XML files and conversely writing the contents of a DOM tree to an XML document.

The DOM tree itself consists of DOM elements (QDomElement). Their start tags may contain attributes. Between the start and end tag, DOM elements may contain text or child elements. In this way the DOM tree is built up from the XML structure, and its elements are without exception DOM nodes (QDomNodes).

QDomNodes know the principle of parenthood: If they are inserted in another part of the tree, they are not copied, but change their location in the tree. The node into which a QDomNode is inserted now functions as its new parent node. Not every node may posess child nodes, however. If you try, for example, to give a child to an attribute node, the object will insert the new node as a sibling node of the attribute node. This deviates from the DOM specification, which at this point divergently demands that an exception should be thrown.

Here a general distinction from the DOM specification can already be seen: Qt does not use exceptions to announce errors, but either uses return values or chooses an alternative behavior. This is why it is recommended that you exclude cases of error in advance of a call by making as many checks as possible in the method's code, and also check return values of methods after calls.

13.2.1 Reading in and Processing XML Files

The following HTML file is written in XHTML:

```
<!DOCTYPE html PUBLIC "-//W3C//DTD XHTML 1.0 Strict//EN"
        "http://www.w3.org/TR/xhtml1/DTD/xhtml1-strict.dtd">
<html xmlns="http://www.w3.org/1999/xhtml" lang="en" xml:lang="en">
  <head>
   <title>Title</title>
  </head>
  <body>
    <p>
      <a href="http://www.example.com">Example.com</a>
      <a href="http://www.example.net">Example.net</a>
      <a href="http://www.example.org">Example.org</a>
    </p>
  </body>
</html>
```

We want to load this into a test application in a QDomDocument and work with it in order to observe different aspects of QDom. For this purpose we open the file with QFile and read out its contents. Then we instantiate a QDomDocument and pass the byte array read out of the file to the QDomDocument with setcontent(). We use using namespace std; to simply write cout (instead of std::cout) to display data on the standard output.

```
// xhtmldomparser/main.cpp

#include <QtCore>
#include <QtXml>
```

```cpp
#include <iostream>

using namespace std;

int main(int argc, char* argv[])
{
  QCoreApplication app(argc, argv);
  QFile file("index.xml");
  if (!file.open(QIODevice::ReadOnly))
    return 1;
  QByteArray content = file.readAll();
  QDomDocument doc;
  QString errorMessage;
  int line, col;
  if (!doc.setContent(content, &errorMessage, &line, &col))
  {
    cout << "Error in Line " << line << ", column " << col
         << ":" << qPrintable(errorMessage) << endl;
    return 1;
  }
}
```

setContent() parses the input and returns a false if there is a parser error. If—like us—you want to learn more about the error, you pass to this function, apart from the bytearray, a pointer to a QString and two integers. If there is an error, the function fills these last three values with the problem description, as well as the relevant line and column in the document.

Figure 13.2:
Every object in the DOM tree generated from the XML is a QDomNode as well.

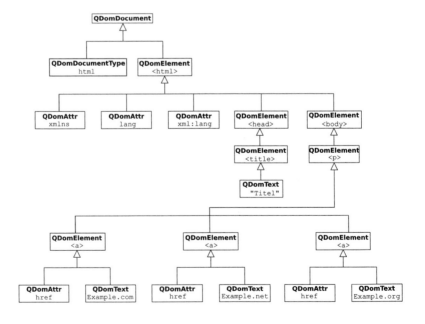

The DOM tree parsed in this way is shown in Figure 13.2. We will now work with this. First we read out the name of the document type and the tag name of the root element in the document. docType() provides us with the document type in a QDomDocumentType object. Its name—that is, the part which stands directly after DOCTYPE—is called html in this case. This is revealed to us through the name() method:

```cpp
// xhtmldomparser/main.cpp (continued)

  QDomDocumentType type = doc.doctype();
  cout << "Document type: " << qPrintable(type.name()) << endl;;

  QDomElement root = doc.documentElement();
  if (root.hasAttribute("xmlns")) {
    QDomAttr attr = root.attributeNode("xmlns");
    cout << "xmlns: " << qPrintable(attr.value()) << endl;
  }

  if (root.hasAttribute("lang")) {
    QDomAttr attr = root.attributeNode("lang");
    cout << "lang: " << qPrintable(attr.value()) << endl;
  }

  QDomNode node = root.firstChild();
  while(!node.isNull())
  {
    if(node.isElement()) {
      QDomElement elem = node.toElement();
      cout << "Child of root node: " << qPrintable(elem.tagName()) <<
endl;
      cout << "Its text: " << qPrintable(elem.text()) << endl;
    }
    node = node.nextSibling();
  }
```

We obtain the root element and save it as a QDomElement via the QDomDocument method documentElement(). The attributes of elements are provided by attributeNode(). In the example we extract the attributes xmlns and lang. If the file does not contain them, attributeNode() would return an empty QDomAttr object. This is why we check whether the element has a corresponding attribute at all, using hasAttribute(). Finally, using value(), we obtain the value of the attribute.

Then we read out all the child nodes of the root element. We use firstChild() to give us the first DOM node (that is, head), and all the others (here, just body) we obtain with nextSibling(). If this is just an element, we convert the node to a QDomElement. If we come across an attribute or comment node, this will not work, of course. To obtain the name of a QDomElements, we use the tagName() method.

The text() method collects the text nodes of an element and its child elements in a QString. Here we receive the text of the headers from the head element, and on the next loop pass the texts of all three reference elements (<a>) beneath the body element.

We now fill the node variable with the next sister nodes and repeat the procedure. If no more sister nodes are available, then nextSibling() returns a null node, which no longer fulfils the loop condition. The output of the above example therefore appears as follows:

```
Document type: html
Root tag: html
Document type: html
xmlns: http://www.w3.org/1999/xhtml
lang: en
Child of root node: head
Its text: Title
Child of root node: body
Its text: Example.comExample.netExample.org
```

The conversion of the QDomNodes returned by firstChild() and nextSibling() into QDomElements can be left out, by the way, if you use firstChildElement() and nextSiblingElement() instead. The procedure used here makes particular sense if you want, for example, to filter out additional comments (represented by QDom-Comment) or text (represented by QDomText and QDomCDATASection).

13.2.2 Searching for Specific Elements

Now that we have seen how we navigate in a DOM tree, we will look at the methods we can use to search specifically for certain elements. DOM provides the elements-ByTagName() function for this purpose. It expects the name of an element type. If you call it as a method of a QDomDocument instance, then it will look through all the elements in the entire document, whereas the method of the same name in the QDomElement class looks through all the elements beneath the element receiving the method call.

Both functions return a QDomList. This is *not* a type definition for QList<QDomNode> but is a different kind of data structure, which is specified in the DOM specifications. We can therefore not process this list with foreach(). Instead we use a for() loop to iterate through the list, as shown here:

```
// xhtmldomparser/main.cpp (continued)

  QDomNodeList anchors = doc.elementsByTagName("a");
  for(uint i = 0; i < anchors.length(); i++) {
    QDomElement anchor = anchors.at(i).toElement();
    QString href = anchor.attribute("href");
    cout << qPrintable(href) << endl;
  }
```

The number of elements is determined by the length() method. Before we can read out the attributes from the current DOM node, we must convert it back to an element. The DOM API always provides only one QDomNodeList for lists. The attribute("href") call is a short form for attributeNode("href").value() and returns the value directly as a QString. The output for our example accordingly appears as follows:

```
http://www.example.com
http://www.example.net
http://www.example.org
```

The QDomNode::childNodes() method returns all subnodes, also in a QDomNodeList.

13.2.3   Manipulating the DOM Tree

Of course, we can also insert new elements into the tree or eliminate existing ones. To delete a DOM node from the tree, you call the removeChild() method of the parent node, which can be determined by parentNode(), and pass the node in question to this method as a QDomElement:

```
// xhtmldomparser/main.cpp (continued)

  QDomElement examplecom = anchors.at(0).toElement();
  examplecom.parentNode().removeChild(examplecom);
```

We now want to convert the remaining links into a nonclickable text, but the text should still be emphasized, for which we use a <b> tag. Ideally, we would therefore change the tag name of the element and remove the href attribute with the following code:

```
// xhtmldomparser/main.cpp (continued)

  for(uint i = 0; i < anchors.length(); i++) {
    QDomElement anchor = anchors.at(i).toElement();
    anchor.setTagName("b");
    anchor.removeAttribute("href");
  }
```

Alternatively we could have created a new element, copied the text, looked for the parent node with parentNode(), and from there replaced the href tag using the replaceChild() method. As arguments, this expects the node to be replaced and then the new node.

Next we create a new partial tree and insert it into the DOM tree. As a basis for partial trees, the class QDomDocumentFragment can be used to save trees that do not have to contain well-formed XML. This means that such a partial tree may contain several direct child elements, whereas in a QDomDocument, one element at the most, the root element, may exist.

QDomDocumentFragments play a special role in methods such as appendChild(), insertBefore(), or insertAfter(): If these contain a fragment as a parameter, then they insert all its sub-nodes.

To create a node (that is, one based on a QDomNode subclass), we must use one of the factory methods from QDomDocument, which all start with create. The only exception is the QDomDocument itself, which we can instantiate directly. If you just instantiate a node without initializing it using the appropriate factory method, then it is considered to be undefined. This behavior represents a source of errors that is not easy to detect.

In the following code we will generate a fragment and insert in it an italic element (i). Into this element we place a text node by first creating a QDomText and then appending it to the italic element with appendChild(). After this we create an XML comment (QDomComment) and insert both the new italic element and the comment into the document fragment:

```
// xhtmldomparser/main.cpp (continued)
```

```
QDomDocumentFragment fragment = doc.createDocumentFragment();
QDomElement italic = doc.createElement("i");
QDomText text = doc.createTextNode("some links for you:");
italic.appendChild(text);
QDomComment comment = doc.createComment("converted links:");
fragment.appendChild(italic);
fragment.appendChild(comment);
QDomNode para = doc.elementsByTagName("p").at(0);
para.insertBefore(fragment, para.firstChild());
```

To enter both elements in our document above the links, we locate the first p element and insert the fragment's components as children, via insertBefore(), in front of what was the first child until now.

13.2.4 The DOM Tree as XML Output

The tree obtained up to this point can again be displayed by QDocument as an XML structure. The methods toString() and toByteArray() can be used for this. The latter is of particular interest if you want to write the XML file back to a QIODevice. The parameter specifies the number of empty spaces that should be used when indenting the XML structure. If this is missing, Qt sets the indent depth to one empty space per level.

In the following example we will write the current status of the DOM tree into the file opened for writing, out.xml. Then we close this and send it to the standard output with toString(). In both cases we use two empty spaces per level when indenting the elements in the output:

```
// xhtmldomparser/main.cpp (continued)

  QFile outfile("out.xml");
  if (!outfile.open(QIODevice::WriteOnly)) {
    cout << "Could not write file: "
         << qPrintable(outfile.fileName()) << endl;
    return 1;
  }
  QByteArray data = doc.toByteArray(2);
  outfile.write(data);
  outfile.close();
  // unicode string representation
  QString string = doc.toString(2);
  cout << qPrintable(string) << endl;
  return 0;
}
```

14

Internationalization

Many programs today are intended to reach users in many different countries. For this reason it is very important that an application can be modified easily and flexibly to the particularities of another language. One aspect of this is the translation of all visible texts into the target language. The direction of text flow, on which the arrangement of widgets is based, is also of central importance.

In this chapter we will first translate the application CuteEdit, which we created in Chapter 4 using the tools of Qt. In addition we will get to know a few useful classes which, when used during the development process, will help to avoid problems later on when translating the software to another language.

14.1 Translating Applications into Other Languages

Qt includes several mechanisms to prepare application programs for translation into other languages later on (see page 50 and also page 123).

We now repeat once again the two most important points: All translatable strings in the program code must always be enclosed by the QObject method tr(). In addition, variables in strings may never be directly concatenated, since it would be impossible to produce the correct word order in the target language, as the following English-to-German sentence conversion illustrates:

```
QString filename = "file.txt";
QString message = tr("Could not save ") + filename;
```

In the German translation, the word order should be "Could file.txt not save," but the expression used to construct the message assumes English word order and so cannot produce the desired phrase. To do the translation correctly, you need to use placeholders, as shown below.

```
QString filename = "file.txt";
QString message = tr("Could not save %1.").arg(filename);
```

Now tr() is able to translate this sentence with the correct inverted (relative to English) word order, Could %1 not save. We will now explain how this works.

14.1.1 Preparing the Application

The CuteEdit version used here is different from the one in Chapter 4, in that it uses English strings in the code. This is not necessary but it does make sense, as English is normally used as the lingua franca, allowing external programmers whose mother tongue is not German to work on the program.

For the translation of Qt-based applications, Qt provides the programs lupdate, linguist, and lrelease. The translation process is not a separate task, completely isolated from the code development, but is integrated into the Qt project management. If our project file up until now looks like this:

```
#cuteediti18n/cuteediti18n.pro

TEMPLATE    = app
SOURCES     = main.cpp mainwindow.cpp
HEADERS     = mainwindow.h
FORMS       = mainwindow.ui
RESOURCES   = pics.qrc
```

then all that is missing is the entry for TRANSLATIONS, which expects one or more translation files as arguments. Adding translation support for German, French, and Italian will look like this:

```
#cuteediti18n/cuteediti18n.pro (continued)

TRANSLATIONS = cuteedit_de.ts \
               cuteedit_fr.ts \
               cuteedit_it.ts
```

Using the lupdate tool, we extract these files from the project sources, the files registered under SOURCES, HEADERS, and FORMS. The following command is sufficient to do this:

```
lupdate cuteediti18n.pro
```

This extracts all the strings in the sources that need to be translated. These *translation sources* are now available in an XML-based format.

If new strings are added during further program development, lupdate cuteediti18n.pro updates the translation sources, and translators can work on the new strings.

14.1.2 Processing Translation Sources with Linguist

The most convenient way to open and edit translation sources is with the program Qt Linguist. This work can be done by people working independently of the Qt software developers, such as freelance translators.

Figure 14.1 shows the main window of the Linguist after it has loaded the file cuteedit_de.ts. The context dock window on the left-hand page gives an overview of the translation context, and it usually displays the name of the class in which a string appears.

If you select a context, the strings for translation in this context will appear. The field in the center provides space for an individual translation.

Since there are standard translations for many commonplace phrases and menu items, you can find suggestions from so-called *phrasebooks*. Qt provides such collections of suggestions for many common languages under Phrases → Open Phrasebook.... If these are loaded, suggestions will appear in the lower-right window if Linguist finds similarities to the word(s) being translated.

Untranslated strings are given a blue question mark, and translated ones an orange question mark. If Linguist discovers an inconsistency in the translation, such as missing "..." in menu items, it places a red exclamation mark in front and displays the problem in the status bar. If you are satisfied with a translation, you confirm it with (Ctrl)+(Enter). It is then given a green checkmark.

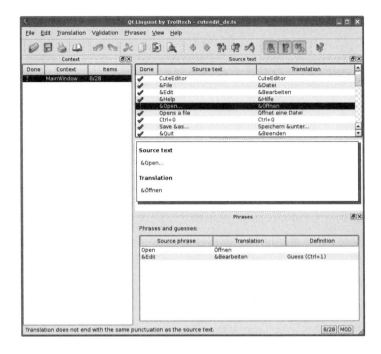

Figure 14.1:
Using phrasebooks,
the Qt Linguist helps
you to find matching
translations and
checks these for
consistency.

When all strings are translated, the results just need to be saved: The .ts file now contains the translated strings. The command

```
lrelease cuteediti18n.pro
```

creates files from (complete or partial) translation sources in a special binary format that the Qt program can use. In our case these are cuteedit_de.qm, cuteedit_fr.qm, and cuteedit_it.qm.

14.1.3 Using Translations in the Program

Loading the correct translation when the program starts is the task of the QTranslator class. It will search for the translation files in the working directory of the application if it is not given a path as the second argument when it is called.

To determine the name of the translation file for the respective system environment, we use QLocale::system(). The static method outputs a QLocale object with information on the current system locale. The name() function returns the locale to us as a string, consisting of a language code and a country code in capitals, which for Germany would be de_DE. Therefore, our filename is cuteedit_de_DE, and this is turned into cuteedit_de_de as a precaution, using toLower():

```
// cuteediti18n/main.cpp


#include <QApplication>
#include "mainwindow.h"

int main(int argc, char *argv[])
{
  QApplication a(argc, argv);

  QTranslator cuteeditTranslator;
  filename = QString("cuteedit_%1").arg(QLocale::system().name());
  filename = filename.toLower();
  cuteeditTranslator.load(filename);
  app.installTranslator(&cuteeditTranslator);
```

QTranslator now looks for the filename according to a fixed pattern: First it adds .qm to the file, then it tries without this extension. If it has still not found anything, it removes all the numbers from the end of the name up to the first underscore or dot, and tries again. In our case the search sequence would look like this:

```
cuteedit_de_de.qm
cuteedit_de_de
cuteedit_de.qm
cuteedit_de
cuteedit.qm
cuteedit
```

The algorithm already found something in the third step. Through the country code, localization is also possible between countries that use the same language but with differences in vocabulary or usage. Thus en usually matches American English, whereas the application would make adjustments aimed toward the language customs of Great Britain if the locale were set to en_UK.

If we include the translation in our QApplication instance with installTranslator(), the application shows a translated user interface after show() has been called.

In addition we install a QTranslator, which contains all the strings of the Qt library.

```
// cuteediti18n/main.cpp (continued)

  QTranslator qtTranslator;
  QString filename("qt_%1").arg(QLocale::system().name());
  filename = filename.toLower();
  qtTranslator.load("qt_" + QLocale::system().name());
  app.installTranslator(&qtTranslator);
```

```
QCoreApplication::setOrganizationName("OpenSourcePress");
QCoreApplication::setOrganizationDomain("OpenSourcePress.de");
QCoreApplication::setApplicationName("CuteEdit");

MainWindow mainWindow;
mainWindow.show();

return a.exec();
}
```

The directory $QTDIR/translations contains the raw translation sources in the file qt_untranslated.ts, together with a series of translations for different languages, such as qt_de.ts and qt_de.qm for Germany. All you need to do is copy the corresponding files to the current directory so that the QTranslator object will find them.

Since the organization and application name, as well as the domain, are used in the path for configurations files, these strings should not be translated.

14.1.4   Adding Notes for the Translation

If a string's meaning is not unique, for example because it just consists of one word, this can lead to problems in translations. For instance, the translator who just sees the word as a single word, and not in its entire usage context, has no clues as to whether the word *stop* means "stop the current operation" or "bus stop." For this reason the tr() method allows a translation comment to be placed as the second argument. The code

```
QString busstop = tr("Stop", "bus stop");
QString stopaction = tr("Stop", "stop action");
```

generates two different strings with corresponding comments, after lupdate has been run on the translation source.

14.1.5   Specifying the Translation Context

For strings occurring in global functions that do not belong to any class, there is no class to use as a default translation context. It is nevertheless possible to assign a context to such a string by calling the actual static method tr() of a particular class:[1]

---

[1] The QApplication method translate() always demands details of the translation context anyway (see page 50).

```
void global_function(MyWidget *w)
{
  QLabel *label = new QLabel(MyWidget::tr("foo"), w);
}
```

lupdate then accepts the label "foo" in the correct correct translation context (in this case, MyWidget).

14.1.6 Internationalizing Strings Outside Qt Classes

For reasons of space, certain data is often stored in a static array. In order that lupdate can also record entries from such char arrays, they must be enclosed by the macro QT_TR_NOOP. tr() then searches for its translations as before from the catalog.

This is illustrated in the following example, in which we store several city names in a static, null-terminated array. After we have instantiated the QCoreApplication object and installed the translator there, the program displays the localized city names, via the tr() instruction, as soon as a translation file is available:

```
// trnoop/main.cpp

#include <QtCore>
#include <QDebug>

int main(int argc, char* argv[])
{
  static const char* cities[] = {
    QT_TR_NOOP("Cologne"),
    QT_TR_NOOP("Munich"),
    QT_TR_NOOP("Rome"),
    0
  };

  QCoreApplication app(argc, argv);

  QTranslator translator;
  filename = QString("trnoop_%1").arg(QLocale::system().name());
  filename = filename.toLower();
  translator.load(filename);
  app.installTranslator(&translator);


  int i = 0;
  while (cities[i])
    qDebug << QObject::tr(cities[i++]);

  return 0;
}
```

Appendixes

A

Debugging Help

Error analysis, often referred to as *debugging*, is one of the most time-consuming activities in software development. Apart from using a debugger, the method of choice is to augment the code with instructions that produce debug output (e.g., the calculations of algorithms) at strategically chosen points. You can also reconstruct how and when various program parts are called by using selected output messages.

A.1 Debugging Functions

There are two different approaches to outputting debugging code, reflecting the differences between C and C++. C developers work predominantly with printf(), whereas C++ programmers prefer to send output through streams, via cout and cerr, since no format string is required in this case.

Both approaches cause problems as soon as program development is finished: Prior to each release, the debugging output must be deactivated, although certain critical messages possibly should remain.

Qt allows an alternative approach that supports both of the commonly used methods and also solves the aforementioned problems: It suppresses debug messages if the QT_NO_DEBUG_OUTPUT macro is defined during the compiling process. This is automatically the case if you build the Qt program without debug support. This is ensured by inserting the CONFIG -= debug line in the project file.

To use the functions and macros described below, no additional includes are necessary—apart from files that otherwise manage without Qt elements. In this case you must include the QtGlobal header:

```
#include <QtGlobal>
```

If QT_NO_DEBUG_OUTPUT is undefined, what is done with the error messages depends on the operating system. Under Unix-type operating systems such as Linux or OS X, the output appears on the standard error output, better known to Unix aficionados as stderr. On Windows machines this output lands in the debugger. If you want to divert the output elsewhere, you can define your own message handler, as described in Section A.1.3 on page 388.

Qt provides three functions that are responsible for the debug output and implement the aforementioned debugging output behavior: qDebug(), qCritical(), and qFatal(). They only vary in terms of their effects, but they are used in an identical manner. Their signatures show close similarities with the C function printf(). They even use the same format options.

A.1.1 Simple Debug Output

qDebug() is the tool of choice for "normal" debug output:

```
void qDebug ( const char * msg, replacement_values_for_format_strings )
```

This function is used, for example, to examine data structures at runtime. The following instruction displays the number of entries in the QList object list:

```
qDebug("Amount of list entries: %d", list.size());
```

In this case qDebug() replaces the formatting placeholders, which are prefixed by the percentage sign, with the actual parameters that have been supplied after the message string, one by one—in this example, thanks to the %d format specifier, qDebug() outputs the number of list entries as a decimal number. The parameter list can be any length at all. Under no circumstances should you specify a variable as the first argument and assume that qDebug() will produce a proper output, since qDebug() accesses the system-dependent printf() for the output, and several printf() implementations first expect a formatting string.

QStrings or byte arrays convert the helper function qPrintable() into C-compliant strings (const char *) that qDebug() can output directly:[1]

```
QString str = "Hello, world!";
qDebug("My first application printed '%s'.\n", qPrintable(str));
```

A considerably more pleasant and more modern type of output is available if you include the <QtDebug> header. Then there is hardly any need for manual serialization,[2] since many Qt types already provide serialization operators for use with qDebug(). For example,

```
qDebug() << "Brush:" << myQBrush;
```

displays all the properties of the myQBrush paintbrush. This works for all major Qt types, so that qDebug() can also display strings and byte arrays without the diversion via qPrintable(). The concept is very similar to redirecting output using cerr, but differs from this in two important points: On one hand, qDebug() adds a space between the various outputs, and on the other hand, it takes care of the line wrap, without a endl having to be explicitly serialized as the final element, as is the case with the C++ operator cout. The serialization operators are defined only for qDebug(), but not for the functions described below.

A.1.2 Errors and Warnings

For error messages occuring during program execution, Trolltech provides the qCritical() method. This works exactly like qDebug(), according to the conventions used for the printf() command:

```
void load(const QString &fileName)
{
```

---

[1] qPrintable() corresponds to the call str.toLocal8Bit().constData(), which returns a const char *. However, the result is only valid for as long as the underlying string remains unchanged. If you require a C string that persists while the Qt string changes, then you must duplicate the result with qstrdup() and delete the created C string later, with free().

[2] *Serialization* is understood as the conversion of an object to a datastream according to a well-defined encoding. This is necessary here if you want to list all the relevant object properties in the debug output.

```
        QFile file(fileName);
        if (!file.exists())
            qCritical("File '%s' doesn't exist!", qPrintable(fileName));
    }
```

Nevertheless, qCritical() does not release the programmer in the slightest from building graceful error-handling capabilities into the application's interface, because (for a graphical application in particular) it cannot be assumed that when something goes wrong, a user will be looking at console output—or, under Windows, even have a debugger running. For this reason, errors should be passed on to the user as often as possible in a comprehensible form, such as via a dialog box.

Another debugging tool option is to use *warnings*. These strings, issued via qWarning(), always appear whenever QT_NO_WARNING_OUTPUT is *not* activated during compilation of the program. If you also set an environment variable by the name of QT_FATAL_WARNINGS, the program will close the first time a qWarning() is issued.

If the program also is to terminate in the release version when a particular behavior occurs, you can use the function

```
void qFatal ( const char * msg, ... )
```

In this case the value 1 is returned. In the debug version the behavior depends on the platform: Under Unix the program tries to generate a core dump, whereas under Windows it announces a _CRT_ERROR, giving the debugger a clue. An example of an error that it would be useful to treat using qFatal() is division by zero:

```
int divide(int a, int b)
{
    if (b == 0)   // Error!
        qFatal("Division by zero is not allowed!");
    return a / b;
}
```

For each of the debug helper functions with C printf()-style semantics—that is, qDebug(), qFatal(), qWarning(), or qCritical()—the internal character buffer is restricted to 8,192 bytes. This includes the terminating \0 character. In addition, Trolltech warns that passing (const char *)0 as a parameter can lead to the program crashing on some platforms. The reasons are flawed implementations of printf(), the function which Qt accesses for debugging functions.

A.1.3   Customizing the Output of Debugging Functions

Under Windows, Qt sends all debug output to a debugger. Developers who are used to the command line and don't work with Visual Studio sometimes have a problem with this. However, Qt allows you to divert debug messages to wherever you want by using so-called *message handlers.*

The following code indicates how to implement your own message handler in case the application is running under Windows. It uses the macro Q_WS_WIN, which only exists in Qt for Windows:

```
int main( int argc, char* argv[] )
{
    QApplication app( argc, argv );
#ifdef Q_WS_WIN
    qInstallMsgHandler(debugWinMsgHandler);
#endif
    ...
}
```

This include guard ensures that the handler really is only accessed under Windows.[3] In general, there is nothing to stop you from activating the handler on all platforms on which console output is preferred. A debug handler that displays debug output in a separate window could look like this, for example:

```
void debugWinMsgHandler(QtMsgType type, const char *msg)
{
    static QTextEdit *edit = new QTextEdit();
    edit->setWindowTitle("Debug window");
    edit->show();

    switch (type) {
    case QtDebugMsg:
        edit->append(QString("<b>Debug:</b> \%1").arg(msg));
        break;
    case QtWarningMsg:
        edit->append(QString("<b>Warning:</b> \%1").arg(msg));
        break;
    case QtCriticalMsg:
        edit->append(QString("<font color=\"red\">
                            <b>Critical:</b></font> \%1").arg(msg));
        break;
    case QtFatalMsg:
        QMessageBox::critical(0, "Debug - Fatal", msg);
        abort();
    }
}
```

The signature of the method, as is usual with callbacks, is defined in advance, but the function name can be freely chosen. It is important only that qInstallMsgHandler() specifies the callback method with its correct name, and also without brackets

---

[3] Alternatively, there exist the macros Q_WS_MAC for Mac OS X, Q_WS_X11 for X11-based platforms, and Q_WS_QWS for the embedded variants of Qt. See http://doc.trolltech.com/4.1/qtglobal.html for a list of all compiler- and platform-dependent macros.

and arguments. You can think of a callback as a pointer to a function. Whoever holds the pointer can invoke the function from an abitrary place in the application at any given time. However, this assumes that the caller knows which arguments the callback function takes. In this case, the required arguments for the message handler callback function are documented in the Qt documentation.

The core of our handler consists of a switch statement that distinguishes between the message types (the QtDebugMsgs given out by qDebug(), the QtFatalMsgs generated by qFatal(), etc.) so that they can be treated specifically.

Our simple implementation shows all debug output in a QMessageBox text window. Since the edit pointer is declared as static, new is used for initialization only on the first cycle. This removes the need to declare global variables and makes a separate class unnecessary. Each time it is invoked with a message, the function ensures that the window is visible and that the new message appears in the window.

Since QTextEdit can understand primitive HTML, we take advantage of this in the code for our debug window to format the text clearly. Only fatal errors, which cause the program to be immediately terminated, are shown by the routine in a modal message box that blocks the rest of the application. If the user confirms such a message by clicking OK, the program terminates immediately.

The routine suggested here does have a small disadvantage, however: The program only terminates when the debug window has been closed by hand.

A.2   Ways to Eliminate Errors

C and C++ already have a wide range of methods for sniffing out errors. Qt adds a few other useful ones, which replace existing functions with more portable variations.

A.2.1   Checking Assertions

The C function assert() interrupts programs compiled in the debug mode if the expression specified in brackets (the *assertion*) evaluates to false. It only works if the NDEBUG macro is *not* defined and requires an additional #include, usually of assert.h.

Qt has the Q_ASSERT() macro, which interrupts the program just like assert() if certain conditions are not fulfilled. It is often used to test preconditions or postconditions for specific code segments of methods. In contrast to assert(), the Qt variant distinguishes between the release and the debugging versions[4] of a program: In the debug version, Q_ASSERT() breaks off with an error message.

---

[4] How you compile a program as a debug or as a release variation is described starting on page 27.

The following Qt assertion instruction, for example, checks whether the program was given one or more arguments:

```
Q_ASSERT(argc > 1);
```

If this is included in the main() function in line 12 of the file main.cpp, the program will output the following to the command line if there is an error:

```
ASSERT: 'argc > 1' in file main.cpp, line 12
```

If we compiled the program in debug mode, the program will then terminate.

In addition to reporting filenames and line numbers, it is often also useful to specify a context that provides information on the purpose of the assertion. Qt has the macro Q_ASSERT_X() for this purpose:

```
Q_ASSERT_X(argc > 1, "main()", "No arguments passed!");
```

This makes the program considerably more verbose and specifies the context for the assertion:

```
ASSERT failure in main(): 'No arguments passed!',
file main.cpp, line 12.
```

A.2.2   Checking Pointers

Unpleasant surprises can often wait in store for developers of portable programs, particularly when you need to allocate large amounts of memory or to reference a pointer across library boundaries. Let's look at the following program extract:

```
char *lots_of_memory= new char[1024*1024*1024];
Q_CHECK_PTR(lots_of_memory);
```

If a pointer allocation goes wrong, new sets the pointer to the value 0 (the null pointer). In this case, the Q_CHECK_PTR() macro used here reacts with an error message as shown below, and terminates the program:

```
In file main.cpp, line 14: Out of memory
```

If you use this macro whenever you require very large amounts of memory, you will save a great deal of work when searching for the causes of memory bottlenecks. This is of immense importance particularly in porting to architectures with little main memory.

Since Q_CHECK_PTR(), just like Q_ASSERT and Q_ASSERT_X, is only executed in debug mode, it is important that you don't use it to carry out operations that may, under some circumstances, influence the normal running of a program. Such operations, also called *side effects*, can in particular cause the program to *only* work correctly in debug mode. For example, the following variation of our above example will most likely always crash in the release version:

```
char *lotsofmemory;
Q_CHECK_PTR(lotsofmemory= new char[1024*1024*1024]);
```

This is because the pointer to the new memory area is never initialized in the release version. That means that any access to lotsofmemory will then be invalid, which will cause the program to crash.

A.2.3 Common Linker Errors

If the linker announces errors containing the keywords vtbl, _vtbl or _ _vtbl, you should first search for the problem in the meta-object compiler moc. It generates an additional file for all classes containing the line Q_OBJECT, which must be linked to the project.

qmake may "forget" about this because of an incorrectly set system time (which can also trigger many other problems, since the build system relies on having the correct timestamps on the source files), but there are also other causes. In this case the problem can be solved by calling qmake by hand.

B

Tulip: Containers and Algorithms

Anyone who wants to program complex algorithms in C++ will often make use of the *Standard Template Library (STL)*, a collection of algorithms and containers that implement data structures. *Containers* are usually created as a template class, whereas *algorithms* operate either on containers or are themselves template functions that work with the data type required in each case.

Yet even now, the STL has various disadvantages: A number of compilers, particularly older ones, do not fully implement some library parts, or implement them incorrectly. Also, since loop contents have to stand in a separate function, some algorithms cannot be expressed in an intuitive manner, as demonstrated in the following code, which outputs to the screen each element of the vector v via the print_element() function:

```
// stl/main.cpp

#include <iostream>
#include <vector>

using namespace std;

void print_element(int element)
{
  cout << element << endl;
}

int main()
{
  vector<int> v;

  v.push_back(1);
  v.push_back(2);
  v.push_back(3);

  for_each(v.begin(), v.end(), print_element);

  return 0;
}
```

Trolltech therefore provides a lightweight addition to the STL with the name of *Tulip*.[1] Tulip is STL-compatible, so it includes all the necessary methods, such as push_back(), but in addition it also has equivalent functions with more intuitive names. Thus push_back() is merely a synonym for append().

In addition, Tulip containers make use of Java-style iterator concepts. They provide their own data structures and matching algorithms for this purpose, which are somewhat easier to handle than those of the STL.

B.1   Iterators

When the elements of a list need to be accessed, many developers use the traditional index-based access within a for loop:

```
QStringList list;
list << "Dog" << "Cat" << "Mouse";
for (int i = 0; i < list.length(); i++)
{
  qDebug() << list[i];
}
```

---

[1] The name is derived from the English term *Tool Lib* (tool library).

This has a number of disadvantages. Basically, iterating via index access is slow for many data structures, especially for structures that do not allow direct addressing via indices (such as some list types, or in trees).[2]

This is why we have *iterators*.[3] These are objects specialized for use in traversing data structures. They point to an element of a data structure and at the same time provide methods to move around within the data structure, starting off from the current element. In this way they abstract the data structure from the iteration, thus avoiding code that uses direct indexed access

Another advantage is that iterators allow the concrete implementation of the data structure on which they operate to be replaced without the need for the iteration code to be modified. If you realize that an embedded list is better for certain problems than a normal pointer-based QList, you can simply substitute the new implementation without this change having any influence on code that uses the iterator.

In addition, iterators provide a certain amount of protection from coding errors that arise because of changes in the container on which they are working. For example, if an element is added to the beginning of a list as the consequence of an iteration (which is often the case in the specialized list QQueue), index-based addressing returns the wrong element on the next access unless the code has been written to adjust the index variable to account for the insertion. This extra care is often unnecessary when writing code that uses iterators to move around the data structure.

Tulip makes a distinction between two iterator typyes: STL-style and Java-style, which are based on different concepts.

B.1.1 STL-Style Iterators

The most well-known iterators in the C++ environment, STL-style iterators are implemented by Tulip in all container classes. STL iterators always point to elements. If they reach the end of the container and are advanced past the final element, they then point to a nonexistent element. If you then try to access the element pointed at by the iterator, the result is undefined.

Using a QStringList, which is basically just a specialized QList<QString>, the example above will look like this:

```
// foriterator/main.cpp

#include <QtCore>
#include <QDebug>
```

---

[2] A good example of this is the QLinkedList discussed on page 398.
[3] In database circles these are known as *cursors*.

```
using namespace std;

int main() {
  QStringList list;
  list << "dog" << "cat" << "mouse";
  QStringList::iterator it;
  for (it = list.begin(); it != list.end(); ++it)
  {
    qDebug() << *it << endl;
  }
  return 0;
}
```

If you apply the * operator to it, you will reach the list element to which the iterator currently points, since Qt overloads the operator * for iterators for this purpose.

In such for loops you must remember to use the pre-increment operator (++it) instead of the usual it++: This operator works without an unnecessary temporary object for each for loop.

If the elements accessed in the loop should only be read but not modified, a const_iterator is used, which ensures improved performance.

B.1.2   Java-Style Iterators

Apart from the STL iterators, Qt also has Java-style iterators. Those are self-contained classes which Trolltech has named according to the pattern Q*container-name*iterator.

Conceptually, Java iterators are fundamentally different from STL iterators in a number of ways. For one thing, they point *between* two elements of a data structure, and not *to* one of them. This results in Java iterators often being easier to handle, but somewhat slower than their STL-compatible colleagues.

Another difference is that by default they do not allow write access to the data structure, in contrast to their brothers of the same kind in the STL world. There are two reasons for this. On one hand, data structures are more often read than written during traversal. An *immutable* (that is, an unchangeable) Java iterator or const iterator (STL) saves time through this. On the other hand, an immutable iterator ensures that the data cannot be changed by an error in the program.

To obtain write access to the elements of the data structure, changeable iterators, or *mutable iterators*, are used. For QList-based lists the changeable iterator is called, for example, QMutableListIterator.

The following example shows how Java-style iterators are handled. It operates on an existing integer QList called list:

```
QListIterator<int> i(list);
```

```
while(i.hasNext())
{
  cout << i.next() << endl;
}
```

hasNext() checks whether the next element exists. next() not only jumps forward, but also returns the next value. After this, the iterator is located *after* this element, since Java-style iterators always "stand in the spaces between elements." If you only want the value of the next element, without moving the iterator, you should use peekNext().

In the same way, hasPrevious(), previous(), and peekPrevious() also exist, allowing iteration in the opposite direction. toBack() takes the iterator just beyond the final element, and toFront() takes it in front of the first one.

Furthermore, findNext() allows searching for elements with a specific value. If such an element exists, the function returns a true value, just like hasNext(), and positions the iterator *after* the element found. Likewise we have findPrevious(), which if successful places the iterator *in front of* the value found. If no element is found, the iterator lands beyond the final element, or before the first one. This is demonstrated by the following code:

```
// qlistdemo/main.cpp

#include <QtCore>
#include <QDebug>

int main() {
  QList<int> intlist;
  intlist << 2 << 5 << 2 << 4 << 2;

  int findings = 0;
  QListIterator<int> it(intlist);

  while (it.findNext(2))
    findings++;
  qDebug() << findings; // output: 3
  // Iterator is positioned after the last '2' element
  while (it.findPrevious(2))
    findings--;
  qDebug() << findings; // : 0
  // Iterator is positioned before the first '2' element
  return 0;
}
```

In addition to this, changeable iterators can insert an element at the current position with insert(), and then jump to its destination. This is illustrated by the next example: It jumps beyond the final element, where it adds a further 2. Because the iterator now stands after this last 2, the algorithm comes up with four matches:

```
// mutableiterator/main.cpp

#include <QtCore>
#include <QDebug>

int main() {
  QList<int> intlist;
  intlist << 2 << 5 << 2 << 4 << 2;

  QMutableListIterator<int> mit(intlist);
  mit.toBack();
  mit.insert(2);
  qDebug() << intlist; // output: (2, 5, 2, 4, 2, 2)

  int findings = 0;
  while (mit.findPrevious(2))
    findings++;
  qDebug() << findings; // output: 4
  return 0;
}
```

The following operations appear somewhat strange, as they violate the immutability principle of Java iterators: They manipulate or inspect elements, although the iterator in fact never directly points to one of them. The operations remove(), value(), and setValue() therefore operate on the final element to be jumped over. The following example deletes all elements with the value 2:

```
// mutableiterator2/main.cpp

#include <QtCore>
#include <QDebug>

int main() {
  QList<int> intlist;
  intlist << 2 << 5 << 2 << 4 << 2;

  QMutableListIterator<int> mit(intlist);

  while (mit.findNext(2))
    mit.remove();
  qDebug() << intlist; // output: (5, 4)
  return 0;
}
```

B.2 Lists

Lists represent fundamental data structures for most applications. Qt has three different types: QList, QLinkedList, and QVector.

These are templates that in their basic form are not specialized to a specific data type. Consequently, you can make a list type out of nearly every class. The class only needs to be assignable, that is, to have a copy operator as well as an assignment operator:

```
class Assignable
{
public:
  Assignable() {}
  Assignable(const Assignable &other); // copy operator
  Assignable&operator=(const Assignable &other); // assignment operator
private:
  ...
};
```

Tulip containers are value based, but they can also handle pointers, since a pointer is, first of all, nothing more than an integer value, namely a memory address. This means that

```
QList<QDate> myDateList;
```

is just as permissible as

```
QList<QDate*> myDateList;
```

It must be remembered here that Qt does not delete the elements behind the pointers when it deletes the list of pointers. This shortcoming is rectified by the helper function qDeleteAll() (see Section B.5.7 on page 418), which accepts either a complete container or two iterators as arguments. In the latter case it only deletes the elements between the start and end iterator, including the element to which begin() points (the last iterator is invalid anyway).

The pointers themselves remain, however. If you want to use the list again—as in the case of the following code—they must additionally be deleted with clear():

```
// listpointerdemo/main.cpp

#include <QtGui>
#include <QDebug>

int main(int argc, char* argv[]) {
  QApplication app(argc, argv);
  QList<QWidget*> widgetList;
  for (int i = 1; i < 10; i++)
  {
     widgetList.append(new QWidget);
```

```
}
// the following is equivalent to qDeleteAll(widgetList);
qDeleteAll(widgetList.begin(), widgetList.end());
// delete all now invalid pointers
widgetList.clear();
// append new item, this is now the first list item
widgetList.append(new QWidget);
return 0;
}
```

If you want to save yourself a lot of typing where containers are concerned, you can define your own names for the desired list types, using the C++ keyword typedef:

```
typedef QList<QDate> QDateList;
```

For read access to list elements, it is advisable to use not the index operator ([]), but the at() method. For code such as

```
QList<QImage> list;
...
QImage image = list[i];
```

the index operator returns only a const reference for a const-declared method. In all other cases it returns a normal reference. Even though this is actually a good thing (after all, const *correctness*[4] helps you to write more efficient programs), you may not always want to immediately generate a complete copy. This problem does not occur if you use the at() method:

```
QImage image = list.at(i);
```

B.2.1 Simple List (QList)

STL programmers frequently use a std::vector because this—in contrast to the STL list container, which is implemented as a linked list—is very fast to iterate over. The QList, the list container most frequently used in Qt is, from the perspective of implementation, an array of pointers that point to objects, in contrast to std::list. Provided that you want to access objects directly, this solution is quicker than an embedded list. Inserting at both ends of a list using prepend() and append() is also very fast—for lists with up to a thousand entries, QList is usually the fastest solution of all those provided by the Qt and STL classes.

---

[4] const *correctness* refers to the use of the const keyword for reference parameters of functions and for member functions that do not modify the object(s) with which they are called. Access methods that pass the internal state of an object to the outside should therefore always be declared as const, for example.

B.2.2 Linked List (QLinkedList)

If you frequently need to insert elements into large data collections, you are better off with a QLinkedList (see Figures B.1 and B.2). This class is implemented as a linked list. It has the disadvantage, however, that access to large lists by means of the index operator or at() can become very slow. This is explained by the way a linked list works: Each element contains a pointer to the next one, and therefore in order to access the element with a specified index, the container must visit all elements from the first one to the one being sought.

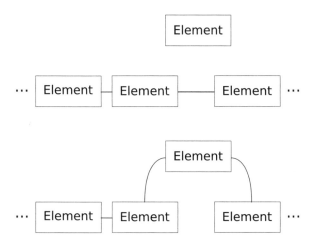

Figure B.1:
To insert an element into a linked list, only one pointer (the longer line) needs to be moved to the new element ...

Figure B.2:
... and another pointer is added, that points from the new element to the one that followed until now.

B.2.3 Vectors (QVector)

A QVector is particularly suitable if you need contiguous memory. If needed, space for new data elements is only allocated immediately after the existing memory. The class thus ensures that the data always lies *adjacent* in memory. The data() method makes use of this fact: It provides an array of the same data type as the one used to declare the vector.

Figure B.3:
QVector *provides a dynamic array, like* std::vector.

A vector behaves like a variable array: Internally, the data structure always reserves slightly more memory than currently required, which is why append operations at the end of the vector are very fast (Figure B.3).

The following example doubles every value stored in vector:

```
// vectordemo/main.cpp

#include <QVector>
#include <QDebug>

int main()
{
  const int n = 10;
  QVector<int> vector(n);
  int *data = vector.data();
  // fill vector
  for (int i = 0; i < n; ++i)
    data[i] = i;
  for (int i = 0; i < n; ++i) {
    data[i] *= 2;
    qDebug() << vector.at(i);
  }
```

The resources used in the second for loop are the same as those used to access a normal C array. In addition only constant costs are caused by the call of data(), since QByteArray works internally with a C++ array. The result of data() is therefore valid only until the size of the vector changes.

The index operator returns a reference to the element at the requested position, provided that the index specified is not larger than the number of elements in the vector. With vectors that are not declared as const, and which are therefore freely writable, you can thus fabricate the following code:

```
// vectordemo/main.cpp (continued)

  QVector<QString> strvector;
  strvector.append("short string");
  if (strvector[0] == "short string")
    strvector[0] = "extra loooong and verbose string";
  qDebug() << strvector;
  return 0;
}
```

Access to a vector element is denoted in the same way as a read access to an array, which—as is familiar from C++—begins at index 0. Here we insert the first element into the vector using append() instead of allocating ten entries in the constructor, as in the previous example with vector(n). This is less efficient than using a QList, but it is still possible.

To be absolutely sure that you never access an index position in write mode by mistake, even if the element is not declared as const, you should use at() instead of the index operator.

B.3   Stacks and Queues

B.3.1   Stacks (QStack)

Stacks are data structures that work according to the so-called LIFO principle (*last in, first out*). As with a real stack, you can only remove the top element, that is, the last element placed on the stack.

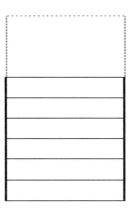

Figure B.4:
QStack *looks like a vector turned on its side by 90 degrees, and the class actually does inherit from* QVector.

Placing a value on a QStack is done by the push() method, which expects an instance of the type used as the QStack type parameter. Conversely, pop() takes the top element from the stack and returns it. The following program outputs the digits entered in reverse:

```
// stackdemo/main.cpp

#include <QStack>
#include <QDebug>

int main()
{
  QStack<int> stack;
  stack.push(1);
  stack.push(2);
  stack.push(3);
  while (!stack.isEmpty())
    qDebug() << stack.pop(); // output: 3, 2, 1
  return 0;
}
```

top() returns a reference to the top element without taking it from the stack. This could be used, as described in Section B.2.3, to look deeper into the stack, since it is actually only a vector (Figure B.4). This would violate the semantics of the stack data structure, however. For this reason it is recommended that you use the methods provided directly by QStack.

As a Java-style iterator, QVectorIterator is used; it functions with the semantics of the QVector base class.

B.3.2 Queues (QQueue)

In many applications you will not be able to avoid having to use a queue. The possibilities are wide ranging—queues are used to implement buffers,[5] as temporary memory for tree-based algorithms such as breadth-first search, and much more.

Qt provides the QQueue class for queues. This is merely a specialization of the QList. It is easy to see the thinking behind this design decision, because a QList performs well when inserting and deleting at the beginning and end of the list.

To get a value into the front of the queue, the enqueue() method is used. As a parameter it expects a value of the type that was used as the type parameter in the declaration of the queue. dequeue() removes the last element from the queue and returns it.

As a Java-style iterator, the iterator of the base class is used (in the same way as QStack), that is, QListIterator.

B.4 Associative Arrays

At first glance, the container classes QMap and QHash seem to serve the same purpose: They save a list of key-value pairs in which access to the resulting collection of values is usually performed by specifying not an index, but a key. Nevertheless, there are differences between the two classes, both in their implementation and in their performance in specific circumstances.

B.4.1 Dictionaries (QMap)

QMap provides a dictionary and is the slower of the two data structures, but it also sorts the key-value pairs automatically. This is of particular relevance to the programmer if he wants to iterate over the data structure: When using QMap iterators, the output is already sorted by key.

The following example shows how a QMap that associates a string to an integer value is created:

---

[5] Not to be confused with QBuffer, which represents an input/output device; see Chapter 11.

```
// mapdemo/main.cpp

#include <QMap>
#include <QMapIterator>
#include <QDebug>

int main()
{
  QMap<QString, int> map;

  map["one"] = 1; // insert using the [] operator
  map["two"] = 2;
  map.insert("seven", 7); // insert using insert()

  qDebug() << map["seven"]; // read using the [] operator
  qDebug() << map.value("seven"); // read using value()

  QMapIterator<QString, int> i(map);
  while (i.hasNext()) {
    i.next();
    qDebug() << i.key() << ":" << i.value();
  }
  return 0;
}
```

With the help of the index operator or by using insert(), we fill up the dictionary map with values. The argument in brackets or the first argument to insert() is the key, for which, in this case, we use values of the QString type. It is worth your while to use insert() rather than the index operator, by the way: The latter is often significantly slower when inserting entries.

Caution must be used when accessing the QMap, however. The value() method and the index operator behave in the same way only with objects declared as const. Otherwise, the index operator has a sometimes nasty side effect: If the key being sought is missing, it creates a new empty entry. As a result, an instance of QMap can become hugely inflated, particularly after many ad hoc queries have been made against it, in which thousands of unsuccessful accesses take place. Accessing the QMap by means of value() protects it from this side effect.

At the end of the example a QMapIterator goes through the list entry by entry. In contrast to the iterators introduced until now, this one has the methods key() and value() to do justice to the nature of the data structure.

Data types that you define must fulfill special conditions in order to be used as keys in dictionaries. A data type whose values will appear as keys in a QMap must implement the less-than operator (operator<()) to allow the members of the QMap to be sorted. We carry this out in the next example using a dataset class that provides a record with fields for an employee's first and last name:

```
// customvaluedemo/datensatz.h

#ifndef DATENSATZ_H
#define DATENSATZ_H

#include <QString>
#include <QHash>

class Record {
  public:
    Record(const QString &surname, const QString &forename)
    {
      m_forename = forename;
      m_surname = surname;
    }

    QString forename() const { return m_forename; }
    QString surname() const { return m_surname; }

  private:
    QString m_forename;
    QString m_surname;
};
```

Now we implement the required less-than operator:

```
// customvaluedemo/datensatz.h (continued)

inline bool operator<(const Record &e1, const Record &e2)
{
  if ( e1.surname() != e2.surname() )
    return e1.surname() < e2.surname();
  return e1.forename() < e2.forename();
}
```

The following program saves some datasets in a QMap, together with an ID that displays the personnel number:

```
// customvaluedemo/main.cpp

#include "datensatz.h"
#include <QHash>
#include <QMap>
#include <QSet>
#include <QDebug>

int main()
{
  Record d1("Molkentin", "Daniel");
  Record d2("Molkentin", "Moritz");
```

```
Record d3("Molkentin", "Philipp");

QMap<int, Record> map;
map.insert(0, d1);
map.insert(1, d2);
map.insert(2, d3);

QMapIterator<int, Record> mi(map);
while ( mi.hasNext() ) {
  mi.next();
  qDebug() << mi.key() << ":"
          << mi.value().surname() << mi.value().forename();
}
```

We require the QHash header file for the extensions on page 410, where we will make our class compatible with hashes.

Requirements of Key Elements

As we have just seen, because a QMap keeps its entries sorted according to key value, the class that is used as the key type must have a less-than operator (here, <), so that the container can set up an ordering of its elements. If you try to define a QMap using a class without such an operator for the key type parameter, the compiler complains that the less-than operator is not defined.

B.4.2   Allowing Several Identical Keys (QMultiMap)

QMap has a further limitation that may be a disadvantage in some situations: It does not allow distinct entries in a container to have keys with the same value. (Thus, the sequence of key values in the sorted container is strictly monotone.) If a second call to insert() is made using an already existing key value, the data value currently associated with the key value is overwritten with the new data value.

But what happens in the following scenario? A sawmill receives daily deliveries of different tree trunks. A worker is tasked to record the number of trunks and the type of wood. However, it is important for the operator to save individual deliveries as separate datasets for later statistical evaluation. A QMap is inadequate here, because it could only represent the most recent deliveries of each type of wood.[6]

Trolltech provides the QMultiMap class for this. This varies considerably from QMap in a number of respects. A QMultiMap can contain several datasets all having the same key value. Also, QMultiMap dispenses with the index operator for technical

---

[6]   Admittedly, in reality such a problem would probably be solved with an SQL database. If you are interested in database access, we refer you to Chapter 9, where the subject of SQL databases is treated in more detail.

reasons. Also, value() and replace() operate on the element that was last inserted into the QMultiMap instance.

To read out all datasets covered by a specific key, values() is the method of choice. When given a specific key value as a parameter, it returns a QList of all values associated with that key.

The following code implements the sawmill example with the help of a QMultiMap. Each insert() instruction inserts a new element without overwriting a possibly existing key. The integer list beech, which is created using values(), contains all the incoming beech trunks starting with the value last inserted:

```
// multimapdemo/main.cpp

#include <QMap>
#include <QDebug>

int main()
{
  QMultiMap<QString, int> trunks;
  trunks.insert("Beech", 100);
  trunks.insert("Umbrella pine", 50);
  trunks.insert("Maple", 50);
  trunks.insert("Beech", 20);
  trunks.insert("Fir", 70);
  trunks.insert("Beech", 40);

  QList<int> beeches = trunk.values("Beech");
  qDebug() << beeches; // output: 40, 20, 100
  return 0;
}
```

QMultiMap also provides the addition operators + and +=, which can be used to combine several associative tables into one single one. For our example this means that we can very simply summarize the incoming goods from several different mills by summing the corresponding QMultiMaps. In this case it may also be worthwhile to make a type definition for the specialization of QMultiMap that is in use:

```
typedef QMultiMap<QString, int> TrunkCountMultiMap;
...
TrunkCountMultiMap mill1result = mill1.incoming();
TrunkCountMultiMap mill2result = mill2.incoming();
TrunkCountMultiMap mill3result = mill3.incoming();

TrunkCountMultiMap total = mill1result+mill2result+mill3result;
```

We assume here that the already defined objects mill1, mill2, and mill3 have a incoming() method, which returns a TrunkCountMultiMap. After the code executes, the total QMultiMap contains the combined goods from all factories.

B.4.3 Hash Tables with QHash

The data structure QHash is very similar to the QMap in how it functions. However, whereas a QMap sorts its entries by key value, QHash uses a hash table internally to store its entries. This means that a QHash is unsorted. Compensating for this, it is slightly faster than QMap when searching for entries with specified keys.

The APIs of the two data structures are almost identical, and so we can rewrite the QMap example from page 404 to use QHash instead just by making some simple substitutions in the code:

```
// hashdemo/main.cpp

#include <QHash>
#include <QHashIterator>
#include <QDebug>

int main()
{
  QHash<QString, int> hash;

  hash["one"] = 1; // insert using [] operator
  hash["two"] = 2;
  hash.insert("seven", 7); // insert using insert()

  qDebug() << hash["seven"]; // value using [] operator
  qDebug() << hash.value("seven"); // value using value()

  QHashIterator<QString, int> i(hash);
  while (i.hasNext()) {
    i.next();
    qDebug() << i.key() << ":" << i.value();
  }
  return 0;
}
```

As with QMap, the index operator in QHash is dangerous, since it inserts a new entry into the container if the key value is not found. A remedy is again provided by the value() method. This generates an empty entry if the value is missing in the hash, but it only returns it, and does not insert it into the hash.

Things become interesting when you start creating your own classes to use as keys. Such classes must implement an equality comparison operator (operator==()) as well as a helper function by the name of qHash() that implements the hash function.

Let's re-implement the example program from page 406. The index operator is quickly implemented: It compares the first and last name strings of both data sets, and returns true if they are equal; otherwise, it returns false.

Calculating a good hash value is much more difficult, because this number must distinguish the element as much as possible from other elements in a QHash instance. Too many elements with the same hash value result in performance penalties. Since the qHash() helper method is implemented for primitive data types and those specified by Qt, we can make use of the specific hash function of the QString class to calculate a hash value for first and last names (instead of doing the calculation entirely from scratch). Combining the results using an exclusive or (^) in turn generates one unique hash value for the entire record from the hash values for the two parts of the record:

```
// customvaluedemo/datensatz.h (continued)

inline bool operator==(const Record &e1, const Record &e2)
{
    return (e1.surname() == e2.surname())
        && (e1.forename() == e2.forename());
}

inline uint qHash(const Record& key)
{
    return qHash(key.surname()) ^ qHash(key.forename());
}

#endif // DATASET_H
```

Now we can use our data structure with QHash in exactly the same way as we did with QMap. For demonstration purposes, the example here also displays the hash value for each entry in the hash:

```
// customvaluedemo/main.cpp (continued)

  QHash<int, Record> hash;
  hash.insert(0, d1);
  hash.insert(1, d2);
  hash.insert(2, d3);

  QHashIterator<int, Record> hi(hash);
  while ( hi.hasNext() ) {
    hi.next();
    qDebug() << hi.key() << ":"
             << hi.value().surname() << hi.value().forename();
    qDebug() << qHash(hi.value());
  }
```

Just like QMap, QHash also has a subclass that allows distinct entries with identical keys to be recorded. It is called QMultiHash, and it changes the behavior of insert() so that it no longer overwrites an already existing entry with a specified key, and it also reimplements replace() so that it replaces the most recently inserted entry if several entries in the hash table have the same key.

Like QMultiMap, QMultiHash also allows you to combine several QMultiHashes into one hash with the + operator.

B.4.4   Hash-based Amounts with QSet

If what you need is not an associative array, but just a simple list that does not have to be sorted and is very fast to search, then QSet may be the best choice.

QSet is implemented internally as a QHash, but it provides many of the semantics of QString, such as cycling through all elements with foreach().

We can illustrate this using our dataset example, in which we first insert some previously generated entries into a customized QSet. To do this we use the << operator. We cycle through the list itself with foreach():

```
// customvaluedemo/main.cpp (continued)

  QSet<Record> set;
  set << d1 << d2 << d3;

  foreach(Record d, set)
    qDebug() << d.surname() << ":" << d.forename();

  return 0;
}
```

In addition, QSet provides all the basic operations for sets known from mathematics, such as set union and set difference. The following example first creates two sets and then forms the set difference of one of the two sets in terms of the other one. The subtract() method responsible for this operates directly on the set object that receives the call, which in this case is set1. It removes from this set all the elements that also exist in the set passed to it as an argument, here set2:

```
// setdemo/main.cpp

#include <QSet>
#include <QDebug>

int main()
{
  QSet<int> set1;
  set1 << 1 << 2 << 3 << 4 << 5 << 6;
  QSet<int> set2;
  set2 << 4 << 5 << 6 << 7 << 8 << 9;
  set1.subtract(set2);
  // output: 1, 2, 3
  qDebug() << "set1 remainders:" << set1;
```

```
    return 0;
}
```

In the same way there are the methods unite(), for the union, and intersect(), for making intersections. These also change the QSet instance with which they are called.

B.5   Algorithms

B.5.1   The foreach Keyword

As an alternative to const iterators, there is the foreach() macro:

```
// stringlistdemo/main.cpp

#include <QStringList>
#include <QDebug>

int main()
{
  QStringList names;
  names << "Patricia" << "Markus" << "Uli";
  foreach(QString name, names)
    qDebug() << name;
  return 0;
}
```

Those who do not like to taint the C++ namespace (C++ inventor Stroustrup is working on a native foreach keyword in the coming language versions) can instead use the synonym Q_FOREACH(). The macro is slightly slower than a const iterator, but this is only noticeable with very large data structures.

In addition Q_FOREACH supports all the validation characteristics for variable declarations that for() also has. This means that a variable declared in the loop header is no longer valid outside the loop for ISO-compatible compilers.

It is important to bear in mind that foreach() creates a copy of the data structure. In the loop shown here, any modification of the list therefore has no effect on the original list. If you are worried that Qt makes a complete copy of the list, you needn't be: Even with lists, Qt makes use of implicit sharing (see page 40).

The fact that foreach() creates copies of the data structure has even more positive aspects:

```
foreach(QString results, results())
  ...
```

If results() contains an operation with cost k before returning the data structure and the function returns a container with i entries, a total cost would arise, with a normal for loop of $k * i$. The copy ensures that there is a caching effect, which brings down the cost for k to a expenditure of $k + i$ with costs of $O(1)$ for k, because results() is only called once.

B.5.2 Sorting

Tulip also contains functions for sorting data inside containers. The most frequently used of these is called qSort() and expects a container as an argument, which it sorts with the heap sort algorithm.

```
// listdemo/main.cpp

#include <QList>
#include <QDebug>

int main()
{
  QList<int> values;
  values << 1 << 10 << 5 << 6 << 7 << 3;
  qSort(values);
  qDebug() << values; // output: ( 1, 3, 5, 6, 7, 10 )
  return 0;
}
```

This is also very efficient with large amounts of data, as it works in linear-logarithmic time $(O(n \log n))$.

During the steps of the sorting process, the qSort() function makes use of the C++ comparison operator operator<() to determine whether two elements should be swapped. If two objects are equal for the purpose of comparison, it is left up to the implementation of qSort() whether they are swapped or not. If operator<() does not compare all object properties, the result may vary subtly.

For this reason there is an additional function qStableSort(), which is also implemented by means of the heap sort algorithm. In contrast to qSort(), however, it ensures that elements that are "equal" to one another always remain in their original sequence in the final, sorted list.

Both functions also have an overloaded variation: Instead of a complete container, they alternatively expect two iterators, the first of which points to the first element to be sorted and the second to the element *after* the last object to be sorted. This variant can accept a function pointer that references a function implementing a comparison operation other than operator<() to be used during the sort. This comparison function must accept and compare two parameters of the same type:

```
// sortdemo/main.cpp
```

```
#include <QStringList>
#include <QDebug>

bool caseInsensitiveLessThan(const QString &s1, const QString &s2)
{
  return s1.toLower() < s2.toLower();
}

int main()
{
  QStringList list;
  list << "AlPha" << "beTA" << "gamma" << "DELTA";
  qSort(list.begin(), list.end(), caseInsensitiveLessThan);
  qDebug() << list; // ( "AlPha", "beTA", "DELTA", "gamma" )
  return 0;
}
```

B.5.3 Sorting in Unsorted Containers

To find a value in a container, Tulip has the function qFind(). This finds the value specified as the third argument, starting from the element to which the iterator named as the first argument points. The last element of the search area is the element *in front of* (that is, before) the object to which the iterator passed as the second argument points. The function returns an iterator pointing to the first matching object if the search value is found, otherwise it returns the iterator value end().

The following example searches in a list of fruit names first for the word *Pear* and then for *Orange*:

```
// finddemo/main.cpp

#include <QStringList>
#include <QDebug>

int main()
{
  QStringList list;
  list << "apple" << "pear" << "banana";

  QStringList::iterator i1 = qFind(list.begin(), list.end(), "pear");
  // i1 == list.begin() + 1

  QStringList::iterator i2 = qFind(list.begin(), list.end(), "orange");
  // i2 == list.end()

  return 0;
}
```

After this code has run, the iterator i1 remains on the second element, whereas i2 points to end(), which according to STL iterator logic is the (undefined) element after banana.

B.5.4 Copying Container Areas

The qCopy() function allows several elements to be copied from one container to another. Here the function expects two iterators, specifying the first element to be copied and the object after the last element to be copied. The third parameter names the position at which the first copied element should appear in the target container:

```
// qcopydemo/main.cpp

#include <QStringList>
#include <QVector>
#include <QDebug>

int main()
{
  QStringList list;
  list << "one" << "two" << "three";

  QVector<QString> vect(list.size());
  qCopy(list.begin(), list.end(), vect.begin());
  qDebug() << vect; // output: ( "one", "two", "three" )
  return 0;
}
```

qCopyBackward() is almost identical to qCopy(), but expects the position of the *last* element to be copied as the third parameter, rather than the first. It inserts the values to be copied from the specified elements of the second container from back to front, so that when read forward they retain their correct order:

```
// backwardcopy/main.cpp

#include <QStringList>
#include <QVector>
#include <QDebug>

int main()
{
  QStringList list;
  list << "one" << "two" << "three";

  QVector<QString> vect(5);
  qCopyBackward(list.begin(), list.end(), vect.end());
  qDebug() << vect; // output: ( "", "", "one", "two", "three" )
```

```
      return 0;
}
```

The example shows that the target container must already have sufficient space before the specified insertion point to hold all of the elements that are copied from the source container. Here, this is ensured for the target QVector by passing the constructor the list size 5 before the call to qCopyBackward() that copies the three elements in the QStringList. This is required because the Tulip algorithms commonly do not allocate extra items.

B.5.5 Binary Search in Sorted Containers

If a list is sorted, the cost of searching it can be reduced from linear ($O(n)$) to logarithmic ($O(\log n)$) time with the help of the binary search algorithm. qBinaryFind() implements binary search in Qt. The function expects the list to be sorted in ascending order, and it takes as parameters two STL iterators, which must point to the positions at the beginning and just after the end of the area to be searched. A third parameter is the value to be searched for. (To sort a list in ascending order, qSort() is ideal; see page 413.)

The following example looks through a list of numbers for the number 6, and the iterator returned as the result of the call to qBinaryFind() points to the third element:

```
// binaryfinddemo/main.cpp

#include <QList>
#include <QDebug>

int main() {
  QList<int> numbers;
  numbers << 1 << 5 << 6 << 7 << 9 << 11;
  QList<int>::iterator it;
  it = qBinaryFind(numbers.begin(), numbers.end(), 6);
  // it == numbers.begin() + 2
  qDebug() << *it; // 6
```

As soon as several values occur that are recognized as equal by the operator<() used, problems arise, however, since it is not defined as to which of the (same) values the returned iterator points:

```
// binaryfinddemo/main.cpp (continued)

  numbers.clear();
  numbers << 1 << 6 << 6 << 6 << 9 << 11;
  it = qBinaryFind(numbers.begin(), numbers.end(), 6);
```

```
  // it == numbers.begin() + 1 or
  // it == numbers.begin() + 2 or
  // it == numbers.begin() + 3
  qDebug() << *it;

  return 0;
}
```

This does not matter if any element matching the search value will suffice, but it becomes crucial to have a well-defined result if the location of the element found will be used to determine the insert position for a new element. For such cases there are the methods qLowerBound() and qUpperBound(). They both expect the same parameters as qBinaryFind() and also perform a binary search. But after this they behave differently.

qLowerBound() returns an iterator pointing to the first occurrence of the search element. If the element sought does not exist in the container, the iterator remains *after* the insert position deemed to be suitable. In either case, a subsequent insert() inserts the value into the correct position, as the following examples show:

```
// upperlowerbound/main.cpp

#include <QDebug>
#include <QList>
#include <QVector>

int main()
{
  QList<int> list;
  list << 3 << 3 << 6 << 6 << 6 << 8;

  QList<int>::iterator it;
  it = qLowerBound(list.begin(), list.end(), 5);
  list.insert(it, 5);
  qDebug() << list; // output: ( 3, 3, 5, 6, 6, 6, 8 )

  it = qLowerBound(list.begin(), list.end(), 12);
  list.insert(it, 12);
  qDebug() << list; // output: ( 3, 3, 5, 6, 6, 6, 8, 12 )

  it = qLowerBound(list.begin(), list.end(), 12);
  list.insert(it, 12);
  qDebug() << list; // output: ( 3, 3, 5, 6, 6, 6, 8, 12, 12 )
```

In contrast to qLowerBound(), qUpperBound() places the iterator *after* the value found. Otherwise it shares all the properties of qLowerBound(). If the search value was not found, the iterator that was passed as first argument is returned.

qUpperBound() and qLowerBound() can thus be used to bracket elements of the same value from both sides, as shown in the following example, which copies a run of equal values into a new container:

```
// upperlowerbound/main.cpp (continued)

  QVector<int> vect;
  vect << 3 << 3 << 6 << 6 << 6 << 8;
  QVector<int>::iterator begin6 =
        qLowerBound(vect.begin(), vect.end(), 6);
  QVector<int>::iterator end6 =
        qUpperBound(vect.begin(), vect.end(), 6);
  QVector<int> vect2(end6-begin6);
  qCopy(begin6, end6, vect2.begin());
  qDebug() << vect2; // output: ( 6, 6, 6 )
```

By subtracting the two iterators from each other we obtain the number of equal elements. We require this to create a vector with a sufficient number of empty elements, because qCopy() does not insert any new elements into the data structure.

B.5.6 Counting the Number of Occurences of Equal Elements

The qCount() method counts how often an object or value occurs within a container. As the first parameter it expects an iterator pointing to the first element to be tested, followed by an iterator pointing to the element after the last element to be tested and an iterator pointing to the object to be counted. This must be of the same type as the type stored in the container. As the last argument, qCount() expects an integer variable in which it saves the number of occurrences. The following example illustrates how qCount() works, using a list of integer values:

```
// upperlowerbound/main.cpp (continued)

  qCount(vect.begin(), vect.end(), 6, count6);
  qDebug() << count6; // output: 3
  return 0;
}
```

B.5.7 Deleting Pointers in Lists

For Qt containers, such as a QList, that are filled with pointers to objects, a simple list.clear() is not sufficient, since this only removes the pointers from the list and does not delete the list or free the objects that are referenced by the pointers.

For this purpose, the qDeleteAll() method is used, which exists in two variations. One expects a container filled with pointers and deletes all the objects that are pointed at by the container's elements. The other expects two iterators and deletes the objects pointed at by the container elements between the two iterators.

The following code example removes from memory all the objects pointed at by the elements in a list of pointers, and then empties the list itself:

```
...
QList<Fruits *> list;
list.append(new Fruits("pear"));
list.append(new Fruits("apple"));
list.append(new Fruits("orange"));

qDeleteAll(list);
list.clear();
...
```

B.5.8 Checking that Data Structures Have Identical Elements

Sometimes it is necessary to compare two lists that, although they are two different data structures, maintain contents of the same type. One example of this is provided by the data structures QStringList and QVector<QString>. The string list corresponds to QList<QString>, so that here, values of the same data type (namely, QString) lie in two different containers.

The qEqual() function is in a position to compare portions of two such structures with one another. In order to do this, it expects three parameters: two STL iterators, one of which marks the beginning of the area in the first data structure containing the elements to be compared, and the other, which marks the end of this area. The third parameter is an iterator on the second data structure and points to the element from which the comparison (which comes to a stop at the end of the container) should start.

The following program accordingly creates two containers and compares all the elements for equality:

```
// qequaldemo/main.cpp

#include <QStringList>
#include <QVector>
#include <QDebug>

int main()
{
  QStringList list;
  list << "one" << "two" << "three";

  QVector<QString> vect(3);
  vect[0] = "one";
  vect[1] = "two";
  vect[2] = "three";

  bool ret = qEqual(list.begin(), list.end(), vect.begin());
  qDebug() << ret; // output: true
```

```
    return 0;
}
```

If we now change one of the elements in one of the data structures (such as in the vector, as follows):

```
vect[2] = "ten";
```

then qEqual() will detect inequalities.

B.5.9   Filling Data Structures

Sometimes it is necessary to fill certain parts of a list with a value. In Qt this is done by the qFill() function, which expects two iterators as parameters: the first one specifies the beginning of the area to be overwritten, and the second specifies the end of the area. The third parameter specifies the value to be filled in.

If we want to overwrite the complete list, we use the begin() and end() iterators of the list:

```
// fillzero/main.cpp

#include <QList>
#include <QDebug>

int main()
{
  QList<int> values;
  values << 1 << 4 << 7 << 9;
  // content of values: 1, 4, 7, 9
  qFill(values.begin(), values.end(), 0);
  qDebug() << values; // output: ( 0, 0, 0, 0 )
  return 0;
}
```

If we use a QVector instead of a QList, we can also use the QVector method fill() instead of qFill(). Usually, QVector is the better choice when filling parts of a container with a specified value is necessary.

B.5.10   Swapping Values

The qSwap() function exchanges the values of any two data containers of the same type, including ordinary variables:

```
int a,b;
a = 1; b = 2;
```

```
qSwap(a,b);
qDebug() << "a=" << a << "b=" << b; // output: a=2 b=1
```

B.5.11   Minimum, Maximum, and Threshold Values

To determine the larger of two elements in terms of value, Qt provides the template functions qMin() and qMax(). Each takes two arguments, both of which must be of the same type. If this type is not a POD[7] but a value-based class, the class must implement the operator < in a valid fashion:

```
// qmindemo/main.cpp

#include <QList>
#include <QDebug>

int main()
{
  // compare instances of a POD and look for minimum
  int max = qMax(100, 200); // max == 200

  // compare instances of a class (QString): looks for
  // the lexicographic minimum
  QString s1 = "Daniel";
  QString s2 = "Patricia";
  QString min = qMin(s1, s2);
  qDebug() << min; // output: "Daniel"
}
```

If it is essential for a value to lie within a specific range, qBound() can be used. This template function takes three arguments: a lower bound, a test value, and an upper bound. It returns the upper or lower limit value if the test value is larger than the upper bound or smaller than the lower bound, respectively. Otherwise, the test value is returned.

The following method for a hypothetical radio tuner class ensures that the user cannot select any frequencies outside the UKW frequencies valid for Europe:

```
int Tuner::createValidFreq(qreal freq)
{
  return qBound(87.5, freq, 108.0);
}
```

Neither qBound() nor qMax() and qMin() change the input data. They return a const reference to the value determined by the function in each case.

---

[7]   *Plain Old Datatype*, that is, all data types defined by the language such as int or bool.

B.5.12 Determining Absolute Value

The C library enables the absolute value of an integer value to be calculated via the abs() function. In the same way that the fabs() function calculates the absolute value for floating-point numbers, Qt defines the qAbs() method, which can calculate the absolute value for all PODs. This works with all classes that implement the unary minus and the comparison operator >= and allows comparison to an integer 0 as the neutral element. The method itself does not allow the programmer to specify a neutral element.

The following code example, which could appear in a window manager class, ensures that the top right point of a window cannot lie above the point $(0, 0)$, that is, the top right corner, and assumes that positive values were actually intended:

```
void WindowManager::placeWindow(WId win, const QPoint& topRight)
{
...
QPoint actualPosition = qAbs(topRight);

...
}
```

B.6   Qt-specific Type Definitions

To ensure that Qt has the same properties on all supported platforms, the library uses its own definitions for most PODs. More detailed information on the requirements for platform-independent data types is provided in a book by Brian Hook.[8] Trolltech defines all these types with the typedef command, so it uses no macros. This has the advantages that the compiler can work with such definitions better and that error messages refer to the Qt types, simplifying error searches.

B.6.1   Integer types

Signed types

- qint8 variables are 8 bits wide (value range: -128 to $+127$).

- qint16 values occupy 16 bits (value range: $-32\,768$ to $+32\,767$).

- qint32 integers use 32 bits (value range: $-2\,147\,483\,648$ to $+2\,147\,483\,647$).

[8]   *Write Portable Code* by Brian Hook (No Starch Press, 2005).

- qint64 values are 64-bit values (value range: -2^{32} to $+2^{32} - 1$). To generate such large values as literals, the Q_INT64_C() macro exists, since a number of compilers do not support 64-bit literals directly:

```
qint64 value = Q_INT64_C(932838457459459);
```

qlonglong is a synonym for qint64.

Unsigned types

- quint8 values are 8 bits in size (value range: 0 to 255).

- quint16 values take up 16 bits (value range: 0 to 65 535).

- quint32 values are 32 bits wide (value range: 0 to 4 294 967 296).

- quint64 integers take up 64 bits (value range: 0 to $+2^{64} - 1$). To generate 64-bit literals, you should use the Q_UINT64_C() macro, because a number of compilers do not support such large integer literals directly:

```
quint64 value = Q_UINT64_C(932838457459459);
```

Similar to qlonglong, qulonglong is a synonym for quint64.

B.6.2   Floating-point Values

With qreal, Qt defines a floating-point number of double precision. This corresponds to the C++ type double.

B.6.3   Shortcuts for Common Types

The following definitions do not improve platform independence, but merely spare the work of having to enter unsigned, for those who do not use the POD type definitions employed by Qt:

- uchar corresponds to unsigned char.

- uint corresponds to unsigned int.

- ulong corresponds to unsigned long.

- ushort corresponds to unsigned short.

Index

Symbols

-= (operator) 28
= (operator) 28
    defining 324
&
    in labeling 90
...
    in menu entries 108
[] *see* index operator
>> (operator)
    defining 325
<< *see* serialization operators
< (operator) 407
16-bit integer
    signed *see* qint16
    unsigned *see* quint16
32-bit integer
    signed *see* qint32
    unsigned *see* quint32
64-bit integer
    signed *see* qint64
    unsigned *see* quint64
8-bit integer
    signed *see* qint8
    unsigned *see* quint8

A

about box 117, 173
    modal 118
abs() 422
absolute value
    determining 422
abstract classes 211
accelerator 107
    vs. shortcut 109

accept() (slot) 71, 162
access control
    for objects 63
accessibility 209
AccessibleDescriptionRole
    in Interview 209
AccessibleTextRole
    in Interview 209
action *see* QAction
Action Editor
    of the Designer 108
Active-X components 47
ActiveQt 47
addition operator
    QMultiHash 411
    QMultiMap 408
addStretch() 148
addWidget() 30, 32, 34, 144, 145
    in QGridLayout 148
    with splitters 150
    with stacked layouts 157
algorithms 412–422
    binary search 416–418
    copy 415–416
    heap sort 413
    search 414–418
    sort *see* sorting
aligning
    DisplayRole data 209
    on a grid *see* QGridLayout
    horizontally *see* QHBoxLayout,
    145
    text 105
    vertically *see* QVBoxLayout
    widgets in QSplitter 150

alpha blending 311
alpha channel 274, 297
alpha transparency 312
alternating background color
    in tables 233
Amarok 264
ampersand *see* &
animation
    in SVG 302
anti-aliasing 277
apparent crashes 186
append() 394
application
    calling 29
    determining name of 169
    generating with qmake 28
    without GUI 44
    quitting 36
Aqua style 88
Arabic characters 40
ARGB32 297, 310
arranging
    on a grid *see* QGridLayout
    horizontally *see* QHBoxLayout
    vertically *see* QVBoxLayout
    widgets 29
artifacts
    due to opaque resizing 151
ASCII 114
assert() *see* assertions
assertions 390–391
assignment operator
    defining 324
Assistant 47–48
    start page 59

use as documentation browser 43, 46
asynchronous device 328, 330
at() 229
attaching
   elements to a list 400
attributes
   of an XML element 369, 371
autoDefault (property) 87

B
background color
   alternating (in tables) 233
   in views 209
backslashes
   in regular expressions 70
backward compatibility
   with Qt3 see Qt3Support
base class 56
   details in class documentation 60
Bezier curve 309
Bidi 156–157
bidirectional languages see Bidi
binary number
   converting to string 72
binary search
   in sorted containers 416–418
blind persons
   alternative description for 209
blocking calls
   with waitForDisconnected() 341
   with waitForReadyRead() 329, 341
breadth-first search 404
Buddy 90
buffer 318, 323, 404
button
   honoring style guide for 83
   push see QPushButton
   radio see QRadioButton
   tool see tool button
ByteArray see QByteArray

C
callback functions 35

Cancel button 162
canceling
   program in case of error see qFatal()
casting
   of objects see qobject_cast
   primitive data types 325
   for QKeyEvent 193
   for QTimerEvent 189
CDATA see QDomCDATASection
centering text 202
central widget 92, 101, 363
cerr 386, 387
changing size
   opaque 151
channel
   with RSS 356
characters
   counting 123
   replacing 123
checkbox 234–237
   in front of actions see QAction, selectable
checking inputs see validator
CheckStateRole 234
   in Interview 209
child objects
   and automatic memory management 31
Chinese characters 40
circle, drawing 278
class
   documentation 59
   name 92
clear mode 314
clicked() (signal) 36
clip region 308
clipboard 201–205
clipping 280, 307–308, 315
closing windows automatically 62
CMYK 274
Code::Blocks 52
collapsible widgets 150
color see QColor
   available options 272
   for DisplayRole data 209
   predefined see GlobalColor

(enumerator)
   selection dialog see QColorDialog
   transparent 272
color gradient
   linear 288, 310
   radial 287
color palette 298
   defining your own 276
color spaces
   CMYK see CMYK
   HSV see HSV
   RGB see RGB
coloring in QPixmap 277
column numbers
   in the QGridLayout 34
combo box 214
   editable 247
command-line program
   with Qt 44
   running 328
comment lines
   removing in a file 320
comments
   reading out from XML documents see QDomComment
comparing
   list contents 419
   objects 290
   QStringList with QVector<QString> 419
comparison operator 409
compatibility
   with Qt3 see Qt3Support
compiler
   affecting length of compiling 44
compiling
   Qt 23, 259
   a Qt program 27–29
   a Visual Studio project 29
compositing
   Porter-Duff 310–315
composition operators 310
.config 136
CONFIG (qmake variable) 386
configuration dialog 161

implementation in KDE 157
  with QStackedLayout 34
configure 23
connection
  closing 336
  delayed see queued connections
connectSlotsByName() 97
const
  as argument type 71
  correctness 400
  declaration of get methods 325
  and inheritance 227
  iterator 396, 412
const char * 387
  as reason for crashing 388
const_cast 247
consumer-producer pattern 342–
  345
container see Tulip
content handler
  registering with QXmlSimpleReader 365
  for SAX see QXmlCon-
  tentHandler
contents
  reading out of a vector 401
context
  in translations 51, 377, 380
control see widget
  element see widget
conversion
  QPixmaps in QImages 297
converting
  to local 8-bit encoding see
  toLocal8Bit()
  to Unicode see fromLocal8Bit()
coordinate system
  of the grid layout 34
  scaling 292
  transforming see QMatrix
coordinates
  storing see QPoint
copying container areas 415–416
counting identical elements 418
Courier 106
cout 386

crash
  apparent 186
  due to const char * 388
  during Interview programming
  225
  due to invalid indices 225
  only in the release version 392
  when using Designer-generated
  classes 93
critical errors
  defining see qCritical()
critical messages see error, dialog
_CRT_ERROR
  generating 388
cursor (database) 395
custom widget 99
Cyrillic characters 40

D

data structures
  filling 420
  thread-dependent 345–347
database see QtSql module
  drivers 258
  support 42, 43, 45
  temporary 265
dataChanged() (signal) 229, 237
datastream see QDataStream
date details see QDate
DB2 database driver 258
DBus 43, 47
deadlock 344
debug libraries
  generating in Windows 28
  installing in Unix 28
debug version
  for an application 64
  generating 28
debugging 385–392
  your own model 227
debugging functions
  changing output of see message handler
  Qt-dependent 386
DecorationRole
  in Interview 209
default button 68, 87

setting 69
default size
  defining see sizeHint()
delegate 210, 228, 245–247
  for database queries 267
  QItem 234
DELETE statement (SQL) 262
deleting QObject-based objects 336
demarshalling 322
demo programs
  included 58
deserializing 322
Designer 48–49, 81–100
  Action Editor 108
  deleting widgets 82
  enabling dock window mode
  81
  file format 49
  Property Editor 56, 109
  Resource Editor 58, 99
  working with view classes 214–
  216
Designer-generated file see ui files
destination mode 311
DestinationAtop mode 313
DestinationIn mode 312
DestinationOut mode 312, 314
DestinationOver mode 311
device
  asynchronous 328, 330
dialog see QDialog
  closing 71
  color selection see QColorDialog
  creating with Designer 82
  for critical messages see error,
  dialog
  editor see Designer
  file selection see QFileDialog
  hiding see hide()
  for information see QMessage-
  Box
  as main window 62
  for messages see QMessage-
  Box
  modal 161–162
  non-modal 163–164, 176

print see QPrintDialog
for questions see question dialog
ready-made 166–184
semi-modal 164
vs. status bar 124
for uncritical messages see information dialog
for warnings see warning dialog
your own file selection 214–221
dictionary see QMap
dimensions
setting see setGeometry()
storing see QSize
direct connections 347
Direct Object Model see DOM
directory
default icon 330
listing contents 332
operations see QDir
selecting 178
directory hierarchy
presenting 212–214
DisplayRole
font type 209
in Interview 209, 224
text alignment 209
text color 209
division
by zero 388
DLLs
of the Qt debug libraries 28
DNS name resolution see QHostInfo
dock window 101, 130–136
dock window mode
enabling in Designer 81
Document Object Model see DOM
document type
determining from XML files 369
documentation 47
browser see Assistant
start page 59
on the Web 59

DOM 43, 45, 353, 366–373
element see QDomElement
nodes see QDomNode
SVG manipulation 46, 301
dotted lines 295
double 423
double buffering 282
switch off 283
drag and drop 194–201, 323
bug in Qt 4.1.2 245
of images 194
implementing in models 241–245
drawing
with Qt 271–317
re-˜ a widget 296
re-˜ the screen 280
on widgets 280–283
drawing path see Painter paths
drop actions
types 244
DTD
handling in SAX see QXmlDTDHandler
dynamic text
generating 124
dynamic_cast 248

E
ECMA script
in SVG 301
editor
Kate 55
widget see QTextEdit
EditRole
in Interview 209, 225
element-based views 251–255
ellipse
drawing 278, 295
filling with pattern 295
ellipsis in menu entries 108
embedded databases 264
embedded version 20
emit (signal designator) 78
empty lines
removing in a file 320
empty space

removing at the beginning and end of line 322
encapsulation 95, 96
Enter key see Return key
enum 105
enumeration types
alignment 105
CheckState 209
DockWidgetFeatures 131
EchoMode 181
format 297
orientation 224
policy 146
SocketError 340
environment
influencing ˜ of a process 328
environment variable
influencing ˜ of a process 319, 329
LANG 329
QT_FATAL_WARNINGS 388
QT_NO_DEBUG_OUTPUT 386
QT_NO_WARNING_OUTPUT 388
reading out ˜ of a process 329
error
critical see qCritical()
dialog 173
fatal see qFatal()
issuing 387–388
linker 392
in multiple inheritance 97
non-integrated layouts 67
searching for see debugging
staticMetaObject 65
unknown signals or slots 64
unresolved signals or slots 79
unresolved symbols 65, 79
vtbl-linker error message 392
error handler
registering with QXmlSimpleReader 365
for SAX see QXmlErrorHandler
error messages
issuing 174
error source
with QMap usage 405
Esc key 162

assigning 168
/etc/xdg 136
event filter 190, 247
event handler 35, 97, 186–190
    for drag and drop 202
    for dropping 199
event listener 35
event loop 26, 31, 185–186, 320
    ending 26, 36
    for non-graphic programs 44
    programming 332
    starting in dialogs 162
    for threads 350–352
events 35, 185–201
    occurring when dropping 198–
        199
    in threads 352
    triggering manually 188
example (directory) see example
    programs
example programs
    included 58
exclusive Or see XOR
exec() 26, 162
Extended Markup Language see
    XML

F
fabs() 422
factory method 153
fatal error
    defining see qFatal()
father see parent widget
FiFo container see QQueue
file
    access 320–322
    default icon 330
    dialog see QFileDialog
    format see format
    open 113, 320
    restricting selection to directo-
        ries 178
    save see saveFile()
    selecting individual 175
    selecting several 177
FILE pointer 113, 320, 322
file selection dialog see QFileDialog

your own 214–221
filename
    selecting 178
fill() 420
filling data structures see qFill()
filtering 212
    data in models 231
    of datasets 234
Firefox
    non-modal dialogs 164
flicker
    avoiding see double buffering
    screen 283
floating dock windows 133
floating number see floating-point
    types
floating-point inputs see getDou-
    ble()
floating-point types
    in Qt 423
font metrics see QFontMetrics
font selection dialog see QFontDia-
    log
font type
    changing 106, 251, 253
    for DisplayRole data 209
FontRole
    in Interview 209, 251
fopen() 113
for loop 394–396
foreach 151, 411–413
    and QDomList 370
foreign key relations
    resolving 266
forever 341
forking 337
format
    images 297
    QDataStream 323
    QImage 297
    RSS 355
    translation sources 377
format strings
    for debug functions 386
    in debug output 386
FORMS (qmake variable) 49
forward declaration 63, 122

fractions
    entering see getDouble()
frame shape 85
free text
    reading in 181
freedesktop.org 43
fromLocal8Bit() 330, 331
FTP see QFtp
    client 45

G
GCC
    undefined symbols 65
    unresolved symbols 79
    for Windows 52
get method 56
getDouble() 180
getInteger() 179
GIF support 23
GlobalColor (enumerator) 272
GNOME 83
Google Earth 19
GPL
    version for Windows 52
gradient
    linear 288, 310
    radial 287
graphics
    integrating 57
    MIME encoding 195
    scaling 100
graying
    actions 129
grid layout see QGridLayout
groups
    of actions 128
    in configuration files 138
GUI
    avoiding locking 332, 337
    design via mouse click see De-
        signer
    editor see Designer
    thread 338
GUI classes
    integrating 43
    not integrating 43

H

handle 34
handler
    classes for SAX 355–361
    for events *see* event handler
handles 125
    adjusting 153
hanging
    because images are too large 305
hash table 409–411
hash value
    calculating 410
hash-based amounts 411
hash-based sets 412
hasNext() 397
hasPrevious() 397
header columns
    for table and tree views 211, 233
header file 26, 43
    adding to projects 106
    multiply included *see* include guards
HEADERS (qmake directive) 64, 106
heap
    generating objects on 32
    with threads 337
heap sort 413
Hebrew characters 40, 156
height
    reading out ˜ of splitter widgets 151
    setting *see* setGeometry()
help
    browser *see* Assistant
    longer help text 110, 129
hexadecimal number
    checking as input value 70
    converting to string 72
hide() 304
home directory
    determining 176
horizontally
    aligning 145
    arranging *see* QHBoxLayout
host name 333

HSV 273
    color selection dialog 275
HTML 354, 367
    centering text 202
    in QMessageBoxes 171, 390
    for tables 226
    in tooltips 226
HTTP *see* QHTTP
    client 45

I

I/O 317–336
icon bar *see* toolbar
icons 125
    for input/output operations 330
    in Interview 209
    selecting for actions 127, 129
    selecting for message boxes 167
    standard 330
    in the status bar 121
identity matrix *see* unit matrix
images *see* graphics
implicit sharing 40, 412
include guards 62, 104
index operator 229, 400
    access to QLinkedList 401
    access to QVector 402
    with QHash 409
    with QMultiMap 408
    vs. value() 405, 409
individual preferences *see* user scope
infinite loop
    with forever 341
info box *see* QMessageBox
    on the program 117, 173
information dialog 171–172
inheritance
    multiple *see* multiple inheritance
    sequence 97
input
    checking 70
    dialogs *see* QInputDialog
    fields for line-by-line input *see*

QLineEdit
    restricting 70
input/output interfaces 317–336
    opening 319
input/output operations
    icons for 330
INSERT statement (SQL) 262
installation path
    defining for Qt 24
integer inputs *see* getInteger()
integer types
    in Qt 422
integer values
    accepting *see* getInteger()
    checking during input 70
    converting strings to 72, 73
inter-process communication 337
InterBase
    database driver 258
internationalization 375–381
interprocess communication 322
intersection
    forming 412
Interview 207–255
    and database access 258, 265–270
introspection 97
invisible widgets
    causes of 67
IP addresses 333
IPv6 333
isNull() 176
ISO 8859-1 114
ISO Latin 1 114
item 207, 251
    cloning 254
    sorting 255
item-based display 207
iterator 394–398
    immutable 396
    Java-style 396–398, 404
    mutable 396
    for QMap 405
    for QQueue 404
    for QStack 404
    STL-style 395–396
    unchangeable 396

J

JavaScript in SVG 301
JUnit 46

K

Kate 55
KDE
Amarok 264
implementation of configuration dialogs 157
media URL 200
non-modal dialogs 164
QMimeData with several URLs 200
Run dialog 164
style 88
KDevelop 53
key binding
application-wide 109
keyboard usage 107
Konqueror
Hebrew 156

L

label *see* QLabel
labeling text 85
landscape (print format) 306
LANG (environment variable) 329
languages oriented from right to left *see* Bidi
layout
adding widgets to *see* addWidget()
automatic *see* layout system
grid *see* QGridLayout
horizontal *see* QHBoxLayout
inserting other layouts into 149–150
manual 141–143
nested 65–68, 149–150
removing in Designer 84
stretch 67, 83
vertical *see* QVBoxLayout
layout system 29, 141–161
advantages 31
LCD display *see* QLCDNumber
lettering *see* labeling text

adjusting for labels 86
libQtCore_debug.so 28
library
generating with qmake 28
LiFo container *see* QStack
lightweight processes *see* threads
line drawing *see* QPen
line edit *see* QLineEdit
line numbers
in the QGridLayout 34
line wrap
preventing 106
removing 123
Linguist 49–51, 376–378
linker
frequent errors 392
problems with undefined ˜ symbols 104
problems with unresolved ˜ symbols 79
Linux
printing large images 305
list view 157–159, 210
without Interview *see* QListWidget
selecting column from the model 227
string-based 207, 221
lists *see* QList
changeable iterators 396
filling 420
linked *see* QLinkedList
QQueue *see* QQueue
QStringList *see* QStringList
QVector *see* QVector
swapping values 420
your own 400
locale 188
determining 378
forcing default 331
forcing standard 329
localization
of an application 49
of images 58
influence on the layout 143
of shortcuts 110, 127
loopback interface

using 336
lrelease 49, 376
ls, calling as external program 332
lupdate 49, 376, 377
recording entries outside classes 381

M

Mac OS X
.plist files 136
project files 53
Qt installation 23
special features of qmake 53
storing settings 137
macros
foreach *see* foreach
forever *see* forever
NDEBUG 390
platform-dependent 389
Q_ASSERT 390, 392
Q_ASSERT_X 391, 392
Q_CHECK_PTR 391–392
Q_FOREACH 412
Q_UNUSED 223
Q_WS_MAC 389
Q_WS_QWS 389
Q_WS_WIN 389
Q_WS_X11 389
QT_TR_NOOP 381
Magic Number 326
main widget 26
central widget 105
creating with Designer 82
separating page list from 153
size grip 118
status bar 118
main window *see* main widget
class *see* QMainWindow
MainActor 19
make 29
Makefile
generating with qmake 28
Makefile.DebugPackage 28
Makefile.ReleasePackage 28
marshalling 322
matrix
inverse 291

singular 291
maxima
    determining 290, 421
maximum size
    setting 151
memory
    allocating 391
    bottleneck 391
memory management 31–33
    automatic 31, 68
    of item classes 251
menu bar 101
    adding in Designer 107–108
    inserting actions into 127
menu entry
    clicking 112
    defining font 129
menu separator 108
message bus 43, 47
message dialog see QMessageBox
message handler 388
    installing 389
message window see QMessageBox
meta-object compiler see moc
MFC 47
Microsoft
    SQL server database driver 258
    styleguide 169
    Visual Studio see Visual Studio
    Windows see Windows (Microsoft)
MIME type
    for the clipboard 201
    for drag and drop 194–195, 242
    your own 194
MinGW 24, 52
minima
    determining 290, 421
minimum size
    defining 289
    setting 143, 145, 150
moc 56–57, 64, 79, 392
    problems 392
    and RTTI 248
moc_file 56
modal dialogs see dialog, modal

modality of a dialog 162
model 208
    for database usage 265–270
    making writable 227
model-view concept see Interview
monitor
    flicker 283
monospaced font
    setting 106
Motif 47
mouse
    events triggered by see QMouseEvent
    wheel 293, 296
mousePressEvent() 295
moving see translation
Mozilla-like splitter handle 153
multiple inheritance
    of Designer-generated interfaces 95
    restrictions 97
multiple selection of files 216
mutable iterator 396
mutex 342
MySQL 45
    database driver 258
    establishing connection 260
    making queries 261
    problems with stored procedures 263

N
name
    of a class created in Designer 92
    determining an application's 169
    resolution 333
namespace
    Qt 105
NDEBUG (macro) 390
network
    integrating ˜ support 43, 332
    programming 42, 45, 332–336
new operator 31
newsfeed 356
next() 397

nmake 29
note
    yellow see tooltip
number() 72, 73

O
object cast see qobject_cast
objectName (property) 92
objects
    counting equal 418
    generating on the stack 32, 33
    hierarchy of 31–33
    names of 85
    serializing 322–328
    tree structure of 31
ODBC database driver 258
OK button 162
Online help see documentation
opaque 273, 274
    resizing 151
OpenGL support 42, 45
OpenSUSE
    installing SQL support 259
operators
    -= 28
    = 28, 324
    << see serialization operators
    addition ˜ for associative arrays 411
    addition ˜ for dictionaries 408
    addition ˜ for QMap 408
    assignment 399
    comparison 409
    composition 310
    copy 399
    defining assignment 324
    defining serialization 325
    index 229, 405, 408, 409
    less than 405–407
    new 31
    operator==() 409
    operator>>() 325
    operator<() 405, 406, 413
    operator<<() 325
    serialization 387
Or
    exclusive see XOR

orientation enumerator 224
overwriting
    areas in data structures *see*
    qFill()

P
page bar
    separating from main widget
    153
page margins
    taking into account when print-
    ing 306
paint event 280, 283
    forcing 296
paintbrush *see* QBrush
Painter paths 280, 309–310, 314
paintEvent() 280–282
palette *see* color palette
parent widget 30
PDF
    generating 306
peekNext() 397
peekPrevious() 397
pen *see* QPen
phrasebook
    for translations 377
pie chart 283
Plastique style 88
.plist files
    generating 136
plugins
    for database driver 259
PODs in Qt 325, 422
pointer
    between two elements 396
    checking validity of 391–392
    deleting in lists 418
polygon *see* QPolygon
Porter-Duff 310
porting
    Qt 3 programs to Qt 4 46
Portland project 175
position
    defining for a widget 152
    setting for a widget *see* setGe-
    ometry()
Post-It note *see* tooltip

PostgreSQL 45
    database driver 259
    integrating drivers 260
preferences
    saving 136–140
    system-wide *see* system scope
    user-defined *see* user scope
preview
    in the Designer 88
previous() 397
print dialog *see* QPrintDialog
print interface *see* QPrinter
printf() 385, 386, 388
printing 302, 305–307
.pro file *see* project file
problems with moc 392
processes
    controlling 328–332
    starting 319, 328–332
processing logic
    separating from GUI 74–76
program crash *see* crash
program names
    defining application-wide 137
    determining 169
progress bar
    during a download 119
    in the status bar 121
project creation *see* qmake
project file
    generating with qmake 27
    integrating Designer files 49
    integrating GUI descriptions 49
    for Mac OS X 53
    for Microsoft Visual Studio 52
    specifying Qt libraries to be
    linked 43
    for Xcode 53
properties 56, 85
    in class documentation 60
    of QAction 109–110
    of QMessageBox 166
    of QSplitter 150
    of QTextEdit 106
    querying 56, 85
    setting 56, 85
    size of 143, 150

of views 216
Property Editor 56, 85, 109
proxy 333
proxy model 231, 270
    designing 237–241
public (objects) 63
push_back() 394

Q
Q_ASSERT (macro) 390, 392
Q_ASSERT_X (macro) 391, 392
Q_CHECK_PTR (macro) 391–392
Q_FOREACH (macro) 412
Q_INT64_C() (macro) 423
Q_OBJECT (macro) 63, 64, 104
Q_UNUSED (macro) 223
Q_WS_MAC (macro) 389
Q_WS_QWS (macro) 389
Q_WS_WIN (macro) 389
Q_WS_X11 (macro) 389
QAbstractButton 42, 87
QAbstractItemDelegate 245
QAbstractItemModel 211, 266
QAbstractItemView 211
QAbstractListModel 211
QAbstractProxyModel 212, 231
QAbstractScrollArea 211
QAbstractSocket 318, 333
QAbstractTableModel 211
QAction 108–110, 126–128
    choose icon 109
    grouped 128
    select icon 127, 129
    selectable 128
    shortcuts 110
    signal when clicking 112
    toggling 126, 129
QActionGroup 128
qApp 112
QApplication 26
    base class for 44
    and QDesktopWidget 304
    quit() 36
    translate() *see* translate()
QAssistantClient 46
qBound() 421
QBoxLayout 42, 145

QBrush 277
    defining color 277
    tiled pattern 295
QBuffer 318, 323, 361, 404
    setting read position to begin-
    ning 365
QButtonBox 83
QByteArray 114, 139, 318
QCheckBox
    in the Qt inheritance hierarchy
    42
QClipboard 201–205
QColor 40
    in the Qt inheritance hierarchy
    42
QColorDialog 275–276
QComboBox see combo box
qCopy() 415
qCopyBackward() 415
QCoreApplication 44, 320, 338
qCount() 418
qCritical() 386–388
QDataStream 243, 322–327
    defining version of the format
    323, 326
    reading in line by line 331
QDate 179, 189
qDebug() 152, 386–388, 390
    displaying database errors 261
qDeleteAll() 399, 418
QDesktopWidget 304
QDialog 161–184
    avoiding bloating 164
    classes inherited from ˜ as main
    window 62
    extensions 164
QDir 176
QDirModel 212–214
    overloaded index() method 213
QDomCDATASection 370
QDomComment 370
QDomDocument 366, 367, 370
QDomDocumentFragment 371
QDomDocumentType 369
QDomElement 366, 369, 370
QDomNode 367
QDomText 370

qEqual() 419
QErrorMessage 174
qFatal() 386, 388, 390
QFile 113, 318, 320–322
QFileDialog 113, 175–178
    flags 175
qFill() 420
qFind() 414
QFont 182
QFontDialog 182–183
QFontMetrics 288
QFrame 41, 42
QFtp 333
QGridLayout 33–34, 148–149, 303,
    362
    addWidget() 34
    column numbers 34
    coordinate system 34
    with Designer 84
    line numbers 34
    in the Qt inheritance hierarchy
    42
QHash 283, 409–411
qHash() 409
QHBoxLayout 33
    in Designer 84
    in the Qt inheritance hierarchy
    42
QHeaderView 211
QHostAddress 333
QHostInfo 333
QHttp 333, 350, 361, 363
QIcon 127
QImage 40, 297–300
    composition modes 310–315
    converting in QPixmap 297
QInputDialog 179–182
qInstallMsgHandler() 389
qint16 422
qint32 422
qint64 422
qint8 422
QIntValidator 70
QIODevice 317–320, 322
    network subclasses 333
    opening 319
QItemDelegate 210, 228, 234, 245

QItemSelectionModel see selection
    model
QLabel
    aligning text 105
    assigning shortcuts 90
    displaying pixmap 197, 278
    displaying strings 38
    markup 102
    properties 85
    in the Qt inheritance hierarchy
    41
    setAlignment() 105
    setNum() (slot) 38
    setPixmap() 197, 277
    setText() 38, 56, 124
    setting image 197, 278
    setting new value 38
    setting text 56, 85, 124
    text (property) 56
    text() 56
QLayout 42, 143–144
    addLayout() 67
    addStretch() 68
    in the Qt Designer 84
QLCDNumber 186
QLinearGradient 288, 310
QLineEdit
    changing input 73
    EchoMode enumerator 181
    restricting input 70
    setValidator() 70
    textChanged() (Signal) 71
    textChanged() (signal) 234
QLinkedList 398, 401
    access via index operator 401
QList 398–402
    as base class for QQueue 404
    mutable iterator 396
QListView 210
QListWidget 157, 251
QListWidgetItem 157, 330, 332
QLocale 378
qlonglong 423
qLowerBound() 417–418
QMainWindow 101–140, 362
    setCentralWidget() 105
qmake 27–29, 51–56, 392

choosing Qt libraries to be linked 43, 257
FORMS variable 49, 91
generating application with 28
generating library with 28
generating Makefile with 28
HEADERS directive 106
help when inheriting from QObject 64
including an SQL module 257
integrating Designer files 49, 91
libraries to be linked by default 43
and moc 56
QT variable 43
RESOURCES directive 57
SOURCES directive 28, 106
special features on Mac OS X 53
special features on Windows 28
TEMPLATE directive 28, 106
TRANSLATIONS directive 376
QMAKEFLAGS (environment variable) 28
QMap 404–407
QMapIterator 405
QMatrix 290–295
qMax() 290, 421
QMenu 127
QMessageBox 116, 166–173, 390
  modal 118, 168
QMimeData 194
qMin() 290, 421
QModelIndex 208, 218, 219
QMouseEvent 186
QMultiHash 411
QMultiMap 407–408
QMutableListIterator 396
QMutex 342
QMutexLocker 344
QNetworkProxy 333
QObject 39–40
  and automatic memory management 68
  connect() 36, 38

deleting ~-based objects 336
deriving from 104
inherited classes 31
inheriting from 39, 63–65
and moc 56
property() 56
setProperty() 56, 85
tr() see tr()
qobject_cast 247
QPaintDevice 276, 302
QPainter 276–278, 280, 282–290
QPainterPath see Painter paths
QPen 277
  defining color 277
  defining thickness 277
  drawing dotted line 295
QPixmap
  converting in QImage 297
  extracting from data stream 200
  filling with color 277
  making screenshots 304
  vs. QImage 297
QPoint 278
  floating-point variants see QPointF
QPointF 279
QPolygon 279, 308
  defining smallest possible rectangle 279
  floating-point variants see QPolygonF
QPolygonF 279
qPrintable() 328, 387
QPrintDialog 302, 306
QPrinter 276, 302, 305–307
QProcess 319, 328–332
  asynchronous usage 330–332
  synchronous usage 329
QProxyModel 212, 231
QPushButton 35
  clicked() signal 36
  clicking on 36
  converting to a toggle button 166
  default button 87
  in the Qt inheritance hierarchy

42
setDefault() 69
size policy 144
QQueue 342, 395, 404
QRadioButton
  in the Qt inheritance hierarchy 42
qrc file 57
qreal 423
QRect 278–279
  floating-point variants see QRectF
  moving 288
  shrinking 280
QRectF 279
QRegExpValidator 70
QRgb 272, 275
QSet 411–412
QSettings 136, 151
QSize 278
  floating-point variants see QSizeF
QSizeF 279
QSizeHint 209
QSlider 38
  set value 38
  setValue() (slot) 38
  value change see valueChanged() (Signal)
  valueChanged() see valueChanged() (Signal)
qSort() 413
QSortFilterProxyModel 231, 232
QSpinBox 38, 180
  set value 38
  setValue() (slot) 38
  value change see valueChanged() (Signal)
  valueChanged() see valueChanged() (Signal)
QSplitter see splitter
QSplitterHandle 153
QSqlDatabase 260
QSqlError 261
QSqlQuery 261
QSqlRecord 262
QSqlRelationalDelegate 245, 267

QSqlRelationalTableModel 266, 268
  problems in Qt 4.1 270
QSqlTableModel 265–266, 268
qStableSort() 413
QStack 403–404
QStackedLayout see stacked, layout
QStackedWidget see stacked, widget
QStandardItemModel 212, 247, 249–250, 356, 357, 365
QStatusBar 118
  addPermanentWidget() 121
  addWidget() 120
  clearMessage() (slot) 120
  showMessage() (slot) 120
QString 40
  arg() 123
  checking if it is empty 182
  converting 8-bit text to/from see fromLocal8Bit()
  converting to number values 72
  internal encoding 114
  outputting via cout 328
  in the Qt inheritance hierarchy 42
QStringList 395
  comparing   with   QVector<QString> 419
QStringListModel 212, 221
QStyle 330
QSvgRenderer 301
QSvgWidget 301
qSwap() 420
Qt
  contents of individual libraries 42
  German translation sources 380
  information box about 173
  installing 23
  open source edition for Windows 24
  size 42
  source code 23
QT (qmake variable) 43, 257, 301,

332, 354
Qt 4.0 42
Qt 4.1 43
Qt 4.2 43
Qt Assistant see Assistant
Qt Designer see Designer
Qt Linguist see Linguist
Qt Solutions 47
Qt-3 classes 46
Qt3Support 43, 46
QT_FATAL_WARNINGS (environment variable) 388
QT_NO_DEBUG_OUTPUT (environment variable) 386
QT_NO_WARNING_OUTPUT (environment variable) 388
QT_TR_NOOP (macro) 381
QTableView 211
QTableWidget 251, 253
QtCore 42, 44, 332
  debug variations 28
QTcpServer 333, 338
QTcpSocket 40, 318, 333, 334, 340
QtDBus 43, 47
QtDebug 387
QTemporaryFile 318
QTestLib 43, 46
QTextBrowser 349, 361
QTextCodec 114
QTextDocument 123
  redo 117
  undo 117
QTextEdit 106, 115, 142
  open new document 116
  preventing line wrap 106
  setDocument() 116
  setting font type 106
  size policy 144
  text format 114
  undo see QTextDocument
QtGlobal 386
QtGui 42, 44–45
QThread see threads
QThreadStorage 345–347
QTime 188
QTimer 334, 350
  singleshot timer 304

QTimerEvent 188, 189
QtNetwork 42, 45, 332
QtOpenGL 42, 45
QTranslator 378, 379
QTreeView 210
QTreeWidget 251, 252
QtSql 43, 45, 257–270
  displaying database errors 261
  establishing connection 260
  making queries 261
  model for Interview 265–270
  temporary database 265
QtSvg 43, 46
QtXml 43, 45, 353–373
QUdpSocket 318, 333
question dialog 169–171
  vs. information dialog 171
questions
  asking 169
queued connections 347, 348
queues see QQueue
quint16 423
quint32 423
quint64 423
quint8 423
quit() 26, 36, 112
qulonglong 423
qUpperBound() 417–418
QUrl 195, 364
  converting to file path 200
QValidator 70
QVariant 135, 200
  converting into native data types 138
  converting to a string 366
QVBoxLayout 30, 144–145
  addWidget() see addWidget()
  creating in Designer 84
  in the Qt inheritance hierarchy 42
QVector 401–402
  filling 420
QVector<QPoint> 279
QWaitCondition 342
qWarning() 341, 388
QWidget 304
  as a basis for all control ele-

ments 40
and layout 141, 143
resize() 105
setWindowTitle() 69, 105
QXmlContentHandler 355, 356
QXmlDefaultHandler 355–361
QXmlDTDHandler 355
QXmlEntityResolver 355
QXmlErrorHandler 355, 356
QXmlInputSource 365
QXmlLexicalHandler 355
QXmlSimpleReader 365

R
rcc 57–58
reading
from right to left see Bidi
rectangle see QRect
redo 117
reference system
fixed 280, 281
reflection 97
Registry
create path 136
saving application data 136
regular expressions
allowing during filtering 234
in Qt 70
in validators 70
reject() (slot) 71, 162
relational databases see QtSql
module
release version
generating 28
repaint 280
resize() 143
resizeEvent() 143
Resource Editor see Designer
resource file 109
resources
choosing icons for actions from
109
compiler see rcc
external 57–58, 99
file 57
localization of images 58
RESOURCES (qmake directive) 57

restricting the view to specific
datasets see filtering
retranslateUi() 92
Return key
assigning 168
RGB
vs. CMYK 274
color selection dialog see
QColorDialog
right alignment 145
roles 135
AccessibleDescriptionRole 209
AccessibleTextRole 209
CheckStateRole 209, 234
DecorationRole 209
DisplayRole 209, 224
EditRole 209, 225
FontRole 209, 251
SizeHintRole 209
StatusTipRole 209
TextAlignmentRole 209
TextColorRole 209
ToolTipRole 209, 225, 251
UserRole 209
WhatsThisRole 209
root element
determining in XML files 369
rotation 293
of the coordinate system 295
RSS parser 355–361
RTTI 248

S
saveFile() 115
saveFileAs() 115
saving
a file see saveFile()
splitter positions 151
under new name see save-
FileAs()
SAX 45, 353–366
default handler see QXmlDefaultHandler
scaling 292
screen
redrawing 280
screen size

and stretch factors 153
screenreader 209
screenshot 302–305
scroll wheel 293, 296
search
in sorted containers 416–418
for specific datasets see filtering
in unsorted containers 414–
415
SELECT queries (SQL) 262
displaying results 267
selectable entries see checkbox
selection model 217
selectionMode (property) 216
semi-modal dialogs see dialog
separator
in menus 108
sequential connections 318
serialization 322, 387
serialization operators 387
defining 325
set difference 411
set method 56
set object see QSet
set operations 411
setGeometry() 141
setupUi() 92, 111
sharing
implicit 40, 412
shearing 293
shortcuts 109
assigning with Designer 90
for labels see Buddy
window-wide 107
show() 163, 164
side-effects
in debug instructions 392
signal
binding to slots by name convention 97
declaring 77
sending 78
SIGNAL() 36
signals and slots 35
connecting with Designer 88
number of arguments 39

sequence of function call 38
  with thread usage 347–350
simplified() 123
singleshot timer 304
size
  changing 87
  defining fixed 281
  fixing 142
  saving a window's 139
  storing *see* QSize
size grip
  for main windows 118
size hint
  providing a *see* sizeHint()
size policy 144, 146
sizeHint() 143, 289
  for SVG files 301
SizeHintRole
  in Interview 209
Skype 19
slider *see* QSlider
slot 36
  binding to signals by name con-
    vention 97
  declaring 71–72
SLOT() 36
socket
  communication via 318, 334,
    338
Socks 5 333
sorting 212, 413–414
  data in models 231
  items in view widgets 255
  with QMap 405
sorting indicator
  in tree views 233
source mode 311
SourceAtop mode 313
SourceIn mode 312
SourceOut mode 312
SourceOver mode 311
SOURCES (qmake directive) 28, 106
spacer 82
  in Designer 82
spaces
  distributing with stretches 67,
    83

removing from beginning and
  end of string 123
spin box *see* QSpinBox
splitter 34, 130, 150–157
  defining size of ˜ widgets 151
  saving position of 151
SQL databases
  support in Qt *see* QtSql
SQLite 45
  compiling support 259
  database driver 259
  integrating drivers 260
  using 264–265
stack
  generating objects on 33
stacked
  layout 34, 157–160
  widget 157
stacks *see* QStack
standard connection (database)
  260
standard locale
  forcing 329, 331
standard output
  directing output to 321
Standard Template Library *see* STL
standard widgets
  manipulating 99
standard-error output *see* stderr
static_cast 189, 193
status bar 101, 110, 114, 118–124
  data to be displayed in Inter-
    view 209
  normal message 119, 120
  permanent message 120, 121
  temporary message 119, 120
status line *see* status bar
status tip
  setting 127
StatusTipRole
  in Interview 209
stderr 386
STL
  compatibility with Qt 393
  iterators 395–396
stored procedures 263
  and SQLite 264

stretch 67, 83, 152
stretch factor 146–148
  in the QGridLayout 148
  and screen size 153
  in the splitter layout 152
string
  converting to numbers 72, 73
  with dynamic elements 124
  list *see* QStringList
  objects *see* QString
  reading 181
string-oriented connections 318
strings
  selecting 181
style 88, 330
styleguide
  on headers in question dialogs
    169
  Microsoft 169
sub-tree
  inserting XML into 372
SVG 43, 46, 300–302
  Basic 301
  file loading 301
  supported profiles 46
  Tiny 301
swapping
  values 420
Sybase Adaptive Server
  database driver 259
synchronous processes 329
system scope
  for preferences 136, 137
system time *see* time

T
tab order 192
tab sequence 48, 87, 89
tab-completion 245
table layout *see* QGridLayout
table view
  of data 211
  of SQL tables 265–266
  without Interview *see* QTable-
    Widget
tabulator *see* tab sequence
tags 366

tar archive
listing contents 328
TEMPLATE (qmake directive) 28, 106
temporary data
storing 318
temporary database 265
temporary directory
determining 176, 319
temporary file 318
temporary memory 404
test cases 43, 46
Testing
inverted Layouts 157
text
color for DisplayRole data 209
document see QTextDocument
dynamically generating 124
editor 101, see QTextEdit
files for Unix and Windows 114
window for messages see QMessageBox
TextAlignmentRole
in Interview 209
textChanged() (Signal) 73
textChanged() (signal) 234
TextColorRole
in Interview 209
threads 40, 337–352
synchronizing 341–345
working with QSettings 136
tiled pattern 295
time
current system 188
determining 333
time object see QTime
timer 188, 189, 295
signal call after timeout 335
timeserver 336
title bar see window title
toggling
actions 126, 133
dock windows 133
via QPushButton 166
toInt() 72, 73
toLocal8Bit() 328
tool button 214

toolbar 101, 125–126
adding in the Designer 109
tooltip 110, 209, 251, 360
setting for actions 129
ToolTipRole
in Interview 209, 225, 251, 360
top-level widget 86, 162
tr() 50, 105, 376
dynamic text parts 123
transactions (database) 264
transformation matrix 290
translate() 50
translation 288, 291
of applications to other languages 49, 375–378
context see context
of the coordinate system 295
sources 377
TRANSLATIONS (qmake directive) 376
transparency
as color 272
of pixels 297
traversing 395
tree structure
of Qt classes 31
tree view 210
of SQL tables 265
without Interview see QTreeWidget
tree-based algorithms 404
Tulip 393–423
type conversion
with signal/slot connections 38
types
PODs 325, 422
Qt-specific 422
typewriter font see monospaced font

U
Ubuntu
installing SQL support later on 259
problems with qmake 27
uchar 423
UDP 318

ui files
format 49
integrating in projects 91–97
uic 49, 92
uint 423
ulong 423
undo 117
stack 117
undocumented features
event filter 247
Unicode 40, 114
converting local 8-bit encoded data to 330, 331
union 135
of sets 412
unit matrix 291–292
unit tests 43, 46
Unix
behavior of qFatal() 388
unsigned char
short form 423
unsigned int
short form 423
unsigned long
short form 423
unsigned short
short form 423
UPDATE statement (SQL) 262
URL see QUrl
usability
accelerators 107
arranging menu bar entries 126
avoiding bloated dialogs 164
defining the default button 87
with drag and drop 197
headers in question dialogs 169
localizing shortcuts 110
non-modal dialogs 163
push buttons for information dialogs 171
status message vs. dialog 124
stretch factor and screen size 153
tab sequence 89
when using QMessageBox 116

yes-no questions 170
use case
    consumer/producer 342–345
user input *see* input
user interface compiler *see* uic
user scope
    for preferences 136, 137
UserRole
    in Interview 209, 360, 366
ushort 423
UTF-8 *see* Unicode

V
validator 70
value ranges
    of floating-point types 423
    of integer types 422
value()
    vs. index operator 405, 409
valueChanged() (Signal) 38
values
    limiting 421
vector *see* QVector
    graphics with SVG *see* SVG
vendor details
    defining application-wide 137
version control 28
vertically arranging a layout *see*
    QVBoxLayout
view 208
    background color 209
    editing entries 246
    element-based without model
    251
    restricting to specific datasets
    234
    selectable entries *see* checkbox
view widgets *see* element-based
    views
viewMode (property) 216
viewport 211
Visual Studio 51, 52
    compiling a Qt application with
    29
Visual Studio project
    compiling 29
    generating from qmake project

file 27

W
WA_QuitOnClose 62
wait condition 342–344
warning dialog 172
warnings 388
webserver
    asynchronous communication
    with *see* QHttp
What's This? help 110, 129, 209
WhatsThisRole in Interview 209
whitespace 123
whole number *see* integer types
widget 29
    adding to a layout *see* addWid-
    get()
    changing properties in the De-
    signer 48
    changing size 105
    collapsible 150
    creating with Designer 82
    drawing on 280, 283
    removing in the Designer 48
    your own 42
width
    reading out ¨ of splitter widgets
    151
    setting *see* setGeometry()
wildcard
    using when filtering 234
window
    changing size 87, 105, 118
    dockable *see* dock window
    for messages *see* QMessage-
    Box
    saving size 139
window title
    setting 69, 86, 105
Windows (Microsoft)
    behavior of qFatal() 388
    development environment for
    open source projects 52
    forking 337
    GPL version 52
    line end of text files 114
    message handler for 389

open source edition 24
platform-specific   extensions
47
Registry *see* Registry
special features of qmake 28
text encoding 114
Windows-XP style 88
words
    counting 123
worker threads 347
working directory
    changing to 332
    determining 176
writing
    allowing in a model 227
WYSIWYG GUI editor *see* Designer

X
X11
    and QImage 297
Xcode 53
XHTML 354, 367
XML 42, 43, 45, 301, 353–373
    determining   document   type
    369
    determining root element 369
    integrating support for 43
    parser 45
    reading files 367
    reading out attributes 369
    translation source format 377
XOR 410
    mode 314
Xt 47

Y
yellow note *see* tooltip
yes-no questions 170

Z
zero
    division by 388
    object 200
zero string
    checking for *see* isNull()